A Field Guide to Wireless LANs

for Administrators and Power Users

Prentice Hall PTR Series in Computer Networking and Distributed Systems

Radia Perlman, Series Editor

Kaufman, Perlman & Speciner	*Network Security: Private Communication in a Public World, Second Edition*
Dayem	*Mobile Data and Wireless LAN Technologies*
Dayem	*PCS and Digital Cellular Technologies: Accessing Your Options*
Dusseault	*WebDAV: Next-Generation Collaborative Web Authoring*
Greenblatt	*Internet Directories: How to Build and Manage Applications for LDAP, DNS, and Other Directories*
Kadambi, Kalkunte & Crayford	*Gigabit Ethernet: Migrating to High Bandwidth LANS*
Kercheval	*DHCP: A Guide to Dynamic TCP/IP Network Management*
Kercheval	*TCP/IP Over ATM: A No-Nonsense Internetworking Guide*
Kretchmar	*Open Source Network Administration*
Liska	*The Practice of Network Security: Deployment Strategies for Production Environments*
Mancill	*Linux Routers: A Primer for Network Administrators, Second Edition*
Mann, Mitchell & Krell	*Linux System Security: The Administrator's Guide to Open Source Security Tools, Second Edition*
Maufer	*A Field Guide to Wireless LANs for Administrators and Power Users*
Skoudis	*Counter Hack: A Step-by-Step Guide to Computer Attacks and Effective Defenses*
Skoudis with Zeltser	*Malware: Fighting Malicious Code*
Solomon	*Mobile IP: The Internet Unplugged*
Syme & Goldie	*Optimizing Network Performance with Content Switching: Server, Firewall, and Cache Load Balancing*
Tomsu & Schmutzer	*Next Generation Optical Networks*
Tomsu & Wieser	*MPLS-Based VPNs: Designing Advanced Virtual Networks*
Zeltserman	*A Practical Guide to SNMPv3 and Network Management*

A Field Guide to Wireless LANs

for Administrators and Power Users

Thomas Maufer

PRENTICE
HALL
PTR

PRENTICE HALL
Professional Technical Reference
Upper Saddle River, New Jersey 07458
www.phptr.com

Library of Congress Cataloging-in-Publication Data

Maufer, Thomas
    A field guide to wireless LANs: for administrators and power users / Thomas Albert Maufer.
        p. cm. -- (Prentice Hall PTR series in computer networking and distributed systems)
    Includes index.
    ISBN 0-13-101406-4
        1. Wireless LANs. I. Title. II. Prentice Hall series in computer networking and
    distributed systems

    TK5105.78.M38 2003
    004.6'8--dc22

                                                                                2003060919

Editorial/Production Supervision: *Techne Group*
Executive Editor: *Mary Franz*
Editorial Assistant: *Noreen Regina*
Marketing Manager: *Dan DePasquale*
Manufacturing Buyer: *Maura Zaldivar*
Cover Design Director: *Jerry Votta*
Full-Service Production Manager: *Anne R. Garcia*

© 2004 Pearson Education, Inc.
Publishing as Prentice Hall Professional Technical Reference
Upper Saddle River, NJ 07458

PRENTICE
HALL
PTR

About Prentice Hall Professional Technical Reference

With origins reaching back to the industry's first computer science publishing program in the 1960s, and formally launched as its own imprint in 1986, Prentice Hall Professional Technical Reference (PH PTR) has developed into the leading provider of technical books in the world today. Our editors now publish over 200 books annually, authored by leaders in the fields of computing, engineering, and business.

Our roots are firmly planted in the soil that gave rise to the technical revolution. Our bookshelf contains many of the industry's computing and engineering classics: Kernighan and Ritchie's *C Programming Language*, Nemeth's *UNIX System Administration Handbook*, Horstmann's *Core Java*, and Johnson's *High-Speed Digital Design*.

PH PTR acknowledges its auspicious beginnings while it looks to the future for inspiration. We continue to evolve and break new ground in publishing by providing today's professionals with tomorrow's solutions.

PRENTICE
HALL
PTR

Peace

Contents

Chapter 2

A Brief History of Networking Standards   33

Chapter 3

Speeds and Feeds   57

Chapter 4

IEEE 802.11's MAC Sub-layer Protocol—Frames, etc.   103

Chapter 5

Dissection of a Probe Response MMPDU   131

Chapter 6

IEEE 802.11's MAC Sub-layer Protocol—Access, etc.   149

Chapter 7

Security Mechanisms for Wireless LANs   191

Preface

My first exposure to the subject of wireless LANs was perhaps in 1999 or 2000, and at the time I was impressed with one simple fact: this is complex technology. Of course, at the time I knew absolutely nothing about wireless local area networks (LANs), so you might argue that by virtue of its very newness combined with my complete ignorance of the subject, it *should* have seemed complicated, but it was much more than just a little different. Nothing about it seemed familiar. It was like learning a new language, or better yet, like learning a new *alphabet*. There were so many new terms; for one small example among many, I could choose SSID, for which I did not even know what the acronym stood for, much less what it really *meant*. And even once I had learned that SSID stood for "Service Set Identifier," I hadn't gained much ground, since it just further exposed the depths of my ignorance, since I didn't know what a "service set" was, or more importantly why it would be necessary or useful for a service set to have an identifier.

These new terms were not only unfamiliar, there was also no easy or obvious way to map them back to something with which I was already familiar. Wireless LANs have virtually no common technological ground with wired LAN technologies. I used to joke that if you gave engineers the task of designing the most complex LAN MAC[1] sub-layer protocol that they could imagine, they would

---

1. The Medium Access Control sublayer is the lower half of the Data Link layer (which is layer 2 in the OSI Reference Model), and which will be discussed in considerable detail in this book.

come up with the Fiber Distributed Data Interface (FDDI). Now that I know much more about wireless LANs, I would change the joke to say that they would come up with IEEE 802.11, which is the official designation of the family of wireless LAN standards described hereinafter.

However, I do not want to imply that the technology is complex for complexity's sake—it really *is* extremely complicated to design a set of physical layer modulations and an associated set of Medium Access Control (MAC) procedures that result in a usable wireless LAN (WLAN) technology. The WLAN protocols that are the subject of this book are the result of nearly 10 years of standards work focused on creating an IEEE standard WLAN technology. The area is evolving rapidly, and it is clear that the current WLAN standards are far from the last word on the subject. There is no end in sight for the evolution of the IEEE 802.11 standards.

While I was busy with other projects at work in 2000 and 2001, wireless LAN products were proliferating, being adopted at an ever-increasing, seemingly feverish, pace. Apparently, there was a pent-up demand that was being served, even by first- and second-generation products that were expensive and didn't work as smoothly as they might have. Throughout 2000–2003, one of the only bright spots in the high-tech economy was the wireless LAN sector. Despite the recession in those years, the growth rate of this market was still in the 20–50% range (depending on whose market analysis studies you read).

Over the last five years, the price of wireless LAN hardware has dropped by about an order of magnitude, and continues to drop. The products are much more robust today, easier to install and use, and in general, much better overall. However, even with the higher prices, poor integration, difficult installation, and marginal performance under anything other than ideal conditions, a non-trivial number of early adopters jumped on the WLAN bandwagon well before there were viable, reliable, easy-to-use standards-based products at reasonable prices. The rate of increase in importance of wireless LANs is such that the book I wrote in 1999 (*IP Fundamentals*) makes no mention of WLAN technology, but today I am writing an entire book devoted to that single topic.

The WLAN market did not really take off significantly until there was a standard in place that had the backing of a large consortium of vendors, who could leverage higher volumes to help drive down costs. Before the ratification of the first IEEE 802.11 standard in 1997, there were pre-standard wireless LAN products, such as those based on HomeRF, for example. There were also numerous purpose-built wireless communications systems using technologies that could be seen as direct forbears of the modern WLAN protocols. Due to a combination of factors, perhaps partially due to the expense of the equipment and the limited ease of use due to minimal integration into PC operating systems of the day, the early pre-standard products were expensive and were not widely perceived as user-friendly. However, the users who managed to get wireless LANs installed and operating were delighted with their newfound freedom and flexibility, unshackled from the wires that had constrained them in the past.

One specific area in which early products came up short was software drivers, especially for client products. It is considerably easier today to use a wireless LAN card with, for example, Windows XP. You simply insert the card, and the operating system auto-detects the hardware, loads the correct drivers, initializes the card, and you're off and surfing. In earlier days, it was a challenge to get products with drivers that were stable, and that could support a range of operating systems (not just different flavors of Windows [e.g., 95 / 98 / NT / 2000 / Me / etc.], but also Linux and MacOS).

Again, this is a complex technology. The best advice I can give you is to try to suppress your natural tendencies to want to map the world of wired LANs that you already understand to the new world of WLANs. The wireless LANs are just different, and ultimately stand apart. WLAN standards, more than any others with which I am familiar, are unique, and have to be understood on their own terms.

Eventually, I began paying much closer attention to WLANs. Now that I have had a chance to synthesize some level of understanding for myself, I hope to be able to share that with a wider audience. In this book, I hope to give the reader a feel for why WLANs *need* to be so very different from and so much more complex than wired LANs. Fundamentally, the conclusion I came to was that WLANs are more complex because they have to be. It's as simple as that.

In the course of my dealings with other IEEE 802.11 Working Group members, I have come to fully appreciate that I do not know everything there is to know about this subject. However, you can rest assured that whatever is in this book is as accurate as I could make it as of the time it was written. It took me a long time to digest the standard(s) (no criticism to the IEEE 802.11 WG, but these documents aren't easy to read!), and I really didn't "get it" until I had the chance to play with some real hardware and put all my knowledge to some actual use. Besides real products, I also have had access to wireless LAN diagnostic tools, such as packet sniffers, which helped me to see what was really going on "under the covers."

I cannot claim to have top-to-bottom knowledge of wireless LAN technology. My knowledge base is centered at the Data Link and Network layers, and I will be the first to admit that I am no expert in Physical layer modulation schemes. In my judgment, this is arcane knowledge (another of my subjective assessments, but I think it would be difficult to convince WLAN users that they needed to understand this stuff any more than Ethernet users could be convinced that they need to understand Differential Manchester encoding). If this sort of thing is what you are looking for, you will find just enough of it here for me to be able to tell you how the various schemes differ, and more importantly, what they are used for. If you want more details on information theory, coding theory, and so forth, there are many excellent books on those subjects. I will make sure that the reader understands the terms FHSS, DSSS, CCK, PBCC, and OFDM (and more) and will be able to tell them apart. I'm not even going to tell you what those mean now. Read Chapter 3, *Speeds and Feeds*, for that information....

I *will* cover the Physical layer technologies in sufficient detail to explain what they do, but I won't try to convince you that I am intimately familiar with their inner workings. I know what they *do*, and I think that's all that most people need to know (heck, if this stuff works smoothly enough, most users won't ever even need to wonder how it works).

When I needed to learn more about WLANs, I found that the best reference was usually the standards themselves, despite their being written less than clearly. The IEEE 802.11-1999 standard is a large enough document that even experienced network software engineers needed "handbooks" to help them find their way through it. At the time, however, WLAN technology was just beginning to mature into a consumer-level technology that needs some basic treatment for mass audiences. By now, that transition is well under way. WLAN-enabled products are hot.

There are other excellent books on wireless LANs if you need to run right out and design your own wireless LAN implementation; however, books for users are few and far between. I hope to ease the acquisition of the new "language skills" that are necessary to become comfortable with this technology. To deploy and use WLANs, much of this knowledge is not required—vendors try to make their products fairly bulletproof to keep their support costs down. However, if you need to set up and manage a WLAN, you'll want to know enough to be effective, without needing to drown in details. If you ever need to go behind the scenes and debug a problem, you will need to have the context that I provide in this book. It's difficult to fix a problem unless you can notice it. To do that, you need to know what the normal behavior is expected to be.

If you want to *use* products based on IEEE 802.11 and need to understand the terminology involved in the standard, so that you can use, deploy, or manage the technology with the minimum of confusion, then this is the book for you. Ultimately, it is my assertion that very few people really need to know about which radio frequencies are being used, or the ways that data is modulated onto those frequencies. I'll include this information for completeness, but I think that most readers can safely skip such sections.

Acknowledgments

The idea for this book was born over dinner at Lupo restaurant at the Mandalay Bay hotel in Las Vegas on May 6, 2002. However, the book would never have been finished without the steady encouragement of the staff at Prentice Hall, especially Mary Franz. There is no amount of gratitude that I can express for her seemingly infinite patience with my slow pace of writing. But that's all behind us now!

I'd also especially like to acknowledge the members of IEEE 802.11's Task Group "*i*" for being so welcoming. In particular, I would like to thank Nancy Cam-Winget, Frank Ciotti, Clint Chaplin, Dave Halasz, Russ Housley, DJ Johnston, Tim Moore, Mike Moreton, Bob Moskowitz, Dorothy Stanley, and Jesse Walker, among many others from within the broader context of IEEE 802.11, including (among others) Duncan Kitchin and Matthew Shoemake. It has been a pleasure to work with all of you, including some of you for whom I only know your first name.

It should be understood that any errors in this book are my own. I have done my best to faithfully describe the pieces of the standard, and the emerging extensions of the standard. It's possible that I have faithfully reproduced something that was incorrect in the first place, and if so, shame on me.

During the course of writing this book, I have found and reported several bugs in emerging IEEE draft standard documents; if I missed one, I apologize for not catching it. It is far more likely that any other mistakes you might find are mine, and if you care to, you can send me email at `<tmaufer@acm.org>` with suggestions for improvements.

IEEE 802® Copyright Notice

Excerpts and adaptations of material from the following cited IEEE standards are reprinted with permission. The IEEE disclaims any responsibility or liability resulting from the placement and use in the described manner.

The author gratefully acknowledges the permission granted by the IEEE Standards Association for this use.

- IEEE 802®-2001, "IEEE Standard for Local and Metropolitan Area Networks: Overview and Architecture". Copyright 2002 by IEEE.

- IEEE 802.1Q™-2003, "IEEE Standards for Local and metropolitan area networks—Virtual Bridged Local Area Networks". Copyright 2003 by IEEE.

- IEEE 802.1X-2001, "IEEE Standard for Local and metropolitan area networks—Port-Based Network Access Control". Copyright 2001 by IEEE.

- IEEE 802.2-1998, "IEEE Standard for Information technology. Telecommunications and information exchange between systems. Local and metropolitan area networks. Specific requirements. Part 2: Logical Link Control". Copyright 1998 by IEEE.

- IEEE 802.3™-2002, "IEEE Standard for Information technology— Telecommunications and information exchange between systems— Local and metropolitan area networks—Specific requirements. Part 3: Carrier sense multiple access with collision detection (CSMA/CD) access method and physical layer specifications". Copyright 2002 by IEEE.

- IEEE 802.10-1998, "IEEE Standards for Local and Metropolitan Area Networks: Standard for Interoperable LAN/MAN Security (SILS)". Copyright 1998 by IEEE.

- IEEE 802.10a-1999, "IEEE Standards for Local and Metropolitan Area Networks: Supplement to Standard for Interoperable LAN/MAN Security (SILS) —Security Architecture Framework". Copyright 1999 by IEEE.

- IEEE 802.10c-1998, "IEEE Standard Interoperable LAN/MAN Security (SILS) Key Management (Clause 3)". Copyright 1998 by IEEE.

- IEEE 802.11™-1999, "Information technology—Telecommunications and information exchange between systems—Local and metropolitan area networks—Specific requirements—Part 11: Wireless LAN Medium Access Control (MAC) and Physical Layer (PHY) Specifications". Copyright 1999 by IEEE.

- IEEE 802.11a-1999, "Supplement to IEEE Standard for Information technology. Telecommunications and information exchange between systems. Local and metropolitan area networks. Specific requirements. Part 11: Wireless LAN Medium Access Control (MAC) and Physical Layer (PHY) specifications High-speed Physical Layer in the 5 GHz Band". Copyright 1999 by IEEE.

- IEEE 802.11b-1999, "Supplement to IEEE Standard for Information technology—Telecommunications and information exchange between systems—Local and metropolitan area networks—Specific requirements—Part 11: Wireless LAN Medium Access Control (MAC) and Physical Layer (PHY) specifications: Higher-Speed Physical Layer Extension in the 2.4 GHz Band". Copyright 2000 by IEEE.

- IEEE 802.11b-1999/Cor 1-2001, "IEEE Standard for Information technology—Telecommunications and information exchange between systems—Local and metropolitan area networks—Specific requirements. Part 11: Wireless LAN Medium Access Control (MAC) and Physical Layer (PHY) specifications Amendment 2: Higher-speed Physical Layer (PHY) extension in the 2.4 GHz band—Corrigendum 1". Copyright 2001 by IEEE.

- IEEE 802.11d-2001, "IEEE Standard for Information technology. Telecommunications and information exchange between systems. Local and metropolitan area networks. Specific requirements. Part 11: Wireless LAN Medium Access Control (MAC) and Physical Layer (PHY) specifications Amendment 3: Specification for operation in additional regulatory domains". Copyright 2001 by IEEE.

- IEEE 802.11g™-2003, "IEEE Standard for Information technology—Telecommunications and information exchange between systems—Local and metropolitan area networks—Specific requirements. Part 11: Wireless LAN Medium Access Control (MAC) and Physical Layer (PHY) specifications Amendment 4: Further Higher Data Rate Extension in the 2.4 GHz Band". Copyright 2003 by IEEE.

- IEEE 802.15.1™-2002, "IEEE Standard for Information technology—Telecommunications and information exchange between systems—Local and metropolitan area networks—Specific requirements. Part 15.1: Wireless Medium Access Control (MAC) and Physical Layer (PHY) Specifications for Wireless Personal Area Networks (WPANs)". Copyright 2002 by IEEE.

- IEEE 802.16™-2001, "IEEE Standard for Local and metropolitan area networks Part 16: Air Interface for Fixed Broadband Wireless Access Systems". Copyright 2002 by IEEE.

- IEEE 802.16a™-2003, "IEEE Standard for Local and metropolitan area networks Part 16: Air Interface for Fixed Broadband Wireless Access Systems—Amendment 2: Medium Access Control Modifications and Additional Physical Layer Specifications for 2–11 GHz". Copyright 2003 by IEEE.

- IEEE 802.16c™-2002, "IEEE Standard for Local and metropolitan area networks Part 16: Air Interface for Fixed Broadband Wireless Access Systems—Amendment 1: Detailed System Profiles for 10–66 GHz". Copyright 2003 by IEEE.

- IEEE 802.16.2-2001, "IEEE Recommended Practice for Local and metropolitan area networks Coexistence of Fixed Broadband Wireless Access Systems". Copyright 2001 by IEEE.

1

Wireless LAN Preliminaries

Why Wireless?

A number of technology trends have been creating an environment in which wireless LAN (WLAN) technology can thrive. WLAN technology did not simply appear out of nowhere...the groundwork to prepare people for mobile computing has been underway for some time. Just as the Internet was able to explode because 1) PCs were abundant, 2) most PCs were connected by LANs, and 3) on the PC, the only thing required to become an Internet node was to install and configure the correct software (in particular, a TCP/IP stack and applications that could use it, such as a web browser). Had PCs not been commonplace, or had LANs not already been deployed, the Internet would not have been able to reach nearly as many people so quickly.

In the case of wireless (or, more generally, mobile) computing, the first enabler was the fact that laptops are getting faster, cheaper, and thus more prevalent. Another enabler was that people had become used to mobility due to the increasing popularity of cellular phones. WLANs enable laptop users to access the network as effortlessly as they can use a cellular phone to call home (provided they are in a location that has a deployed WLAN, of course). Finally, there are a number of application scenarios at home and at work for which the requirements ideally match the capabilities of WLAN technology.

Wireless and mobile communications are a feature that people increasingly have come to expect in relation to the user experience of computing. Mobility is becoming the norm, for the convenience and flexibility it affords. Eventually, it is likely that WLAN chips will find their way into most types of objects. There are a number of interesting vertical applications of WLAN technology, besides the obvious vertical application known as wireless Internet access.

For one example, in certain restaurants, orders are now directly entered at tableside by waiters using PDAs with WLAN capabilities.[1] This is an excellent example of integration of appropriate technology to enable smoother business practices, since the PDA-based data entry gets the order into the system immediately, and the wait staff do not need to spend their valuable time doing data entry of the order (when they could be serving other customers).

Or in a hospital, one might imagine that doctors could use WLAN-equipped PDAs or laptops to pull up patient information at bedside, and be able to interact with that data much more fluidly than if it were a sheaf of papers. It is generally the case that hypertext capabilities are difficult to implement in nonelectronic documents. With regard to medical applications of WLANs, it turns out that certain types of hospital equipment may use the same frequency bands as certain WLAN technologies, so care would have to be taken to avoid interference. Such issues are avoidable if the WLAN technology is chosen such that it cannot interfere with the critical functions of various installed medical equipment; this could be accomplished by either physically separating the equipment or by using a different frequency so the two types of equipment cannot interfere with each other.

Chapter 2, *A Brief History of Networking Standards*, will cover the range of Physical layer choices for WLANs, and will make it clear what options exist for using two or more different types of communications equipment, via different operating frequencies, different modulations, or other parameters.

Rise of Laptops

Laptops are becoming the preferred type of personal computer, particularly for business users. When laptops were first brought to market, users lucky enough to have a laptop typically had both a desktop machine and a laptop, since laptops typically had less computing power than a comparably priced

---

1. The author knows of at least one restaurant that has implemented such a system. One wonders if the next step might be to offer wireless Internet access over the same infrastructure, thereby creating a revenue stream from the installed equipment.

desktop machine and were only useful as an extension of their desktop PC, not as their primary machine. In addition to their initial high cost, early laptops tended to be heavy and not have very long battery life. These impediments tended to restrict laptops to applications in which mobility was mandatory, and for which the performance achievable on those early platforms was adequate. As time passed, laptops became lighter, their battery life was extended, and they became more powerful. Most importantly, they became cheaper—so much so that for many users they are beginning to supplant the desktop machine.

Given that modern laptops have sufficient performance for most business applications, and that they have a significant edge in terms of portability, compared to desktop machines, their popularity has been rising, and the percentage of PCs sold that are laptops has been increasing[2] as a result. It has become very common for a corporate user to only have a laptop. For home users, laptops are not as common, but the trend is that they are becoming more common, especially if one considers the term "laptop" in its broadest sense, and include new mobile PC product categories like tablet PCs that are designed around mobility from the start. In fact, one might observe that a tablet PC is relatively useless without a wireless infrastructure, so the WLAN has become an enabler for a new class of computing platform.

Networking Became Pervasive

Until WLAN technology arrived on the scene, the only networking option for laptop users was Ethernet. There is nothing wrong with Ethernet. 10/100 Mbps Ethernet was (and is) ubiquitous in laptops, as it is in desktops. In the 2004 time frame, 10/100/1000 should begin to become "standard equipment" in new PCs, even in laptops. In corporate settings, Ethernet is the dominant networking technology, and a cubicle typically has from two to four network jacks. Part of

---

2. In fact, according to a news story on July 2nd, 2003, the market research firm NPD Group has stated that in May 2003, revenues from the sale of laptop PCs exceeded revenues from non-laptop PCs for the first time. In terms of units, laptops still only account for 40% of the market, but since they are more expensive, they accounted for 54% of the market in terms of revenue in the month of May 2003. The trend is clear, however, and it would be reasonable to expect that laptops will soon lead the PC market in both revenue and unit terms.

the convenience of Ethernet derived from its use of the RJ-45[3] connector, which is easy to use and is not easily dislodged once it is connected.

However, using Ethernet requires that a user be near an available Ethernet hub or switch port to obtain network connectivity. This might sound like an obvious observation, and this is not an unreasonable requirement for a desktop PC. However, mobile users with laptop computers are always in search of a network (or telephone) jack from which they can obtain connectivity. While the laptop was portable, there was a certain lack of convenience in unplugging the Ethernet (or telephone) cable every time the user needed to move to a new location.

Ethernet was an acceptable (barely) "roaming" technology inside an office building, in which it was possible that all conference rooms and some common areas were equipped with network jacks and/or tabletop switches to which users could attach. Theoretically, providing wiring to conference rooms allowed a primitive form of roaming, but a room with four network jacks would be unable to provide network connectivity for five or more people, unless one brought his or her own hub or switch (and then the number of available power outlets in the room might become an issue!).

However successful Ethernet has been in corporate deployments, due to the widespread availability of network jacks, the typical home or apartment environment typically does not have an abundance of Ethernet jacks (or even phone jacks) in every room (in California, landlords are only required to provide a single phone jack in an apartment, and only newer homes have been pre-wired for networking). Deploying networking technology at home has, until the advent of WLAN technology, involved adding a wired infrastructure to serve the places that the homeowner thinks will need network connectivity.

Emergence of Cellular Phones

At the same time that laptops were emerging as the leading type of PC sold, cellular phones were becoming increasingly affordable, through a combination of competition and expansion to a larger user base. In fact, cellular phones have been in existence since the 1980s, but it is only in the recent past that cellular

---

3. RJ-45 stands for *Registered Jack-45*, an 8-pin connector used commonly to connect computers onto an Ethernet-based LAN. RJ-45 connectors look similar to the ubiquitous RJ-11 connectors that are used as modular telephone jacks, but RJ-11 jacks are somewhat narrower, as they involve only 4- or 6-pin connectors.

phones have become so prevalent as to be considered commonplace. In terms of public perception, it is now more unusual for someone to *not* have a cellular phone. So-called "mobile professionals" armed with laptops and cell phones are a common sight almost everywhere you go these days. Who hasn't seen people driving with one hand and taking notes on a dashboard-mounted notepad with the other while using a hands-free cell phone headset while shaving?

Cell phone networks are pretty good at delivering "good enough" voice communications, but a limiting issue with cell phones is that there is very limited bandwidth available for data services in today's existing cell phone networks. While it is possible to connect a laptop to a cell phone and dial out using a modem, as if the cell phone were a regular telephone line, the connection will rarely be faster than 9.6 kbps. Existing cell phone networks, even those that are digital, are optimized for voice, not data.

To remedy this situation, the world's telephone companies have proposed to enhance cell phones by upgrading to a new third-generation (often abbreviated as "3G") infrastructure, so that Internet-enabled wireless communications will be the norm, rather than the exception. In 3G networks, data performance will be much better (on the order of 100 kbps, or perhaps even higher). However, to get to this 3G "nirvana," an enormous investment in new infrastructure must be made. Moreover, the user base must adopt the new technology by purchasing new telephones capable of supporting Internet features.

Despite the existence of some agreements on 3G wireless standards, there have been few widespread deployments to date, and one reason may be that it is not certain how to cost-justify the investment. Will the new capabilities generate sufficient return on investment? Such questions were not asked in the late 1990s, when large sums of money were invested in infrastructure with little consideration of whether the investment would lead to increases in future income, and whether the possible increases were sufficient to justify making the investment. Now that the pre-3G investments are paying off, it seems like the business decision has been made to extract as much "bang for the buck" from the initial investment as possible, while doing trial 3G deployments to try to find out what new services users are willing to pay for. (It is amusing to note that the difficulties of getting 3G networks deployed have caused some vendors to start talking about 4G networks. Luckily, the evolution of cell phone network infrastructures is beyond the scope of this book.)

Even with the potential of 3G (or 4G, if you will) wireless technologies, such networks are not "LAN-like" and do not match the way people are used to interacting with networked content, especially with respect to billing. One of the major differences between surfing the Web at home or at work versus using advanced cell phone based data services is that the billing model is significantly different. In addition, to the author's mind, surfing the Web on a two-inch diagonal screen is of limited usefulness (and two inches is a large screen by cell phone standards).

Internet Billing: Wireless versus Wired

In the cell phone world, the providers seem to want to be able to create "value-added" services that they can charge extra for. There is no good reason that they should not behave this way. This is also how traditional telephone companies handle billing. Beyond your basic touch-tone telephone service, you can order additional services such as caller-ID, distinctive ringing, call waiting, voice mail, and so on. Typically, there is a per-use fee, or an "unlimited use" fee that is billed monthly.

There are probably some truly compelling mobile-oriented applications that phone companies will be able to offer as a data-dependent value-added service (things like "I'm at the following intersection…please make me a reservation at the nearest Chinese restaurant and tell me how to get there"). Value-added services like that would have a user interface that could be simple enough to put on a small screen.

Of course, the same application could be offered on a laptop via a Web browser, but how many people carry their heavy laptop with them everywhere[4]? General Web surfing and email[5] are probably not going to be popular applications for cell phones, which are otherwise getting smaller and smaller.

---

4. Even if a practical one-pound laptop existed, it would still be over five times heavier than my cell phone…. Most people would agree that when it comes to mobile application platforms, lighter is better.

5. In some cases, email is a useful mobile application, such as the BlackBerry® "über-pagers" by Research in Motion (RIM) Limited. A Blackberry is like a miniature laptop, in that it has a usable screen and a small keyboard, and some models even have limited Web-browsing capabilities (next-generation models will be able to be used as cell phones). These devices use a variety of pre-3G wireless data networks to maintain access in most major metropolitan areas, worldwide.

However, on a typical Internet connection, whether at dial-up or broadband (e.g., DSL or cable-modem) speeds, you usually get "All the Internet you can eat" (limited only by the speed of your access line) for a simple monthly fee. Once connected, Internet users are free to access whatever networked applications interest them, from the very popular World-Wide Web (WWW) to file transfer applications, to voice over IP (VoIP), and so on, only limited by the speed of their access method.

To an ISP, charging by the byte or by the connection would represent a vast amount of overhead in their billing systems, so Internet access is almost always a flat-rate service. Where optional fee-for-service "products" exist, they typically involve things like firewall service, or an extra IP address for nominal monthly charge(s), or some amount of online file storage, which may or may not be included in your monthly fee, on which you can store a Web site or email or what have you. Internet providers (that provide access via dial-up or via dedicated "always-on" technologies like DSL or cable modems) typically do not do their billing on a per-packet, per-message, or per-connection basis.

However, such charging models are not unheard of in the "Internet provider" context, as they are more likely to be seen in the "wireless Internet" offerings that are based on advanced cellular phones that double as Web browsers. The fact that the wireless Internet services are significantly bandwidth-constrained means that bandwidth is a scare resource; scarcity equates to value, so they need to set a price for every byte that a user consumes that reflects at least the basic value of the bandwidth consumed, plus some additional profit margin. If wireless bandwidth were significantly more plentiful, the pricing models would probably be different. As long as the bandwidth is scarce, it will be priced accordingly (i.e., it will be expensive!).

Wireless: Applications versus Devices

Today, wireless applications tend to be tied to a particular access device, with the laptop being the most general purpose, but also the heaviest, and devices like cell phones and pagers being on the other end of the scale, for very specific applications such as voice communications and interactive text messaging.

This situation of application-specific devices resembles the early days of mainframe computing, in which each application (or type of application) often required a dedicated terminal. It was not uncommon for someone to have two or more terminals on his or her desk, each devoted to just one type of application. Eventually, the "terminals" became software-based and all migrated into a general-purpose platform (initially, as special multi-window terminals, then the terminals evolved into programs running in the PC), sharing a single connection to the network.

At some point, the interactive terminal model itself (in which the applications, including the user interface and all the necessary support software ran on the mainframe) was replaced by networked applications using client/server paradigms, in which the user interface runs locally on the PC, and connects to a back-end server that provides access to some form of database or other networked service.

However, it remains to be seen whether there will ever be a "converged" wireless device that will satisfy the needs of a variety of applications. At this point, it seems more likely that application-specific devices will be the norm for some time to come, although some degree of convergence may occur as they all migrate to common delivery technologies based on the Internet Protocol (IP), perhaps over a future infrastructure based on 3G wireless technology, but also over other types of access networks, such as those based on WLANs, or perhaps wireless MANs.

It is also possible that application-specific wireless devices in close proximity to each other could pool their talents using short-range wireless technology such as Bluetooth®. In such a scenario, users could assess their needs and assemble a set of wireless products (and their associated services) to match, obviating the need for an "all things to all people" common wireless device. For example, a PDA with a database of contact information could be queried by a cell phone so that when the cell phone rings, it can look up the calling party's number and display the caller's name instead of a telephone number. This approach is more flexible and modular, and theoretically more scalable, since it avoids the need to input the same information (i.e., the name and telephone number) into both the PDA and the cell phone.

As of early 2003, many late-model cell phones have Bluetooth capabilities, and once laptops and PDAs also have Bluetooth, this type of integration will just be a matter of software, since the connectivity will be available to enable all the devices to expose their unique services to the others, and allow the user's collection of devices to operate as a collective, seeming to be greater than the sum of its parts.

WLANs Arrive on the Scene

With WLANs, finally a networking technology has been designed that matches the way people use laptops. It is likely that the large extant pre-existing population of potential users (i.e., laptop owners with spare PC Card slots) enabled the rapid adoption of WLAN technology as soon as the first "fast enough" (up to 11 Mbps) cards became cheap enough for mass-market adoption. Based on the rapid acceptance of these products, the market was clearly ready and waiting for them.

So, wireless has the edge in convenience, but will probably always fall short in terms of ultimate performance.[6] Luckily, in order to be successful, WLANs need not be fastest (or even as fast as wired LANs), just "fast enough to be useful." The most common application in today's home networks is to inexpensively and conveniently extend Internet access to machines throughout the house. Given that typical broadband access download speeds are only on the order of 750 kbps or so (perhaps as high as 1.5 or 1.6 Mbps), the 11 Mbps speed of today's most common WLAN technology is more than adequate (for this application).

Applications of WLANs

These initial WLAN products were indeed fast enough to be usable, but not fast enough to be a wired LAN replacement. However, WLAN connectivity has become an ideal complement to a wired LAN connection. WLAN technology has become an integral part in most laptop product lines, even to the point of being integrated across the board.

Corporate Deployments

Wireless has become very popular with business users, and many corporate networks have installed WLANs to complement their wired LANs. Initial deployments were in places like conference rooms, but for convenience reasons, the deployments tended to spread. One good aspect for users is that they can simply install and manage their own WLAN by attaching a wireless bridge to a free network jack in their cubicle.

---

6. As compared to a switched Ethernet LAN, which is often configured to dedicate at least 10 Mbps to each user (frequently 100 Mbps), as opposed to sharing 11 Mbps among all the active users as is done in IEEE 802.11*b*.

In fact, it is so easy to deploy WLAN technology that corporate IT departments need to have tools with which to patrol their networks in search of unauthorized wireless hubs. (There are security implications when naive end users expose the corporate network to eavesdroppers that may be sitting and listening in from their position outside in the parking lot.)

The ease of deployment is very good for users, and mimics the way that wired LANs appeared in corporations in the late 1980s and early 1990s; in other words, enthusiasts who were operating outside the boundaries of the MIS department installed them.

However, due to security aspects of wireless networking, this easy deployment of WLANs is very bad for the MIS department, since WLANs are often installed inside of the corporate firewall, which exposes the corporate network to unauthorized users. It is possible to deploy (currently proprietary) WLAN products with better security, but such products are often tightly integrated into a user authentication database to provide strong authentication and better forms of encryption than the basic WLAN product offerings; this integration causes an added load on the MIS department if they never had such a user authentication database in the past. Understanding the topic of security and WLANs is very important, and therefore it will be explained in detail later in the book.

Wireless "Hot Spots"

Besides corporate deployments of WLANs, by MIS departments and otherwise, there is an emerging industry in which enterprising companies providing public WLAN access have begun setting up wireless "hot spots" in places where business users congregate, such as airports, hotels, and conference centers. Wireless "hot spots" also tend to be near universities. In Cupertino, CA (home of Apple Computer and De Anza College), there is a donut shop called the Donut Wheel (open 24 hours, every day, even Thanksgiving and Christmas) that is renting out its airspace to such a service provider. Anyone with a WLAN-capable device can purchase 24 hours of Internet access for $2.00—which sounds like a bargain to me. Companies that operate such "Internet over WLAN" access services may sometimes be known as WISPs (i.e., wireless ISPs).

There is an interesting market segmentation that is possible (even desirable) in the relationship between the hot spot operator and the actual WISPs. In practice, many WISPs may want to provide access in the same local geographical area. However, there is a limit to how many non-overlapping channels exist within the various RF bands over which WLANs operate, and if every WISP installed its own local wireless infrastructure, they would all interfere with each other, and none of their customers would be able to use the services that the WISPs were trying to offer.

In the wireless access business, there is a natural place for a third party to exist, a "WLAN provider" that actually installs and manages the local physical infrastructure, over which the WISPs' customers access their respective WISPs. There is no directly analogous separation in the wired Internet access business, primarily because a single party owns the wires over which the service is offered, and because only a single customer can use a given physical facility at a time.

The WLAN operator would need to have a way of communicating with the various WISPs that have contracted with it, so that only valid users can gain access to the otherwise public airwaves.[7]

Note that although a number of companies are trying to set up such businesses, there seem to be just as many local anarchists who are setting up free WLANs. Yes, you read that correctly, *free*. As in open access, no charge, high-speed Internet service. While many different companies have expressed interest in building and operating WLAN-based wireless Internet infrastructures—from the traditional telephone companies, to wireless phone providers, to local ISPs, and others—it is not clear whether the "free wireless access" movement will be a minor annoyance or a real impediment to turning WLAN-based access into a profit-generating venture.

Deployments at Home

Another ideal usage scenario for WLANs is in the home, since most houses do not have networking jacks in every room, and WLANs just use the air that most people already have at home in abundance. Even though the natural platform for WLANs so far has been laptops, it is also possible to add a WLAN interface card to a standalone PC. In fact, the typical home PC is probably not a laptop,

---

7. Luckily, such protocols do exist, and are already being employed to a certain extent in enterprise networks; for example, the same protocols that corporations use to validate their dial-up users' identities can be (and will be) applied to WLANs. The topic of authentication will be covered in detail in the chapters on WLAN security.

at least at this point in time. Trends in the business world tend to repeat themselves at home, so it is likely that laptops will become increasingly prevalent at home, eventually. In 2002, and into 2003, the largest portion of the WLAN market, based on revenue, was due to home-based WLANs, to the extent that over two-thirds of the revenue was attributable to home-based WLAN deployments.

Other home-networking technologies have been created, including the Ethernet-like products from the Home-Phoneline Networking Alliance (HomePNA™[8]). Despite being able to perform the technically difficult trick of operating Ethernet over the telephone wiring in a house, the fact remains that there is a practical obstacle that must be overcome—there aren't telephone jacks in every room of the house.[9] Moreover, the HomePNA™ network is a shared network of approximately the same speed[10] as 11 Mbps WLANs (and 54 Mbps WLANs are already on the market). Therefore, the fact that WLANs do not require any physical changes, such as additional wiring, is a *big* advantage for most home users.

The one downside for WLANs in the home is that most homes have many walls, and drywall is fairly opaque to 2.4 GHz radio waves (even more so to 5 GHz RF radiation). Empirical data suggests that for each wall that a 2.4 GHz RF signal must pass through, it loses between 20 and 35 percent of its signal strength. Consequently, after passing through at most four walls, there will be virtually no remaining signal over which to provide wireless connectivity. One way to solve this problem would be to strategically locate a small number of additional wireless base stations, which are more properly known as "Access Points" (a.k.a., APs) throughout the house. Deploying APs is considerably easier than adding additional telephone or network jacks, although the APs will need to be attached to a wired network.

---

8. For more information on HomePNA™, go to www.homepna.org.

9. To have an extra phone jack added to my residence, the author paid a handyman over $100 to climb around in my ceiling, find the phone wiring, drop a new extension down between the walls, and install a wall jack. Adding more than a few extensions to an existing telephone system can be rather expensive.

10. HomePNA™ products can achieve between 1 and 10 Mbps of throughput, although future versions will be faster. The actual speed will depend on the quality of the existing wiring, how much noise is on the lines, and other factors. However, future HomePNA™ will continue to suffer from the fact that it will still be a shared medium, and it will still be limited to use by devices that are near telephone jacks.

One network topology that can be very useful at home is to have a WLAN "backbone" connecting little islands of wired connectivity, as in Figure 1–1, which depicts one such island. Note that it is possible that the AP functionality may one day be integrated into the PC itself (e.g., Microsoft's rumored "Soft AP" implementation). It is also conceivable that, given the right software, any WLAN card could enable a PC to become an AP.

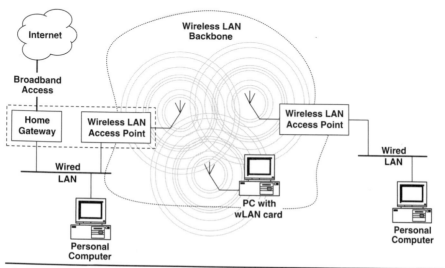

Figure 1–1   A wireless LAN home "backbone"

The WLAN demonstrably has sufficient bandwidth to enable the users in a home to share broadband access to the Internet. In the future, more bandwidth-intensive applications, such as network-based audio and video distribution in the home, may require that higher-speed WLANs be used, perhaps in conjunction with expanded wired LANs if the applications' demands cannot be met with a purely wireless infrastructure.

For now, the most interesting application and the speed available are a good match for each other. In fact, as indicated in Figure 1–1, newer models of Home Gateway devices are often sold with an integrated AP.

Components of IEEE 802.11 LANs

An IEEE 802.11 LAN Basic Service Set (BSS) can operate in one of exactly two modes, specifically "independent" or "infrastructure." A BSS in infrastructure mode is also sometimes referred to as being part of an ESS (Extended Service Set; a collection of more than one BSS and the necessary wired LAN Distribution System (DS) that ties them together), which behaves logically like an extended BSS. To make a collection of BSS WLANs into an ESS, they must all identify themselves using the same Service Set Identifier (SSID, or ESSID, or BSSID, depending on the context, but in any case it's the same thing, a string of up to 32 characters that identifies each BSS.[11]

Each infrastructure-mode BSS has exactly one AP. Independent BSS LANs do not have an AP. The lack of an AP, a form of network infrastructure that the independent BSS lacks, is why the term *ad hoc* is sometimes used when referring to a WLAN in IBSS mode (IBSS is the abbreviation of Independent BSS).

There is significant opportunity for confusion since the term *IBSS* could reasonably be taken to mean either "independent BSS" (correct) or "infrastructure BSS" (incorrect). Table 1–1 translates the terms in the standard into the words that are frequently used in conversation to describe the types of WLANs.

Table 1–1   Types of IEEE 802.11 LANs

IEEE 802.11 Standard	Common Usage
Independent BSS	*ad hoc*
IBSS	*ad hoc*
BSS	infrastructure
Infrastructure BSS	infrastructure
ESS	infrastructure

In this book, the author will tend to use the terms of the standard whenever possible, since they are more precise.

Infrastructure Mode

A WLAN in infrastructure (or BSS) mode consists of a control station (STA) known as an AP and a collection of client STAs.[12] Figure 1–2 illustrates a

---

11. For example, the author's home WLAN's SSID is "police line—do not cross".

typical infrastructure-mode WLAN, consisting of a single BSS with an AP and several STAs.

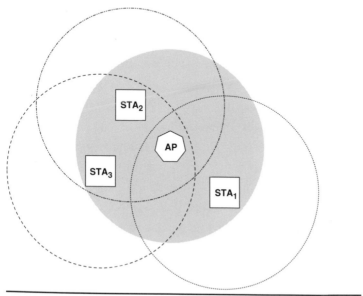

Figure 1–2   A single wireless LAN BSS in infrastructure mode

The gray background centered on the AP indicates the AP's radio coverage (due to nonlinear propagation effects, the actual coverage domain is unlikely to be a circle). An STA is not able to be a part of the WLAN unless it is within range of the AP. The STA must also complete the procedures necessary to join the WLAN (a process comprising both authentication and association).

All traffic in an infrastructure WLAN must pass through the AP. This restriction has a cost, which is that every frame must be sent across the wireless medium (WM) two times.[13] However, the benefit of this scheme is that all the stations need not be in range of each other; the BSS must only meet a much less restrictive constraint, namely that each STA must be able to hear the AP, and

---

12. Some people pronounce STA as "stay," and others pronounce it as "stah." The author uses the former, but it's likely that both are equally valid.

13. An enhancement under consideration by the IEEE 802.11*e* Task Group may allow stations to negotiate "side channels" (properly known as "Direct Links") to enable two STAs within range of each other to exchange high-bandwidth traffic, without needing to send the traffic through the intermediate hop of the AP, thereby reducing the number of frames that must cross the wireless medium by half.

vice-versa. Every silver lining has a cloud, though, since by allowing STAs to be out of range of each other's radios, we have created a "hidden node" problem that increases the complexity of the access control procedures.

Realistically, however, the hidden node problem is only one aspect of the fundamental difference between the wireless medium and the wired medium with which we are all familiar, Ethernet.

Ethernet detects collisions by simply listening for them while a transmission is in progress. A collision is an event that happens on the entire LAN segment simultaneously. The sender and all other members of the LAN can tell when it happens. However, in a WLAN, it is possible for a frame to be interfered with by some form of local interference at the receiver, without the interference being detectable by the sender. The way that the wireless LAN standards compensate for this is to require that most types of frames be acknowledged, which is not a reliability mechanism, but a remote collision detection mechanism. Therefore, there is no need for WLAN devices to incur the cost of duplex-capable radios (that can listen while they transmit; i.e., to try to detect collisions or other interference).

The only requirement for WLANs is that the radio must be simplex; in other words, at any given time it is either a transmitter or a receiver, but it never needs to be both. Figure 1–3 shows a "hidden node" configuration in which STA_2 and STA_3 can both hear each other (as well as the AP), but STA_1 can only hear the AP.

Moreover, STA_4 is not part of the WLAN…at least not until it moves closer to the AP. The fact that STA_1 can hear STA_4 is irrelevant—although the possibility exists that STA_4 could interfere with STA_1's ability to participate in the WLAN (i.e., if STA_4 happens to transmit a frame while the AP is sending a frame to STA_1). In the latter scenario, the AP would have no way to know that its transmission to STA_1 was interfered with, because the AP is not within range of STA_4.

Even if two STAs happen to be within range of each other's radios (and the AP's, of course), the traffic flowing between the STAs still must pass through the AP. Note that even though STA_2 and STA_3 are both within range of each other's radios in Figure 1–3, their traffic still must pass through the AP. This may seem like a waste in the case of these two stations, but note that STA_1 cannot directly reach STA_2 or STA_3…its only means of sending traffic to those two

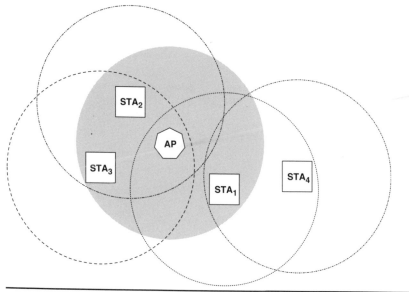

Figure 1–3   Hidden nodes

stations is via the AP. Therefore, even though using an AP has the effect of making the message cross the airwaves twice, this enables all stations in range of the AP to send traffic to each other, regardless of their actual proximity.

If STA_3 wants to send a frame to STA_1, STA_3 first sends the frame to the AP. The frame has now crossed the air once (the STA_3-to-AP hop). The AP then forwards the frame on to its destination, namely STA_1. The frame has now crossed the air a second time (the AP-to-STA_1 hop). This has the effect of reducing the maximum capacity of the WLAN approximately in half. This may seem wasteful, but this "waste" is necessary, since in this example, STA_1 and STA_3 are not in range of each other's radios, so without the AP there would be no way for them to communicate. Each time the frame crossed the wireless medium, it is acknowledged (i.e., the ACK is hop-by-hop, not end-to-end).

IBSS (*Ad Hoc*) Mode

In IBSS mode, a WLAN has no AP. Without the AP as a central control point, the STAs have to assume many of the duties of an AP. Because the AP function is not part of an IBSS-mode WLAN, a practical constraint on the layout of an *ad hoc* network is that all the STAs need to be reachable by all the other STAs. There can be no hidden nodes in an IBSS-mode WLAN.

In Figure 1–4, we see four STAs in an IBSS-mode WLAN. The intersection of the coverage circles of the STAs represents the edges of the WLAN.

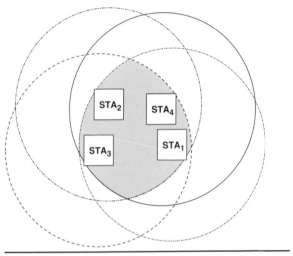

Figure 1–4   Independent BSS (*ad hoc*) mode

For example, another function that an AP performs is to buffer traffic directed to a dozing STA (i.e., the state known as "dozing" occurs when the STA's radio is in power-save mode), the AP will buffer frames that are intended for that STA. In an IBSS, each STA must perform its own buffering in the event that another STA has temporarily dozed.

Also, in an infrastructure BSS, the AP sends a periodic "Beacon" frame to coordinate the activities within the BSS, whereas in an IBSS, each STA takes turns sending the Beacon frame. IBSS WLANs also have a unique capability, in that they must support the merging of two IBSS-mode WLANs with the same SSID if they wander near enough each other.

There are other differences, but these few samples should give the reader the correct impression that there are many fundamental differences between an IBSS-mode WLAN and an infrastructure-mode WLAN.

Summary: Differences between Wired and Wireless LANs

One major difference between wired LANs such as Ethernet, and WLANs, is that in a WLAN, each STA has both limited transmitter power capacity and limited receiver sensitivity. On an Ethernet LAN, it is an assumption that all the stations can hear each other's transmissions, and can all speak loudly enough that all the other Ethernet stations can hear them. In addition, it is a presumption that the Ethernet transmitters can receive while they transmit, so that they can detect a collision as soon as it happens. In a WLAN, not all the STAs may be within range of a given STA's radio transmitter. Conversely, not all STAs may have sufficiently sensitive receivers to hear the transmissions of all the other STAs. Consequently, WLANs have a so-called "hidden-node" problem that wired LANs cannot have.[14]

Because of the hidden node problem, among other challenges specific to wireless media, the IEEE 802.11 MAC protocol supports an explicit ACK for unicast traffic. In a wired LAN, specifically Ethernet, there is an implicit requirement that a station will be able to tell on its own if its transmission was interfered with. In IEEE 802.11, however, the source may complete a transmission and never be able to hear the interference—even if it had listened for it, the source of the interference may be close enough to the receiving STA to interfere with the frame it is receiving, but too far from the sending STA for its interference to be detected at the sender.

In a WLAN, what matters is the noise environment *at the destination*, which is not necessarily the same as the noise environment at the source. The only way for the sender to be sure that its frame was received correctly is for the destination to acknowledge receipt of the frame. This ACK mechanism is not meant to make the IEEE 802.11 MAC protocol into a reliable data-link protocol; it is simply intended to compensate for the variation of RF noise and other interference across the WLAN.

Another important fact to remember about WLANs is that the medium is inherently shared, so the MAC protocol is limited to what is effectively half-duplex operation (sometimes abbreviated as HDX), but the WLAN STAs are simplex devices, since at any given time they are either a transmitter or receiver, but never both. In plain English that means that only one station can be speaking at any given time. In HDX mode, the entire bandwidth of the channel is used completely by a single station for as long as the protocol allows, and the rest of the stations are idle while any given station is transmitting. In contrast,

---

14. To be clear, a properly functioning wired LAN cannot have hidden nodes, but the author has seen Ethernet devices that could receive traffic but not send it, or vice-versa, so the node might appear to send traffic, but could not receive it.

switching has brought full-duplex (FDX) operation to Ethernet's Medium Access Control (MAC) layer protocol, which was originally limited to HDX operation. In FDX mode, collisions are impossible and a station may be transmitting and receiving frames simultaneously.

As will be seen in a subsequent chapter, the WLAN MAC sub-layer protocol is designed to function in the presence of hidden nodes, and other wireless-specific "challenges" with which wired LAN protocols do not need to be concerned.

Before exploring the innards of the plethora of WLAN standards, it is useful to understand the organization that is producing these standards.

Where Do Wireless LAN Standards Come From?

The short answer is that they come from the Institute of Electrical and Electronics Engineers (IEEE), which is a nonprofit technical professional association with 380,000 members in 150 countries (as of June 2003). The IEEE oversees more than 900 active standards, with 700 under development, one of which is known as Project 802, responsible for creating standards for local area networks (LANs) and metropolitan area networks (MANs).

In Project IEEE 802's own words[15]:

> "The first meeting of the IEEE Computer Society 'Local Network Standards Committee,' Project IEEE 802, was held in February of 1980. There was going to be one LAN standard, with speeds from 1 to 20 MHz[16]. It was divided into media or Physical layer (PHY), Media Access Control (MAC), and Higher Level Interface (HILI). The access method was similar to that for Ethernet, as well as the bus topology. By the end of 1980, a token access method was added, and a year later there were three MACs: CSMA/CD[17], Token Bus, and Token Ring.

---

15. This text was extracted from: http://grouper.ieee.org/groups/IEEE 802/overview2000.pdf.

16. The author does not know why they used the unit "MHz" rather than "Mbps."

17. Carrier Sense Multiple Access with Collision Detection (CSMA/CD) is the name for the protocol by which bandwidth is shared on half-duplex Ethernets. The terms "CSMA/CD" and "Ethernet" have become somewhat synonymous in certain circles, but modern switched Ethernet networks have full-duplex capability, and therefore do not use CSMA/CD; they simply preserve Ethernet's original frame format, transmission rate(s), and inter-frame timing from the "classic" Ethernet protocol.

In the years since, other MAC and PHY groups have been added, and one for LAN security as well. The unifying theme has been a common upper interface to the Logical Link Control (LLC) sub-layer, common data framing elements, and some commonality in media interface. The scope of work has grown to include Metropolitan Area Networks (MANs) and higher data rates have been added. An organizational change gave us the 'LMSC' name and more involvement in the standards sponsorship and approval process."

Therefore, IEEE Project 802 is more commonly known as the IEEE LAN/ MAN Standards Committee (or [the] LMSC for short), and has been in existence since 1980. Over the decades in which the IEEE's LMSC has been in existence, it has had a large number of Working Groups (WGs), each corresponding (roughly) to a given type of LAN or MAN technology.

The IEEE LMSC is divided into WGs, each of which is identified by a decimal number after the "802". For example, there is an IEEE 802.3 WG that has defined the standards for Ethernet, an IEEE 802.5 WG that defined the standards for Token-passing Rings, and the IEEE 802.1 WG defined the standards for bridging and other inter-LAN issues. The IEEE 802.1 WG is notable in that it has not standardized any particular LAN or MAN technology *per se*; rather it has defined the interworking rules that allow the various LAN and MAN technologies being produced by the LMSC's WGs to interoperate.

As has been alluded to already, the subset of the IEEE's LMSC that has been chartered with the standardization of WLANs is called the IEEE 802.11 WG. The term *IEEE 802.11* refers to the 11th WG under IEEE Project 802. The first meeting of the IEEE 802.11 WG was in 1990.

Figure 1–5 illustrates numerous interactions between the IEEE 802.11 WG and other WGs, and depicts a simplified[18] version of the top-level structure of the LMSC, with the WGs inter-relationships shown in a "protocol stack" view, showing how the various WGs and their associated specifications map to the Data Link and Physical layers.[19]

---

18. The sheer number of entities that make up Project IEEE 802 is why Figure 1–5 can only show a subset of the structure—a full diagram would be unreadable. Table 1–1 contains the complete listing.

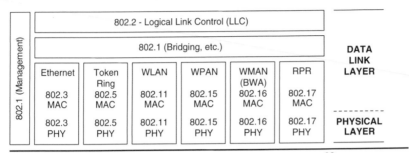

Figure 1–5   Top-level structure of IEEE Project IEEE 802[20]

Figure 1–6 shows the relationship of Project IEEE 802's Data Link layer standards to the IP at the Network layer. Note that in the case of Ethernet, the intermediate IEEE 802.2 (LLC) layer is not always required.

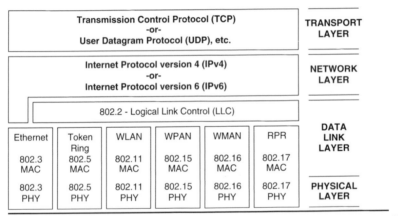

Figure 1–6   Relationship of Project IEEE 802 protocols to the IP stack[20]

As can be seen in Figure 1–6, IP can be layered directly over Ethernet, or it can be layered over IEEE 802.2 LLC, which in turn operates over IEEE 802.3. However, IEEE 802.2 LLC *is* a required layer when IP is operating over, for example, IEEE 802.11 and IEEE 802.5. Essentially, LLC is required in all IEEE 802 technologies except for Ethernet, where it is optional.

In regard to IEEE 802.11, these protocols and their exact usage will be detailed later in this book. For now, this treatment is just to establish the lay of

---

19. The Data Link layer and Physical layer are layers two and one of the Open Systems Interconnection (OSI) Reference Model, respectively.

20. Adapted from IEEE Std. 802®-2001, copyright 2002. All rights reserved.

the land. The case of IPv4 or IPv6 over Ethernet is special, in that neither of those protocols need be layered over the IEEE 802.2 LLC sub-layer in order to operate over Ethernet. Such an encapsulation is possible, but the default is for IPv4 or IPv6 to be directly encapsulated in Ethernet.

The remaining IEEE 802 standards over which IP can operate, including IEEE 802.11, all require the presence of the LLC sub-layer protocol(s) between IP and the MAC sub-layer header. For the case of IEEE 802.11, these issues will be covered in great detail later in the book.

Table 1–2 gives a complete list of all the entities that are (or have been) elements of IEEE Project 802. Currently active groups are in **boldface** type.

Table 1–2   Complete Constituents of Project IEEE 802

	802.1	**WG**	**Higher Layer LAN Protocols (e.g., bridging and management)**
(inactive)	802.2	WG	Logical Link Control
	802.3	**WG**	**Ethernet**
(inactive)	802.4	WG	Token Bus
(inactive)	802.5	WG	Token Ring
(inactive)	802.6	WG	Metropolitan Area Network (DQDB/SMDS)
(inactive)	802.7	WG	Fiber Optic
(disbanded)	802.8	TAG	Broadband
(inactive)	802.9	WG	Isochronous LAN
(inactive)	802.10	WG	Security
	802.11	**WG**	**Wireless Local Area Network (WLAN)**
(inactive)	802.12	WG	Demand Priority
<never used>	802.13		
(disbanded)	802.14	WG	Cable Modem
	802.15	**WG**	**Wireless Personal Area Network (WPAN)**
	802.16	**WG**	**Broadband Wireless Access (WMAN; fixed and mobile)**
	802.17	**WG**	**Resilient Packet Ring**
	802.18	**TAG**	**Radio Regulatory**
	802.19	**TAG**	**Coexistence**
	802.20	**WG**	**Mobile Broadband Wireless Access (MBWA)**

Note that there have been three Technical Advisory Groups (TAGs) in addition to the 16 WGs that have been defined since the beginning of Project IEEE 802. The TAGs have contributed to Project IEEE 802's work in various ways, depending on the situation that necessitated the creation of the TAG. In some cases, the TAG may be doing "technical fact finding" and producing reports that provide important information to one or more WGs. In other cases, the TAG may be a quasi-WG, or a co-WG. The main difference between TAGs and WGs is that TAGs do not produce standards. Some inactive groups may be "hibernating," which means that they can be reactivated for some purpose deemed relevant to their original charter, should a need arise.

The fact that there are four WGs and one TAG active in the general area of standardizing wireless technologies indicates that wireless standardization is very important to the IEEE LAN/MAN Standards Committee (LMSC, a.k.a. IEEE Project 802), and by extension, to the companies and their customers in the data communications industry. Specifically, the following activities are underway that are relevant to wireless technology:

- The IEEE 802.11 WG is developing WLANs. The standards it has produced, and the products based on them, are the subjects of this book.
- The IEEE 802.15 WG is developing WPANs (wireless personal area networks (WPANs)), based on Bluetooth and other short-range wireless technologies.
- The IEEE 802.16 WG is developing standards for fixed and mobile broadband wireless MANs (WMANs).
- The IEEE 802.18 TAG has been formed to provide input and technical guidance to the various wireless WGs within Project IEEE 802. This TAG is concerned with the regulatory issues surrounding the use of radio-based wireless standards.
- The IEEE 802.19 TAG, like IEEE 802.18, is another TAG that is operating as a coordinating body across all wireless standardization within the IEEE LMSC. To paraphrase their charter: "The IEEE 802.19 Coexistence TAG will develop and maintain policies defining the responsibilities of [IEEE] 802 standards developers to address issues of coexistence with existing standards and other standards under development. It will also, when required, offer assessments regarding the degree to which standards developers have conformed to those conventions, and may also develop coexistence documentation of interest to the technical community outside [IEEE] 802."
- Finally, the IEEE 802.20 WG is designing a set of standards for mobile broadband wireless access (MBWA).

An overview of the IEEE 802.15 and IEEE 802.16 technologies (with minor coverage of IEEE 802.20) is presented in Chapter 8, *Applications and Deployment of Wireless Technology*, but a full treatment of the standards that have been, and are being, developed by these WGs is beyond the scope of this book. Interested readers can find a good introductory treatment of IEEE 802.15 and IEEE

802.16 in the fourth edition of Dr. Andrew Tanenbaum's *Computer Networks*, published in 2002.

Within any given IEEE Project 802 WG, work is often divided among various dedicated "Task Groups" (TGs). For example, the IEEE 802.3*ae* TG has developed standards that will allow Ethernet to operate at 10 Gbps (that standard, until it is incorporated into a future revision of IEEE 802.3, is known as IEEE 802.3*ae*-2002).

Within the IEEE 802.11 WG are numerous TGs that are actively standardizing various aspects of WLANs. In fact, there are so many IEEE 802.11 TGs that it may be daunting for people new to WLANs (or those who have not read this book!) to keep them straight in their minds.

To whet your appetite (and hopefully not scare you away!), this book will eventually describe IEEE 802.11, IEEE 802.11*a*, IEEE 802.11*b*, IEEE 802.11*c*, IEEE 802.11*d*, IEEE 802.11*e*, IEEE 802.11*f*, IEEE 802.11*g*, IEEE 802.11*h*, IEEE 802.11*i*, IEEE 802.11*j*, IEEE 802.11*k*, and IEEE 802.11*n*.

As of June 2003, the WG has produced its base standard, and five of IEEE 802.11's TGs have finished their respective task(s). Specifically, the completed TGs are IEEE 802.11*a* through IEEE 802.11*d*, and IEEE 802.11*g*. These TGs have all produced officially approved standards of the IEEE, and products exist that implement them. By the time you read this, it is likely that IEEE 802.11F and IEEE 802.11*h* will exist as approved standards, rather than as drafts.

The other TGs are in varying stages of completeness, and one may possibly be approved as a standard in 2003, namely IEEE 802.11*j*. The remainder of the list represents the wide variety of ongoing work that is being done to further define what a wireless LAN can do, and how it can do it.

Overview of IEEE 802.11's Structure and Output Thus Far

The IEEE 802.11 WG is producing the standards for WLANs at both the MAC layer and the Physical (PHY) layer. So far, it has specified one MAC and several PHYs that operate under that MAC. This is a big job, and as noted earlier it has been ongoing since 1990 (the original IEEE 802.11 WG was trying to design WLAN standards for use in the U.S. Industrial, Scientific, and Medical (ISM) band, at 915.0 ± 13 MHz).

Over time, the WG's horizons were expanded as new spectrum became available (e.g., the 2.4 GHz unlicensed ISM band (2.450 ± 0.050 GHz)), and as new technology made higher performance possible (e.g., Digital Signal Processors (DSPs) that are capable of implementing advanced modulation schemes). For all but historical purposes, it is safe to ignore the IEEE 802.11 WG's early work on PHYs that were designed to operate in the 915 MHz ISM band. The first PHYs to gain widespread market acceptance operated in the 2.4 GHz ISM band.

The first "real" IEEE 802.11 specification, namely IEEE 802.11-1997, defined a MAC layer and two different PHYs that allowed operation at either 1 or 2 Mbps in the 2.4 GHz unlicensed ISM band. IEEE 802.11-1997 also included a specification for a PHY based on "diffuse infrared" signals. The diffuse infrared PHY will not be discussed further, other than to note that its range is 10 meters (it could perhaps be pushed to as much as 20 meters), and it is limited to operation at either 1 or 2 Mbps, matching the speeds of the RF PHY in the base IEEE 802.11 specification. The main IEEE 802.11 specification was updated in 1999, so IEEE 802.11-1999 is the latest version.

IEEE 802.11*b* (a.k.a. Wi-Fi™) defined "higher speed" extensions to the original IEEE 802.11-1997 specification. There were two new PHY modes that allowed operation at either 5.5 or 11 Mbps, also within the 2.4 GHz unlicensed ISM band. IEEE 802.11*b* products typically support all four rates: 1, 2, 5.5, and 11 Mbps.

At the same time that the IEEE 802.11*b* TG was working on their "high rate" extensions to IEEE 802.11-1997, the IEEE 802.11*a* TG was working on specifying a new PHY designed to operate within the 5 GHz unlicensed national information infrastructure (U–NII) band, which partially overlaps the 5 GHz ISM band, which is at 5.800 ± 0.075 GHz. IEEE 802.11*a* uses a modulation technique known as Orthogonal Frequency Division Multiplexing (OFDM).

When completed, IEEE 802.11*a*-1999 offered speeds of <u>6</u>, 9, <u>12</u>, 18, <u>24</u>, 36, 48, and 54 Mbps. The underlined speeds, namely 6, 12, and 24 Mbps, are the data rates that every IEEE 802.11*a* implementation must support, but two of the three "mandatory" rates, namely 6 and 12 Mbps, are virtually identical to IEEE 802.11*b*'s 5.5 and 11 Mbps rates. IEEE 802.11*a*'s real appeal, initially, was the possibility of much higher top-end speeds than IEEE 802.11*b*. For a variety of reasons, IEEE 802.11*a* has failed to garner much market share (or mindshare), at least so far. There are indications that this is changing, but only time will tell how popular products based on IEEE 802.11*a*-1999 will become.

Figure 1–7 shows the various WLAN speeds that have been standardized at the time of this writing, as well as indicating which standard is associated with each speed.

Standard	Type	Speed
802.11a+g	(optional)	54
802.11a+g	(optional)	48
802.11a+g	(optional)	36
802.11g	(optional — PBCC)	33
802.11a+g	(mandatory)	24
802.11g	(optional — PBCC)	22
802.11a+g	(optional)	18
802.11a+g	(mandatory)	12
802.11b	(mandatory)	11
802.11a+g	(optional)	9
802.11a+g	(mandatory)	6
802.11b	(mandatory)	5.5
802.11	(mandatory)	2
802.11	(mandatory)	1

Figure 1–7   IEEE 802.11 WLAN standards and speeds (Mbps)

Now that the IEEE 802.11g-2003 standard is available, products can legitimately claim to support it. Eager vendors began shipping products based on the drafts of the standard in 2002, and even without a Wi-Fi™ logo program for IEEE 802.11g-based products, they sold *very* well.

IEEE 802.11g-2003 offers speeds up to 54 Mbps while operating at 2.4 GHz ISM band, by combining IEEE 802.11*a*'s OFDM modulation with commodity 2.4 GHz radios to achieve speeds equivalent to those available in IEEE 802.11*a*. Moreover, IEEE 802.11*g* is backward compatible with IEEE 802.11*b*, and should be a natural migration path from IEEE 802.11*b*-based WLANs.

IEEE 802.11g-2003 also provides two speeds that are not available with IEEE 802.11*a*, namely 22 and 33 Mbps (both of which use the optional modulation scheme known as Packet Binary Convolutional Coding, or PBCC). Full details on all of these Physical layer choices are provided in Chapter 3, *Speeds and Feeds*.

What Is Wi-Fi™? Is It the Same as IEEE 802.11?

Wi-Fi™ is a registered trademark of the Wi-Fi™ Alliance. Wi-Fi™ is a brand, in a way, that represents a certification program, and is the associated logo that represents that brand. End users can have confidence that any two products that display the Wi-Fi™ logo will interoperate. The moniker "Wi-Fi™" is to IEEE

802.11 as "Ethernet" is to IEEE 802.3, although Ethernet never really had an industry consortium that was testing and certifying standards compliance, then conferring a logo on devices. Wi-Fi™ stands for "wireless fidelity," and is a user-friendly name that has been created to refer to a common type of WLAN products.

The Wi-Fi™ Alliance is a nonprofit organization that certifies the interoperability of products based on the IEEE 802.11 standards. The Wi-Fi™ Alliance was founded in 1999—the same year that the updated WLAN base specification was finalized (designated IEEE 802.11-1999), along with IEEE 802.11*b*-1999 and IEEE 802.11*a*-1999. The initial members of the Wi-Fi™ Alliance[21] were Agere Systems, Cisco Systems, Intersil Corporation, Nokia Inc., Symbol Technologies, and 3Com Corporation. By July 1, 2003, over 180 companies had become members of the Wi-Fi™ Alliance. The Wi-Fi™ Alliance's Web site is located at www.wi-fi.org.

Originally, the Wi-Fi™ logo only applied to products based on the IEEE 802.11*b*-1999 standard. Such products may operate at speeds of 1, 2, 5.5, and 11 Mbps in the 2.4 GHz unlicensed Industrial, Scientific, and Medical (ISM) band (specifically, 2400 to 2500 MHz). The Wi-Fi™ logo has been extended to apply to other types of physical layers that can be used with IEEE 802.11.

The Wi-Fi™ Alliance certifies those products from member companies that have been certified as complying with the applicable IEEE 802.11 standard(s), as well as meeting some basic performance and throughput targets. Once certified, a product is granted the right to display the Wi-Fi™ logo, as shown in Figure 1–8.

Figure 1–8   The Wi-Fi™ logo[22]

---

21. The original name of the Wi-Fi™ Alliance was WECA, which stood for the Wireless Ethernet Compatibility Alliance. WECA changed its name in July 2002.

22. Note well: The display of this logo in no way confers endorsement of this book by the Wi-Fi™ Alliance.

For a product to become Wi-Fi™-certified, which enables the vendor to display the Wi-Fi™ logo on the certified product's packaging, the vendor must pay annual membership dues to the Wi-Fi™ Alliance, on the order of $25,000 per year, and submit their product for certification testing by the Wi-Fi™ Alliance. Having paid the annual membership fee, a company can certify any number of it products, provided the company pays the Wi-Fi™ Alliance a per-product testing and certification fee of $15,000. However, if a company terminates its Wi-Fi™ Alliance membership, it can no longer display the Wi-Fi™ logo.[23]

Products conforming to IEEE 802.11a operate in the 5 GHz unlicensed ISM band (in the United States, from 5725 through 5875 MHz), and must be able to transmit at speeds of 6, 12, and 24 Mbps. IEEE 802.11a products may optionally also support transmission at speeds of 9, 18, 36, 48, and 54 Mbps. Subsequent sections of the book will cover all the relevant technical details of IEEE 802.11a-1999 and IEEE 802.11b-1999, as well as the emerging IEEE 802.11g-2003.

The Wi-Fi™ Alliance had been planning to create another logo, for IEEE 802.11a products, known provisionally as "Wi-Fi5" (where the "5" refers to the fact that the IEEE 802.11a products operate in a subset of the 5 GHz radio frequency spectrum, as opposed to IEEE 802.11 and IEEE 802.11b, which both operate in portions of the 2.4 GHz spectrum). However, due to the overwhelming market awareness of the Wi-Fi™ logo, it was decided to extend the Wi-Fi™ logo to cover products based on IEEE 802.11a, rather than create a new logo. The first Wi-Fi™-certified IEEE 802.11a products became available in late 2002.

Summary

For certain applications, wired LANs—of which the canonical example is Ethernet—will always be superior to WLANs if the only means of comparison were raw throughput. For one thing, the wired LAN is much more resistant to radio-frequency (RF) interference, which is a major factor that can affect

---

23. Note that the membership fee and per-product testing fees may have changed by the time you read this. The information cited here was the latest available on the Wi-Fi™ Alliance's Web site, as of July 1, 2003. Future versions of the Wi-Fi™ Alliance's Frequently Asked Questions (FAQ) document may have updated information. This FAQ can be viewed at www.wi-fi.org.

WLAN throughput. Twisted-pair wiring is extremely immune to RF interference.[24] The highest-performance wired LANs are based on optical fiber and are the most resistant to both electrical and RF interference. Moreover, any advances in data modulation techniques can be applied equally well to both wired and wireless media.

Therefore, given the inherent advantages of wired media, notably excellent signal-to-noise ratio compared to almost any wireless medium you could imagine, it's very likely that wired media will always be faster than wireless media.

The frequency spectrum in which 11 Mbps WLANs operate is not dedicated to their use. A great benefit to easing deployment of WLANs is that they operate in unlicensed spectrum, but this means that there is no way to prevent nearby "operators" of WLAN devices from interfering with each other. The limited range of WLAN devices helps prevent interference (best case is outdoors, with no line-of-sight obstructions, at 150 meters or so; indoors, usable WLANs rarely have a radius of more than 20–30 meters).

Even if WLAN operators had a guarantee that there were no other WLAN devices operating close enough to interfere with theirs, there would still be naturally occurring radio interference, especially given that modern PC CPUs typically operate near these frequencies and may become a source of RF noise (harmonics from a CPU clock running as slow as 1.2 GHz could generate 2.4 GHz noise, and CPU chips in the 2.4 GHz range are becoming more widely available in PCs targeted at the home user, but luckily, PC cases are usually well-shielded against leakage of RF energy). In fact, there are other sources of RF interference near the 2.4 GHz frequency band besides improperly shielded PC motherboards, including 2.4 GHz cordless telephones and microwave ovens.

Despite the lack of dedicated RF spectrum, the unlicensed nature of WLANs ensures their widespread deployment. The degree to which interference affects throughput will vary depending on the number of devices attempting to operate in the same area, as well as the prevalence of natural or man-made sources of RF interference. WLANs are remarkably robust over a

---

24. However, the fact that there is still an electrical connection between two devices means that one device can still interfere with another; for example, if there is a power surge near one device, that electrical impulse may be carried to the other device and cause significant damage. However, the improved transmission media of twisted pair and optical fiber allow for far higher speeds that are likely to be achievable over a wireless medium.

usable radius, so that acceptable performance may be achieved even in less than perfect environments. Later in the book, we will see how the MAC protocol deals with the challenging RF transmission environment, through the use of explicit ACKs, retransmissions, MAC-layer fragmentation, and being able to switch to more robust (albeit slower) modulations.

2

A Brief History of
Networking Standards

This chapter is meant as background material for readers who may not be familiar with all the types of networking standards there are, and the organizations that produce them. Readers who are already familiar with terms like CCITT, OSI, IEEE, IETF, ITU-T, TCP/IP, X.25, and so on can proceed to Chapter 3, *Speeds and Feeds*[1].

In practice, there are two kinds of standards, *de facto* and *de jure*. The latter are formally created by organizations that are specifically chartered with producing them, and often have the force of law or treaties behind them. The former were perhaps never intended to become standards, but due to popularity or influence became entrenched in the marketplace.[2] The standards to be discussed next were *de jure* standards created under the auspices of the international group known as the CCITT.[3]

The original reason for creating them was partly to offer an alternative to an emerging proprietary networking protocol suite, namely IBM's Systems

---

1. The information in this short chapter is provided for completeness. There is an unwritten rule that all books that have to do with networking must at some point mention the OSI Reference Model.

2. In the context of this chapter, the standards we discuss are generally the *de jure* variety.

3. The acronym stands for *"Comité Consultatif International Télégraphique et Téléphonique."* The group still exists. The portion of the CCITT that standardized networking protocols and conducted related activities has been relocated to the International Telecommunications Union, Telecommunications Standardization Sector (abbreviated: ITU-T), which is a component of the United Nations.

Network Architecture (SNA), which for many years did achieve *de facto* standard status until it was displaced by TCP/IP. Pre-OSI networking protocols of the era (mid-1970s and onward), such as IBM's proprietary SNA, were very different from the eventual OSI model in many ways, but shared many architectural features in common with OSI's structure, including the number of layers, and their basic functionality. Although there was not a perfect functional alignment between the OSI-RM and IBM's SNA, it seems rather clear that there was some cross-pollination of ideas among the groups involved in the creation of the two protocol stacks.

One key observation about IBM's SNA is that it had a *strong* design preference for connection-oriented protocols, and it provided for reliable delivery at many layers, whereas the OSI protocol stack usually offered either connection-oriented or connectionless operation for protocols implementing layers above the Physical layer, which is (of course) inherently connection-oriented.

There is no ambiguity in the term *de jure*. However, there are multiple ways that a standard can be *de facto*, including the way it was created and the way it is used. For example, a *de jure* standard could be used in a way that the authors never intended. If that usage becomes popular, that particular use of the standard could be deemed *de facto*. For example, certain protocols may have been designed with a certain scope in mind, for example, LAN protocols are typically expected to operate within an area that is "local". However, if that technology later evolves such that it is deployed in larger contexts, that might or might not align with the protocol designers' intentions.

Another way that protocols can evolve is exemplified by the way that Ethernet is beginning to see so-called "jumbo" frames being supported by equipment that supports gigabit Ethernet, however, the IEEE 802.3 committee (which is the name of the working group that is managing the evolution of the standards governing what we typically call "Ethernet") does not recognize such an implementation as being in compliance with the standard. In all other ways, an Ethernet product that supports jumbo frames would be interoperable with earlier devices, but mixed networks might exhibit strange behavior, such as one-way traffic flows for large frames, and other bizarre effects.

The only reason we mention these examples is that it is important to understand that there are no subtleties in the term *de jure*, but the meaning of the term *de facto* may be context-dependent, and it is possible to have a *de facto* usage of a *de jure* standard.

The Mother of All Networking Standards

The old ironic aphorism that the great thing about standards is that there are so many to choose from is funny because it is so true. The profusion of data networking standards partially derives from the many different organizations that create such standards, such as ANSI, CCITT, IEEE, IETF, ITU-T, and so forth, and partially from the many different layers at which standards may be defined. Private companies also espouse their own protocols, and frequently "embrace and extend" openly created protocols for their own purposes. The main system of classifying data networking standards is the OSI-RM, which illustrates an idealized protocol stack that supports functionality distributed throughout seven interdependent layers.

During the Open Systems Interconnection (OSI) networking protocol suite standardization effort, which started in the mid-1970s and continued through the late 1980s and early 1990s, a form of division of labor was employed such that a different WG designed each protocol layer, in such a way that the details of the internal operation of any given protocol layer were irrelevant, as long as each layer provided a certain set of well-defined services to the layer above it. Each layer likewise depended on a different set of well-defined services that would be exposed by the layer below it.

In the early days of the standardization of the protocols that would eventually comprise the seven layers of the OSI Reference Model (OSI-RM), the lower layers were understood best, and thus their standardization was completed first. These well-understood layers consisted of the Physical[4] and Data Link layers (some Network layer protocols were already understood as well, such as the connection-oriented Network layer of CCITT X.25). Figure 2–1 shows the complete seven-layer protocol stack defined by the OSI-RM.

In most cases, a layer has well-defined interfaces that are used to either accept data from higher layers, or to indicate the presence of data to a higher layer. Typically, there are also control interfaces between the layers that allow a higher

---

4. A device that implements a Physical layer protocol is frequently referred to verbally and written shorthand, namely as a "PHY" device.

Application
Presentation
Session
Transport
Network
Data Link
Physical

Figure 2–1
OSI Reference Model

layer to configure a lower layer according to administrative preferences, operating conditions, and so forth.

The internal operation of a layer is invisible to the layers above or below it; the important thing is that the layer must operate according to its configuration and support the functionality that is expected of it. Figure 2–2 illustrates the relationships between a given layer and the ones above and below it.

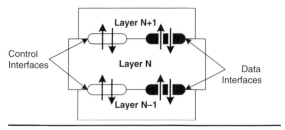

Control
Interfaces   Layer N+1

                  Layer N   Data
                                   Interfaces
                  Layer N–1

Figure 2–2   Layered protocol model

The "transmit" direction is down the stack, and the "receive" direction is up the stack. Each layer is communicating with a peer process at the same layer on another machine, using the services provided by the layers below it in the stack. Logically, the interaction is as if the peers were communicating directly, a fiction that is achieved through the presence of the lower layers. Figure 2–3 shows the logical (horizontal) and physical (vertical) operation of the layered protocol model.

To understand the function of the Data Link layer, of which the MAC sub-layer is a part, and which is the layer occupied by IEEE 802.11, we must examine the context in which the Data Link layer is located. The Data Link layer is also referred to as "layer 2" of the OSI-RM, which is an abstract representation

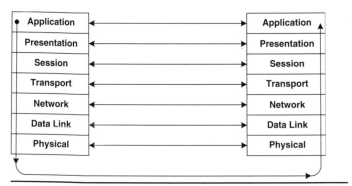

Figure 2–3   Operation of the layered protocol model

of a protocol stack that divides the job of sending and receiving data over a network into layers, each with its own well-defined function(s). The choice of seven layers was somewhat arbitrary, and had as much to do with politics than technology.[5]

The OSI-RM's seven abstract layers each perform a specific function. Layers 2 through 6 (the middle layers) have a common characteristic, in that they perform a service (or set of services) for the layer above, and expect a service (or set of services) from the layer below. In other words, they are simultaneously "clients" of the layer below, while they offer "services" to the layer above. The reason that layer 1 and layer 7 are different is that they have no layer below or no layer above, respectively. Therefore, layer 1 only provides service(s) to layer 2 because layer 1 is at the bottom of the protocol stack, and there is no lower layer; similarly, due to its position at the top of the protocol stack, layer 7 only uses services offered by layer 6.

The protocol stack manifests itself in a nested series of headers that are prefixed to data that is passed down from the layer above, as illustrated in Figure 2–4. In the ideal case, the extra header added by each layer is treated as if it were data by the layer(s) below. In practice, it is occasionally more efficient to peek into the next higher-layer protocol's header to make more accurate forwarding

---

5. There was an existing proprietary protocol suite that was very successful when the OSI standardization effort was begun, namely IBM's Systems Network Architecture (SNA). If IBM needed seven layers, then certainly the standard protocol suite couldn't have fewer. Anecdotally, there was also a natural structure of the committees that were participating in the OSI standardization effort that favored seven WGs, which mapped nicely to seven layers.

decisions, but that is an implementation choice and doesn't change the basic model described here, in which each layer adds its own header.

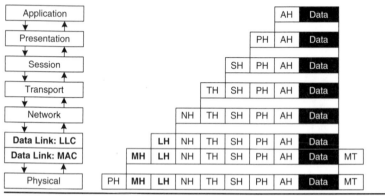

Figure 2–4   Layered headers in the OSI-RM

Each layer's headers either implicitly indicate the identity of the next higher layer protocol (as in the way that IEEE 802.2 LLC is expected to follow the IEEE 802.11 MPDU header), or a layer's header will contain an explicit pointer to the proper higher-layer protocol entity, if it is possible to have more than one such higher-layer protocol.

Note that the MAC layer also adds a trailer, containing a frame check sequence. The non-MAC-layer protocols simply add a header, and each protocol layer is equivalent, logically, to one of the set of headers pre-pended to the data being transferred between the two peer entities.

Functions of the OSI-RM's Layers

The Physical Layer

The very bottom of the protocol stack is occupied by the Physical layer, which deals with the details of transmitting bits onto a wired or wireless physical medium, using electrical, optical, radio frequency, and other signals. Early Physical layer protocols tended to be oriented toward wired point-to-point serial communications links, since broadcast-capable LANs had not yet been invented when the initial work on the OSI protocol suite was begun. The Physical layer defines what constitutes a bit (or a symbol that represents a well-defined set of some number of bits).

A bit stream may be represented by any of the following physical phenomena:

- Electrical voltage modulation (analog)
- Electrical voltage modulation (a.k.a., digital baseband)
- Optical transmitted power (i.e., brightness or amplitude) fluctuations
- Optical frequency modulation (i.e., wavelength division multiplexing)
- Optical phase modulation
- Optical polarization modulation
- RF amplitude modulation[6]
- RF frequency modulation
- RF phase modulation
- RF polarization modulation
- Semaphores
- Smoke signals
- Some combination of RF amplitude, frequency, phase, and/or polarization modulation

Finally, a Physical layer typically operates at a given fixed speed (once the station has attached to the medium and discovered that speed), and the bit encodings are typically defined such that the receiver may easily synchronize itself to the sender's Physical layer clock, so that the receiver can interpret each bit at the proper time, which helps the receiver avoid misinterpreting the data.

To summarize the features of the Physical layer, we have seen that the Physical layer is responsible for tasks that directly relate to sending and receiving bits over the medium. The Physical layer defines the encoding of bits on the medium, may control the establishment and tear-down of connections, and can perform monitoring of the medium, such as when a modem bases its modulation on the measured characteristics of a connection, to find the best speed for the evolving conditions on the call. The bit encoding on a Physical medium may include support for Forward Error Correction (if the medium is expected to be noisy).

---

6. Radio Frequency signals can be carried over the air (as in a WLAN), or they can be carried over coaxial cable (e.g., 10BROAD36 Ethernet and cable television, for two examples of wired RF technologies). This footnote applies to all the RF entries in the bulleted list after the line with this footnote reference.

The Physical layer is fundamentally connection-oriented, since if a device is not connected (in some sense) it cannot send or receive bits. There may even be Physical layer headers that are transmitted ahead of a frame that describe the modulation or other aspects of the succeeding frame. In IEEE 802.11, such a PHY protocol exists that allows different stations in a wireless LAN to operate at varying speeds.

The Data Link Layer

Early Data Link protocols tended to be reliable, since early physical data communications media were so error-prone. The earliest reliability mechanisms employed by the first Data Link layer protocols tended to use simple "ping-pong" reliable transmission schemes, in which a new frame may only be transmitted after the current frame has been acknowledged. Later, more advanced "sliding window" protocols enabled a station to have multiple unacknowledged frames "in flight" to a destination, up to a limit defined by the window size (typically at least seven frames).

These "acknowledgment-oriented" schemes were used to provide for reliable transmission of data over the slow and error-prone physical infrastructures that were common in the 1970s and 1980s; in particular, the media did not support high-speed transmission, and they frequently had very poor signal-to-noise ratios. In this timeframe, even digital transmission facilities could be extremely noisy (measured by bit-error-rate), and were quite slow.[7] It was the job of the Data Link layer to take whatever steps were necessary so that the physical medium would appear error-free to the Network layer.[8] Early Network layer protocols tended to be oriented toward packet-switched "cloud" technologies such as X.25.

By the time that broadcast-capable Data Link layer technologies, such as LANs, had matured sufficiently to warrant their incorporation into the OSI-RM framework, it was easy to integrate these new types of Data Link layers into

---

7. In the 1970s, a dedicated 56 kbps digital circuit was considered fast, which is amazing when one considers that DSL and cable modems today offer speeds on the order of 20 times faster. So-called "T-1" circuits became more common in the 1980s, but were quite expensive initially, primarily due to regulatory issues.

8. As long-haul (MAN and/or WAN) fiber-optic transmission technology was deployed in the late 1980s and early 1990s, the quality of data circuit facilities, as measured by signal-to-noise ratio or by bit-error-rate, increased by several orders of magnitude.

the OSI-RM without needing to make substantial changes to the definition of the Network layer due to the layer abstraction. As long as the new LANs exposed the control and data interfaces that the Network layer expects, the Network layer will be satisfied with the situation. The changes necessary to integrate LANs into the OSI-RM framework were primarily isolated to the Physical and Data Link layers, although Network layer protocols might need small changes to accommodate the availability of certain optional Data Link layer features (or to avoid trying to use features that are not currently available). In order to accommodate certain Data Link layers that do not provide reliable transport, higher layer protocols may provide their own forms of error recovery mechanisms.

The IEEE LMSC (a.k.a. Project 802) is now in its third decade of operation, and has made substantial contributions to the Physical and Data Link layers, defining over a half-dozen MAC sub-layer protocols, and specifying the associated PHYs over which these MAC sub-layer protocols operate. This group has generated, and continues to make progress on, the standards for wireless LANs, namely IEEE 802.11.

As conceived by the OSI-RM, the Data Link layer is responsible for enabling long frames (up to thousands or tens of thousands of bits) to be received intact across an unreliable Physical layer. The Data Link layer protocol's job is to delimit frames and it will typically provide a capability for error detection on a per-frame basis, but may optionally also include a capability for forward error correction or for robust delivery (through retransmissions). Even lacking the capability of forward error correction, different Data Link protocols provide for varying degrees of robustness in their ability to detect (and correct for) errors. The amount of effort expended will be inversely proportional to the expected performance of the associated Physical layer medium (i.e., reliable media might not need really robust error detection, whereas noisy channels may need more sophisticated algorithms, or combinations of algorithms). The Data Link layer is also responsible, where appropriate, for defining mechanisms to allow a Physical medium to be shared among a set of stations.

The Data Link layer is the lowest layer to incorporate the concept of an "address," which is in this case limited to use within the span of the underlying physical medium, or perhaps more broadly within the domain of operation of the Data Link layer protocol. In the IEEE's model, the addressing occurs at the MAC sub-layer, which is why these addresses are often referred to as "MAC addresses."

The Data Link layer protocol is also responsible for providing a label indicating which Network layer protocol owns the encapsulated payload within the frame, and therefore which Network layer protocol should handle the frame at the receiver. For example, two Data Link layer entities could be exchanging frames, with some of the frames being associated with the AppleTalk Datagram Delivery Protocol (DDP), others with the IP (IPv4), and still others with the Address Resolution Protocol (ARP). Without some form of label, a receiving Data Link entity would have no idea how to pass the contents of the frame up the protocol stack.

This de-multiplexing concept repeats itself in certain higher-layer protocols, in that a given layer may have several possible higher-layer client protocols, and there must be either an implicit or explicit means to indicate which of the possible higher-layer protocols is actually contained in the frame payload portion of this Data Link layer frame.

The OSI Data Link layer may be connection-oriented or connectionless. Many examples of connection-oriented Data Link protocols happen to support reliable delivery, but it is not mandatory that this be the case. In fact, IEEE 802.11 is one example of a MAC sub-layer protocol that supports a primitive type of reliability, yet it is a connectionless protocol.

The Network Layer

The Physical layer is completely unconcerned with the structure of the bit-stream that it is carrying. In that respect, the Physical layer is unaware of its payload. The Data Link layer is similarly unaware of a frame's payload, which is commonly a Network layer protocol, or some other "client" protocol of the Data Link layer, such as a control or setup protocol. For example, certain protocols only need to send Data Link layer frames. They are, in a sense, simple "applications" that are operating directly over the Data Link layer. Even in this latter case, however, the Data Link layer is unaware of the structure or contents of the frame.

The Network layer provides for end-to-end addressing, and a Network layer path can encompass many different types of Data Link layers. The Network layer protocol can be either connection-oriented or connectionless. Due to the ever-increasing deployment of the IP (which is connectionless), it is becoming more difficult to find real-world examples of connection-oriented Network layer protocols. There are probably still many networks that use X.25, which is a WAN-oriented Network layer protocol that emerged in the late 1970s that happens to be an example of a Network layer protocol that is connection-oriented and supports reliable delivery. In addition to addressing information, the header of a Network-layer protocol will include some way to indicate the proper higher-layer client protocol.

The Transport Layer

The Transport layer is used to create logical connections or associations between software entities on two communicating devices. In the OSI-RM, this is the lowest layer that creates a formal binding between two network endpoints for exchanging data between them. It is possible for the Transport layer protocol to be either connection-oriented or connectionless.

In the TCP/IP protocol suite, the TCP is the Transport layer protocol that provides a (connection-oriented) reliable octet stream service to the communicating endpoints. The User Datagram Protocol (UDP) provides a connectionless Transport layer service that supports certain applications, but is also used as a multiplexing layer over which other Transport layer protocols are operated. There are Transport layer protocols in the OSI protocol suite, but they do not provide useful examples because they are much less well known than TCP and UDP.

In the case of IP, the "Protocol" field in the IP header is only one octet in length, so there is a limit of 256 unique protocols that may be carried by IP. By using UDP as a de-multiplexing layer, that number can be expanded considerably. For example, the Real-time Transport Protocol (RTP), which is by its very name clearly a transport protocol, is layered over UDP, which is another transport protocol.

All UDP-based protocols together only consume the one IP "protocol" value (UDP is IP protocol number `0x11`), and there are 2^{16} UDP ports by which to identify applications. Examples of UDP-based applications include certain types of Domain Name Service (DNS) traffic, Dynamic Host Configuration Protocol (DHCP), Network Time Protocol (NTP), Routing Information Protocol (RIP) and RIP Next Generation (RIPng), the Simple Network Management Protocol (SNMP), and the Trivial File Transfer Protocol (TFTP).

Other examples of Transport layer protocols exist in the TCP/IP suite, including the new Stream Control Transmission Protocol (SCTP), which is a new protocol that was designed to carry signaling information for telephone switching over IP networks, but which is being considered as a transport for iSCSI (SCSI over IP), and for other uses.

The Session Layer

The TCP/IP suite has no specific protocols that map to either layer 5 or layer 6 of the OSI-RM. Layer 5, the OSI Session layer, is used to create a higher-level abstraction of a Transport layer connection. There are certain requirements of iSCSI that could benefit from an Internet-standard Session layer protocol. Because such a protocol does not exist, the iSCSI protocol designers had to invent what is effectively a Session layer protocol specifically for iSCSI, to enable peer entities to use multiple TCP connections (for performance reasons) and still be able to preserve the SCSI commands and responses in the proper order. The IETF has considered creating Session layer abstractions in the past, but these efforts have not gained much traction, except in certain limited settings (iSCSI is one, and HTTP version 1.1 is another). In each case, the "Session Layer" protocol that was created is highly specific to the application. Perhaps there is no generically useful set of Session layer protocol primitives that could serve a broad class of applications, and it is better to design new Session layer protocols as needed.

The Presentation Layer

The OSI Presentation layer is responsible for encoding higher-layer (Application layer) data structures into a form suitable for transmission. This could involve using a self-describing encoding such as Abstract Syntax Notation One (ASN.1), or it could involve the definition of data structures that support certain types of application needs. The point of the Presentation layer was to provide a set of data representation types that can be leveraged by various applications. Many popular IETF protocols seem to prefer ASCII-coded human-readable protocol exchanges, such as are used to exchange commands between peer entities using the File Transfer Protocol (FTP), HyperText Transfer Protocol (HTTP), and the Simple Mail Transfer Protocol (SMTP).

The Presentation layer could also support compression, encryption, or almost any other conceivable transformation of the application's data stream that might be generically useful (application-specific data representations can also be supported). One of the better known OSI Presentation layer "protocols" is the ASN.1 data representation, which is used in several IETF protocols, most notably SNMP.

The Application Layer

In the OSI world, there are a number of defined protocols at the Application layer, including X.400 (email), VT (Virtual Terminal protocol, sort of like TEL-NET in the TCP/IP world), X.500 (directory services), and so on. There are many more applications in the TCP/IP world, from video games to email (i.e., SMTP), network management (i.e., SNMP), World Wide Web (i.e., HTTP), file transfer (e.g., FTP, TFTP, etc.), networked file systems, etc. The application defines whatever primitives it needs to send and receive data, to send and receive status and error codes, and so forth.

Aside: The IETF[9] and TCP/IP Standards

Before exploring the Data Link layer in more detail, this is a good time to mention the other major protocol suite (which has effectively supplanted the OSI protocol suite); namely, the TCP/IP family of protocols.

The IETF was a completely different type of standards organization, which placed "rough consensus and running code" ahead of excessive formality. The IETF grew out of networking research efforts funded by the United States Defense Advanced Research Projects Agency (DARPA, occasionally known as ARPA). The Transmission Control Protocol/Internet Protocol (TCP/IP) protocol stack emerged in the early 1980s.[10]

TCP/IP was not based on the OSI model (in fact, the designers of TCP/IP had significant philosophical differences with the way that *de jure* networking standards were created at the time; e.g., by the CCITT and ISO. The TCP/IP "reference model" actually only has four layers, namely Subnetwork (maps roughly to the OSI Physical and Data Link layers), IP (maps closely to the OSI Network

---

9. IETF stands for Internet Engineering Task Force.

10. Specifically, the Internet (well, it was the ARPANET at the time) cut over to use TCP/IP instead of the original packet-switching protocol NCP on January 1, 1983.

layer), Transport (maps roughly to the Transport and Session layers of the OSI stack), and Application (maps roughly to the Session, Presentation, and Application layers of the OSI stack).

Although TCP/IP was developed in an *ad-hoc* fashion by an international team of engineers, and was eventually adopted by users on every continent, it was not an international standard in the traditional sense of the word. However, it was nonproprietary and many vendors supported it (partially because it was free[11]), making it a *de facto* standard, which evolved over time into a real international standard, perhaps eventually becoming a victim of its own success.[12] Because of the near-universal deployment of the TCP/IP suite, and the fact that the IETF has achieved the necessary international-level recognition from the "official" standards community, the IETF's standards process can legitimately be said to produce *de jure*, not *de facto* protocols.

Referring back to the concept of a connection, TCP/IP restricts its notion of a connection to its Transport layer, although modern technologies like Multi-Protocol Label Switching (MPLS) are adding lightweight connection-oriented features just below the Network layer (i.e., the IP layer in the TCP/IP "reference model").

Because of its flexible design, TCP/IP was, and is, readily adaptable to run over any lower-layer technology, as one can see by looking at how many types of "IP over foo" standards there are in the IETF's RFC library. More information about the IETF can be found at their Web site, www.ietf.org.

---

11. Much of TCP/IP's early success can be attributed to the fact that it was freely included with BSD UNIX® distributions in the 1980s. Once implementations of the OSI protocols became available, they were typically expensive, and by the time they came to market, many early adopters were already familiar with TCP/IP. Many organizations that were forced by policy to acquire OSI software opted to keep their OSI software safe inside its shrink-wrap rather than learn something new.

12. The IETF "process" is becoming more and more well-defined, which is both good and bad (in the author's opinion). There was always a degree of brazenness about the IETF process, such as it was. The IETF motto was "rough consensus and running code." Their standards were written, implemented, tested, and improved, in a very informal, yet very productive fashion. IETF folks eschewed the formal standards organizations as ossified relics, and ridiculed their output as excessively complex and not grounded in real-world implementation experience. No standard took more abuse than the OSI suite of protocols. The early 21st-century IETF is a very different beast, with progressively more well-defined processes and the intrusion of terms like "normative references" into their specifications. At this point, the IETF has taken its place alongside the "real" standards bodies like the IEEE, ANSI, and ITU-T.

IPv4 and IPv6 Encapsulation in IEEE 802 LANs

The IEEE has standardized the LAN technologies over which IP operates, with the notable exception of Ethernet, which pre-dated the inception of the IEEE's Project 802 (the LAN/MAN Standards Committee, or LMSC), the group that was created to standardize LAN technology within the OSI-RM context.

Each LAN technology is given a name according to the working group within the LMSC that has been chartered to develop that standard. For example, the IEEE 802.11 working group is creating standards for wireless LANs. In the next section, the structure of the IEEE LMSC will be described in more detail. For now, suffice it to observe that the IEEE LMSC divided the Data Link layer into medium-specific and medium-independent sub-layers.

The medium-independent sub-layer is known as the Logical Link Control (LLC) sub-layer, and is defined by IEEE 802.2. There are two layered protocols in the LLC sub-layer, one which is called LLC, and is required to be present over all the MAC sub-layer protocols that the IEEE has defined, and the other which is called "SNAP" and is optionally available over LLC when carrying certain higher-layer protocols, in particular IPv4, ARP, and IPv6.

The LLC sub-layer protocol uses the concept of a Service Access Point, which is just a number that identifies what sort of payload is within the payload that follows the LLC sub-layer protocol header. If SNAP is in use, the LLC SAP is set to 0xAA.

Although a unique IEEE 802.2 LLC SAP value was assigned to IPv4, IPv4 is rarely (if ever) seen transmitted over IEEE 802.2 LLC alone—the recommended practice for transmitting IPv4 and ARP over IEEE 802 LANs is to encapsulate them in both IEEE 802.2 LLC and IEEE 802.2 SNAP. While it is technically possible to transmit "IPv4 over 'raw' IEEE 802.2 LLC" packets on FDDI or Token Ring LANs, that practice violates RFC-1042, which has been a full Internet Standard for a very long time. However, other protocols such as IPX, NetBEUI, and OSI Connection-Less Network layer Protocol (CLNP), among others, may be layered directly over IEEE 802.2 LLC sub-layer protocol without requiring the presence of the IEEE 802.2 SNAP sub-layer protocol.

Finally, note that there is no IEEE 802.2 LLC SAP value for IPv6, which also must be encapsulated over non-Ethernet (i.e., IEEE 802) LANs in both IEEE 802.2 LLC and IEEE 802.2 SNAP headers (although to differentiate itself from IPv4, IPv6 uses a Type value of `0x86DD`, compared to IPv4's Type value of `0x0800`).

Figure 2–5 illustrates the common protocol stack used when TCP/IP packets are transported over any IEEE 802 LAN medium. As indicated in the diagram, both IPv4 and IPv6 share the same basic encapsulation. The MAC sub-layer protocol for IEEE 802.11 is highlighted.

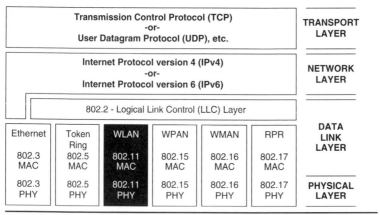

Figure 2–5   TCP/IP layering over various IEEE 802 media

When IPv4 or IPv6 is encapsulated in IEEE 802.3 Ethernet (with the "Length" as opposed to "Type" interpretation of the frame), the protocol stack using the LLC sub-layer is used. However, if the original "Type" form of Ethernet is used, the IP header can be layered directly over Ethernet with no intervening IEEE 802.2 LLC sub-layer protocol(s). Figure 2–5 shows both possibilities, only in the case of IEEE 802.3/Ethernet.

The presence of a "Type" field in the original Ethernet header is the main thing that distinguishes it from the protocols that were subsequently developed by the IEEE LMSC, since all of those subsequent protocols rely on the LLC sub-layer protocol (and possibly the SNAP sub-layer protocol) to identify the contents of the frame.

IEEE LAN Standards

The job of developing LAN standards, which are occupants of the Data Link layer, was assumed by the IEEE Project 802 LAN/MAN Standards Committee (LMSC), which has developed a number of LAN standards, including those based on bus topologies and ring topologies. Two examples of the former are "Ethernet" (known as CSMA/CD[13]) and "Token Bus," products of the IEEE 802.3 and IEEE 802.4 WGs, respectively. Wireless LANs based on standards defined by the IEEE 802.11 WG don't have a "topology" in the same physical sense as a wired LAN, but logically could be considered a bus. Actually, Token Bus is a hybrid technology, since although it is physically a bus, it is logically a ring. Examples of pure ring topologies include Token Ring, the product of the IEEE 802.5 WG, and Fiber Distributed Data Interface (FDDI[14]), which was produced by ANSI X3T9.5.

The IEEE LMSC's partitioning of the Data Link layer allows the LLC sublayer to be independent of the details of the Physical layer, with a standardized interface to the MAC sub-layer. The MAC sub-layer protocol is typically paired with at least one type of Physical layer medium (many MAC sub-layer protocols can operate over more than one type of Physical layer medium). For example, Ethernet can run over many types of media that support baseband (digital) transmissions, including two types of coaxial cable, single-mode and multimode optical fiber, and twisted pair copper wire. An Ethernet PHY was also defined to allow operation over analog broadband media (specifically, a pair of closed circuit television channels), but that form of deployment (known as 10BROAD36) was never very popular.

Even though FDDI was a product of the American National Standards Institute, and not the IEEE LMSC, it *was* designed such that it required the IEEE 802.2 LLC (and possibly SNAP) protocols for its proper operation. This is proof of the wide applicability of the IEEE LMSC model of Data Link protocols. So, ANSI X3T9.5 designed FDDI as a MAC sub-layer protocol that required LLC, despite the fact that FDDI was not a product of the IEEE LMSC. As of the late 1990s, FDDI became obsolete, since the necessary PHY components necessary to build FDDI "NICs" or FDDI interfaces for hubs (concentrators), switches, or routers were no longer produced. Faster technologies displaced FDDI; although it was one of the most reliable LAN technologies ever invented, it was never designed to scale up to gigabit speeds.

---

13. CSMA/CD stands for "Carrier Sense Multiple Access with Collision Detection."

14. For an *excellent* reference on FDDI, the reader is referred to Gary Kessler's 1992 book, entitled *Metropolitan Area Networks: Concepts, Standards, and Services.*

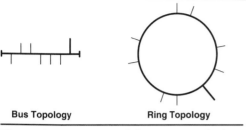

Bus Topology   **Ring Topology**

Figure 2–6   Bus and ring LAN topologies

Figure 2–6 illustrates the two basic LAN topologies. Each of the short line segments emanating from the bus or ring represents a single device attached to the LAN. In each case, one of the attachments is drawn as a longer, thicker line, which represents a link from this LAN segment to an intermediate device; for example, a bridge or router (or, if you prefer, a layer-2 or layer-3 switch). Note that in either case, the topology can easily support delivery of broadcast frames (special frames that may be received by every station on the medium), which is one key property that distinguishes LANs from point-to-point or point-to-multipoint WAN-oriented Data Link protocols.

In the course of defining its LAN-oriented (i.e., broadcast capable) Data Link layer protocols, the IEEE LMSC has divided the Data Link layer into two sub-layers, as follows. This logical subdivision of the Data Link layer is undetectable by adjacent layers.

- The upper sub-layer of the Data Link layer is known as the LLC sub-layer, which is defined in the IEEE 802.2-1998 standard (or its successor). The LLC sub-layer is responsible for abstracting the actual MAC sub-layer details to provide a common interface to the Network layer protocol(s).[15] The LLC sub-layer may be decomposed into two protocols, one called (confusingly) "LLC" and the other called the Sub-Network Access Protocol, or "SNAP." The most common form of the LLC

---

15. Note that in the TCP/IP "reference model" there is no explicitly defined interface between the IP layer and what the TCP/IP model refers to as the "subnetwork" layer, which may be a point-to-point subnetwork, a nonbroadcast multiple access subnetwork, or a broadcast-capable multiple access subnetwork. The last category encompasses LAN technology, the first is, obviously, point-to-point WAN links, and the middle one maps to packet-switched "cloud" technologies such as X.25, frame relay, and ATM, which easily support unicast delivery at the Data Link layer to multiple neighbors over the same physical interface, but that do not have the ability to support multicast or broadcast delivery (other than by frame replication).

sub-layer protocol occupies three octets, and the SNAP protocol consumes another five octets. The two LLC sub-layer protocols provide certain MAC-layer-independent control and demultiplexing services and provide an interface that is not dependent on (or aware of) the internal operation of the lowest sub-layer of the Data Link layer, the MAC sub-layer.

- The IEEE defines the MAC sub-layer to be the lower portion of the OSI-RM's Data Link layer, and is concerned with implementing medium-specific operations to ensure that data is properly transmitted and received. A typical protocol stack, such as that depicted in Figure 2–7, shows the relative positions of the LLC and MAC sub-layers. In the IEEE LMSC's protocol architecture, the MAC sub-layer consists of only one protocol. Figure 2–7 also places the Data Link layer in the context of the IETF's TCP/IP protocol stack.

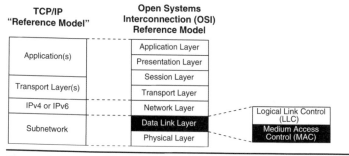

Figure 2–7   Data Link sub-layers relative to the OSI and TCP/IP models

The Data Link layer's job, in its entirety, is to ensure that the bit-transmission facility (or facilities) of a particular physical medium appears error-free to the Network layer. For media that are shared among multiple stations, the Data Link layer also specifies procedures by which the stations fairly share access to the medium.

By "error-free" we mean that the Data Link layer only delivers frames up to the Network layer if they have passed some level of testing and been found to be free from errors. Ultimately, the responsibility for ensuring that the data is uncorrupted lies with the Application, which may use techniques such as strong cryptography to ensure that any data it receives is exactly what the sender intended.

In order to determine if a frame has an error or not, most Data Link protocols compute simple but effective frame check sequences which allow the Data Link layer to certify that a frame is probably not corrupted, though most of the algorithms used for this purpose are capable of being fooled into accepting a frame that was modified en route. One reason is that the frame check sequence only protects a frame while it is on the wire, not when it is inside a switch being sent from one interface to another. If part of a frame was modified while it was inside a switch, the outgoing interface will compute a correct frame check sequence that reflects the new contents of the frame, and the receiver will not be able to tell if the frame check sequence is the same as that sent by the original sender. This is why the real responsibility for ensuring accuracy in data transport falls to a higher layer.

Some Data Link layer technologies provide for reliable delivery via explicit acknowledgments (with retransmissions when necessary), or via forward error correcting codes, but LAN-oriented Data Link protocols tend to act in an "unreliable" mode. Due to the implicit lack of acknowledgments, this could also be called "unacknowledged" mode. Because Physical-layer errors are assumed to be quite rare in LAN media, and because the speeds are high and transmission latencies are low, it is reasonable to expect that higher-layer protocols can recover quickly based on the low rate of errors that are expected.

The point-to-point or point-to-multipoint WAN-oriented Data Link protocols that pre-dated LAN technology had to cope with noisy lines. Due to the speed advantage enjoyed by LANs, it became more efficient to just send the data as quickly as possible, and recover from the occasional rare error, rather than to operate in a much slower "explicit acknowledgement" mode that was virtually guaranteed to be error-free.

While LAN-oriented Data Link layer protocols are admittedly unreliable (actually, they are very reliable, if installed properly), unacknowledged Data Link layer protocols, such as those that are used over LAN media, do still retain at least an error-detecting code, so that the frames that are handed up to the Network layer are believed to be error-free. Typically, either the Network layer will have its own reliability mechanism(s), or the Network layer will punt the ultimate verification of the data's validity to the Transport layer or above. One reason for this shift of responsibility to a higher layer is that LAN media are typically so much faster and provide a significantly more robust transmission medium than did the older media that required low-layer reliability mechanisms.

This latter statement is not strictly true in the context of wireless LANs, since the medium over which wireless LANs operate is not dedicated to their use, and interference from other sources may corrupt the frames that are "in flight" between WLAN stations. The MAC sub-layer protocol that has been defined for use in IEEE 802.11 WLANs has specific features that are designed to make the best of a challenging situation.

Wired LAN and WAN media are now extremely reliable, as measured by bit error rates, but it is no longer the case that LAN media are implicitly faster than WAN media. Today, certain point-to-point WAN data circuits operate at SONET[16] OC-192 speeds, sending data at just less than 10 Gbps,[17] whereas common LAN speeds in early 2003 top out at "only" 1 Gbps (e.g., 1000BASE-T). A version of Ethernet known as IEEE 802.3*ae* has been defined that operates at 10 Gbps,[18] but it is not yet in common use (even in LAN backbones), and will probably not be used outside of WAN backbones for quite some time.[19]

Introduction to IEEE 802.11's MAC Sub-layer Frame Structure

Besides defining access control and resource sharing capabilities for multiple stations contending for a common LAN medium, one of the other key operations performed by the Data Link layer is known as "framing," which is the process of

---

16. Synchronous Optical Network (a very similar technology is known as the Synchronous Digital Hierarchy (SDH) in Europe).

17. Synchronous Optical Network (SONET) Optical Carrier level 192, operates at a bit transmission speed of 192*51.84 Mbps, or 9953.28 Mbps (9.953280000 Gbps). The payload capacity of an OC-192 circuit is about 4 percent less than the bit transmission speed, due to the overhead of framing and other PHY layer signaling and control information.

18. As of early 2003, there are several fiber-based PHYs and a short-range copper PHY, but no 10GBASE-T has yet been defined, although discussions in that direction have already begun. It remains to be seen whether a practical 10GBASE-T standard will emerge, or whether the world will finally begin to use optical fiber instead of twisted pair wiring.

19. Efforts within the IEEE to define 10GBASE-T are in the earliest stages of discussions in early 2003, but this author can't imagine what applications would require that kind of bandwidth to be deployed to the desktop; of course, when the author first heard about 10 Mbps Ethernet, he couldn't imagine who could possibly use that much speed (at the time, the applications were terminal-oriented, so why would you ever need speeds that could deliver text to you at many times the speed at which you could read it?). Who knows, some future virtual telepresence technology may require presently unimaginable amounts of bandwidth.

encapsulating the higher-layer protocol packet (which may or may not be a Network layer protocol packet) in a set of Data Link layer headers, and appending a Data Link layer trailer, which is often simply an error-detecting sequence.

The Data Link layer header will include *at least* the following items:

- MAC sub-layer Destination Address (i.e., MAC-DA)
- MAC sub-layer Source Address (i.e., MAC-SA)

Another common Data Link layer header element is a "type" or "protocol" field that indicates which kind of higher-layer packet is embedded in the frame, but strictly speaking, this is an LLC sub-layer[20] function, and IEEE 802.11 only specifies a MAC sub-layer protocol. In fact, the IEEE 802.3 standard specifies two versions of Ethernet, wherein one variety interprets the two-octet field following the MAC-SA field as a "Type", and the other variety of the Ethernet header interprets this two-octet field as a "Length" value, which pushes the higher-layer protocol demultiplexing tasks up to the LLC sub-layer.

The LLC sub-layer protocol provides a form of demultiplexing for higher layer protocols via its two one-octet Destination and Source Service Access Point (DSAP and SSAP) fields. Due to the LLC sub-layer protocol's limited number of SAP values, there is another protocol in the LLC sub-layer known as the Subnetwork Access Protocol (SNAP), which has a full two-octet Type field and is layered on top of the LLC protocol. SNAP also has an OUI field, which means that everyone who acquires an OUI has access to the complete set of 2^{16} (i.e., 65,536) Type values, while setting the OUI to `0x000000` causes the Type field to be interpreted as if it were the Ethernet Type field.

IEEE 802.11 MAC Sub-layer Protocol's Idiosyncrasies

One cannot avoid comparing IEEE 802.11 to Ethernet. On one hand, Ethernet is the best-known example of a LAN technology, so it is a logical basis for comparison, and on the other hand, IEEE 802.11 is sometimes misleadingly referred to as "wireless Ethernet." The latter moniker is genuinely misleading. Other than the fact that IEEE 802.3 and IEEE 802.11 both define MAC sub-layer protocols and their associated PHYs, there is almost nothing in common between IEEE 802.3 and IEEE 802.11.

---

20. Note that the author did not say "LLC sub-layer protocol."

- The IEEE 802.11 MAC sub-layer protocol has no higher-layer protocol demultiplexing features of its own, and thus *requires* the presence of the IEEE 802.2 LLC sub-layer protocol headers to perform the higher-layer protocol demultiplexing function. The presence of the IEEE 802.2 SNAP sub-layer protocol's headers is optional.
- In wireless LANs based on IEEE 802.11, the stations must explicitly "join" the LAN, which is the equivalent of plugging in an Ethernet cable. The procedures that govern the joining and leaving processes have no exact equivalent in the world of the Ethernet MAC protocol.
    - To be fair, Ethernet does have an "autonegotiation" feature that allows two Ethernet peer entities to determine the best combination of speed (e.g., 10, 100, or 1000 Mbps) and duplex setting (e.g., full- or half-duplex). However, this negotiation happens below the MAC sub-layer.
- There is no implicit or explicit form of authentication in Ethernet as there is in IEEE 802.11.

Summary

We have seen that the landscape of networking standards is littered with a figurative alphabet soup of standards bodies and their output. The Data Link layer is only one of the seven layers of the OSI-RM, an abstract model of a layered protocol stack. The TCP/IP protocol suite is much less formal than the OSI-RM, but layers similar functions in hierarchically similar ways.

The IEEE has developed numerous standards at the Data Link layer, and in doing so has created the logical partition of the Data Link layer into the Logical Link Control (LLC) and Medium Access Control (MAC) sub-layers.

Wireless LANs, which operate at the Data Link layer, are being standardized by the IEEE 802.11 working group, which has produced a fairly complex set of specifications which is laced with its own unique terminology, owing to the fact that operating a MAC sub-layer protocol over a wireless medium is much more challenging than over any wired medium.

The IEEE 802.11 MAC sub-layer protocol, which will be explored in depth in the subsequent chapters, relies on the IEEE 802.2 LLC sub-layer protocol (and optionally IEEE 802.2 SNAP, which may be layered over LLC) to encapsulate higher-layer protocols such as IPv4 over a wireless LAN.

3

Speeds and Feeds

In this chapter, we discuss the Physical (PHY) layer[1] protocols that have been developed for IEEE 802.11-based WLANs, with the focus on the speeds and throughput that can be achieved by each. The discussion in this chapter covers the PHY-layer protocols that were defined in the following documents:

- IEEE 802.11-1999 (the base specification)
- IEEE 802.11*a*-1999
- IEEE 802.11*b*-1999

This chapter also covers the work that has just been completed in the IEEE 802.11 Working Group's Task Group "*g*" (TG*g*), which has produced a document that is known as IEEE 802.11*g*-2003. In terms of the speeds at which the IEEE 802.11*g*-2003 standard operates, there is a significant overlap with the IEEE 802.11*a*-1999 standard.

This chapter contains the following information. The first sections involve an overview of the performance of the various PHYs. For many readers, this will be all they want to know about IEEE 802.11 PHY layer protocols, since it summarizes the speeds and modulations that are employed. The overall structure of an IEEE 802.11 implementation is described, including the PHY (which includes the radio frequency (RF) unit and the Baseband Processor (BBP, the modulation/demodulation circuitry), and the MAC, which leads naturally into the next chapter, which begins to cover the MAC sub-layer protocol. This chapter also

---

1. Chapter 2 includes a discussion of the OSI-RM, of which the PHY is the lowest layer.

includes some lower-level details, including the PHY layer encapsulations, and high-level details of the modulation schemes used to achieve the various bit rates over either 2.4 GHz or 5 GHz frequency bands.

Overview of IEEE 802.11 PHYs

There are a remarkable number of Physical layer choices that may be used in the context of IEEE 802.11 WLANs. The large number of choices arises because there are a number of different physical media over which the frames can be transmitted, including diffuse infrared optical, as well as several different radio frequency bands, including a set of channels in the 2.4 GHz *unlicensed* ISM[2] band (2.450 ± 0.050 GHz, which is a total RF bandwidth of 100 MHz), as well as several other *unlicensed* bands in the neighborhood of 5 GHz, for whom usability depends on the regulatory domain (i.e., country or geographical region) in which the product is being used.

The IEEE 802.11*b*-1999 and IEEE 802.11*g*-2003 standards, in the United States (and in most of the world), actually use a subset of the 2.4 GHz band, ranging from 2.401 to 2.4835 GHz. However, in Japan, frequencies up to 2.495 GHz may be used.

The fact that WLANs operate in *unlicensed* spectrum is a critical distinction from other wireless data standards such as PCS, 3G, or 4G wireless [WAN] networks. The spectrum for those services was sold at a very high price, and it must be frustrating to the operators who spent literally billions of dollars to build these networks that now it is possible to deploy technologies that have much better performance and can operate in spectrum that has no associated cost. Operators of WLAN-based access networks may have a substantial advantage over operators of competing technologies.

---

2. There are numerous unlicensed Industrial, Scientific, and Medical (ISM) bands scattered throughout the RF spectrum in the United States. The FCC manages the spectrum and defines how each slice is used. Other countries have their own regulatory agencies, and they may or may not have parallel spectrum assignments that are functionally equivalent to the U.S. ISM bands.

Due to the richly inter-related nature of the concepts and issues involved in WLAN PHYs, including the physical RF spectrum allocation, the modulation schemes, and the regulatory issues surrounding product development and deployment, the author will first discuss the PHYs together, to show their similarities, and then summarize each individual PHY in its own section. The author believes that the similarities between the IEEE 802.11 PHYs are more important than their differences and that the differences are best appreciated when you don't focus on them alone.

This chapter does not go into substantial detail with respect to Frequency Hopping Spread Spectrum (FHSS) techniques such as are specified in IEEE 802.11-1999 for use in the 2.4 GHz band to achieve speeds of 1 or 2 Mbps. FHSS technology has been widely deployed in the context of other wireless communication systems, and there is a large installed base of FHSS-based systems deployed today. However, the frequency hopping variety of spread spectrum is effectively a dead-end technology insofar as WLANs are concerned. The Direct Sequence Spread Spectrum (DSSS) techniques covered in this chapter are scalable to much higher throughput rates. This sidebar gives a "just the facts"-level of coverage of FHSS.

The IEEE 802.11-1999 FHSS PHY uses the 2.4 GHz band in a completely different way than the Barker code, which is a form of Direct Sequence Spread Spectrum (DSSS) that also achieves 1 or 2 Mbps, using either 2GFSK (two-level Gaussian Frequency Shift Keying) or 4GFSK (four-level GFSK) coding, respectively.

Regardless of the speed at which it is operating, the FHSS PHY relies on a pseudo-random frequency-hopping sequence that is communicated in advance to all the FHSS STAs. In North America and Europe (although not Spain or France), there are 79 channels within the 2.4 GHz band when it is used for FHSS operation, and they are mapped by a simple formula: Take the channel number and multiply it by 1 MHz, and then add it to 2400 MHz and the result is the channel frequency in MHz. There is no channel 1—the first channel is 2 and the 79th is 80, so the range of frequencies available to the FHSS PHY is from 2.402 GHz to 2.480 GHz. The random hopping sequence mentioned earlier is advertised by the AP so that all the STAs will be able to synchronize themselves with the hopping pattern.

In Japan, 23 channels are available (from 2.473 to 2.495 GHz, numbered as shown previously, except instead of 2 through 80, Japan uses 73 through 95). Finally, Spain uses channels 47 through 73, and France uses channels 48 through 82.

No discussion of FHSS would be complete without mentioning that the author has never seen an IEEE 802.11-1999 product that implements the FHSS PHY. The author would not want to give the impression that he has seen everything; however, he believes that FHSS is not worth covering in detail, as it is distracting from the IEEE 802.11 WLAN PHYs that readers are likely to encounter in the real world (e.g., IEEE 802.11*a*-1999, IEEE 802.11*b*-1999, and IEEE 802.11*g*-2003).

While FHSS may be important to someone studying signal processing, it is the author's opinion that FHSS is not of direct practical interest, nor is it the basis for future progress in WLANs. There are numerous books on signal processing and wireless communications theory in which a sufficiently motivated reader can find arbitrarily detailed information on FHSS technology.

The IEEE 802.11 wireless LAN standards have a number of different physical layers, most of which operate in various channels within certain well-known RF bands. It probably goes without saying, but a product that operates in the 5 GHz band has a 5 GHz radio subunit, and only receives or transmits energy in this part of the radio frequency spectrum. In particular, unless the product also has a 2.4 GHz radio subunit, it cannot receive or transmit 2.4 GHz signals.

One reason that a 2.4 GHz system can't receive a 5 GHz signal (or vice versa) is that it takes completely different Physical-layer radio circuitry (including tuners, mixers, amplifiers, etc.) to receive or transmit at either frequency. Each frequency band requires a completely different analog radio subunit to receive and transmit signals at a given frequency.

In addition, each frequency uses a different antenna length. For reasons that are too complex to describe here, antennas are most efficient when they are approximately one quarter as long as the wavelength of the radio waves that they are designed to receive. Basic physics of wave phenomena tells us that the frequency of a wave times its wavelength is equal to the group velocity of the wave.

In the case of electromagnetic radiation, the wave's group velocity is "c" (the speed of light, which is accepted to be 299,792,458 meters per second, or 299,792,458,000 millimeters per second). By simple algebra, we find the quarter-wavelength by dividing c by four times the frequency. By such a calculation, an optimal antenna for the 2.4 GHz band is about 30.75 mm (299,792,458,000/(4×2,437,000,000)).[3] A similar calculation shows that an optimal antenna for the 5 GHz band is about 14.28 mm (299,792,458,000/(4×5,250,000,000)).[4]

For those of us who are more comfortable with English units of measure, the ideal 2.4 GHz antenna is just over 1 3/16 inches long, and the length of the ideal 5 GHz antenna is about 9/16 of an inch.

Beyond the actual differences in the radio subunits, and the need for different antennas for each of the RF subunits, there are other, related issues, such as the fact that certain analog RF components, such as power amplifiers, are designed to work efficiently only across a certain frequency range.

Some products may appear to have two antennas, but they are not always both in use, because the radio may (on a frame-by-frame basis) select the antenna with the best signal quality when receiving data. This feature is known as *antenna diversity.* In some early products, one of the "antennas" was just a dummy (i.e., an empty piece of plastic), since presumably a product with two antennas looked more capable than a product that only had one. In a product with two RF subunits (i.e., one at 2.4 GHz and another at 5 GHz), each plastic antenna housing could easily accommodate two discrete antennas (since they are so short), one for 2.4 GHz and one for 5 GHz.

There are, in fact, dual-band products on the market that support both IEEE 802.11*a*-1999 and IEEE 802.11*b*-1999, and now that IEEE 802.11*g*-2003 has been standardized, we can expect to see dual-band products incorporating all three standards, and such devices are often known by the shorthand moniker "a/b/g."

---

3. 2.437 GHz is the center frequency of Channel 6 in the 2.4 GHz band, which is the default channel for most products based on IEEE 802.11*b*.

4. 5.25 GHz is the center frequency of the 5.15–5.35 "U-NII lower band," which is where IEEE 802.11*a*'s eight contiguous non-overlapping channels are located (there are four other non-overlapping channels in a disjoint portion of the U-NII spectrum (the upper band)).

A dual-band wireless STA will presumably always associate with the fastest AP available, unless the signal quality from that AP would not result in a good-quality connection. Such decisions are out of the scope of the standard, and are an implementation choice for the vendor of the dual-band device.

One important thing to keep in mind about the different modulations that can be used with IEEE 802.11 is that (in general) higher speed modulations have shorter range. A wireless AP using IEEE 802.11*b* might in theory be able to service a circular area[5] that is 300 feet (90–100 meters) in radius, but the closer a STA is to an AP, the stronger the signal will be, and the more successful the STA will be in using a higher-speed modulation. For STAs based on IEEE 802.11*a*, the core area in which the signal is strong enough to support the fastest modulations may only be 60–90 feet in radius (i.e., up to 30 meters or less, depending on the number of users). This smaller radius is due to the different propagation characteristics of 5 GHz RF energy relative to the propagation of 2.4 GHz RF energy. Paradoxically, lowering a STA's transmit rate may actually improve throughput, since slower modulation schemes are more robust.

For the RF-oriented[6] PHYs that have been defined for use with IEEE 802.11, Figure 3–1 shows the valid combinations of frequency band (e.g., 2.4 or 5 GHz), and the associated modulations that are usable within that band to achieve the speeds on the left.

Several observations are immediate, first being that there are a *large* number of optional modulations for IEEE 802.11*g*. An implementation of IEEE 802.11*g* that supported all these optional encapsulations would be more complex, but the mandatory parts are relatively easy for anyone who has implemented IEEE 802.11*a* and IEEE 802.11*b*. In IEEE 802.11*g*, the modulation

---

5. Due to physical obstructions, the design of the radiating antenna, multipath effects, and other nonlinear effects, the coverage area will not be exactly a circle. As can be seen in Chapter 8, common large-scale WLAN designs create a hexagonally packed array of circles with a radius of between 60 and 120 feet (18 to 37 meters).

6. IEEE 802.11-1999 also defined a PHY based on diffuse infrared technology that could operate at 1 or 2 Mbps. The author is not aware of any mass-market products that implemented this type of PHY.

	2.4 GHz				5 GHz		
	IEEE 802.11b		IEEE 802.11g			IEEE 802.11a	
1	B		B				1
2	B		B				2
5.5	C	P	C	P			5.5
6			O		DO	O	6
9				O	DO	O	9
11	C	P	C	P			11
12			O		DO	O	12
18				O	DO	O	18
22				P			22
24			O		DO	O	24
33				P			33
36				O	DO	O	36
48				O	DO	O	48
54				O	DO	O	54

Barker (mandatory)	B	O	OFDM (optional)	
CCK (mandatory)	C	P	PBCC (optional)	
OFDM (mandatory)	O	DO	DSSS-OFDM (optional)	

Figure 3–1   Valid IEEE 802.11 operating parameters[7]

scheme of IEEE 802.11a, and thus the BBP chip design, has effectively been grafted onto an IEEE 802.11b radio.[8]

The tricky parts with IEEE 802.11g are interoperating with legacy IEEE 802.11b devices, which can no longer decode the modulations of all the frames that might be flowing across the 2.4 GHz medium. These changes are primarily in two places, namely the MAC sub-layer, and the Physical Layer Convergence Protocol (PLCP) sublayer, which is part of the PHY layer. However, for now, think of IEEE 802.11g as essentially the modulation scheme from IEEE 802.11a (OFDM[9]) grafted onto the radio from IEEE 802.11b.

OFDM modulation is employed in the same way in both IEEE 802.11a and IEEE 802.11g. Wherever an OFDM-based speed is mandatory in IEEE 802.11a, that speed is also mandatory in IEEE 802.11g. Likewise, wherever an ODFM-based speed is optional for IEEE 802.11a, it is also optional for IEEE 802.11g. Also, within IEEE 802.11g, observe that wherever OFDM is either

---

7. Adapted from IEEE Std. 802.11™-1999, copyright 1999, IEEE Std. 802.11a-1999, copyright 1999, IEEE Std. 802.11b-1999, copyright 2000, and IEEE 802.11g-2003, copyright 2003. All rights reserved.

8. This is not actually as straightforward as it might sound…the RF components for IEEE 802.11g will require better linearity and in general need to be of higher quality to support IEEE 802.11g. Clearly, such a higher quality RF subunit can obviously still support IEEE 802.11b.

9. OFDM stands for Orthogonal Frequency Division Multiplexing.

optional or mandatory to achieve a given speed, CCK[10]-OFDM is an optional modulation that can be used to achieve that same speed (although CCK-OFDM is *always* optional in IEEE 802.11g, regardless of whether OFDM is mandatory for that speed).

The implementation rules for both IEEE 802.11a and 802.11g are the same as well, in that if an implementer wants to support the highest rate (54 Mbps)—which is *not* mandatory—then that implementation must support all slower optional rates. Every OFDM-based implementation, in order to be compliant with the standard, must include support for the mandatory rates of 6, 12, and 24 Mbps.

Thus, an implementation that supported *only* 6, 12, 24, and 54 Mbps would not be considered compliant with either IEEE 802.11a or IEEE 802.11g because an implementation that supports 54 Mbps must also support the complete set of optional rates, viz. 9, 18, 36, and 48 Mbps.

Within a given channel, a modulation scheme will either use the center frequency of the channel as its sole carrier frequency over which its transmissions are modulated, or it will break up the channel into multiple [orthogonal] subcarrier frequencies. For example, in IEEE 802.11a and IEEE 802.11g, OFDM actually breaks up a channel into 52 subcarriers, of which 48 actually carry data. This is true whether OFDM is being used within one of the channels in the 2.4 GHz band (i.e., in a product based on the eventual IEEE 802.11g standard), or within one of the channels in the 5 GHz band (in a product based on IEEE 802.11a-1999).

This "carrier" frequency concept is not the same thing as the "non-overlapping channels" that will be discussed in more detail shortly. With respect to the number of carriers in each modulation, the only multicarrier schemes are the ones based on OFDM (DSSS-OFDM[11] included). All the other modulation schemes are based on a single carrier frequency:

---

10. CCK stands for Complementary Code Keying, another form of direct sequence spread spectrum (DSSS) communications, which is the most common modulation that is used with IEEE 802.11b. In the CCK-OFDM (also known as DSSS-OFDM), the PLCP header of the frame uses the CCK form of DSSS, while the PLCP payload (the MAC frame) is modulated using OFDM.

11. DSSS-OFDM is a hybrid of CCK and OFDM in which the usual OFDM PHY header is replaced with a CCK-style PHY header. The term *CCK-OFDM* may be used interchangeably with *DSSS-OFDM* (the IEEE 802.11g-2003 standard uses the latter terminology).

- Barker with DBPSK or DQPSK
  - Supports speeds of 1 Mbps (using DBPSK) and 2 Mbps (using DQPSK)
  - Defined by IEEE 802.11-1999
    - Mandatory-to-implement
- Complementary Code Keying (CCK)
  - Supports speeds of 5.5 and 11 Mbps
  - Defined by IEEE 802.11*b*-1999
    - Mandatory-to-implement
- Packet Binary Convolutional Coding (PBCC)
  - Supports speeds of 5.5 and 11 Mbps
  - Defined by IEEE 802.11*b*-1999
    - Optional-to-implement
  - Extended by IEEE 802.11*g*-2003 to provide speeds of 22 and 33 Mbps[12]
    - Optional-to-implement

Channels within the 2.4 GHz Band

Within the 2.4 GHz domain, there are 14 channels that may be used by either IEEE 802.11*b* or IEEE 802.11*g*. Each channel is numbered according to its center frequency, starting with 2412 MHz, incrementing by 5 MHz for each successive channel up through channel 13 at 2472 MHz. The channels that would have been centered at 2477 and 2482 MHz are not defined, but Channel 14, at 2484 MHz, has been defined (specifically, Channel 14 is only defined for use in Japan; this channel is centered 2 MHz higher than the expected…had the existing pattern been extended, the second channel above Channel 12 would have been centered at 2482 MHz).

Each of these channels is 22 MHz wide, meaning that they range from the point 11 MHz below the channel's center frequency, to the point 11 MHz above

---

12. PBCC was defined in IEEE 802.11*b* as an optional modulation scheme, offering the same speeds as CCK, namely 5.5 and 11 Mbps, so its appearance in IEEE 802.11*g* is not surprising, although you may never have heard of it before. The IEEE 802.11*g*-2003 variant of PBCC achieves higher speeds (e.g., 22 and 33 Mbps).

the channel's center frequency. This means that, for example, Channel 1 runs from 2401 to 2423 MHz, since it is centered at 2412 MHz. Channel 2 overlaps almost completely with Channel 1, since it spans the range from 2406 to 2428 MHz (centered on 2417 MHz).

It turns out that one has to move all the way up to Channel 6, which begins at 2426 MHz, is centered on 2437 MHz, and ends at 2448 MHz, to find the first channel above Channel 1 that does not overlap with Channel 1's range of frequencies. Similarly, one must then skip all the way to Channel 11 before one finds a channel that does not overlap with Channel 6. Channel 11 is bounded by 2451 MHz and 2473 MHz, centered on 2462 MHz. This is why the channel allocation within the 2.4 GHz band is said to provide for three non-overlapping channels. The three channels that do not overlap are Channel 1, Channel 6, and Channel 11.

A WORD ON NOTATION

Since 1 GHz is exactly the same as 1000 MHz, it is equally correct to refer to a frequency as either 2472 MHz or 2.472 GHz. By extension, the same frequency could be referred to as 2,472,000 kHz, 0.002472 THz (because 1 terahertz (THz) is exactly 1000 GHz), or 2,472,000,000 Hz. The author may choose to refer to frequencies in both the 2.4 GHz and 5 GHz bands in units of either MHz or GHz, depending on which is more convenient in a given context.

Figure 3–2 clearly shows that while 14 channels are defined inside the 2.4 GHz band for use within the context of IEEE 802.11*b*, there is no regulatory domain in which all of these 14 channels are concurrently usable.

Figure 3–2 is actually a synthesis of several tables from IEEE 802.11*b*-1999 and IEEE 802.11*b* Corrigendum 1-2001[13] and shows the low, center, and high frequencies for each channel on the left, and on the right shows the defined regulatory domains in which each channel may operate. The left portion of Figure 3–2 shows the frequency boundaries that define each channel in

---

13. A "corrigendum" is similar to an errata sheet. Webster's Dictionary defines the word as follows: "an error in a printed work discovered after printing and shown with its correction on a separate sheet."

	Low	Center	High		0x10 (FCC)	0x20 (IC)	0x30 (ETSI)	0x31 Spain	0x32 France	0x40 Japan	0x41 Japan	
1	2401	2412	2423	1	X	X	X				X	1
2	2406	2417	2428	2	X	X	X				X	2
3	2411	2422	2433	3	X	X	X				X	3
4	2416	2427	2438	4	X	X	X				X	4
5	2421	2432	2443	5	X	X	X				X	5
6	2426	2437	2448	6	X	X	X				X	6
7	2431	2442	2453	7	X	X	X				X	7
8	2436	2447	2458	8	X	X	X				X	8
9	2441	2452	2463	9	X	X	X				X	9
10	2446	2457	2468	10	X	X	X	X	X		X	10
11	2451	2462	2473	11	X	X	X	X	X		X	11
12	2456	2467	2478	12			X		X		X	12
13	2461	2472	2483	13			X		X		X	13
n/a	2466	2477	2488	n/a								
n/a	2471	2482	2493	n/a								
14	2473	2484	2495	14						X		14

Figure 3–2   IEEE 802.11*b*/*g* Channelization within the 2.4 GHz Band

the 2.4 GHz band. The non-overlapping channels 1, 6, and 11 are highlighted in gray.

On the right side of the table, each column corresponds to a different regulatory domain, and indicates whether that channel is legally usable in that domain. The leftmost column corresponds to the United States (regulated by the Federal Communications Commission). The second column is Canada (regulated by Industry Canada (IC) formerly the Department of Communications). Those European countries that follow ETSI (European Telecommunications Standards Institute) regulations are grouped together in the third column). Several individual European countries have their own rules, viz. Spain and France. Japan has two unique regulatory domains, (which actually has two different regulatory domain identifiers, one in which only Channel 14 is usable, and the other in which Channels 1 through 13 are all usable, similar to the characteristics of the ETSI domain).

An observant reader will note that there is 3 MHz of separation between both pairs of the non-overlapping channels (i.e., between Channels 1 and 6, and between Channels 6 and 11). As it is currently defined, Channel 14 happens to be adjacent to Channel 11, and strictly speaking, does not overlap with it, although there is no space between Channel 11 and Channel 14. So, it would seem that the reason why Channel 14 was not centered on 2477 or 2482 MHz (the two "unused" channels in Figure 3–2) is that if Channel 14 had been defined to use either of those channels, it would definitely have overlapped with Channel 11.

Curiously, if Channel 14 had been defined to be centered on 2487 MHz, then it would have constituted a fourth non-overlapping channel, since its low-end frequency would have been 2476 MHz, which is 3 MHz above the highest frequency in Channel 11 (2473 MHz). Such a definition for Channel 14 would not have pushed the top of Channel 14 outside the U.S. ISM band, since such a definition of Channel 14 would have topped out at 2498 MHz, which isn't as close to the top of the U.S. ISM band as Channel 1 is to the bottom of the U.S. ISM band. This is mostly a moot point, however, since Channel 14 is only defined for use in Japan. Moreover, in the United States and in many other parts of the world, the spectrum for IEEE 802.11*b* and IEEE 802.11*g* tops out at 2.4835 GHz (i.e., just beyond the top of Channel 13). As of this writing, Japan is the only country that has defined a channel beyond 2.4835 GHz.

As can be seen in Figure 3–2, in the majority of countries, Channels 1 through 11 are usable, but in parts of Europe it is possible to use Channels 12 and 13, and in Japan a Channel 14 has been defined (Channel 14 is only available in Japan). Almost more important than the "extra" channels that one may be able to use in some locations are the apparently "normal" channels that *cannot* be used in certain places—note that in Spain and France, Channels 1 through 9 are *not* usable. Spain would appear to be the most restrictive country with respect to the 2.4 GHz band, as only two channels are available for use in Spain.

Most vendors of equipment based on IEEE 802.11*b* have chosen Channel 6 as the default for their WLAN devices. However, from a regulatory perspective, this would appear to be a less than optimal choice. Specifically, note that Channel 11 is usable in all but one regulatory domain, while there are several regulatory domains in which Channel 6 is not legally usable.

A case could be made for making Channel 11 the default channel, but that is not the case in the real world where Channel 6 is, in fact, the default channel in most IEEE 802.11*b* products on the market. However, this has minimal impact since when a STA is activated in a new location, it uses MAC-layer mechanisms to determine which channel(s) is (are) available for its use, so the choice of default is not as important as it might seem to be (at least for STAs; in an AP, the default channel should be chosen as a result of entering the regulatory domain in which the AP is located).

Channel Selection by a STA

If you have spent any time digging around in the user interface of your WLAN card, you probably found an interface that allows you to display the currently selected channel on which your WLAN card is operating. To be more precise, the control panel or configuration utility allows you to see what channel the *driver* has selected—the user typically cannot pick the channel arbitrarily; rather, the driver software dynamically finds a channel in which an AP has a nice strong signal (other criteria may also be important in the selection of the best channel), and then associates with the AP that is in control of that channel.

When a WLAN card is initialized, the driver spends some time looking for an AP, and uses internal rules to pick the best one (strongest and/or best quality RF signal; acceptable security policy; legal authorization to use a certain channel in a certain location; etc.). The control panel shows the user what channel has been selected by the driver. The author's laptop is running Microsoft Windows 2000, and has a WLAN card.

Figure 3–3 shows the user interface that is exposed by the WLAN card's configuration utility under Widows 2000[14]. In this user interface, clicking the Rescan button forces the card to change channels.

For most products based on IEEE 802.11*b* and IEEE 802.11*g*, the configuration utility should be able to display Channels 1 through 11—or conceivably Channels 1 through 14, if the card was designed to support up to Channel 14. The range of available channels will depend on the capabilities of the radio in the WLAN card, as well as the driver software (i.e., it's possible that a WLAN card that seemingly doesn't support Channel 14 could be upgraded to support Channel 14 simply by updating its firmware and/or driver software; in other words, it's possible that the radios in many existing IEEE 802.11*b* products would be able to "tune in" to Channel 14 if their software was capable of directing them to do that).

Figure 3–4 shows the similar configuration utility from Red Hat Linux 9.0's NEtwork Administration Tool (neat). The terminology used within

---

14. Other than showing this generic screen shot, I won't identify the brand here (not that I have anything particularly bad or good to say about the card; it has a Wi-Fi logo, and it works). If you recognize the brand from this screen shot, you should not infer any endorsement of the associated product, product line, or corporation.

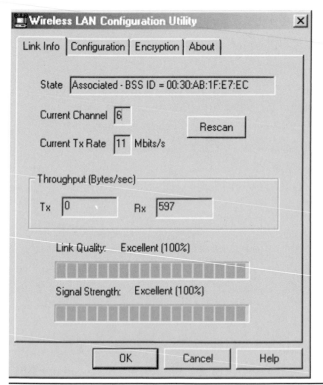

Figure 3–3   Windows 2000 User Interface of an
IEEE 802.11*b* STA showing channel selection

`neat` is somewhat unique, in that the tool refers to three types of WLAN, viz. "Managed," "Ad-Hoc," and "Auto." The former is what we normally see referred to as "infrastructure" (i.e., basic or extended service set (BSS or ESS)) while "Ad-Hoc" refers to an "independent" basic service set (IBSS). "Auto" mode allows the driver to choose to join whatever WLAN it discovers nearby, if any, perhaps requiring user input if more than one WLAN is available from which to choose.

Figure 3–5 shows the same screen with the mode set to Ad-Hoc.

Note that in Red Hat Linux 9.0, as well as in Microsoft Windows 2000, the WLAN configuration utilities both ask for the following information: 1) the SSID, 2), the mode of operation (essentially, the latter boils down to IBSS (ad-hoc) vs. infrastructure (BSS or ESS) mode).

In the Windows user interface, the indicators of signal strength and quality are on the same screen as the SSID prompt, while the mode switch is on a different

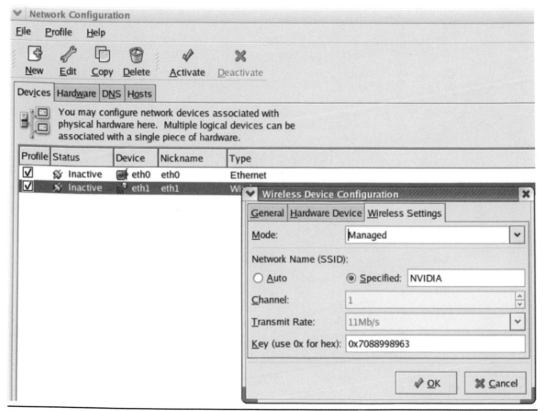

Figure 3–4   Red Hat Linux 9.0 ″neat″ User Interface of an IEEE 802.11*b* STA showing channel selection in ″Managed″ (infrastructure) mode

screen. Figure 3–6 shows the other configuration screen for the author's WLAN card configuration utility, again under Microsoft Windows 2000.

One other difference between the Red Hat Linux 9.0 and Windows 2000 configuration utilities is their treatment of Wired-Equivalent Privacy (WEP) encryption configuration. The WEP key is displayed on the main neat screen, but it is in a separate screen under Windows 2000.

These differences are only cosmetic, as there is no "standard" arrangement for the configuration screens. Different products might choose to present the configurations in different ways. As long as they all allow the SSID and mode to be chosen, along with (optionally) the WEP key(s), then a given device will be able to participate in the WLAN.

Figure 3–7 shows the encryption configuration screen for the author's WLAN card configuration utility, again under Microsoft Windows 2000.

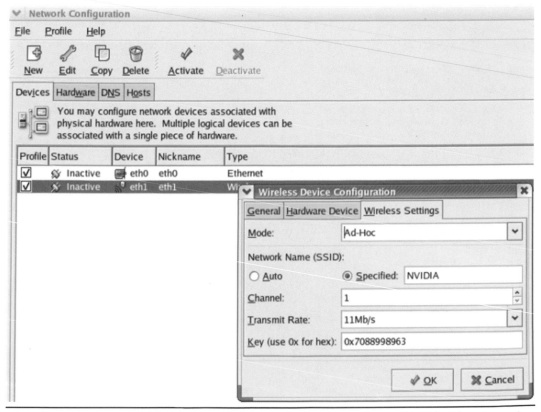

Figure 3–5   Red Hat Linux 9.0 "neat" User Interface of an IEEE 802.11*b* STA showing channel selection in "Ad-Hoc" mode

For completeness, Figure 3–8 shows the configuration screen of a Macintosh computer equipped with an AirPort WLAN card, using the MacOS 9 operating system. As you can see, the same information is presented, differing only in the layout of the configuration screens.

Note that in the Apple AirPort user interface, the term "ad-hoc" does not appear; it is replaced by the term "Computer to Computer." By not choosing "Computer to Computer" the user is implicitly choosing infrastructure mode (in the authors opinion, Apple has done a good thing by removing the jargon from their configuration utility).

Most APs have similar user interfaces—typically web-based so its appearance does not depend on the client browser's operating system—that allow the user to specify the channel on which the AP will operate, as well as the SSID

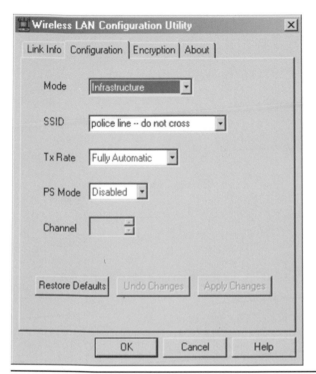

Figure 3–6   Windows 2000 User Interface of an IEEE 802.11*b*
STA showing SSID and Power Save mode controls

(in the case of my AP, the term used is ESSID, which is also equivalent to the
term BSSID and SSID).

Figure 3–9 shows the main configuration screen of the author's Access Point.
This is a cropped screen shot of a portion of a web page exposed by the management utility within the Access Point.

The particular user interface on the author's AP exposes the active WEP key
to the view of the management client, so the author deleted the key before taking the screen shot. Normally, in the particular case of the implementation of
the author's AP's web-based configuration utility, the key would be displayed as
26 hex digits (since the key is 104 bits, or 13 bytes, in length, and each byte is
represented as two hexadecimal digits).

The main configuration difference between a STA and an AP is that a STA
discovers the channel that it thinks is best, while a network manager must
configure an AP with the channel on which it will operate, and must define
the SSID for the local WLAN centered on the AP (if multiple APs are in the

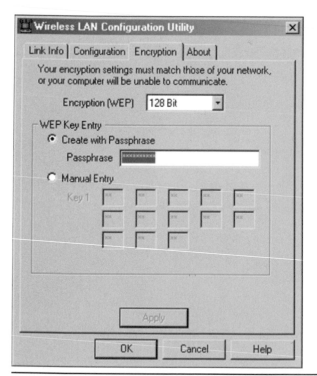

Figure 3–7   Windows 2000 User Interface of an IEEE 802.11*b*
STA showing encryption mode controls

WLAN, it is known as an "Extended Service Set," hence the term ESSID—
a single-AP WLAN is a "Basic Service Set," hence the term BSSID).

The STA is not statically configured with a channel number. A STA also can
discover which SSIDs are nearby, and present the user with a choice. In principle, a STA needs no *a priori* settings, unless it desires to use WEP encryption.

Roaming 'Round the World

Different parts of the world have different regulations controlling acceptable use
of the radio frequency spectrum. These rules may apply on a scale as small as a
country, or be a regional regulation (e.g., being defined uniformly throughout a
region, such as Europe). Other rules may apply only in very small areas, such as
on a military base.

Ideally, users should be able to roam to any geographical area they choose,
and their WLAN adapter should detect its location and automatically adapt its

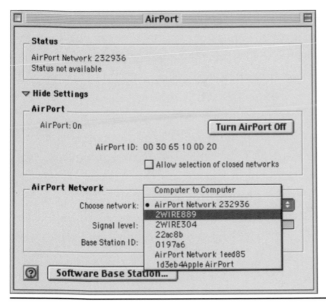

Figure 3–8   Apple MacOS 9 AirPort User Interface of
an IEEE 802.11*b* STA showing SSID and implicit mode selection

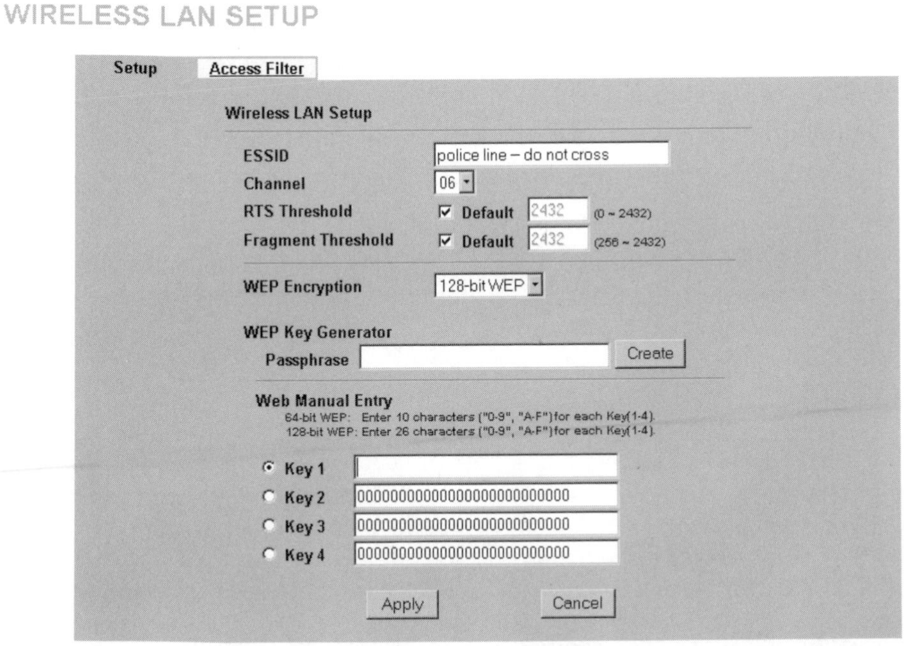

WIRELESS LAN SETUP

Setup	Access Filter

Wireless LAN Setup

ESSID   police line – do not cross

Channel   06

RTS Threshold   ☑ Default   2432   (0 ~ 2432)

Fragment Threshold   ☑ Default   2432   (256 ~ 2432)

WEP Encryption   128-bit WEP

WEP Key Generator

Passphrase   [   ] Create

Web Manual Entry
64-bit WEP: Enter 10 characters ("0-9", "A-F") for each Key(1-4).
128-bit WEP: Enter 26 characters ("0-9", "A-F") for each Key(1-4).

⦿ Key 1   [   ]

○ Key 2   00000000000000000000000000

○ Key 3   00000000000000000000000000

○ Key 4   00000000000000000000000000

Apply   Cancel

Figure 3–9   Web-based User Interface of an IEEE 802.11*b* AP showing SSID,
encryption, and channel selection controls (among others)

transmitter to comply with local regulatory requirements. Clearly, to help WLAN users adhere to local regulations, a mechanism is needed to help STAs seamlessly discover where they are (in the coarse geographic sense of the word *where*), so that they know which channels are legally available for their use.

The IEEE 802.11 WG has defined specific procedures that attempt to maximize interoperability, while still providing mechanisms to allow users in many countries to use WLANs, while complying with local laws and/or regulations. End users should never have to wonder what the legal configuration of their STA's WLAN card is. The card should learn from the AP any relevant restrictions on its operation, before it ever transmits anything.[15]

As shown in Figure 3–2, the original specification for IEEE 802.11*b*-1999 defined various "handles" to label each regulatory domain, to enable this automatic "domain discovery" capability. This is exactly the function of the IEEE 802.11*d*-2001 specification, entitled: "Amendment 3: Specification for operation in additional regulatory domains."

For example, the IEEE 802.11*d*-2001 specification allows an AP to advertise the regulatory domain in which it is operating (as configured by the network manager—this *cannot* be automatic!). IEEE 802.11*d* applies to any PHYs operating in the 2.4 GHz portion[16] of the RF spectrum. STAs within range of an IEEE 802.11*d*-capable AP will then use the information that the network manager configured regarding the regulatory domain that the AP is operating within. A suitably configured AP can then operate according to whatever legal constraints are imposed for radio frequency devices within that regulatory domain. Based on the configuration of the AP, nearby STAs will also be given the information that they need in order to make decisions about which channel(s) are legally available to them.

---

15. It is possible that a STA may transmit for a brief time while it is trying to find an AP. A STA has two choices…either wait for an AP to identify itself, or actively probe all the channels until an AP answers. Once the AP's response is heard, the STA can restrict future transmissions so that they always use one of the allowed channels.

16. IEEE 802.11*h*, which is currently under development, but is almost finished being standardized (should be published in 2003), brings similar regulatory domain detection functionality to the 5 GHz domain, as well as enhanced power control to support the various limits on transmitted power in different regulatory domains. The title of IEEE 802.11*h* is (verbatim): "Spectrum and Transmit Power Management extensions in the 5GHz band in Europe."

IEEE 802.11 Operation at 5 GHz—IEEE 802.11*a*

The use of the 5 GHz spectrum by PHYs based on IEEE 802.11*a*-1999 is quite different from the uses of the 2.4 GHz spectrum by either IEEE 802.11*b*-1999 or IEEE 802.11*g*-2003. The most obvious difference is that the 5 GHz spectrum is not contiguous with the 2.4 GHz spectrum. Devices that operate at 5 GHz cannot interfere with those that operate in the 2.4 GHz spectrum, which means that one could operate two WLANs in the same physical space such that they would not interfere with each other. In fact, because IEEE 802.11*b* supports three non-overlapping channels, and because IEEE 802.11*a* supports twelve non-overlapping channels, one could actually operate 15 unique WLANs in the same physical space.

The IEEE 802.11*a*-1999 standard was written to allow operation over the United States "Unlicensed National Information Infrastructure" (U-NII) band. The U-NII was allocated to support devices that provide high-speed wireless digital communications for short-range, fixed, and point-to-point applications on an unlicensed basis. The U.S. U-NII band comprises a lower band (5.15–5.35 GHz), and an upper band (5.725–5.825 GHz). Due to different limits on radiated power, each band is suitable for slightly different applications.

Although the U-NII would appear to have two bands[17], the U-NII is actually divided into three logical bands, as shown in Figure 3–10, with each of the three bands occupying 100 MHz. The difference in the bands is the maximum power allowed by the FCC.

The 5.15–5.25 GHz portion of the lower U-NII band has the most restrictive power limits, yet is still suitable for indoor or other short-range applications (e.g., WLANs). The power is restricted to this extent to keep these devices from interfering with mobile satellite service operations. The 5.25–5.35 GHz portion of the lower U-NII band has reduced restrictions on radiated power, so it is additionally suitable for use between buildings, as well as within them. Finally, the upper U-NII band (5.725–5.825 GHz) has the least-restrictive regulation with respect to radiated power, allowing for longer distance (on the order of a few kilometers) operation when the signal is guided with directional antennas.

---

17. The two U-NII bands consist of the 200 MHz "lower band" that ranges from 5.15–5.35 GHz, and the 100 MHz "upper band," which spans from 5.725 to 5.825 GHz. The upper and lower bands are not contiguous.

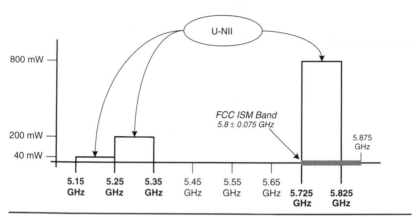

Figure 3–10   Definition of the U-NII band

A device operating in the upper band need not feel the need to always use more power than a device designed for the lower bands, just because it can. It is up to the designers of an IEEE 802.11*a* product whether they want to support only the lower U-NII band, or want to provide a radio that is tunable across a much wider range.

As an aside, there is also an ISM band in the 5.0 GHz spectrum (5.8 ± 0.075 GHz, or from 5.725 to 5.875 GHz), of which the upper U-NII band is a subset. The upper end of the ISM band extends beyond the top end of the U-NII band. The spectrum that extends beyond the defined top end of the upper U-NII band is not available for use by IEEE 802.11*a* products (as of the time of this writing).

Channel Definitions within the U-NII Band

Channel spacing within the IEEE 802.11*a* specification is based on 5 MHz multiples. Effectively, this gives 200 channels, numbered 0 through 200, in the 1000 MHz range between 5 and 6 GHz. For example, Channel 40 would be at 5200 MHz, and Channel 41 would be at 5205 MHz.

To keep some separation between the IEEE 802.11*a* channels and the edges of the U-NII spectrum, the IEEE 802.11*a*-1999 standard specifies that there be 30 MHz of unused space on either side of the 5.15–5.35 GHz U-NII band (the lower band). As depicted in Figure 3–11, the remaining 140 MHz of spectrum in the lower U-NII band can accommodate eight 20 MHz channels, in which the separation between the centers of two adjacent channels is 20 MHz.

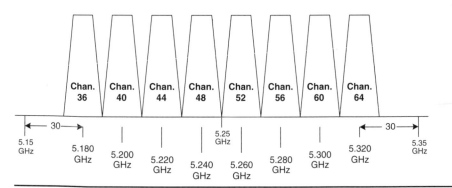

Figure 3–11   Eight contiguous IEEE 802.11a channels in the lower U-NII band

These eight channels are all non-overlapping. For readers who have heard some things about IEEE 802.11*a*, these are the "eight non-overlapping" channels that vendors of IEEE 802.11*a* products tout as being one reason to claim superiority over IEEE 802.11*b* products (which are limited to three non-overlapping channels).

In addition, IEEE 802.11*a*-1999 defines four more channels in the upper U-NII band, with 20 MHz of guard space between the edge of the band and the channels within it. Figure 3–12 shows the layout of these four additional non-overlapping channels.

Despite the fact that IEEE 802.11*a*-1999 offers a total of 12 non-overlapping channels, some early implementations seem to have restricted themselves to the lower band of the U-NII, which only has eight non-overlapping channels.[18]

The worldwide availability of RF spectrum in the 5 GHz region is not uniform, and as this book is being written, there are numerous efforts underway to "harmonize" spectrum allocations and the standards that depend on them, such that there will be a greater degree of similarity in the end-users' WLAN experience as they roam around the planet. IEEE 802.11*h* is an emerging standard that can allow IEEE 802.11*a* devices to operate in Europe, similar to the way that IEEE 802.11*d*-2001 permits the operation of IEEE 802.11*b*-1999 devices in different regulatory domains.

---

18. It is possible to make a radio that can operate within both the upper and lower U-NII bands, but a radio that is tunable over a wider range of frequencies may be slightly more expensive than one that is limited to a smaller frequency range. Such "wideband" radios do exist on the market, and this capability may be a practical necessity for "globally tunable" radios in the 5 GHz neighborhood of the RF spectrum.

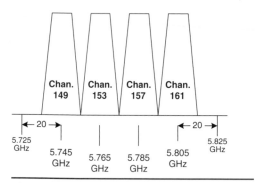

Figure 3–12   IEEE 802.11*a* channels in the upper U-NII band

The IEEE 802.11*h* draft is on its way to approval in 2003, but the author is not willing to make any statements about potential spectrum allocations or regulatory changes in Europe, Japan, or elsewhere. Worldwide regulations of devices operating in the 5 GHz spectrum are hopefully going to be converging over the next one to three years, but exactly how the dust will settle is far from clear at this point.

The IEEE 802.11 WG recently formed a new Task Group "*j*" to define an IEEE 802.11*a*-like PHY for use in Japan, in their 4.900–5.000 GHz and 5.030–5.091 GHz unlicensed bands. Some manufacturers' "5 GHz" radios are already tunable down into the 4.9 GHz frequency band, but there are not yet defined procedures for using that band in accordance with Japanese law (these procedures are being defined by TG*j*).

The IEEE 802.11*j* standard will also support operation in the 5.15–5.25 GHz band in Japan, which happens to be the same frequencies as the lowest U-NII band over which IEEE 802.11*a*-1999 operates. However, a product using these frequencies in Japan must adhere to the procedures defined in the forthcoming IEEE 802.11*j* standard. A TG*j*-compliant PHY may also operate in the middle and upper U-NII bands that are used by IEEE 802.11*a*-1999 PHYs.

One difference between the forthcoming IEEE 802.11*j* and IEEE 802.11*a*-1999 will be that STAs that support the eventual IEEE 802.11*j* standard *will not be able to transmit on those frequencies until they have heard an AP tell them that it is permissible to do so.* This implies that STAs based on such PHYs will not be able to operate within an independent BSS (IBSS).[19]

Another implication is that any STA incorporating a PHY based on IEEE 802.11*j* will not support active scanning to join a WLAN, since that would involve transmitting RF energy at those frequencies before the station knew that it was safe to do so.

Again, a STA based on IEEE 802.11*j* must wait to hear from an AP that it is safe to operate before it can emit any RF energy in these frequency bands. TG*j*'s activity began in 2002, as a study group, but the real business of TG*j* did not begin until the IEEE 802.11 WG meeting in January 2003. Due to the straightforward nature of the work (adopting IEEE 802.11*a*'s OFDM modulation to operate in a slightly different frequency band, as well as defining a few necessary MAC sublayer protocol changes), TG*j* appears to have made quick progress. It is possible, bordering on probable, that the IEEE 802.11*j* draft standard will be ready for Sponsor Ballot by the end of 2003.

The issue with spectrum allocations in the neighborhood of 5 GHz is complicated by the fact that many military and civilian radar systems (and things like microwave landing systems that help planes to land in bad weather) also occupy the same spectral neighborhood. Different countries may have significant issues with a product that works fine in one country, but that interferes with military radar in their country.

In the immediate-to-short term, IEEE 802.11*a* products *are* available now, and are now being certified by the Wi-Fi Alliance, so that customers can buy 5 GHz products with a Wi-Fi logo with the same confidence that they have had in purchasing IEEE 802.11*b* products in the 2.4 GHz band. Once the regulatory issues are resolved, the products that people are purchasing today will not become obsolete, although there may be new software that will allow operation in new geographies. Depending on the ability of radios to be tuned to a wide range of frequencies, it may not even be necessary for a user to buy a new product—new software and drivers may suffice.

Bring on the Noise

Much has been made of the fact that radio frequency interference is a problem in the 2.4 GHz ISM band, since microwave ovens, 2.4 GHz cordless phones,

---

19. IBSS mode is colloquially known as *ad-hoc* mode, and in this mode all the STAs associate with each other without relying on a central AP.

and so forth all emit RF radiation in this band. The noisiness of the 2.4 GHz band is one reason that vendors of IEEE 802.11*a* equipment cite when listing the advantages of their products.

However, the 5 GHz spectrum is not as pristine as it once was, since noise is now creeping into the band (e.g., 5 GHz cordless phones[20]). Moreover, besides interference from new categories of home-based devices, there are many other types of devices that have been designed to operate in the U-NII.

For example, there are devices that bridge an Ethernet LAN to a "T-3" circuit over the air (for point-to-point applications of the U-NII, the author has seen products that can operate in either the 5.8 GHz portion of the U-NII, or in both the 5.2 and 5.8 GHz portions), and several network access providers are using the 5.8 GHz portion of the U-NII band to provide broadband Internet access (DataCentric Broadband, for just one example).

As IEEE 802.11*a* products begin to be operated in the 5.8 GHz portion of the U-NII, there is the potential that they will be exposed to interference from some of these other devices that take advantage of the unlicensed spectrum in the U-NII band. It is even the case that point-to-point wireless bridges operating in the lower (5.2 GHz) portion of the U-NII band might possibly interfere with IEEE 802.11*a* products operating along the line of sight from the transmitter. Granted, these devices might not be that common, but neither are 5 GHz cordless phones…yet. The assertion that the 5 GHz band is cleaner than the 2.4 GHz band will be less true as time goes by.

The fact is that noise can be a problem in any frequency band. In practice, if end users know that they are deploying a WLAN in a commercial kitchen, then it might be wise for them to use IEEE 802.11*a*, since it won't be affected by the RF background noise from the microwave ovens. Similarly, if a facility uses a lot of cordless phones, then a wise choice of WLAN technology would be one that does not interfere with their installed phones. The cordless phone users will also appreciate the lack of interference (the author can hear static on his cordless phone when his WLAN is active).

---

20. This is another marketing triumph. The vendors sell 5 GHz cordless telephones to customers based on the unstated assumption that 5 is bigger than 2.4, so it must be better. The same thing happened when cordless phone vendors moved from the 900 MHz ISM band to the 2.4 GHz ISM band. Now, the ironic thing is that as end users have moved out of the 900 MHz band into higher bands, the 900 MHz band has become much cleaner for people who still have "old" 900 MHz cordless phones. Ah, progress. J

If an installation is not near an obvious source of noise, in either the 2.4 GHz or 5 GHz band, then noise need not be the driving criterion when making a choice of WLAN technology.

Remember that in some countries the 5 GHz band also overlaps with military and commercial radars, which do present significant, high-powered sources of noise in the 5 GHz spectrum. A signal that is considered noise by one person may be a valuable signal to another person. One of the features of the IEEE 802.11*h* specification is that it will enable IEEE 802.11*a* devices to peacefully coexist with radars, both by detecting their presence and by adjusting their output power in order to share the RF spectrum, which is preferable to not having access to that spectrum at all. It is not clear how much the WLAN device would affect the operation of the radar, especially at a distance, but the radar's power is sufficient to cause significant interference to the WLAN device for nontrivial bursts of time.

The reason this is mentioned is not to discourage investment in IEEE 802.11*a* devices, just to dispel the myth that the 5 GHz spectrum is a very low-noise environment. If you are considering deploying a WLAN and you are going to make a purchasing decision, be sure to base it on an actual site survey, not a gut feeling. Especially with the imminent availability of products based on IEEE 802.11*g*-2003, there is no reason to feel that IEEE 802.11*a* is the only high-performance option, and if this level of performance is important to you, it would behoove you to determine whether you'd be better off deploying 2.4 GHz WLANs or 5 GHz WLANs (and some users may choose not to decide at all, but to use both frequency bands!).

AUTHOR'S NOTE

IEEE 802.11*a* and IEEE 802.11*b* were standardized in 1999. Some vendors make an argument that says that IEEE 802.11*a* is "just as mature" as IEEE 802.11*b*. Well, maybe...if the only metric is the age of the standard. A significant reason why IEEE 802.11*a* did not garner market share as quickly as IEEE 802.11*b* did was that it was far more difficult to design CMOS-based RF circuitry that could operate in the 5 GHz band, in compliance with the IEEE 802.11*a* standard.

In addition, the modulation techniques that IEEE 802.11*a* uses to encode bits on the wireless medium were also much more complex than those required by IEEE 802.11*b*. The fact that IEEE 802.11*a* implementations had to overcome these technical challenges gave a head start to IEEE 802.11*b*.

Atheros Communications was one of the first companies to do what many people initially believed to be impossible (or at least too expensive to be cost effective)…they implemented IEEE 802.11*a* in CMOS. However, by the time IEEE 802.11*a* components became widely available, IEEE 802.11*b* products had already been in the marketplace for well over a year, and had increased in popularity very quickly after their debut.

There are some practical reasons why IEEE 802.11*a* is less attractive. For one thing, 5 GHz radio waves do not penetrate walls as well as 2.4 GHz radio waves do. Such a limitation may be more important in a home setting than in a corporate deployment. Moreover, the 5 GHz band is not uniformly allocated across the different regulatory domains (i.e., countries) of the world, which means that an IEEE 802.11*a* product that can legally be used in one country might be illegal to operate in another country. This problem is also solvable, by making products that can select their RF operating frequency based on the regulatory domain in which they find themselves.

IEEE 802.11*a* does have some significant benefits. Most notably among its benefits is that the standard has many more non-overlapping channels in which to operate. As a result, it can support more users in the same area, or the same number of users in a given area at higher speeds than IEEE 802.11*b* can.

With all of that said, IEEE 802.11*a* products are just now appearing on the market that are comparable (in the usability sense) with the existing IEEE 802.11*b* products. In addition, the Wi-Fi™ Alliance began certifying IEEE 802.11*a* products in late 2002, so it is now possible to purchase such products with the same degree of confidence that users have had in IEEE 802.11*b* products.

The IEEE 802.11 PHY in Context

To help put all the concepts of radio frequency channels and these other concepts into context, we can place them into a block diagram of a typical WLAN product, as depicted in Figure 3–13. The RF subunit contains the analog electronics that actually drives energy onto the wireless medium (WM), and receives energy from the WM. The BBP is the subunit that acts like a modem, encoding the digital data from the IEEE 802.11 frames into an analog form. The BBP also performs the reverse operation on received data from the WM. Finally, the MAC subunit is where the frames are generated and received, the inner workings of which will be discussed in the next chapter.

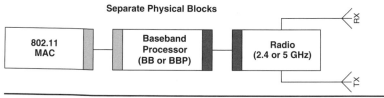

Figure 3–13   Functional blocks of a WLAN adapter

One can envision these modulation techniques as equivalent to similar techniques employed by modems, which also need to send digital data over an inherently analog medium. The job is the same, logically, although the techniques differ due to the different noise characteristics of the wireless medium (vs. a dial-up line), and due to the different speeds that are being achieved. In contrast, modulation onto a wired medium, either fiber or copper (twisted pair), is "baseband" (or carrier-less) style modulation, which is not really modulation at all…the transmitter simply transmits an electrical or optical representation of the digital data stream.[21]

Whether baseband (digital) or carrier-based (analog) modulation is being used, the modulation is not always done on a bit-by-bit basis…some modulation schemes encode multiple bits into a single "data symbol" for transmission onto the medium. Even some digital wired media don't directly transmit bits onto the wire; for example, consider the case of FDDI, which used a 4B/5B code and ran at 125 mega-symbols per second, where each five-bit symbol encoded four bits of actual data.[22]

To continue with the FDDI example, there are practical reasons for using such a technique, one being that of the 32-symbol (5-bit) "alphabet," there are

21. It is also possible to operate broadband (analog) modulations over wired media, which is what modems do over phone lines. The wireless medium is not the only non-baseband medium in use by data networking protocols.

also 16 nondata symbols beside the 16 symbols that represent each possible 4-bit group of data. The nondata symbols can be used for various control and signaling functions (since they are not legally able to appear within the data itself). Finally, the clock speed can be reduced from 200 MHz, which is what it might have taken to do certain one-bit-at-a-time baseband modulations, to 125 MHz, which was important at the time that the standard was defined, since it would not have been economically feasible to produce FDDI products unless the clock speed was kept as low as practical, while still achieving the goal of 100 Mbps operation.

The three logical blocks from Figure 3–13 may be integrated into one common piece of silicon that incorporates MAC, BBP, and RF subunits on one chip. There would still be a need for some external chips, such as power amplifiers between the RF output and the antennas, however. The author is not aware of such a highly integrated component, but two other pairings are common, as depicted in Figure 3–14.

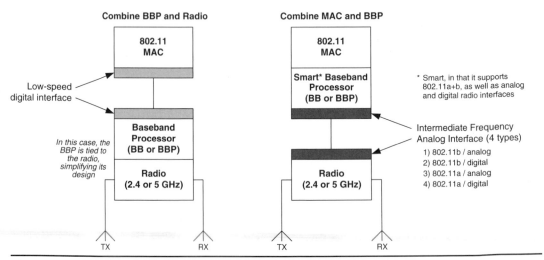

Figure 3–14   Common pairings of WLAN PHY subunits

22. Gigabit Ethernet is similar, in that some of its PHYs make use of an 8B/10B code (in which data is transmitted 256 bits at a time, using symbols taken from a 1024-element "alphabet"). Thus the link's clock speed will need to be on the order of 1250 MHz to carry 1000 Mbps (i.e., because a 10-bit symbol only transmits eight bits worth of data, there is a 10/8 (or 1.25) multiplier).

The pairing on the left puts the BBP and RF subunits near each other, or even integrates them together. This kind of makes sense since moving analog signals around inside a computer is a tricky thing to do, especially as the carrier frequencies get higher. The MAC and BBP are exchanging data at, worst case, about 50 Mbps, in only one direction at a time. There are many possible solutions that can make it very easy to move such a low-speed digital signal around inside a PC.

The pairing on the right of Figure 3–14 integrates the MAC and the BBP, which may make sense for certain applications, such as integration into PC core logic chipsets. In fact, this latter approach is being standardized by the JEDEC JC-61 committee, so that there is a common interface between chipsets with integrated BBP (and perhaps MAC as well) with external radio devices.

The signal between the BBP and radio is either analog or digital. If analog, it will probably take the form of a so-called "intermediate-frequency" signal that will be directly used to modulate the carrier wave in the radio, prior to the finished signal being amplified for transmission over the antenna, with a similar process occurring in the receive direction. If digital, then a digital representation of the modulated data stream is sent to the radio chip.

Because of the existence of the JC-61 interface, which will be standardized in the first half of 2003, we can expect to see radio vendors producing chips with such an interface, so their radios can easily be integrated with BBPs that also will have a JC-61 interface. This will give computer designers more flexibility in choosing the best MAC/BBP (or just BBP) and the best radio for their unique application. They can choose to optimize for best features, best cost, or any other metric they consider important.

Supporting Multiple Speeds Simultaneously

WLAN media have one attribute that is unique compared with LANs that are based on physical wires. In a WLAN, it is possible for stations on a shared-medium network to be operating at different speeds. While Ethernet supports 10 and 100 Mbps attachments to switched networks, these interfaces are dedicated collision domains that are limited to the two stations that share the link, one being the attached device, and the other station being the switch to which the device is attached. In short, any given wire only ever runs at 10 or 100 Mbps.

Based on the current definition of Ethernet, a wire can't carry both 10 Mbps and 100 Mbps signals simultaneously.

The speed mismatch between ports running at different speeds is handled by buffering within the Ethernet switch. By allowing stations in a WLAN to operate at different speeds, the WLAN is able to optimize itself to the local needs of each station, without requiring that all the stations be forced to go no faster than the "weakest link." Just as wired switches buffer frames to support multiple link speeds, in the wireless world the AP is responsible for buffering frames to each member STA in a WLAN, and the speed used will be dependent on the configuration of the STA, which is communicated to the AP during the "association" procedure.

It would be natural to wonder why a STA wouldn't always want to run at the fastest speed. The fact is that each STA is probably a different distance from the AP, and each STA has a different local noise environment. Also, due to non-linear propagation effects caused by reflections and absorption of radio waves, even two STAs that are equidistant from an AP may see different signal strength. Based on all these factors, it is likely that the signal strength, as well as the signal-to-noise ratio, that the STA sees from the AP can be presumed to be different for every station.

The modulations that achieve the fastest speeds generally require the signal strength to be above a certain threshold, and require a signal-to-noise ratio that allows the STA to recover the frame from within the signal. In IEEE 802.11, the goal is to provide a number of modulations of graduated robustness, so that the STA can gracefully scale back its own transmit speed until it achieves an acceptable ratio of successful transmissions. In the subsequent chapters that discuss the IEEE 802.11 MAC layer protocol, specifically its procedures for sharing access to the wireless medium, we will see that there is a capability for retransmission of IEEE 802.11 frames.

The STA expects to see an ACK within a short time after sending a frame, which is how it can tell that it might need to modify its data transmission speed (i.e., the lack of a single ACK might not cause the STA to infer that it is now too far to use a given speed, but if several ACKs are lost in a short time, plus if the signal strength and/or signal-to-noise ratio is deteriorating, the STA may choose to "down-shift" and use a slower modulation).

One thing that is important to remember, and can be confirmed by looking back at Figure 3–3, is that the STA's speed is the transmit speed. In Figure 3–3, look for the "Current Tx Rate" parameter, which in my case was 11 Mbps, the fastest transmit speed possible for a device based on IEEE 802.11*b*-1999. The speed on receive may be different, since it will depend on the choice of transmission speed by the communicating peer STA, or in the case of an infrastructure WLAN, all STAs are in communication with the AP, not directly with each other.

There is also a MAC-layer capability to perform frame-level fragmentation, since it is possible that a large frame will not be able to get through since it takes longer to transmit and is therefore more vulnerable to interference. However, if the MAC can break that frame up into smaller chunks, then each chunk might have a chance to make it to the other side without encountering interference. In the end, it might take longer to send the sequence of frame fragments to the other side than it would have taken to get the entire frame across, but it's possible that the large frame would never have made it across, no matter how many retransmission attempts the STA was willing to make.

In the end, a STA might stay at a higher speed if all the retransmission and fragmentation tricks were sufficient, but a STA can also reduce its own transmit speed as a way to better handle noisy transmission environments. Based on the increased robustness of the modulation schemes as one lowers the transmit speed, it is reasonable to expect that the frames will be more likely to be successfully transmitted at lower speeds. In fact, at lower speeds it's even possible that the STA will see higher overall throughput, since most of its packets will get through without needing to be retransmitted or fragmented. This is because the modulations for lower speeds are generally more robust against noise than the modulations that can achieve faster speeds.

In the event that a STA had responded to frame transmission errors by reducing transmit speed, it can revert to a higher speed after a suitable time has passed. The standard doesn't specify or recommend how to detect situations when using a slower speed might be a good choice, nor does it specify how long to wait before trying again at the next-faster speed. It is up to each vendor to decide how to gracefully handle noise, the presence of which is a fact of life in the wireless domain. In the end, a slow transmission is better than no transmission.

What's really interesting is how different speed frames can coexist on the WM. The trick is that all the modulations that can share the same frequency band begin with a common "prelude" that describes what type of modulation will follow. All STAs must be able to understand this prelude, even if the song that follows is in a language they can't understand. Figuratively, they may be able to tell that music is playing, but they won't be able to understand it. However, most importantly for correct operation of the WLAN, they will still be able to detect that another STA is active on the channel, and will know how much time the STA has reserved for transmission. Typically, a STA will reserve enough time for the frame to be transmitted, and for the associated ACK to be received, which is just a small additional amount of time.

The length of the frame-to-be-transmitted is not specified in octets, but in microseconds, because in order for receivers to do anything meaningful with the length in octets, they would need to divide by the transmission speed to get the expected transmission time. However, receivers may not be able to tell what modulation scheme is in use, which will mean that they'll have no clue as to how fast it is. Only the sender knows how fast its intended modulation is, and can predict with great accuracy the expected duration of its transmission.

The following figures expose the contents of this "prelude" protocol, PLCP, which is actually a sublayer of the PHY layer. Before delving into the structure of the PLCP header, Figure 3–15 shows the layering of PLCP within the PHY and relative to the rest of the IEEE 802.11 protocol stack.

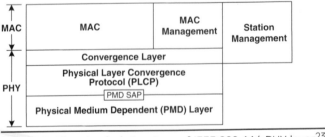

Figure 3–15   Logical structure of IEEE 802.11*b* PHY layer[23]

No single IEEE 802.11 protocol architecture diagram applies to all of IEEE 802.11's PHYs, however, Figure 3–15 depicts IEEE 802.11*b*'s protocol architecture, and the other PHYs have similar structures. IEEE 802.11*a* has an OFDM-based PLCP, and the FHSS and DSSS schemes from IEEE 802.11-1999 both have similar, but simpler, versions of this diagram.

---

23. Adapted from IEEE Std. 802.11™-1999, copyright 1999. All rights reserved.

The Physical Medium Dependent (PMD) layer handles all the work of transmitting PHY Protocol Data Units (PPDUs) onto and receiving PPDUs from the WM. In addition, the PMD handles medium-specific configuration and tuning necessary to maintain optimal performance. The PMD Service Access Point is the interface through which the PLCP layer sends PPDUs across the PDM sublayer. Above the PLCP sublayer is the Convergence sublayer, which serves to expose a common interface to the MAC, regardless of which PMD sublayer is actually in use.

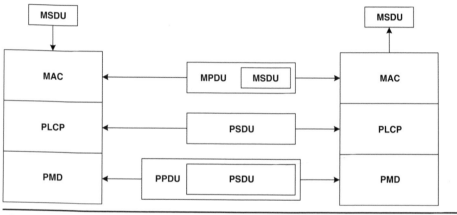

Figure 3–16   IEEE 802.11 PDU layering

Figure 3–16 shows the names of the PDUs that are exchanged between each layer in Figure 3–15. The job of the MAC Service is to exchange MAC Service Data Units (MSDUs). To accomplish this task, the MAC layer adds a MAC Protocol Data Unit (MPDU) header before the MSDU and a Frame Check Sequence (FCS; in this case the FCS is the MPDU trailer) after the MSDU. The resulting MPDU is accepted as a PHY Service Data Unit (PSDU) by the PHY's PLCP sublayer.[24]

Just as the MAC layer protocol's job is to exchange MSDUs, the PHY layer's job is to exchange PSDUs. In order to exchange the PSDUs successfully across the WM, the PHY layer adds a PLCP header to build a PPDU. Unlike the MPDU, there is no PPDU trailer. The PLCP header is what enables each frame to travel at a different speed. Figures 3–17a and 3–17b show the PLCP header formats for IEEE 802.11*b*.

---

24. Note that the MAC layer also exchanges Control frames and MAC Management Protocol Data Units (MMPDUs) that are also treated as PSDUs by the PHY's PLCP sub-layer.

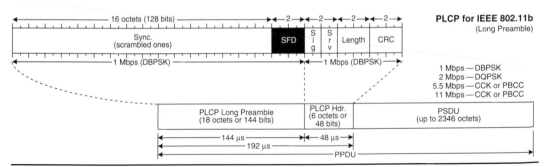

Figure 3–17a   IEEE 802.11*b* PPDU format—Long Preamble

As with Ethernet, the frame begins with a preamble that is used to allow the receiver to synchronize itself with the exact bit transmission speed of the sender. The expectation is that a receiver can maintain a "lock" on the sender's clock for the duration of a maximum-sized frame.

In the case of IEEE 802.11*b*, the PLCP preamble is available in one of two sizes. The first size, depicted in Figure 3–17a, is the "Long Preamble," which is 144 bits in length and is transmitted using the Differential Binary Phase Shift Keying (DBPSK) modulation at 1 Mbps. At 1 Mbps, each bit takes 1 μs to transmit, so the temporal length of the PLCP Long Preamble is 144 μs.

The preamble is created by sending a 144-bit all-ones pattern through the IEEE 802.11*b* scrambler. The preamble concludes with a Start-of-Frame Delimiter (SFD), which is 16 bits long. The SFD always contains the same value (the rightmost bit is transmitted first): `11110011 10100000`, or `0xF3A0` in hexadecimal notation.

The other preamble size, depicted in Figure 3–17b, is the "Short Preamble," which is 72 bits in length (exactly half of the length of the Long Preamble), and just like the Long Preamble, it is transmitted using the Differential Binary Phase Shift Keying (DBPSK) modulation at 1 Mbps. At 1 Mbps, each bit takes 1 μs to transmit, so the temporal length of the PLCP Short Preamble is 72 μs. The bit pattern of the Short Preamble is created by sending a 72-bit all-zeros pattern through the IEEE 802.11*b* scrambler.

As a final differentiator between the Long and Short Preambles, the Short Preamble concludes with an SFD, which is a bit-reversed image of the SFD in the Long Preamble (this is why the graphic in Figure 3–17b shows "(DFS)" below "Short SFD." The "DFS" is meant to remind us that the SFD in the Short Preamble is in the reverse order compared to the SFD in the

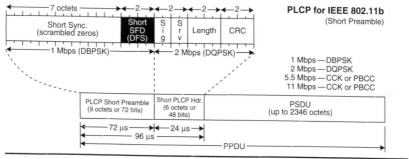

Figure 3–17b   IEEE 802.11*b* PPDU format—Short Preamble

Long Preamble. The Short Preamble's SFD, then, always contains the same value (the rightmost bit is transmitted first): 00000101 11001111 (0x05CF in hexadecimal notation).

Since supporting the PLCP Short Preamble is not mandatory for STAs based on IEEE 802.11*b*-1999, STAs that do not support it will not be able to detect that a frame has started, since they will not see a valid SFD (at least, not valid for a STA that only supports PLCP with Long Preamble). Note that the PLCP Short Preamble is exactly half the duration (in microseconds) of the PLCP Long Preamble.

Following either the PLCP Long Preamble or the PLCP Short Preamble is the PLCP Header, which consists of four fields. The first field to be transmitted is the "Signal" field, which is one octet in length. This field is used to indicate the speed at which the PSDU will be transmitted. In IEEE 802.11*b*, the speed is encoded in 0.1 Mbps increments, starting with a minimum value of the field of 0x0A (decimal 10, or 1 Mbps when multiplied by 0.1 Mbps). The other values of the field in IEEE 802.11*b* are 0x14 (decimal 20, which is 2 Mbps when multiplied by 0.1 Mbps), 0x37 (decimal 55, which is 5.5 Mbps when multiplied by 0.1 Mbps), and finally, 0x6E (decimal 110, which is 11 Mbps when multiplied by 0.1 Mbps).

The PLCP Header following the PLCP Short Preamble is structurally and semantically identical to the PLCP Header that follows the long preamble; however, when the Short Preamble is in use, the PLCP Header is transmitted twice as quickly—at 2 Mbps, using Differential Quaternary Phase Shift Keying (DQPSK). Thus, the 48 bits of the PLCP Header are transmitted in only 24 μs.

The PLCP Length field carries the time to transmit the PPDU, as derived from the transmit data rate and the size of the MPDU (a.k.a. PSDU). Finally, the PLCP Header concludes with a CRC-16 checksum that protects the Signal, Service, and Length fields.

The PLCP "Service" field is used to help qualify the exact nature of the modulation scheme that is being used to transmit the PSDU. For example, if PBCC coding is in use, the Service field will be marked to indicate that fact. Figure 3–18 shows the meaning of the bits in the Service field, comparing the definition of the field as defined in IEEE 802.11*b*-1999 with the version in IEEE 802.11*g*-2003. The figure shows the meaning and usage of each bit in both IEEE 802.11*b* and IEEE 802.11*g*. Note that the only two bits that have revised meanings are bits 5 and 6.

IEEE 802.11*b*-1999			Bit	IEEE 802.11*g*-2003		
	reserved	r	Bit 0	r	reserved	
	reserved	r	Bit 1	r	reserved	
0: not locked / 1: locked	Locked Clocks	LC	Bit 2	LC	Locked Clocks	0: not locked / 1: locked
0: not PBCC / 1: PBCC	Modulation Selection	MS	Bit 3	MS	Modulation Selection	0: not PBCC / 1: PBCC
	reserved	r	Bit 4	r	reserved	
	reserved	r	Bit 5	LE-P1	Length Extn. (PBCC)	Used to resolve ambiguities in the PLCP Length calculation when using 22 and 33 Mbps PBCC modulations.
	reserved	r	Bit 6	LE-P2	Length Extn. (PBCC)	
Improves accuracy on Length field for 11 Mbps PHYs	Length Extension	LE	Bit 7	LE	Length Extension	Improves accuracy on Length field for 11 Mbps PHYs

Figure 3–18   IEEE 802.11*g*-2003's PLCP Service field as compared to IEEE 802.11*b*-1999's PLCP Service field[25]

As usual, in IEEE 802.11 standards, bit 0 is the first bit to be transmitted since it is the least-significant bit.

The "Locked Clocks" bit indicates that the transmit frequency and symbol clocks are derived from the same oscillator. If this is true, then the transmitting STA sets this bit; otherwise, it remains clear.

In IEEE 802.11*b*, the Length Extension bit in the PLCP Header's Service field is only valid for PPDUs that are transmitted at 11 Mbps (according to the contents of the Signal field). To quote the IEEE 802.11*b*-1999 standard: "Since there is an ambiguity in the number of octets that is described by a length in

25. Adapted from IEEE Std. 802.11*b*-1999, copyright 2000, and IEEE Std. 802.11*g*™-2003, copyright 2003. All rights reserved.

integer microseconds for any data rate over 8 Mbps, a length extension bit shall be placed at bit 7 in the PLCP Header's Service field to indicate when the smaller potential number of octets is correct." The calculation that drives the setting of the Length Extension bit in IEEE 802.11*b* is equally applicable to both the CCK-11 and PBCC-11 modulations.[26]

Finally, the PLCP Header's Service field has a Modulation Selection bit (b3) that is used to determine whether CCK or PBCC is in use for any speed where either could be used, in particular, 5.5 and 11 Mbps. Along with the Signal field in the PLCP Header, a receiving STA can use the combination of MS and MS2 to determine the modulation that is being used.

For the purposes of computing the CRC-16 that protects the PLCP Header, all the Service field bits that are not defined are set to zero. This behavior has been carried forward into IEEE 802.11*g*, although there are only three reserved bits in the Service field as defined by IEEE 802.11*g*-2003.

Based on the setting of the modulation selection bit, and the value in the Signal field, the modulation can be uniquely determined. If the Signal field indicates a speed of 6, 9, 12, 18, 24, 36, 48, or 54 Mbps, then the DSSS-OFDM mixed modulation scheme must be in use (pure OFDM has its own unique PLCP header, so if those speeds are used in the OFDM PLCP header's Signal field, then the modulation is uniquely determined since the only modulation that can follow an OFDM PLCP header is OFDM). Figure 3–19 shows the OFDM PLCP PPDU structure that is used in both IEEE 802.11*a* and IEEE 802.11*g*.

If the speed in the Signal field is 22 or 33 Mbps, then the PBCC modulation must be in use. In addition, bit 3 of the Service field would be set in this case. If PBCC were only usable at 22 or 33 Mbps, there would be no need to define bit 3, but since PBCC is also usable at 5.5 and 11 Mbps, and since CCK is also usable at those speeds, bit 3 is needed to determine whether or not PBCC or CCK is in use for 5.5 or 11 Mbps. For 1 and 2 Mbps, the only valid modulation is Barker.

In summary, if the Signal field tells us that the PSDU is going to be transmitted at 6 Mbps, then there are only two choices for modulation, either OFDM or DSSS-OFDM. It follows that when the CCK-style PLCP Header is used, the

---

26. The two additional Length Extension bits (in bit positions 5 and 6) that have been defined by IEEE 802.11*g* are applicable only to PBCC-22 and PBCC-33, similar to the IEEE 802.11*b* LE bit, based on a somewhat more complex algorithm that determines which of the two bits shall be set in any given situation.

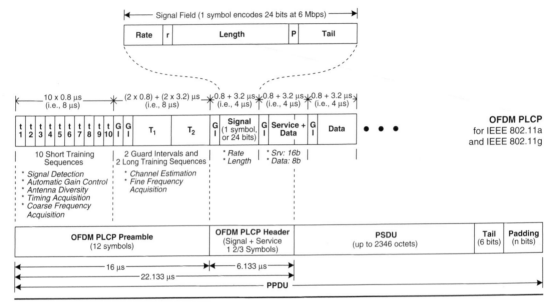

Figure 3–19   OFDM PLCP Header and PPDU structure

only real choice *for this modulation speed* is DSSS-OFDM. The MS bit must be zero in this case, which does not imply CCK modulation (as MS=0 would only be meaningful if the speed were 5.5 or 11 Mbps).

By the way, note that just as the CCK-style PLCP Header is transmitted using one of the mandatory modulations that all IEEE 802.11*b* devices can be expected to understand,[27] the OFDM PLCP Header is also transmitted at one of the mandatory rates (in this case, 6 Mbps). At this speed, each symbol carries 24 bits in 4 µs, which works out to 6 Mbps (24 bits divided by 4 µs is 6 Mbps).

Summary of IEEE 802.11 PHYs

The naming of the various PHYs defined in the context of IEEE 802.11 is not as descriptive as one might hope. The original RF-based PHYs were named Frequency Hopping Spread Spectrum (FHSS) and Direct Sequence Spread

---

27. All PLCP preambles using CCK modulation are transmitted at 1 Mbps using the Barker/ DBPSK modulation. When long preambles are used (the default for IEEE 802.11-1999 and IEEE 802.11*b*-1999), the PLCP header (which is situated between the PLCP preamble and the PSDU's header) is also transmitted at 1 Mbps. However, when short preambles are used, the PLCP header is transmitted at 2 Mbps using Barker/DQPSK modulation.

Spectrum (DSSS). In addition to these RF-based PHYs, the IEEE 802.11-1999 specification also specified a diffuse infrared PHY. All of those PHYs operate at either 1 or 2 Mbps. There was no specific "marketing" name for the 1 and 2 Mbps PHYs, other than "IEEE 802.11."

IEEE 802.11*a*

The IEEE 802.11*a*-1999 standard specifies a "High-Speed Physical Layer in the 5 GHz Band." To quote the standard, the following describes the actual attributes of IEEE 802.11*a* PHYs:

- The radio frequency LAN system is initially aimed for the 5.15–5.25, 5.25–5.35, and 5.725–5.825 GHz unlicensed national information structure [sic] (U-NII) bands, as regulated in the United States by the Code of Federal Regulations, Title 47, Section 15.407.

- The OFDM system provides a [W]LAN with data payload communication capabilities of 6, 9, 12, 18, 24, 36, 48, and 54 Mbps. A WLAN product claiming to support IEEE 802.11*a* *must* be capable of transmitting and receiving data at rates of 6, 12, and 24 Mbps.

- The OFDM system uses 52 subcarriers that are modulated using binary phase shift keying (BPSK), quadrature phase shift keying (QPSK), 16-quadrature amplitude modulation (16-QAM), or 64-QAM.

Figure 3–20 shows which modulations are used to achieve which speeds. The "coding rate" expresses the parameters governing forward error correction at a given speed.

Data Rate (Mbps)	Modulation	Coding Rate (R)	Coded Bits per Subcarrier	Coded Bits per OFDM Symbol	Data Bits per OFDM Symbol
6	BPSK	1/2	1	48	24
9	BPSK	3/4	1	48	36
12	QPSK	1/2	2	96	48
18	QPSK	3/4	2	96	72
24	16-QAM	1/2	4	192	96
36	16-QAM	3/4	4	192	144
48	64-QAM	2/3	6	288	192
54	64-QAM	3/4	6	288	216

Figure 3–20   OFDM modulations and their resulting speeds[28]

28. Excerpted from IEEE Std. 802.11*a*-1999, copyright 1999. All rights reserved.

There are actually 12 non-overlapping channels that have been specified in IEEE 802.11*a*, of which eight contiguous channels occupy the "lower" U–NII band, and a disjoint four contiguous channels occupy the "upper" U–NII band. The increased number of non-overlapping channels is a significant deployment advantage for WLANs based on IEEE 802.11*a*, since it is possible to overlay many more APs in the same physical space.

IEEE 802.11*b*

The IEEE 802.11*b*-1999 standard is called "Higher Speed Physical Layer Extension in the 2.4 GHz Band." The IEEE 802.11*b* PHYs are commonly known as the "High Rate" (or simply "HR") PHYs, and include two different modulation choices in the 2.4 GHz band. The mandatory modulation scheme is known as Complementary Code Keying (CCK), and an alternate scheme is also defined, known as Packet Binary Convolutional Coding (PBCC). Both of these defined modulation schemes support operation at two speeds: 5.5 and 11 Mbps.

IEEE 802.11*b* is defined to operate between 2.401 GHz and 2.4835 GHz, which is a proper subset of the 2.4 GHz ISM band in the United States, and which is also similarly available for unlicensed use in many other parts of the world. The channel definition within the 2.4 GHz band, as specified in IEEE 802.11*b*-1999, allows for three non-overlapping channels: Channel 1, Channel 6, and Channel 11.

The complete name for the CCK PHYs is "High Rate Direct Sequence Spread Spectrum" (or HR/DSSS). They are "high rate" compared to plain DSSS that was defined by the original IEEE 802.11-1999, which operated at either 1 or 2 Mbps. There is an optional variant of HR/DSSS that uses the Short PLCP Preamble, which is known as HR/DSSS/short. In addition, there are two names for the PBCC-based PHYs, namely HR/DSSS/PBCC and HR/DSSS/PBCC/short, wherein the PLCP Header is preceded by the optional Short Preamble.

In all these cases, the PLCP Header is modulated such that any STA could understand it, to enable backward compatibility, so the PLCP header is modulated at either 1 Mbps or at a combination of 1 and 2 Mbps. The Short Preamble variants defined in IEEE 802.11*b*-1999 are able to be demodulated by DSSS STAs, but since there was no Short Preamble option defined at that time, these STAs would not be able to parse the PLCP Preamble of these frames.

IEEE 802.11*d*

IEEE 802.11*d*-2001 is not a PHY standard, but it is very deeply related to the IEEE 802.11*b* standard, so it is worth mentioning here. The IEEE 802.11*d* standard, entitled "Amendment 3: Specification for operation in additional regulatory domains," provides mechanisms that can enable products based on IEEE 802.11*b*-1999 to roam across differing regulatory domains.

Based on information conveyed by an IEEE 802.11*d*-capable AP, an IEEE 802.1*d*-capable STA will learn the regulatory domain in which it is operating, and thereby cease using channels that are not legal to use in that domain.

IEEE 802.11*g*

IEEE 802.11*g*-2003 adds the OFDM modulations based on IEEE 802.11*a*-1999 to the lower-cost radios of IEEE 802.11*b*-1999. It also extends the PBCC modulation, which optionally was defined to operate at 5.5 and 11 Mbps in IEEE 802.11*b*-1999, to the speeds of 22 and 33 Mbps. Additionally, a hybrid modulation is provided which uses the DSSS-style PLCP header, with OFDM-modulated data. The PHYs in the IEEE 802.11g standard are known as "Extended Rate PHYs" and have the following names:

- ERP-DSSS (5.5 and 11 Mbps using CCK with Short Preamble)
- ERP-OFDM (6, 9, 12, 24, 36, 48, and 54 Mbps)
- ERP-PBCC (22 and 33 Mbps)
- DSSS-OFDM (6, 9, 12, 24, 36, 48, and 54 Mbps)

The Short Preamble support, which was optional-to-implement in IEEE 802.11*b*, is mandatory-to-implement in IEEE 802.11*g*. The AP decides when it is safe to enable that mode of operation (e.g., when most, or all, of the associated STAs are ERP-STAs). IEEE 802.11*g*-2003 specifies rules to help the ERP-STAs safely interoperate with HR-STAs.

WINNERS AND LOSERS

The proliferation of PHY choices in the IEEE 802.11 marketplace leads many to wonder which PHY will "win" over the others. As of late 2002, there was a selection of Wi-Fi-logoed products based on IEEE 802.11*b*-1999, plus the so-called "b+" products that offered 22 Mbps performance using PBCC at that speed (as well as at 5.5 and 11 Mbps). Products based on IEEE 802.11a-1999 were also on the market, and began to be issued with Wi-Fi logos as of late 2002. Several vendors also supported dual-band products; in other words, products that included support for both IEEE 802.11a-1999 and IEEE 802.11b-1999.

At the very end of 2002, and more so as 2003 got under way, products based on pre-standard IEEE 802.11g began to appear, to a warm welcome from the marketplace, despite their pre-standard status, and despite the fact that they lacked the Wi-Fi™ "seal of approval." Products in the latter category are implicitly b/g combinations, and several vendors have announced chipsets that will enable future products to support all three PHYs (a, b, and g).

Based on past experience, it is likely that not all of the products may have equivalent mass-market success; however, niche applications may exist for the non-mass-market choice(s), perhaps even to the extent that there will be solid business justification for finding and serving those markets. Early indications are that IEEE 802.11g will be a winner, since it offers a logical upgrade path for users who have already deployed IEEE 802.11b equipment in the 2.4 GHz ISM band.

There was a time when the "conventional wisdom" was that IEEE 802.11a would displace IEEE 802.11b as soon as products supporting IEEE 802.11a were available. However, what actually happened was that IEEE 802.11b products became wildly popular, and their costs dropped rapidly, which further encouraged their adoption. There is no dispute that IEEE 802.11a has some considerable technical advantages over IEEE 802.11b, but the market would appear to be saying (at least for now) that IEEE 802.11b is good enough (at least for today's applications).

In the author's opinion, it is not likely that any of IEEE 802.11a, IEEE 802.11b, or IEEE 802.11g will disappear in a short time (due to obsolescence by a superior standard). It is more likely that they will all find some degree of market acceptance. The author is making no predictions as to which will still be in existence in five years, although by that time we should be beginning to see next-generation WLAN products based on the standards that will emerge from the new "High Throughput" Task Group that is being created within IEEE 802.11 in 2003 (we're already hearing talk about IEEE 802.11*n*, even though TG*n* doesn't even begin its formal existence until September, 2003...).

The Future's So Bright...

Rather than spending too much time imagining the future, we will get on with the task of understanding today's WLAN standards. Even though researchers are busy pushing back the wireless frontier, it's not likely that products using their breakthroughs will be available for a while, whereas the existing IEEE 802.11 standards are already quite a lot to wrap our minds around, are important today, and are likely to remain important for a rather long time to come. Despite the long evolutionary road ahead of WLAN standards, the current generation will probably have a long half-life, and an understanding of how these standards operate should be very useful to end users and administrators alike.

What about Faster Speeds?

Many IEEE 802.11*a* vendors already have proprietary (non-interoperable) methods to achieve twice the bandwidth of IEEE 802.11*a*; in other words, 108 Mbps. This sounds great on paper, but few such products ever get more than 40 Mbps throughput in real environments.

The progress of WLAN standards so far has been in multiples of 5, as can be seen in Figure 3–21. If that trend holds, we can expect to see 250 Mbps WLAN products in a few years. Despite the shockingly high bandwidth, such speeds are actually within reach of modern Digital Signal Processors, although products supporting the extremely high-order modulations will be expensive to produce for some time, and their peak speeds will only be reached under ideal operating conditions; however, it is certain that speeds of well over 200 Mbps should be achievable, and even practical, within 5 years.

In an effort to bring interoperability to the >50 Mbps speed regime, the IEEE 802.11 WG has begun work to form the High Throughput Task Group, to begin in September 2003 and be known as IEEE 802.11*n*, to define WLAN standards that should offer a minimum of 100 Mbps throughput.

It is clear that despite its success so far, WLAN technology is still in its infancy. This observation is not meant to diminish the accomplishments to date

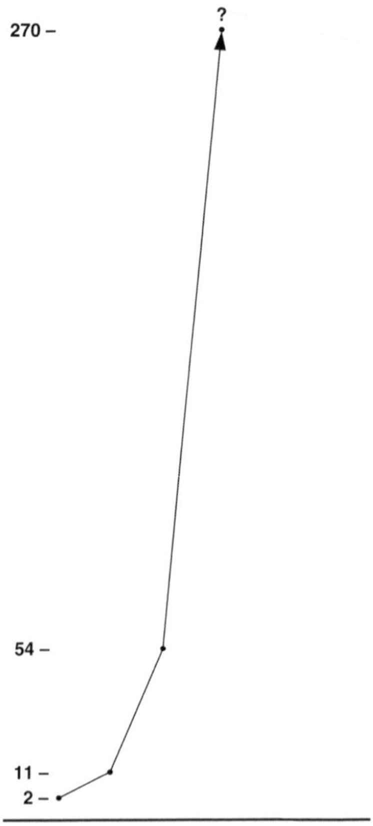

Figure 3–21   Evolution of top
speeds of IEEE 802.11 PHYs

of the IEEE 802.11 WG, the Wi-Fi Alliance, or of the hundreds of vendors who have built and marketed IEEE 802.11-compliant products, but just to remind everyone that there is a lot of room for improvement in WLAN technology. There is no doubt that wireless is the future, and that the future has already begun.

4

IEEE 802.11's MAC Sub-layer Protocol— Frames, etc.

While the Physical layer options discussed in Chapter 3 are of fundamental importance (and are very tangible to the end user, because they are directly related to perceivable characteristics such as the performance of the WLAN), the unifying feature that all IEEE 802.11-based WLANs have in common is their MAC sub-layer protocol. In contrast to the PHY protocol(s), the MAC sub-layer protocol is virtually invisible to end users, except when they initially configure their WLAN adapter.

In this chapter, we describe the MAC sub-layer protocol that has been developed for IEEE 802.11-based WLANs. The discussion in this chapter is based on the MAC sub-layer protocol that was specified in the document IEEE 802.11-1999, which is the base standard for IEEE 802.11 WLANs.

The MAC sub-layer is formally the lower portion of the Data Link layer, but the upper sub-layer, known as the Logical Link Control (LLC) sub-layer, is comprised of up to two protocols. In contrast, there is exactly one MAC sub-layer protocol at the MAC sub-layer of the IEEE's subdivided OSI Data Link layer. Confusingly, one of the two protocols at the LLC sub-layer is named LLC, which might lead one to conclude that, as with the MAC sub-layer, there is only one LLC sub-layer protocol. The other LLC sub-layer protocol is known as the Sub-Network Access Protocol (SNAP), which if used must be layered over LLC. However, LLC can be used alone...SNAP is optional, but LLC is mandatory over all IEEE MAC sub-layer protocols. In an attempt to avoid confusion, the author will make every effort to distinguish between the LLC sub-layer and the LLC sub-layer protocol(s) whenever the context is not clear.

Besides examining the inner workings of the IEEE 802.11 MAC sub-layer protocol, in this chapter we will also examine the remainder of the Data Link layer in detail, at least as it pertains to IEEE 802.11-based WLANs. Besides learning facts such as the mandatory usage of the LLC sub-layer protocol over IEEE 802.11's MAC sub-layer protocol, which has already been alluded to, there are a number of fundamental (and mandatory) MAC sub-layer features, and there are some optional extensions, which are either defined in the original IEEE 802.11-1999 specification or in an extension document (e.g., IEEE 802.11e or IEEE 802.11i, the two most prominent examples of MAC sub-layer protocol enhancements under way in the IEEE 802.11 WG). One of the most important invariant features is the MAC sub-layer's frame formats, as well as the basic channel access method, known as the Distributed Coordination Function (DCF).

The MAC sub-layer protocol design for IEEE 802.11 is in the process of evolution, being marginally extended and modified by various TGs within the IEEE 802.11 WG. Because of the importance of the MAC sub-layer protocol, there is reluctance to modify it very much. To a greater or lesser extent, TGs "e," "h," "i," and "j" are modifying part of the behavior of the MAC sub-layer protocol, because of necessary functionality that the IEEE 802.11 WG perceived to be missing in the IEEE 802.11-1999 specification.

Keep in mind that anything that the author states regarding the output of the existing TGs of IEEE 802.11 is based on the specifications as they existed when this book was finished. As such, it is possible that the details may have been changed between when this book was written and whenever the TG ultimately completed work on its standard. At the time of this writing, the most recent TG is "n," and it is not expected to have its first official meeting until September, 2003. In order to minimize the divergence, the author is trying to only refer to the parts of each draft that seem to be the most "solid," but there is no guarantee that the details of even these portions of the draft(s) will not change. Please look at the completed drafts for the final information. The IEEE gives away its standards for free after they have been finished for 6 months; search the web for the "Get IEEE 802" program.

Task Group "*e*" is adding facilities to enable "Quality of Service" within WLANs. This affects the basic WLAN frame header (in QoS-enhanced data frames, there is an additional two-octet "QoS Control" field that is appended at the very end of the frame's header that allows the frame to be marked according to the desired QoS parameters). TG*e* is also defining some procedures to enable two STAs to establish a "Direct Link" with each other, so that they can exchange traffic without sending it through the AP. This feature, if approved in TG*e*'s final draft, will optimize certain traffic since that traffic will only need to cross the wireless medium once (instead of needing to cross it twice, once to the AP, and once from the AP).

Task Group "*f*" has defined an independent IEEE 802.11*F*-2003 standard (known as a "recommended practice") for inter-AP procedures. TG*f*'s standard was approved in June of 2003 and was published in July 2003.

Task Group "*i*" is defining new procedures that will enable STAs to join and leave a wireless LAN securely. As the reader may be aware, the security that was defined in IEEE 802.11-1999 (known as "Wired-Equivalent Privacy," or WEP) has been found to be so weak as to be virtually useless. TG*i* will be defining techniques that enable a STA to securely associate with an AP, and also to send and receive encrypted data. Finally, TG*i* will likely also define procedures to enable "fast roaming" to happen while maintaining the strong security protection that has already been negotiated for an association between a STA and an AP. By "fast" we mean that the secure roaming from one AP to another can happen rapidly enough that a user who is engaged in, for example, a Voice-over-IP-over-WLAN phone conversation, would not notice any degradation in the quality of the sound conveyed through the phone, such as an audible dropout or click. In order to protect a higher-layer data packet as it crosses the wireless medium, TG*i* has defined several new "encapsulation" headers that carry the necessary information to help a receiver (in possession of the negotiated keys) decode the frame. Security will be discussed in considerably more detail in a later chapter.

Task Group "*g*" has made some minor adjustments to the usage of one of the basic MAC-layer Control frames. TG*g*'s standard was published in June of 2003 as IEEE 802.11*g*-2003.

Task Group "*h*" was discussed in the previous chapter, and it provides control mechanisms for a STA to discover the regulatory domain in which it is located, and to make necessary accommodations to the other non-WLAN users that might be sharing the channel, such as being able to detect if a periodic radar system is in use. TG*h* also provides mechanisms to control the output power of the WLAN device, to permit it to share the medium with other non-WLAN users. TG*h*'s work is nearly complete, and seems likely to be published in 2003. It is actually debatable whether or not TG*h* is modifying the MAC or PHY layer—it has aspects of both.

Task Group "*j*" is a new PHY similar to IEEE 802.11*a* that supports operation in Japan's 4.9 and 5.0 GHz bands. Due to the fact that this portion of the radio frequency spectrum is not dedicated to WLANs, STAs that support the TG*j* PHY are not permitted to send any traffic until they have heard from an AP first, so only "passive scanning" is allowed..."active scanning" is prohibited. IEEE 802.11's MAC sub-layer protocol, as amended by TG*j*, relies on the presence of a properly configured AP. In particular, this prohibits TG*j* devices from operating in "*ad-hoc*" mode. TG*j* may complete its work in 2003, but publication in early 2004 is more likely.

IEEE 802.11 MAC Sub-layer Frame Structure

No book on IEEE 802.11 would be complete without a description of the MAC sub-layer protocol's frame structure. One of the key operations performed by the MAC sub-layer of the Data Link layer is known as "framing," which is the process of encapsulating the higher-layer protocol packet (which may or may not be a Network layer protocol packet) in a set of MAC sub-layer headers, and appending a MAC sub-layer trailer, which most often is simply an error-detecting sequence. Framing also includes defining an interface to the Physical layer that can support the successful exchange of long sequences of bits across the Physical medium, which in the case of WLANs is especially unreliable.

The Data Link layer header will include *at least* the following three items:

• MAC sub-layer Destination Address (MAC-DA)
• MAC sub-layer Source Address (MAC-SA)
• Information to identify the higher-layer protocol payload (carried in the LLC sub-layer, by either the LLC sub-layer protocol or the LLC sub-layer protocol in conjunction with the Sub-Network Access Protocol (SNAP)

The first two items are MAC sub-layer items, and the third item in the list is frequently found in the form of a "type" or "protocol" field that indicates which kind of higher layer packet is embedded in the frame. Strictly speaking, this is an LLC sub-layer function. Note that I did not say "LLC sub-layer protocol," since it is possible to have Data Link protocols that are not divided into LLC and MAC sub-layers. The original Ethernet is an example of such a Data Link layer protocol.

The IEEE 802.2 LLC sub-layer protocol does provide a limited form of de-multiplexing for higher layer protocols via its one-octet Destination and Source Service Access Point (DSAP and SSAP) fields. Due to the limited number of LLC SAPs, there is another protocol in the LLC sub-layer known as the Sub-network Access Protocol (SNAP), which has a full two-octet Type field and is layered on top of the LLC protocol.

Figure 4–1 shows the decomposition of the LLC and MAC sub-layers into their constituent protocols (of course, the MAC sub-layer has only one proto-col). The most common form of the LLC sub-layer protocol occupies three octets, and the SNAP protocol, if present, consumes a further five octets.

Figure 4–1   LLC and MAC sub-layers versus
MAC, LLC, and SNAP protocols[1]

The MAC Sub-layer versus the Data Link Layer

Before continuing with the discussion of the IEEE 802.11 MAC sub-layer pro-tocol, we should emphasize that the Ethernet header represents more than just a MAC sub-layer protocol header…it is actually a complete Data Link layer header. This point bears repeating, since the terms "MAC layer" and "Ethernet" are frequently used almost interchangeably. In the IEEE world, the MAC layer has very specific functions, and Ethernet is not, in fact, a MAC-layer protocol, hence the opportunity for confusion.

---

1. Adapted from IEEE Std. 802®-2001, copyright 2001, and IEEE Std. 802.2-1998, copy-right 1998. All rights reserved.

The Ethernet protocol was designed before there was such a thing as a MAC or LLC sub-layer, so Ethernet's header structure had to support all the functions of the Data Link layer. Thus, the Ethernet frame's header ends with a two-octet "Type" field that is used to identify the higher layer protocol payload within the Ethernet frame body.[2] The reason to belabor this point is that it is not the case that IEEE 802.11 has such a field, which implies that (unlike Ethernet) IEEE 802.11 requires the presence of the IEEE 802.2 LLC sub-layer protocol in all of its data frames.

The IEEE 802 version of Ethernet, IEEE 802.3, uses the two-octet field (which Ethernet uses to indicate the higher layer protocol's Type) as a Length field. When the final two octets of the "Ethernet" header are used in this way, the "multiplexing" function is forced to lie within a higher layer; in other words, in the LLC sub-layer protocol header.

In modern terms, the MAC sub-layer protocol portion of IEEE 802.3's header consists of simply the Destination Address and Source Address fields. The structure of an Ethernet frame (very similar to an IEEE 802.3 frame) is shown in Figure 4–2.

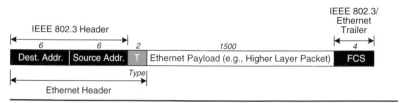

Figure 4–2   Structure of an Ethernet frame[3]

The "FCS" in the Ethernet frame's trailer stands for Frame Check Sequence. The MAC sub-layer protocols produced by the IEEE (including IEEE 802.3 and IEEE 802.11, among others) tend to use the 32-bit Cyclic Redundancy Check (CRC-32) as their FCS algorithm. This algorithm is not perfect—it cannot detect all types of transmission errors—but it is a "quick and dirty" way to determine if a frame is probably error-free.

---

2. This is probably a good place to point out that the author uses the word "frame" to refer to a layer-2 protocol data unit (PDU), whereas he uses the term "packet" to refer to a layer-3 PDU. In certain contexts (i.e., TCP), the term "segment" is appropriate as a term for a layer-4 PDU.

3. Adapted from IEEE Std. 802.3™-2002, copyright 2002. All rights reserved.

Not shown in Figure 4–2, but still present, are Ethernet's seven-octet preamble and its one-octet SFD,[4] both of which are transmitted immediately prior to the Ethernet Destination Address, to allow the receiver to precisely synchronize its clock to the sender's clock. After a frame has been completely transmitted, there is also an inter-frame gap, nominally 96 bit-times in length, that must be observed by MAC sub-layer entities, to give the medium a chance to "settle" prior to the transmission of the next frame. Other MAC sub-layer protocols may or may not have the equivalent of Ethernet's inter-frame gap.

The receiver must be able to maintain synchronization throughout the duration of the frame. Once the receiver's clock is synchronized to the sender's (which happens during the preamble), the bits or symbols (sets of bits) that are transmitted thereafter typically have a self-synchronizing capability that allows the receiver's clock to remain locked to the sender's precise rate of transmission.

The LMSC concept of the MAC sub-layer involves issues such as conveying information necessary to get the frame on to and off of the medium, such as frame synchronization, frame control information, frame addressing information, and so on. The higher layer protocol multiplexing function is technically part of the LLC sub-layer protocol(s).

Structure of the IEEE 802.11 MAC Sub-layer Frame

The IEEE 802.11 MAC sub-layer protocol structure follows the IEEE LMSC model, and thus has no higher-layer protocol demultiplexing features of its own. Therefore, the IEEE 802.11 MAC sub-layer protocol relies on the LLC sub-layer[5] headers to perform the higher layer protocol de-multiplexing function.

Besides defining the format of a MAC-layer frame, the IEEE 802.11 MAC sub-layer protocol specification must also define the means by which stations gain access to and share the medium, such that it is shared as fairly as

---

4. Actually, the original Ethernet did not have a "Start of Frame Delimiter" (SFD in IEEE 802.3 parlance), it had an eight-octet preamble that consisted of alternating 1s and 0s (which is just what the seven-octet IEEE 802.3 preamble consists of).

5. The LLC sub-layer consists of the LLC sub-layer protocol, and optionally the SNAP sub-layer protocol.

possible. Once a wireless station (frequently abbreviated as "STA" in the wireless LAN standards) has successfully joined a wireless LAN, it must obey the "rules of the road" that govern access to the wireless medium.

Chapter 5, *Dissection of a Probe Response MMPDU*, describes the "access" aspects of the IEEE 802.11 MAC sub-layer protocol, while this chapter focuses mostly on the frame-oriented aspects. This division of content is admittedly somewhat arbitrary, but the two subjects deserve to be described independently.

IEEE 802.11's MAC sub-layer access control protocol is comprised of a number of mechanisms that are collectively known as Carrier Sense Multiple Access with Collision Avoidance (CSMA/CA). The IEEE 802.11 standard refers to CSMA/CA, along with certain related procedures, as the Distributed Coordination Function (DCF).

The IEEE 802.11 MAC sub-layer protocol uses CSMA/CA in a manner similar to the way that Ethernet uses its Carrier Sense Multiple Access with Collision Detection (CSMA/CD), in that CSMA/CD's rules were defined to govern medium access in half-duplex shared (i.e., non-switched) Ethernet networks.

All IEEE 802.11 frames begin with the two-octet Frame Control (FC) field, the structure of which is depicted in Figure 4–3.

Bit 0	Bit 1	Bit 2	Bit 3	Bit 4	Bit 5	Bit 6	Bit 7	Bit 8	Bit 9	Bit 10	Bit 11	Bit 12	Bit 13	Bit 14	Bit 15
Protocol Version		Type		Subtype				To DS	From DS	More Frag.	Retry	Pwr. Mgt.	More Data	Prot. Frm.	Ord.

Figure 4–3   IEEE 802.11's Frame Control field[6]

The Protocol Version (bits 0 and 1) defined by IEEE 802.11-1999 is "0x00". The Type (bits 2 and 3) and Subtype (bits 4 through 7) fields define the format of the subsequent frame, and are listed in Figure 4–4.

The frame's two-bit Type subfield permits a total of four IEEE 802.11 frame types, of which three were defined in IEEE 802.11-1999, viz.:

---

6. Excerpted from IEEE Std. 802.11™-1999, copyright 1999, with the naming of Bit 14 shown as modified by IEEE 802.11*i* (work in progress; *subject to change before publication*). All rights reserved.

Type Value b3 b2	Type Description	Subtype Value b7 b6 b5 b4	Subtype Description	Frame Class
0 0	Management	0 0 0 0	Association Request	2
0 0	Management	0 0 0 1	Association Response	2
0 0	Management	0 0 1 0	Re-association Request	2
0 0	Management	0 0 1 1	Re-association Response	2
0 0	Management	0 1 0 0	Probe Request	1
0 0	Management	0 1 0 1	Probe Response	1
0 0	Management	1 0 0 0	Beacon	1
0 0	Management	1 0 0 1	Announcement Traffic Indication Message (ATIM)	1
0 0	Management	1 0 1 0	Disassociation	2
0 0	Management	1 0 1 1	Authentication	1
0 0	Management	1 1 0 0	De-authentication	2,3
0 1	Control	1 0 1 0	Power Save Poll (PS-Poll)	3
0 1	Control	1 0 1 1	Request to Send (RTS)	1
0 1	Control	1 1 0 0	Clear to Send (CTS)	1
0 1	Control	1 1 0 1	Acknowledgment (ACK)	1
0 1	Control	1 1 1 0	Contention Free End (CF-End)	1
0 1	Control	1 1 1 1	CF-End + CF-ACK	1
1 0	Data	0 0 0 0	Data	3,1*
1 0	Data	0 0 0 1	Data + CF-ACK *any PCF-capable STA or the Point Coordinator (PC)*	3
1 0	Data	0 0 1 0	Data + CF-Poll *only the Point Coordinator (PC)*	3
1 0	Data	0 0 1 1	Data + CF-ACK + CF-Poll *only the Point Coordinator (PC)*	3
1 0	Data	0 1 0 0	Null Function (no data)	3
1 0	Data	0 1 0 1	CF-ACK (no data) *any PCF-capable STA or the Point Coordinator (PC)*	3
1 0	Data	0 1 1 0	CF-Poll (no data) *only the Point Coordinator (PC)*	3
1 0	Data	0 1 1 1	CF-ACK + CF-Poll (no data) *only the Point Coordinator (PC)*	3
1 0	Data	1 0 0 0	QoS Data	3,1*
1 0	Data	1 0 0 1	QoS Data + CF-ACK *any PCF-capable STA or the Point Coordinator (PC)*	3
1 0	Data	1 0 1 0	QoS Data + CF-Poll *only the Point Coordinator (PC)*	3
1 0	Data	1 0 1 1	QoS Data + CF-ACK + CF-Poll *only the Point Coordinator (PC)*	3
1 0	Data	1 1 0 0	QoS Null Function (no data)	3
1 0	Data	1 1 0 1	QoS CF-ACK (no data) *any PCF-capable STA or the Point Coordinator (PC)*	3
1 0	Data	1 1 1 0	QoS CF-Poll (no data) *only the Point Coordinator (PC)*	3
1 0	Data	1 1 1 1	QoS CF-ACK + CF-Poll (no data) *only the Point Coordinator (PC)*	3

QoS   CF-ACK

Null   CF-Poll

* May be used as a Class 1 frame only if both the ToDS and FromDS bits are clear (i.e., set to zero)

Figure 4–4   Management, Control, and Data Frames in IEEE 802.11[7]

- Bit 3 (0) + Bit 2 (0)—Management
- Bit 3 (0) + Bit 2 (1)—Control
- Bit 3 (1) + Bit 2 (0)—Data
- Bit 3 (1) + Bit 2 (1)—Undefined

7. Adapted from IEEE Std. 802.11™-1999, copyright 1999. All rights reserved. Augmented by draft 4.4 of IEEE 802.11*e* (work in progress, subject to change before publication.).

The bit ordering within multi-bit fields in Figure 4–3 are in "little-endian" form (which matches the IEEE 802.11-1999 specification), but Figure 4–4 displays them in "big-endian" form, since the author finds that more easily understandable. In order to ease conversion between the two formats, Figure 4–4 includes the bit position numbers at the top of the chart. Chapter 5 contains several detailed examples that should help clarify the relationship between the different representations.

Through the use of the 4-bit Subtype field, each of IEEE 802.11's frame Types may have up to 16 Subtypes. The Subtype field is stored in the fourth through seventh bit positions of the FC field. When the Type subfield indicates a Data frame, each of the four bits of the FC's Subtype subfield has a particular meaning (whereas the subtypes of the Management and Control Types are just numbers, with no structure). In Figure 4–4, the meanings of each bit offset within the Subtype field of the Data Type is illustrated by enclosing each bit in a vertical box with the label at the bottom.

Only half of the Data Subtypes were defined in the IEEE 802.11-1999 standard, with the remainder being reserved. These have now been allocated to the IEEE 802.11 WG's TG "e," which is enhancing the MAC sub-layer protocol to provide features that can support QoS. These eight Data subtype values that were originally reserved mirror the functions of the first eight, except that these formerly reserved Data subtypes now all denote QoS-enhanced frames.

The Data frame types in italics are associated with the IEEE 802.11e TG,[8] and will only become valid once that standard has been approved, probably not in 2003.

Three-quarters of the Data subtypes are only valid during PCF mode (see Chapter 6). PCF mode, in which the AP polls the STAs for frames, was an early attempt at providing a latency-bounded MAC service. Any Data subtypes with "CF" in their names are used only during Contention-Free operation; in other words, only when the BSS is operating in PCF mode. Of these, half of them

---

8. The working title for the IEEE 802.11e draft standard is "Medium Access Control (MAC) Enhancements for Quality of Service (QoS)."

may only be sent only by the Point Coordinator (PC) function in the AP, whereas the other half may either be sent by the Point Coordinator (PC) or by any other STAs in PCF mode. Given that PCF mode is virtually not implemented, these subtypes should be rarely seen in the real world.

Summary of the Frame Control Field

- Bits 0 and 1 (which comprise the Protocol Version field) have been defined by IEEE 802.11-1999 as "0x00".
- The Type (bits 2 and 3) and Subtype (bits 4 through 7) fields define the format of the subsequent frame.
- Bit 8 (the "ToDS"), and bit 9 (the "FromDS" bit), will be covered in Chapter 6. These two bits control the interpretation of the "Address" fields in the MPDU and MMPDU headers.
- Bit 10, the "More Frag." (i.e., More Fragments) bit, indicates (if it is set to "1") that this MPDU or MMPDU is a fragment of a larger MSDU or MMPDU, and that this is *not* the last fragment. If the bit is clear, then this frame is the last fragment, or the frame was never fragmented. Note that when a STA performs MAC-layer fragmentation, each MSDU or MMPDU fragment is transmitted in order, and is individually acknowledged before the next fragment of that MSDU or MMPDU can be sent.
- Bit 11, the "Retry" bit, is set when this MPDU or MMPDU is a retransmission of an earlier MPDU or MMPDU. The Retry bit allows the receiving STA to detect and eliminate any duplicate MPDUs or MMPDUs that it happens to receive. If a STA receives a MPDU or MMPDU and acknowledges it, but the ACK control frame does not reach the sending STA, then the sender will retransmit the frame with the Retry bit set. In this case, the receiving STA will get more than one copy of the frame, but only the first copy will have the Retry bit clear, while all the rest will have it set. The receiving STA will be able to use this extra information to ensure that it only receives a single copy of the frame.
- Bit 12, the "Pwr. Mgt." (i.e., Power Management) bit, is used to indicate what power management state the sending station will enter upon successfully completing the transmission of the current MPDU or MMPDU. When a STA sets this bit, it is advertising that it will be

entering "power-save" mode after it completes sending this frame and it receives the ACK indicating that the frame was received. If this bit is clear, the STA is going to remain in an active state.

- Bit 13, the "More Data" bit, is used when talking to a STA that is in power-save mode, to let it know that after this frame, there are still more frames buffered for it. Upon receiving a frame with this bit set, the receiving STA could choose to stay awake a little longer to collect the frames that are queued for delivery to it. If the receiving STA chooses to conserve power and doze anyway, the AP will buffer the frames until the receiving STA's next scheduled awake time.

- Bit 14, the "Prot. Frm." (i.e., Protected Frame) bit,[9] is used to indicate that a frame is protected by one of the cipher suites supported by IEEE 802.11 (see Chapter 7, *Security Mechanisms for Wireless LANs*, for more details).

- Bit 15, the "Ord." Bit, is set to indicate that a given MSDU is being sent using the "strictly ordered" service class provided by the 802.11 MAC. The other service class type is "re-orderable multicast." If an MSDU is being sent with the Order bit set, then no other MSDUs may be sent to a STA until this MDSU has been completely transmitted (e.g., in the case where an AP has multiple frames buffered for that STA, any frames with the Order bit set must be transmitted in order). A STA may not simultaneously receive traffic using the strictly ordered service class if it has already elected to use power management. If a STA wishes to receive frames of the strictly ordered service class, it may not doze.

Structure of the IEEE 802.11 MAC Frames

As we saw previously, there are three types of frames, and in this subsection they will be discussed in the following order: Control, Management, and Data.

---

9. This bit was formerly known as the "WEP" bit (Wired-Equivalent Privacy) in the original IEEE 802.11-1999 standard, but the IEEE 802.11*i* TG is changing its name (as indicated in the text). The author has chosen to use the newer name, but to keep the original name alive via this footnote. Purists may object to my referencing a draft document, but the author is willing to take the risk that IEEE 802.11*i* will be ratified during the shelf life of this book.

IEEE 802.11 Control Frames

Figure 4–5 shows the format of all six types of Control frames, which are all very short. The first four types of Control frames (Request-to-Send, Clear-to-Send, Acknowledgment, and Power-Save Poll) are the most common.

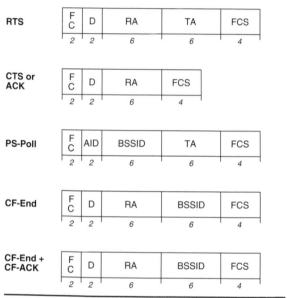

Figure 4–5   IEEE 802.11 Control frames

RTS and CTS

The RTS/CTS mechanism can be used to protect the transmission of an MPDU or MMPDU, by reserving the medium in advance of the actual transmission of the frame. The RTS/CTS mechanism is used on a hop-by-hop basis; in other words, the sending STA could use this mechanism when sending a frame to the AP, but the AP may make its own decision as to whether or not to use the RTS/CTS mechanism to protect the transmission of the frame to the receiving STA. By "protect" we mean that the RTS/CTS mechanism reserves the medium for a time interval long enough to transmit a frame and to receive the associated ACK frame. This "reservation" obviously only applies to STAs that were present to hear the RTS/CTS exchange, so it is still possible that a STA could jump in and interfere with an allegedly protected exchange (although the MAC entity is supposed to listen before talking, this can't prevent a roaming STA, which listened first, found the medium idle, began transmitting, then roamed into the middle of another WLAN in which another transmission was in progress).

The Request-to-Send (RTS) frame is 20 octets long as is optionally used to reserve the medium for a subsequent frame transmission. After the corresponding Clear-to-Send (CTS) is received, the STA that sent the RTS will know it can safely send its frame, since all STAs in the BSS will have heard the CTS from the AP. The CTS frame is only 14 octets long. Once the receiving STA (which could be an AP) has the frame, a separate decision is made if the receiving STA is not the frame's final destination.

At each hop, a decision must be made as to whether the RTS/CTS mechanism will be used to protect the frame on its next hop, or whether it will send it directly. The STA (or AP) has a configuration parameter known as the RTS threshold that determines whether a frame is preceded by an RTS/CTS exchange. Frames that are smaller than the RTS threshold are not preceded by the RTS/CTS exchange, with the exception that multicast frames are never preceded by an RTS/CTS exchange regardless of their size.

ACK

The Acknowledgment (ACK) Control frame (14 octets) is used to indicate successful reception of a frame by the next-hop receiver. If the sender does not receive an ACK during the expected time window after it finished transmitting its frame, it will re-send the frame at its next opportunity. The ACK is used in a slightly modified fashion in the event of MAC-layer fragmentation, which is covered in Chapter 6.

The ACK in IEEE 802.11 is not used to implement a reliable Data Link layer protocol (many reliable Data Link protocols do use ACK-based schemes to provide for retransmissions). The usage of the ACK in IEEE 802.11 actually serves to indicate to the sender whether a collision has happened. A collision is inferred by the lack of an ACK.

PS-Poll

The PS-Poll (Power-Save Poll) Control frame (20 octets) is used when a STA sees that an AP has frames buffered for it. The STA sends the PS-Poll so the AP knows that the STA is ready to receive the buffered frame(s). This mechanism is used when the STA has been dozing and now wants to collect the frames that the AP buffered while the STA was dozing.

"CF-End" and "CF-End + CF-ACK"

These two Control frames are used only in PCF mode, which is covered briefly in Chapter 6. Note that both of those frames are sent to the broadcast address, and both of them have their Duration field set to indicate zero microseconds.

IEEE 802.11 Management Frames (MMPDUs)

Figure 4–6 shows the format of all 11 types of Management frames.

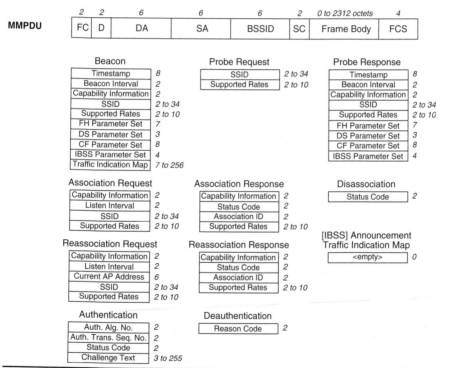

Figure 4–6   IEEE 802.11 Management frames (MMPDUs)[10]

The use of these frames will be covered later in this chapter, or in Chapter 6. A general statement that can be made about MMPDUs is that they are all used

---

10. Adapted from IEEE Std. 802.11™-1999, copyright 1999. All rights reserved.

in infrastructure mode, except for the ATIM message, which is only used in IBSS mode. Anything to do with Association must involve an AP, and so Association-related MMPDUs are not usable in IBSS mode. Authentication MMPDUs can be used in either infrastructure or IBSS mode. Likewise, Probes and Beacons are usable in both modes.

IEEE 802.11 Data Frames (MPDUs)

All of the IEEE 802.11 variants, regardless of the frequency band in which they operate, use the MAC sub-layer protocol frame format depicted in Figure 4–7. The formal name for this structure is the MAC Protocol Data Unit (MPDU). The Address 4 and QC fields have a gray background because they are optional (their presence depends on the contents of the FC field).

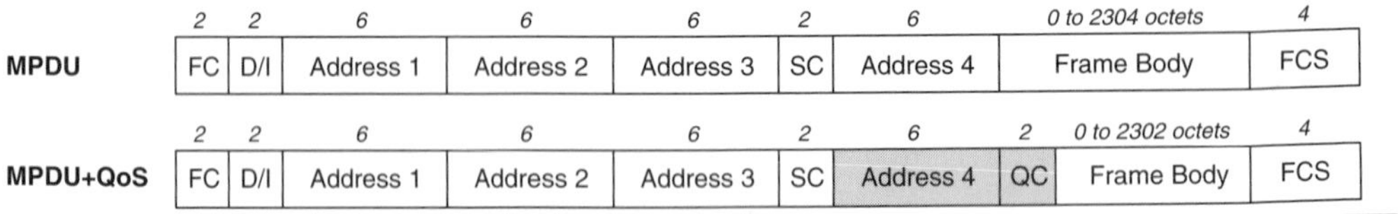

	2	2	6	6	6	2	6	0 to 2304 octets	4
MPDU	FC	D/I	Address 1	Address 2	Address 3	SC	Address 4	Frame Body	FCS

	2	2	6	6	6	2	6	2	0 to 2302 octets	4
MPDU+QoS	FC	D/I	Address 1	Address 2	Address 3	SC	Address 4	QC	Frame Body	FCS

Figure 4–7   Overall structure of an IEEE 802.11 MPDU[11]

Figures 4–5, 4–6, and 4–7 are all drawn to the same scale. (The only exception is that the MMPDU and MPDU frame body fields are not drawn to scale, since they are variable-length and can be so much larger than the rest of the components of the frame.) The labels in Figure 4–7 are as follows:

FC	IEEE 802.11	Frame Control
D	IEEE 802.11	Duration
SC	IEEE 802.11	Sequence Control
QC	IEEE 802.11*e*	QoS Control
FCS	IEEE 802.11	Frame Check Sequence

The maximum size for an IEEE 802.11 MPDU is 2346 octets. Of that, the IEEE 802.11 frame's MAC header (24 or 30 octets) plus the MAC trailer (i.e.,

---

11. Adapted from IEEE Std. 802.11™-1999, copyright 1999, as amended by IEEE 802.11*e* draft 5.0 (a work-in-progress, which is subject to change before its publication). All rights reserved.

the FCS, at four octets) consumes a total of 28 or 34 octets, which leaves a remainder of 2312 or 2316 octets in which to carry the MPDU payload. These sizes did not consider the effect of the IEEE 802.11*e* QC field, which would consume two octets if it were present. The entire frame, including the MAC sub-layer protocol header, the MPDU payload, and the FCS, comprises the MAC MPDU, or in the case of Management frames, the MAC MMPDU.

IEEE 802.11 with IEEE 802.1Q

In **Ethernet**, an IEEE 802.1Q VLAN tag is inserted into the frame and effectively removes four octets from the frame's capacity (Ethernet defines "frame extension" in which a frame may be allowed to have a full-size 1500-octet payload, a 14-octet Data Link header, the usual four-octet FCS, and the four octets of VLAN information, for a total of 1522 octets (the usual maximum frame size for Ethernet is 1518 octets, without VLAN information present).

Because the presence of the two-octet IEEE 802.1Q Tag Control Information Header is indicated by using Ethernet Type `0x8100`, the insertion of the TCIH consumes four octets of the Ethernet frame's payload capacity.

Figure 4–8 illustrates the addition of the IEEE 802.1Q VLAN tag to the Ethernet (or IEEE 802.3) header. The "VT" field is the "VLAN [Ethernet] Type", `0x8100`. The TCI is the IEEE 802.1Q Tag Control Information Header (TCIH).

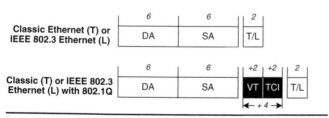

Figure 4–8   IEEE 802.1Q VLAN tag in Ethernet and IEEE 802.3[12]

However, in IEEE 802.11 (and in all other non-Ethernet LAN protocols that rely on LLC sub-layer protocol encapsulation), the "Type" field of `0x8100` is still the only way to indicate that the TCIH is present. To get a TCIH into

---

12. Adapted from IEEE Std. 802.3™-2002, copyright 2002, augmented by IEEE Std. 802.1Q™-2003, copyright 2003. All rights reserved.

the stack, one needs a three-octet LLC sub-layer header (because the LLC sub-layer protocol must always follow the IEEE 802.11 MPDU header), and a five-octet SNAP sub-layer header, with the Type field of the latter set to 0x8100 (the SNAP sub-layer header is present to provide a way to encode the "Type" field in the context of LLC...when the SNAP OUI is set to the value of 0x000000, the value in the SNAP "Type" field is interpreted as if it were in the Ethernet "Type" field). The two-octet TCIH then follows the SNAP type field (only when the SNAP Type field contains 0x8100).

A total of 10 octets have been consumed, which are no longer available to carry MPDU payload. Said another way, the presence of the IEEE 802.1Q header has reduced the carrying capacity of the MPDU by a total of 10 octets. Contrary to the situation with IEEE 802.3, there is no concept of "frame extension" in IEEE 802.11 to accommodate the IEEE 802.1Q VLAN header.

In either case, after the inserted IEEE 802.1Q VLAN tag (consisting of the TCIH and whatever it takes to prefix it with a Type of 0x8100), the frame resumes with whatever has been displaced by the insertion of the VLAN tag. In Ethernet, frequently another "Type" field follows the TCIH. In IEEE 802.11, which normally requires the MPDU payload to begin with the LLC sub-layer protocol header, we can conclude that the item immediately following the IEEE 802.1Q TCIH will be an LLC sub-layer header, which encapsulates the frame's "real" higher layer protocol payload.

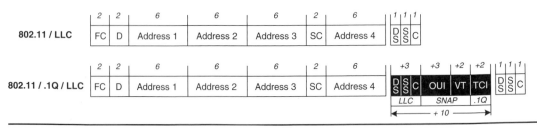

Figure 4–9   IEEE 802.1Q VLAN tag in IEEE 802.11[13]

Figure 4–9 illustrates the insertion of the IEEE 802.1Q-2003[14] VLAN tag after the IEEE 802.11 MPDU header.

---

13. Adapted from IEEE Std. 802.11™-1999, copyright 1999, augmented by IEEE Std. 802.1Q™-2003, copyright 2003. All rights reserved.

14. IEEE 802.1Q was originally standardized in 1998.

Data Link Protocol Stacks Based on IEEE 802.11

The field labels in the IEEE 802.11 MAC header are the expected ones, and the remaining labels are as follows. DS and SS are DSAP and SSAP, respectively, and C is Control. Those three are the three octets of the LLC sub-layer protocol header. The OUI is the SNAP Organizationally Unique Identifier (which is set to 0x000000 in this case, since the interpretation of the SNAP Type field is the normal Ethernet Type interpretation).

Figure 4–10 illustrates the possible Data Link protocol stack that might be based on IEEE 802.11's MAC sub-layer protocol. The base of the stack is either the 24-octet (b) or 30-octet (B) IEEE 802.11 MPDU header. That layer is required, and the 24-octet form is more common. The other mandatory layer is the 3-octet IEEE 802.2 LLC sub-layer.

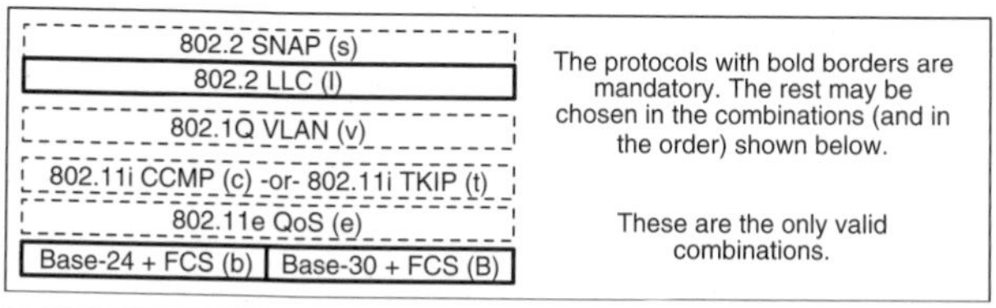

Figure 4–10   Possible Data Link protocol stack based on IEEE 802.11[15]

Starting from the bottom of the stack, we see that the forthcoming IEEE 802.11*e* standard will optionally add a 2-octet QC field at the end of any QoS-enhanced MPDU's header (indicated by (e) in Figure 4–10). In the event that IEEE 802.11*i* encryption is in use, there are two options. Headers related to CCMP (indicated by (c) in Figure 4–10) will consume 16 octets of the MPDU's effective payload, while TKIP (indicated by (t)) will consume 20 octets. Next, above the IEEE 802.11 layer is the IEEE 802.1Q layer, which (if present) requires 10 octets (this header is indicated by (v) in Figure 4–10).

Finally, completing the Data Link layer protocol stack is the IEEE 802.2 LLC sub-layer protocol (indicated in Figure 4–10 as (l)), and optionally the IEEE 802.2 SNAP sub-layer protocol (indicated as (s)), which consumes five

---

15. Adapted from IEEE Std. 802.1Q™-2003, copyright 2003, IEEE Std. 802.2-1998, copyright 1998, and IEEE Std. 802.11™-1999, copyright 1999, as amended by IEEE 802.11*e* draft 5.0 and IEEE 802.11*i* draft 5.0 (both works-in-progress as of this writing, which are subject to change before their eventual publication). All rights reserved.

octets when it is present. The LLC sub-layer protocols, LLC and SNAP, are both part of the MPDU payload, but taken as a whole they comprise the top of the Data Link layer protocol stack. The size of this total stack affects how much data the Network layer can send at a time, in other words, it affects the maximum capacity of the MSDU. In the case of IP, the IP layer refers to the Maximum Transmission Unit (MTU) of a subnetwork technology, which is the payload size of the subnetwork. In the case of Ethernet, a 1500-octet IP packet can fit into a 1518-octet Ethernet frame. In the case of IEEE 802.11, a 2346-octet MPDU can hold an amount of data that depends on how "deep" the Data Link layer protocol stack is.

In a moment, you will see that the deepest stack is 74 octets, which results in an MTU of 2346-74 octets (i.e., 2272 octets) of capacity in the eyes of the IP layer. There are actually 12 "basic" combinations of headers, from which all the possible Data Link layer header sets formed from IEEE 802.11 can be derived, which are illustrated in Figure 4–11.

802.11

These are the 12 valid "base" combinations of IEEE 802.11, IEEE 802.11e, and IEEE 802.11i headers.		
b 28	B **34**	**28** b
B **34**	Bc **50**	**44** bc
c 16	Bt **54**	**48** bt
t 20	Be **36**	**30** be
e 2	Bec **52**	**46** bec
	Bet **56**	**50** bet

Figure 4–11 The 12 basic Data Link protocol stacks based on IEEE 802.11[16]

There are four different ways to "complete" these basic headers to make complete Data Link layer headers. One could add LLC, or LLC + SNAP, or VLAN + LLC, or VLAN + LLC + SNAP. The four groups of resulting headers are shown in Figure 4–12.

Figure 4–13 breaks down the 48 header combinations by size, showing the various ways that headers can be arranged to form valid Data Link protocol stacks based on the IEEE 802.11 MPDU.

One might be surprised that it is possible, in certain (probably rare) circumstances, to have a Data Link layer header set that is up to 74 octets in length.

---

16. Adapted from IEEE Std. 802.11-1999, copyright 1999, as amended by IEEE 802.11*e* draft 5.0 and IEEE 802.11*i* draft 5.0 (both works-in-progress as of this writing, which are subject to change before their eventual publication). All rights reserved.

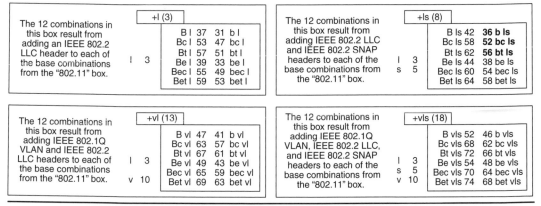

Figure 4–12   The 48 possible Data Link protocol stacks based on IEEE 802.11

```
        -31- b    l                    -36-  b    ls
        -33- be   l                    -38-  be   ls
        -37- B    l                    -42-  B    ls
        -39- Be   l                    -44-  Be   ls
        -41- b    vl                   -46-  b    vls
        -43- be   vl                   -48-  be   vls
B   vl  -47- b c  l          B   vls  -52-  b c   ls
Be  vl  -49- bec  l          Be  vls  -54-  bec   ls
        -51- b t  l                    -56-  b t   ls
B c  l  -53- bet  l          B c  ls  -58-  bet   ls
        -55- Bec  l                    -60-  Bec   ls
B t  l  -57- b c  vl         B t  ls  -62-  b c   vls
Bet  l  -59- bec  vl         Bet  ls  -64-  bec   vls
        -61- b t  vl                   -66-  b t   vls
B c vl  -63- bet  vl         B c vls  -68-  bet   vls
        -65- Bec  vl                   -70-  Bec   vls
        -67- B t  vl                   -72-  B t   vls
        -69- Bet  vl                   -74-  Bet   vls
```

Figure 4–13   Sizes of Data Link header stacks based on
IEEE 802.11

The most common combinations of headers are likely to be the "bls", "bcls", and "btls", at 36, 52, and 56 octets, respectively. Those are the short (24-octet) IEEE 802.11 MPDU with IEEE 802.2 LLC and SNAP, or that set with CCMP encryption, or that set with TKIP encryption. These formats are the most likely because IP packets (IPv4 or IPv6) are encapsulated in LLC and SNAP over IEEE 802.11, and IP represents the majority of data communications traffic today (and at this point, that is predominantly IPv4, though from an encapsulation perspective, IPv6 is just like IPv4, it just uses a different EtherType).

Because we have constructed complete Data Link layer header sets, the payload capacity for higher layer protocols represents the capacity that will be seen by the higher layer protocol. Just as IPv4 sees a 1518-octet Ethernet MTU and knows it can fit a 1500-octet IPv4 packet into that frame, in the case of IEEE 802.11, the upper layer protocol stack must be aware of the various types of Data Link layer headers, since the payload could range from 2346-74 octets (i.e., 2272 octets) at worst, or 2346-31 octets (i.e., 2315 octets) at best.

IEEE 802.11 Data Exchange Interfaces

In MPDUs, the necessary LLC sub-layer protocol header consumes three octets of payload capacity within the IEEE 802.11 MPDU's frame body. The LLC sub-layer protocol header and whatever follows it is part of the MSDU, although strictly speaking, the MSDU is the data structure that is passed from LLC to the MAC. The MSDU is encapsulated in an MPDU header, and the MPDU is exchanged between MAC entities. The MSDU is essentially what is passed between MAC sub-layer entities (see Figure 4–14).

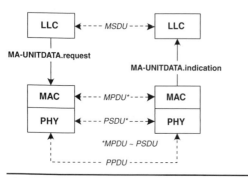

Figure 4–14 MLME interfaces for sending and receiving data

The MPDU header contains various control information that is important to ensure that the receiver can properly interpret the frame, and to facilitate the proper operation of the IEEE 802.11 MAC sub-layer protocol's arbitration techniques.

The MSDU

The MSDU is a data object that is handed from the LLC to the MAC layer through the IEEE 802.11 "MA-UNITDATA.request" interface primitive.

Similar interface primitives[17] have been defined by other IEEE MAC sub-layer protocols (the names differ slightly among the standards, but tend to be quite similar).

> MA-UNITDATA.request (
>
>> source address,
>> destination address,
>> routing information,
>> data,[18]
>> priority,
>> service class
>>)

The routing information field is not employed by IEEE 802.11. The priority field is used to indicate Contention (DCF) or Contention-Free (PCF) operation (DCF is the default), and the service class is used to indicate Reorderable Multicast or Strictly Ordered service (Reorderable Multicast is the default). Note that only the addressing and this other control information must be passed from the LLC layer to the MAC layer across the MA-UNITDATA.request interface. The MAC sub-layer protocol knows all the remaining information to enable it to construct the rest of the IEEE 802.11 MAC sub-layer protocol header.

The MPDU and PSDU

The MPDU is effectively analogous to the PLCP PSDU, in that the PSDU is what is exchanged by PHY-layer entities (as the MSDU was what was exchanged by MAC-layer entities). The PSDU is encapsulated in a PPDU header, just as the MPDU header encapsulated the MSDU.

---

17. For example, IEEE 802.3 has equivalent interfaces, which are referred to as "MA-DATA.request" and "MA-DATA.indication."

18. This includes the LLC header plus whatever higher layer protocol data is encapsulated within LLC. It is also possible that the "data" argument will be null, which is allowed in IEEE 802.11, and might be used by a STA to tell an AP that it is entering power-save mode. It is also possible that a non-null data frame can be used for the same purpose.

The PPDU

At the lowest layer, the PLCP PPDU is what is actually transferred between two STAs. The PPDU consists of a PLCP header and the PSDU.

Higher-Layer Protocol Encapsulation

The frame payload of the IEEE 802.11 MPDU must always start with an LLC sub-layer protocol header, since the IEEE 802.11 MAC sub-layer protocol header has no ability to describe the encapsulated higher layer protocol. The LLC sub-layer protocol identifies its higher layer protocol payloads using assigned Service Access Point (SAP) values. Certain higher layer protocols can be layered directly over the LLC sub-layer protocol header (e.g., Novell's Internetwork Packet Exchange (IPX), NetBEUI, etc.).

Due to the small size of the LLC SAP fields (eight bits each, of which only six bits are really usable[19] to enumerate higher layer protocols), the LLC sub-layer protocol provides an "escape valve" by defining the IEEE 802.2 SNAP. One DSAP/SSAP value has been reserved to indicate that the five-octet SNAP header is present. Since far more than 64 protocols exist that can operate over IEEE 802 LAN technologies, the SNAP "escape valve" is absolutely necessary. The IEEE 802.2 SNAP header contains a full two-octet Type field, with values used exactly as in Ethernet's Type field. The presence of the five-octet SNAP header is indicated by setting the LLC header's Destination SAP (DSAP) and Source SAP (SSAP) fields to the reserved SAP value of 0xAA.

The MTU, and thus the payload capacity, of IEEE 802.11 MPDUs is considerably larger than that of Ethernet, which can "only" send 1500 octets of payload at a time.[20] Either TCP's Maximum Segment Size (MSS) negotiation or Path MTU Discovery will allow wireless stations to send frames to Ethernet-attached stations, without placing an undue packet-level fragmentation and

---

19. To be precise, because the SAP values are structured, not even a full eight bits are available to enumerate higher layer protocols. There is actually a maximum of 64 unique SAP values, rather than the full 256 that one might expect to be supported in an 8-bit field.

20. In the case of IEEE 802.3, the MTU would be 1492 octets since the higher layer protocol payload must be reduced by eight octets to allow for the eight octets that were consumed by the LLC and SNAP sub-layer headers. The IEEE 802.3 MTU is further reduced to 1488 octets when the IEEE 802.1Q TCIH is present (in addition to the LLC/SNAP headers).

reassembly burden on the AP (even if this were a good idea, which it is not, the purported "IP fragmentation-aware AP" could only be used with Network layer protocols that naturally support packet-level fragmentation through native header structures; an example of such a protocol is IPv4; IPv6 is *not* such a protocol…).

In many early IEEE 802.11 drivers, the interface that the IP stack saw looked a lot like Ethernet (because the OS's IP stack only knew how to talk to an Ethernet-style driver). As a result, most IEEE 802.11 LANs have MPDUs with reduced maximum payload sizes of 1500 octets (including a 1492-octet IP packet, and eight octets of LLC and SNAP headers). Regardless of how large a Data Link layer header set is added here, the total length will still be well less than the maximum IEEE 802.11 MPDU size of 2346 octets.

A "native" driver, in order to be safe, might still want to allow for all possible Data Link header combinations, by limiting the IP packet size to 2250 octets. This size would allow any of the Data Link protocol stacks to be pre-pended to the IP packet, and still remain under the 2346-octet MPDU size limit.

Table 4–1 gives a comparison of the "vital statistics" for IEEE 802.3 versus 802.11 MAC sub-layer framing comparing the MAC sub-layer protocols without the other elements of the Data Link layer stack that might be present.

Table 4–1   IEEE 802.3 Framing versus
IEEE 802.11 Framing

	802.3	802.11
Minimum Data Frame Size	64	28 or 34
Maximum Data Frame Size	1518	2346
Frame Header Size	14	30
Frame Trailer Size	4	4
Maximum Data Frame Payload Size	1500	2312

Table 4–1 may appear to be a bit of an apples-to-oranges comparison, but IEEE 802.3 is not the same as Ethernet, despite their names being used interchangeably in many contexts. Contrary to the case of Ethernet, IEEE 802.3 is a pure[21] MAC sub-layer protocol, because it also depends on the higher LLC sub-layer's protocol(s) for medium-independent frame control and demultiplexing functions.

---

21. The IEEE 802.3 specification does still permit the "Type" form of "classic Ethernet," even though it does not strictly adhere to the IEEE 802 MAC/LLC abstract sub-layer model.

The IEEE 802.3 form of Ethernet header has no Type field, just as the IEEE 802.11 header lacks a Type field. In a 14-octet IEEE 802.3 frame header, the MAC sub-layer addresses consume 12 octets, and the remaining two octets consist of a "Length" field.

Encapsulation of IP over Ethernet and IEEE 802.11

Although a unique IEEE 802.2 LLC SAP value was assigned to IPv4, IPv4 is rarely (if ever) seen transmitted directly over the IEEE 802.2 LLC sub-layer protocol—the recommended practice for transmitting IPv4 and ARP over IEEE 802 LANs is to encapsulate them in both IEEE 802.2 LLC *and* SNAP, with the OUI in the latter set to 0x000000, and the SNAP Type field set to 0x0800 for IPv4 and 0x0806 for ARP (or 0x86DD for IPv6).

While it is possible to transmit "IPv4 over 'raw' LLC" packets on FDDI or Token Ring LANs, that practice violates RFC-1042, which has been a full Internet Standard for a very long time now. However, note that it is possible for other protocols, such as IPX, NetBEUI, OSI, and others, to be layered directly over LLC without using SNAP. Finally, note that there is no LLC SAP value for IPv6, which also must be encapsulated over non-Ethernet (i.e., IEEE 802) LANs in LLC and SNAP headers.

Modes of Operation

There are two different usage models for IEEE 802.11, namely infrastructure Basic Service Set (BSS or ESS) and independent Basic Service Set (IBSS). Even though both kinds of BSS could be called IBSS, the "I" in IBSS means "independent." IBSS mode is also known informally as "*ad hoc*" mode, and in this mode, STAs that are near enough to each other may communicate directly with each other, station-to-station, without needing to use an AP. In IBSS mode, all the STAs must be able to hear each other, so hidden nodes are impossible by assumption.

An Extended Service Set is formed by the concatenation of two or more *infrastructure* BSSs that share the same SSID. Infrastructure BSS mode is often referred to as simply "BSS," or "ESS" mode. Communications between stations within an infrastructure BSS, or between one node in one BSS and another node in a different BSS within a single ESS is facilitated by at least one special intervening node known as an AP. In order to get a frame between two wireless stations, it may be necessary for the frame to cross more than one AP, but always at least one AP, unless the WLAN is in IBSS mode and therefore has no AP.

An AP advertises its presence by issuing periodic "Beacon" frames that allow the wireless stations to detect its presence. Before data may be transmitted by a client, an "association" must be negotiated between the client and the AP. If an AP is present, all traffic between WLAN clients must go through the AP. Beacons are also used in IBSS mode, but in IBSS mode, each STA takes turns sending the Beacon. The BSSID is determined by the first STA to create the IBSS mode BSS with a given SSID. In an infrastructure mode BSS, the BSSID is the MAC address of the STA in the AP (every AP is logically a STA as well).

The AP provides essential management functions in the WLAN, but the cost of an AP is that every frame between WLAN clients on the same BSS must traverse the RF medium twice—even if they are within range of each other's radios—thereby reducing the effective throughput of the medium to about half of the theoretical maximum bit transmission rate.[22] On the plus side, the AP (or set of APs) enables communication between stations that would otherwise be too far apart for their own radios and antennas to hear each other, and thus the AP can prevent STAs that are mutually out of range from interfering with a STA that is in range of both of those STAs. The presence of the AP, and the protocols used to gain access to the medium, allow for the presence of so-called "hidden" nodes in an infrastructure BSS. No node is hidden from the AP, but some nodes can be out of range of other nodes.

Besides forwarding traffic amongst the WLAN clients, the AP usually also includes a "Portal" function that enables traffic from the WLAN's clients to be bridged to a wired LAN, typically an Ethernet. The IEEE 802.11 term for the wired infrastructure that connects APs together is the "Distribution System" (DS). The Portal function is optional…it's possible to have a wireless station act as an AP and provide no access to a DS. The combination of the AP and its

---

22. *Ad hoc* mode works fine for stations located within range of each other, but an AP is required if connectivity beyond the WLAN is desired. The Portal function enables this connectivity. APs that are deployed primarily to facilitate communication between wired and wireless stations probably aren't impeding the station-to-station traffic on the WLAN, since most traffic on such WLANs will probably be going to, or coming from, the wired side of the AP.

associated Portal acts like any other mixed-media LAN bridge, in that it learns which MAC addresses are reachable via which of its interfaces.

Among other things, the Portal function makes sure that frames transmitted onto the Ethernet are never larger than 1518 total octets (inclusive of Ethernet's 14-octet header and its 4-octet trailer (Frame Check Sequence, or FCS), and also translates the MAC header format so that frames from stations on the WLAN can be recognized by stations on the Ethernet, and vice versa. For example, IP packets that are encapsulated in LLC/SNAP on the WLAN need to be translated into DIX (Classic Ethernet) format on the Ethernet side. If an IEEE 802.11 frame had an IEEE 802.1Q-2003 VLAN header, the Portal function could translate that frame into an Ethernet frame with an appropriately formatted IEEE 802.1Q header set.

Conversely, DIX-encapsulated Ethernet packets that are received by the Portal in the AP from the DS need to be converted to LLC/SNAP-encapsulated frames before they are transmitted onto the WLAN. If an LLC-encapsulated frame arrives from the Ethernet side, then the only transformation of the frame is that the MAC sub-layer portion of the IEEE 802.3 header (the first 14 octets) will be replaced by the necessary IEEE 802.11 MAC sub-layer header, probably 24 octets long.

Summary

We have seen the formats of the IEEE 802.11 MAC sub-layer Control, Management (MMPDU), and Data (MPDU) frames, and enumerated all possible combinations of headers, taking into consideration IEEE 802.11*e* and IEEE 802.11*i*, as well as IEEE 802.1Q-2003 VLANs. We have described the structure of the FC field, the first two octets of every type of IEEE 802.11 MAC sub-layer protocol frame, which defines the structure and format of the frame that follows. We have compared the usage of IEEE 802.1Q-2003 VLANs in IEEE 802.11 against their usage in Ethernet. We have differentiated the characteristics of IBSS (*ad hoc*) vs. infrastructure WLANs. We have related the MSDU to the MPDU, and compared the MSDU/MPDU relationship to the PSDU/PPDU relationship at the PLCP layer.

5

Dissection of a Probe Response MMPDU

The main portion of Chapter 4 was concerned with a high-level depiction of the frame formats used by IEEE 802.11.

In this chapter, the structure is examined in microscopic detail by taking apart a Probe Response MMPDU from an actual packet trace, to see how the theoretical treatment of the main body of Chapter 4 matches up with what is actually sent on the wireless medium. This material is in its own section because the author does not believe that this information is likely to be equally useful to every reader. If a reader someday needs to analyze a frame from a network analyzer, he or she might find this material useful. Because it is not necessary for the understanding of the remainder of the book, and because it is excessively detailed to keep in the body of Chapter 4, the author chooses to place this information on its own, in this chapter. Readers who want to skip this section will probably not regret it.

Reprise of IEEE 802.11's MMPDU Structure

All of IEEE 802.11's MMPDUs have a common overall structure, which is shown in Figure 5–1 and might be referred to as the "MMPDU skeleton," since it represents the overall format of every MMPDU.

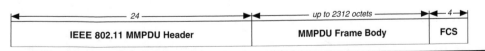

Figure 5–1   MMPDU frame format

The MMPDU header is expanded in Figure 5–2.

F C	D	DA	SA	BSSID	S C
2	2	6	6	6	2

Figure 5–2   MMPDU header format

The D subfield in Figure 5–2 represents the MMPDU's Duration, the DA and SA represent the Destination and Source MAC addresses, and the BSSID is the MAC address of the STA in the AP (in infrastructure mode), or the randomly computed BSSID that has been computed for the WLAN (in IBSS mode). The SC subfield is the Sequence Control subfield, which is used to sequence each frame and to support MAC-layer frame fragmentation. Observe that the MMPDU header is always only 24 octets, while the MPDU header can be either 24 or 30 octets in length.

All IEEE 802.11 frames begin with this two-octet FC field, which determines the format of the frame to follow, be it a Control frame, a Management frame (MMPDU), or a Data frame (MPDU). For the reader's convenience, the format of the FC field will be repeated here, in Figure 5–3. The definitions of all the bits in the FC field can be found in the main body of Chapter 4.

Bit 0	Bit 1	Bit 2	Bit 3	Bit 4	Bit 5	Bit 6	Bit 7	Bit 8	Bit 9	Bit 10	Bit 11	Bit 12	Bit 13	Bit 14	Bit 15
Protocol Version		Type		Subtype				To DS	From DS	More Frag.	Retry	Pwr. Mgt.	More Data	Prot. Frm.	Ord.

Figure 5–3   The Frame Control (FC) field

For MMPDUs, the FC field's Type and Subtype values help determine the unique structure of each of the possible MMPDU frame types. The main body of Chapter 4 showed the format of each type of MMPDU. The FC field of every IEEE 802.11 frame's header always has the format depicted in Figure 5–3, regardless of whether the frame is a Control frame, a Management frame (MMPDU), or a Data frame (MPDU).

What Causes a Probe Response?

The simple answer is that a Probe Request MMPDU does. Under what circumstances is such a frame sent?

A STA seeking to join a WLAN has a choice between listening on successive channels, waiting on each channel to hear a Beacon from an AP (this is known as a passive scan), or performing an "active scan" of the network, in which the STA transmits Probe Request MMPDUs on all available channels until the STA finds an AP, a timer expires and the user gives up, or until the device's battery runs out.

One disadvantage of a passive scan is that the STA does not know *a priori* which channel(s) are in use in a given physical location, so it must listen for a potential Beacon on each channel for some amount of time before moving to the next channel and listening there. It is possible that a STA might not hear a Beacon frame for quite a while.

In contrast, an active scan puts the STA in the driver's seat. The STA broadcasts[1] a Probe Request on every channel that its physical layer supports—waiting long enough to hear a Probe Response—before testing the next channel for the presence of an AP by sending a Probe Request on that channel. Figure 5–4 shows the structure of both the Probe Request and the Probe Response MMPDU. The Probe Request has the usual MMPDU header and two mandatory (variable-length) fields in the MMPDU frame body. The Probe Response has many optional Information Elements (IEs), but those that are present must be in the order listed in Figure 5–4.

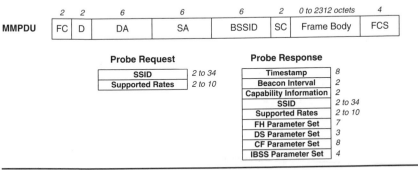

Figure 5–4   Structure of the Probe MMPDUs

---

1. By using the verb "broadcast," we literally mean that the MAC-DA in Probe Request MMPDUs is 0xFFFFFF-FFFFFF. In Probe Request MMPDUs, the BSSID is also set to the "broadcast address" (since the STA does not yet know the BSSID value of the local BSS). Not surprisingly, the MAC-SA in the Probe Request MMPDU is the STA's own MAC address. The STA will learn the BSSID in the Probe Response MMPDU, if it ever hears one.

The first three fields of the Probe Response are mandatory (because they are fixed-length fields) and they can be decoded because the receiver knows how long each of them is. For this to work properly, these must always be in the same order. The TLV-encoded fields may appear in any order. The one that is not listed that may be present is the Robust Security Network (RSN) IE (the RSN IE is being defined by the IEEE 802.11*i* TG; see Chapter 7, *Security Mechanisms for Wireless LANs*, for a description).

Certain of the parameter sets are mutually exclusive. For example, if an FH (Frequency Hopping) parameter set is present, then a DS (Direct Sequence) parameter set won't be present (and vice versa). The CF parameter set is only in Beacons or Probe Responses from APs in which a Point Coordinator is operating. The IBSS parameter set is only sent from STAs that are operating in IBSS mode (and, obviously, never from APs).

The Probe Response MMPDU has a much richer structure than the Probe Request, and strongly resembles a Beacon MMPDU. That similarity is not surprising, since the two types of MMPDUs are both sent by APs, and they are both serve similar functions. They both serve to advertise the parameters under which the WLAN operates, and are frequently referred to as a pair (i.e., "Beacon and Probe Response" or "Beacon or Probe Response").

Dissection of an Actual Probe Response

Rather than discuss the structure of the Probe Response MMPDU hypothetically, we will examine an actual Probe Response MMPDU, which happens to be 86 octets long, and was captured with the outstanding "Ethereal" protocol analyzer (Ethereal[2] is the product of an open-source programming project). While dissecting this MMPDU, we will also have an excellent opportunity to explore the concepts of "little-endian" versus "big-endian" bit and octet ordering.

---

2. In some ways, Ethereal is actually superior to commercial packet analysis tools costing thousands (or tens of thousands) of dollars. What Ethereal lacks in user interface polish, it more than makes up for in protocol coverage. I highly recommend that you do a Web search on "Ethereal" if you need such a tool. Ethereal is available for Linux and Windows, but the Windows version cannot be used as a WLAN sniffer, though it can open files created by commercial WLAN sniffers. The Linux version can act as a sniffer for wireless, as well as Ethernet (Ethernet sniffing is supported on Windows as well as Linux).

Figure 5–5 shows an actual MMPDU that we will examine. The fields alternate in boldface or plain text to make it easier to follow along with the description to follow (referencing the order of the fields in the Probe Response MMPDU header, as depicted in Figure 5–4, then continuing into the Probe Response payload, which we will decode shortly).

```
0000   50 00 3a 01 00 07 50 ca fc 3c 00 40 96 41 ff 78
0010   00 40 96 41 ff 78 a0 dd 4a 53 36 f2 00 00 00 00
0020   64 00 31 00 00 07 74 73 75 6e 61 6d 69 01 04 82
0030   84 8b 96 03 01 06 85 1e 00 00 4c 0d 07 00 ff 03
0040   11 00 41 50 33 35 30 2d 34 31 66 66 37 38 00 00
0050   00 00 01 00 00 22
```

Figure 5–5   An actual Probe Response MMPDU

The column of numbers on the left side of Figure 5–5 is the octet number (in hexadecimal), so the first row contains the first 16 octets, numbered 0x00 through 0x0F, and the second row contains the next 16 octets (0x10 through 0x1F), and so on. Ethereal has written these octets in "big-endian" notation.[3]

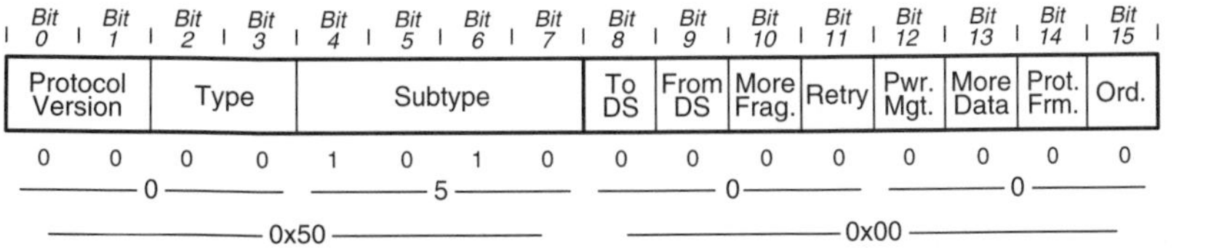

Bit 0	Bit 1	Bit 2	Bit 3	Bit 4	Bit 5	Bit 6	Bit 7	Bit 8	Bit 9	Bit 10	Bit 11	Bit 12	Bit 13	Bit 14	Bit 15
Protocol Version		Type		Subtype				To DS	From DS	More Frag.	Retry	Pwr. Mgt.	More Data	Prot. Frm.	Ord.
0	0	0	0	1	0	1	0	0	0	0	0	0	0	0	0
	—— 0 ——		—— 5 ——					—— 0 ——				—— 0 ——			
	—————— 0x50 ——————							—————— 0x00 ——————							

Figure 5–6   The FC field of the Probe Response MMPDU of Figure 5–5

Figure 5–6 illustrates—in the case of the two-octet FC field—how one converts from the FC field structure that is defined in IEEE 802.11-1999 to what is seen in Ethereal. In this figure, and other similar figures to follow, the graphical packet structure will always be on top, with the bit numbering in place to reinforce the correct relative bit order (in the order specified in the standard).

Regardless of whether it is written on the left or right, bit-0 is always the least-significant bit. In figures that have example binary data, that data will appear immediately below the graphic, and the bits will be summarized into nybbles in the next line down. Finally, in the lowest line of the figure, the octets will be written in Ethereal's "big-endian" notation, which reverses the order of

3. In big-endian notation, the first octet to be transmitted is at offset 00, the next is at offset 01, and so forth. Moreover, each octet is written as if the most-significant bit were on the left.

the nybbles (i.e., 0x9A in little-endian notation would be written as 0xA9 in big-endian notation).

In Figure 5–6, we see the structure of the two-octet FC field, including the bit ordering, which indicated little-endian notation since the highest-numbered bit of the two-octet field is on the right. The bits in this field are numbered 0 through 15, with the least-significant bit (numbered 0) on the left. The IEEE LMSC tends to use this notation—little-endian notation—in its standards. (The IEEE LMSC is not perfectly consistent, there are exceptions to this rule, but it is a fairly accurate statement.) The IETF tends to write numbers in the opposite way; their so-called "network order" is big-endian, which can cause confusion for people who need to work both sides of the Data Link/Network layer fence.

There is no right or wrong way to write binary numbers, but for consistency (and to help minimize confusion) on must choose to either put the least-significant bit on the right or the left—and to stick with one's decision. Besides being written on the left in the IEEE LMSC's standards, the least-significant bit of the least-significant octet is usually the first bit to be transmitted onto the medium.

One thing to keep in mind about the hexadecimal representation of the frame is that the frame arrives one octet at a time, so Ethereal does not know that the first two octets are one field. The order in which the octets are displayed is the order in which they arrived from the physical medium. If one was writing the entire FC field in little-endian notation, it would cover all 16 bits, and would be written as 0x0050. Yet, since the 0x50 was the first octet off the "wire," and the 0x00 was the second, we actually see the first two octets of the hexadecimal representation of the frame as 0x5000.

The first (i.e., leftmost) octet consists of the following bit pattern: "00001010", which would be interpreted as 0x0A *if this field were interpreted as having been written using big-endian notation*, but big-endian notation is *not* being used in this case. In little-endian notation, we must interpret the bits within the octet in the reverse order, as if they were written as "01010000", which is 0x50 in its hexadecimal representation.

There is no conflict between these notations, since it is still the case that in the binary representation of 0x50, the least-significant nybble[4] is 0x0, and the

---

4. A "nybble" is a four-bit field and the term is a play on words (think of the 8-bit "byte" that sounds like "bite" and see how a nibble is a small bite. A nybble corresponds to a single hexadecimal digit (in the hexadecimal representation of a one-octet number, there are two digits…each digit is a nybble). A nybble can take on any value from 0x0 to 0xF (i.e., 0000 to 1111 in binary).

least-significant bit is part of the "Protocol Version" number. As shown in Figure 5–6, the first (least-significant) nybble is 0x0, and the next-most-significant nybble is 0x5 (when the bits are interpreted in little-endian notation). We combine those two nybbles into 0x50, in which the "5" is written first.

If we look back at Table 4–1, we see that when the "Type" field within the FC field is set to 00, we have an MMPDU (i.e., an MMPDU). Moreover, when the Subtype is set to "0101," we have a Probe Response MMPDU. Note that the bit patterns in Table 4–1 are listed in "big-endian" format for convenience of comparing them to the packet decodes you might encounter in the real world.

We will now work our way through the actual captured packet in Figure 5–5, taking advantage of the fact that alternate fields have been set in boldface type. After the two-octet FC field (value: 0x5000), we have the "Duration" subfield, which is also a two-octet field (whose format is shown in Figure 5–7).

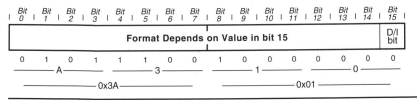

Figure 5–7   The Duration subfield of Figure 5–5's Probe Response MMPDU

The contents in this case are "0x3A01" (the value from Figure 5–5 has been illustrated here in Figure 5–7). We can use our knowledge of little- and big-endian number formats to interpret this field. First, we reverse the order of the hexadecimal digits (nybbles) to yield "0x013A". This hexadecimal number is equivalent to the decimal number 314, which is what Ethereal computed in the packet decode (see Figure 5–10).

The meaning of the D/I field (in an MMPDU, it is always a "D" field; in fact, the only time it is interpreted as an "I" field is when it contains an Association ID, which is the case in a PS-Poll Control frame) depends on the most-significant bit. Figure 5–8 shows how bits 15 (and 14) of the D/I subfield control the interpretation of the values in this subfield. The bits in the case of this frame indicate a Duration interpretation, which is what would be expected of any MMPDU.

The first row in Figure 5–8 is the overall structure of the D/I subfield. If the most significant bit (bit-15) is 0, this two-octet subfield is interpreted as a "Duration" field (this is always the case for MMPDUs); otherwise, this subfield

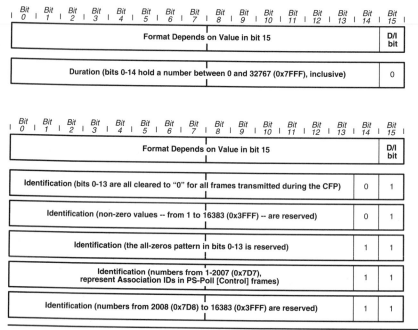

Figure 5–8   Interpretation of the Duration/Identification subfield

is interpreted as an "Identification" field. When the D/I subfield is a Duration subfield, the 15 bits that are less significant than the D/I bit hold a little-endian encoded value from 0 to 32,767 (0x7FFF). There are basically two sub-cases when the D/I field is set to "1", which correspond to bit-14 being set to 0 or 1.

- The first case is when bit-15 is 1 and bit-14 is 0, and the 14 remaining bits (numbered 0 through 13) are also set to 0. This setting is used for all frames that are transmitted during the Contention-Free Period (CFP; see the description of contention versus contention-free later in the chapter). The other possible values of this field—from 1 to 16,383 (0x3FFF)—are reserved.

- The other major case is when bit-15 is 1 and bit-14 is also set to 1. There are three ranges of values in the remaining 14 remaining bits that have been defined. Two of the ranges are reserved, one range being when all 14 of the bits are set to 0, and the other being little-endian-encoded values from 2008 (0x07D8) through 16,383 (0x3FFF). The defined values from 1 to 2007 (0x07D7) correspond to Association ID numbers, and this usage of the D/I subfield is only valid in Power-Save-Poll Control frames. In little-endian binary (in a 14-bit field), the range of 1 to 2007 can be represented numerically in binary as 10 0000 0000 0000 to 11 1010 1111 1000, and 2008 has the binary value of 00 0110 1111 1000.[5]

The next subfield in Figure 5–5 is the MAC-DA. This field contains the MAC address of the STA that sent the Probe Request that generated this Probe Response. The value in this field (translated to big-endian notation) is 0x000750cafc3c.

The subsequent two subfields are the MAC-SA and the BSSID, in that order. In this case, the two fields contain the same value, viz. 0x00409641ff78. In this case, the AP that transmitted the Probe Response frame was also the AP that defined its own MAC address to be this BSS's BSSID, which is why these two fields contain the same MAC address. Since there is typically one AP per BSS, this will be the typical situation for packets sourced by the AP.

In general, however, these two fields could contain different values, such as when the AP is forwarding a packet from one node to another; for example, a multicast Data frame. The MAC-SA in that case will be the original sender's MAC address, but the AP will tag the frame with its own BSSID so that receiving STAs (that may be in range of multiple APs) can filter which multicasts they receive based on the BSSID of the BSS that the STA has actually joined.

After the BSSID is the final subfield in the MMPDU header, namely the Sequence Control (SC) subfield. Figure 5–9 shows the format of the SC subfield, which encodes two values, the Fragment Number and the Sequence Number.

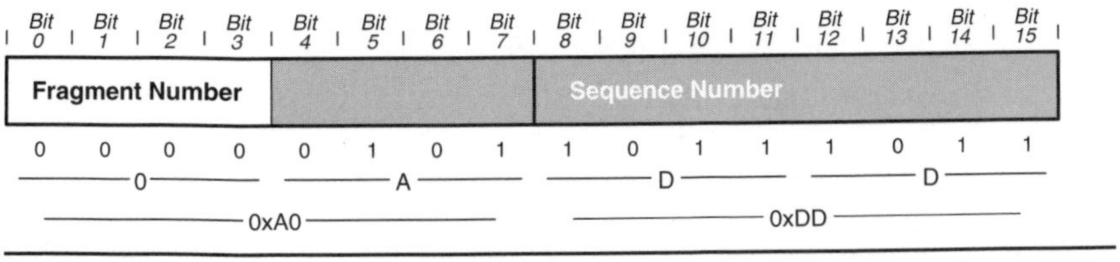

Figure 5–9   The Sequence Control subfield in the MMPDU header

The values below the diagram in Figure 5–9 show the values from the packet capture in Figure 5–5, which was 0xA0DD. Breaking that down and reversing it

---

5. The numbers 2007 and 2008 can actually both be represented using only 11 bits, so including the three most-significant zero-bits is only done to make the numbers fit the available 14-bit field.

into little-endian representation, we see that the Fragment Number field is set to 0x0 (it is just a single nybble), and the Sequence Number field contains 0xDDA, which is 3546 in decimal notation, and this number agrees with the Ethereal packet decode shown in Figure 5–10.

Since the More Fragments bit in the FC field of the MMPDU header is clear, this is not fragment number zero of a series of MMPDUs that are fragments of a larger MMPDU (both Management and Data frames are eligible for fragmentation; Control frames are too short to need that service). To put the previous discussion in perspective, Figure 5–10 illustrates the complete Ethereal decode of the MMPDU header, which is the first 24 octets of any MMPDU.

```
Type/Subtype: Probe Response (5)
Frame Control: 0x0050
    Version: 0
    Type: MMPDU (0)
    Subtype: 5
    Flags: 0x0
        DS status: Not leaving DS (or network is operating
                   in AD-HOC mode)
        .... ...0 = To DS
        .... ..0. = From DS
        .... .0.. = More Fragments: This is the last fragment
        .... 0... = Retry: Frame is not being retransmitted
        ...0 .... = PWR MGT: STA will stay up
        ..0. .... = More Data: No data buffered
        .0.. .... = WEP flag: WEP is disabled
        0... .... = Order flag: Not strictly ordered

Duration: 314

Destination address: 00:07:50:ca:fc:3c (Cisco_ca:fc:3c)
Source address: 00:40:96:41:ff:78 (Ciron_41:ff:78)
BSSID: 00:40:96:41:ff:78 (Ciron_41:ff:78)

Fragment number: 0
Sequence number: 3546
```

Figure 5–10   Ethereal decode of the MMPDU header

The Probe Response frame body may contain a number of Information Elements (IEs). This particular complete MMPDU is a total of 86 octets in length. Figure 5–11 shows the ordering of these IEs, along with a brief description of each. The figure also shows the length (or range of possible lengths) for each IE.

Order	Field Name	Size	Description
1	Timestamp	8	
2	Beacon Interval	2	
3	Capability Information	2	
4	SSID	3–34	
5	Supported Rates	3–10	
6	FH Parameter Set	7	The FH Parameter Set information element is present within Probe Response frames generated by STAs using frequency-hopping PHYs.
7	DS Parameter Set	3	The DS Parameter Set information element is present within Probe Response frames generated by STAs using direct sequence PHYs.
8	CF Parameter Set	8	The CF Parameter Set information element is only present within Probe Response frames generated by APs supporting a PCF.
9	IBSS Parameter Set	4	The IBSS Parameter Set information element is only present within Probe Response frames generated by STAs in an IBSS.

Figure 5–11   Ordering of the Probe Response MMPDU's Payload fields

The first three fields (Timestamp, Beacon Interval, and Capability Information) are each a fixed length, and total 12 octets in all. The subsequent fields are
all TLV-encoded, and if they are not necessary, they are omitted.

The first field in the data portion of the MMPDU frame is the Timestamp
field, which is simply an eight-octet, little-endian-encoded, numerical value. Its
purpose is to help keep the entire membership of STAs in a given BSS running
on the same clock. The Timestamp field is expressed in units of microseconds
(abbreviated µs; the abbreviation "us" is frequently used when the Greek letter
"mu" (µ) is not available).

The Timestamp field is also used to keep all the STAs in the BSS aware of
the latest BSS parameters. If a Beacon or Probe Response is received that has
parameters that differ from those that the STA has on record, it will adopt the
new values only if the Timestamp field is newer than the Timestamp that was
associated with the most recent Beacon or Probe Response data of which the
STA has a record.

In the case of the packet we have been examining from Figure 5–5, the contents of the Timestamp field are `0x4a5336f200000000`. To make it easier to
read this long hexadecimal number, each successive octet is either underlined (or
not) so that each octet is easily identified. As one would expect, the Timestamp
field, like any other counter, is incremented by adding to the least-significant
portion of the value. Consistent with little-endian notation, the value is stored
in the leftmost portion of the Timestamp field. If we examine only the portion
of the field that has been set (i.e., the least-significant four octets), we can interpret the value in this field. Figure 5–12 breaks out these four octets into their little-
endian representation.

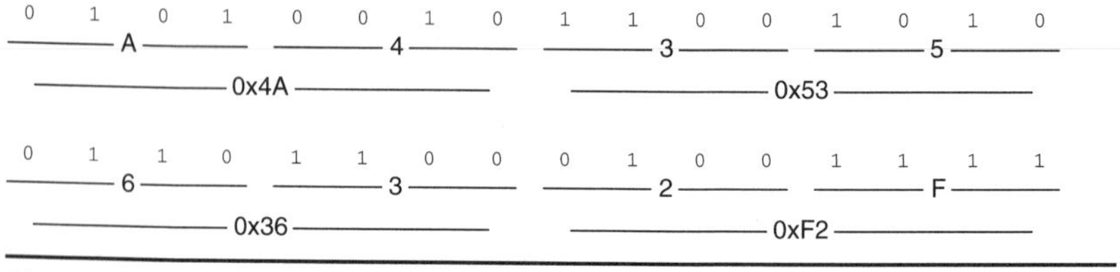

0	1	0	1	0	0	1	0	1	1	0	0	1	0	1	0

———— A ———— ———— 4 ———— ———— 3 ———— ———— 5 ————

———————— 0x4A ———————— ———————— 0x53 ————————

0	1	1	0	1	1	0	0	0	1	0	0	1	1	1	1

———— 6 ———— ———— 3 ———— ———— 2 ———— ———— F ————

———————— 0x36 ———————— ———————— 0xF2 ————————

Figure 5–12   The Timestamp field of Figure 5–5

After converting this four-octet binary number to its decimal equivalent, we obtain a value of 4,063,646,538 μs, or a value just slightly less than 4,064 seconds.[6] The IEEE 802.11 MAC header's usage of the Timestamp field allows the STAs to remain in synchronization with the AP to within 4 μs, plus the maximum delay involved in propagating a frame across the BSS (provided the speeds being used in the BSS are at least 1 Mbps).

The next subfield in the Probe Response MMPDU's payload is the Beacon Interval subfield. It is a simple two-octet numerical field. The number indicates the desired time interval between the Target Beacon Transmission Times (TBTTs). If the medium is busy when the AP becomes ready to transmit a Beacon, it will allow the existing communication to finish before transmitting its Beacon. Thus, the interval between Beacon frames will not be *less than* the Beacon Interval, but it is possible for the interval between Beacons to exceed the value specified in the Beacon Interval field.

The units for the Beacon Interval field are kilo-microseconds (1,024 μs). In the IEEE 802.11-1999 specification, the term "Time Unit" is introduced, and defined such that one Time Unit is equal to 1 kμs (i.e., one Time Unit is equal to 1.024 ms). Figure 5–13 shows the Beacon Interval field from the packet capture in Figure 5–5.

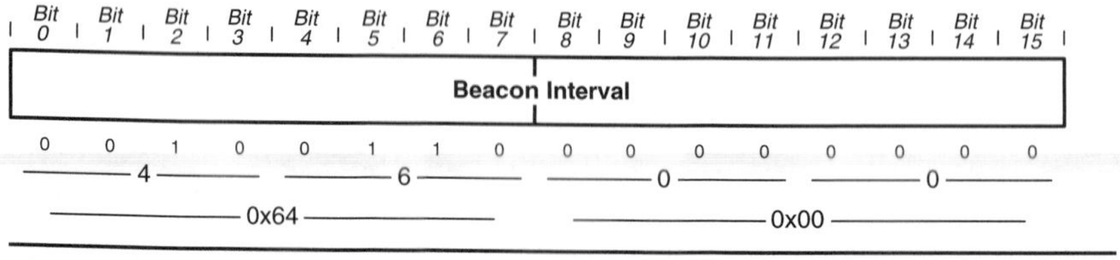

Bit 0	Bit 1	Bit 2	Bit 3	Bit 4	Bit 5	Bit 6	Bit 7	Bit 8	Bit 9	Bit 10	Bit 11	Bit 12	Bit 13	Bit 14	Bit 15
							Beacon Interval								
0	0	1	0	0	1	1	0	0	0	0	0	0	0	0	0

———— 4 ———— ———— 6 ———— ———— 0 ———— ———— 0 ————

———————— 0x64 ———————— ———————— 0x00 ————————

Figure 5–13   The Beacon Interval field of the MMPDU in Figure 5–5

In the case of the Beacon Interval field from the MMPDU frame in Figure 5–5, we see that the Beacon Interval is 64 Time Units, or 64×1024 μs,

---

6. To be precise, the value works out to 67 minutes, 43.646538 seconds.

which is the same as 65,536 µs, or 65.536 ms (milliseconds...the conventional kind, i.e., exactly 10^{-3} seconds, or $1/1000^{th}$ of a second). In order to express the Beacon Interval without any confusing notation, the value in this example works out to 0.065536 seconds.

Following the Beacon Interval field is the Capability Information field. This field tells the STAs some of the configuration choices the network manager has made. The Capability Information field, along with the values from the packet in Figure 5–5, is shown in Figure 5–14.

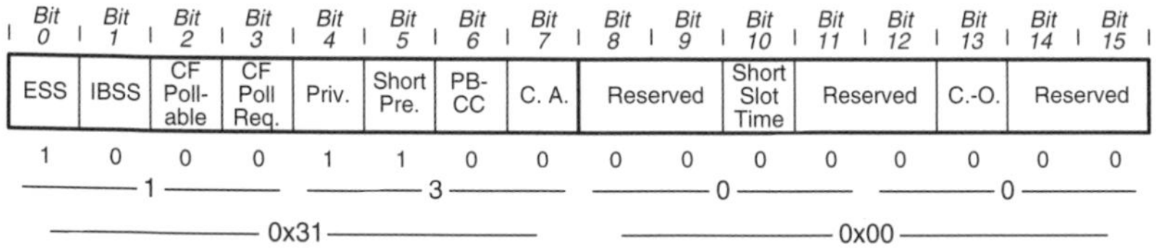

Bit 0	Bit 1	Bit 2	Bit 3	Bit 4	Bit 5	Bit 6	Bit 7	Bit 8	Bit 9	Bit 10	Bit 11	Bit 12	Bit 13	Bit 14	Bit 15
ESS	IBSS	CF Poll-able	CF Poll Req.	Priv.	Short Pre.	PB-CC	C. A.	Reserved		Short Slot Time	Reserved		C.-O.	Reserved	
1	0	0	0	1	1	0	0	0	0	0	0	0	0	0	0

—————— 1 ——————   ——— 3 ———   ——— 0 ———   ——— 0 ———

—————— 0x31 ——————   ——————— 0x00 ———————

Figure 5–14   The Probe Response Capability Information field

Since there are only two BSS modes, namely "infrastructure" or "independent" BSS, it is strange that the IEEE 802.11 MAC protocol designers chose to give each choice its own control bit. If the ESS bit is set, the transmitter is basically declaring itself to be an AP. When operating in IBSS mode, a STA sets the IBSS bit in its Beacon[7] or Probe Responses. In the case of the MMPDU from Figure 5–5, the ESS bit (Bit 0) is set, and the IBSS bit (Bit 1) is clear.[8]

Bits 2 and 3 are used to control aspects of the Point Coordination Function (PCF) mode of medium access control. As a preview of PCF, suffice it to say that in PCF mode, a central control entity known as the "Point Coordinator" (in the AP) acts to collect frames from WLAN STAs by polling each STA, rather than by allowing each STA with data to send to independently contend for access to the medium. The "CF" abbreviation in each of the labels for Bits 2 and 3 means "Contention-Free," as distinguished from the access method that is based on contention.

---

7. In IBSS mode, the STAs all take turns sending Beacons, which is different from the situation in infrastructure mode, in which the AP is the "designated Beacon sender."

8. Given that ESS mode and IBSS mode are mutually exclusive, it is not obvious why there are two bits, since there are only two possibilities, and one bit could easily represent the two possibilities.

Bit 4 is labeled "Priv." and is more completely known as the "Privacy" bit. This bit is used to indicate that the sender of the Probe Response packet supports data privacy protocols, if desired. Bit 5 in the Capability Information field has been defined to indicate whether an AP supports the "Short Preamble" format at the PLCP layer. You will recall this concept from Chapter 3, *Speeds and Feeds*. In IEEE 802.11*b*, the Short Preamble was not mandatory-to-implement, and in order for a STA to use it, the STA needed to know whether the AP could receive a frame that was sent using a different preamble than was defined in IEEE 802.11-1999.

Bit 6 indicates that the AP can support frames encoded using Packet Binary Convolutional Coding (PBCC). PBCC support is defined in IEEE 802.11*b*-1999 as an optional modulation technique. PBCC modulation only affects the 5.5 Mbps and 11 Mbps speeds that were added by IEEE 802.11*b*-1999. The default modulation technique for the two "High Rate" speeds (i.e., 5.5 and 11 Mbps) is known as Complementary Code Keying (CCK).

Bit 7 indicates that the sender of the Probe Response MMPDU supports "Channel Agility." This capability is used to indicate that a STA can support both FH and DS mode PHYs at the same time. Such a capability would be useful to an AP, but a STA in IBSS mode would also perhaps find this useful. When the Channel Agility bit in the Capability Information field is set, we should expect to see both a DS Parameter Set and an FH Parameter Set (see Figure 5–11). Devices with PHYs that only support Frequency Hopping or Direct Sequence (DS) Spread Spectrum will clear this bit and only transmit the IE that defines their local configuration.

The next bits were defined in IEEE 802.11*g*-2003.

Bit 10 is defined in IEEE 802.11*g* to indicate support for the optional Short Slot Time capability. Bit 13 is defined to indicate support for the optional modulation scheme known as CCK-OFDM. The bits in the remainder of the Capability Information subfield are undefined at the time of this writing, and should be considered reserved for future use.

All the remaining IEs are "Type-Length-Value" encoded. For now, suffice it to say that by "TLV-encoded," we mean that each field is self-describing, since it starts with a one-octet Type field, followed by a one-octet Length field, and finally a field containing the Value that is being conveyed in a given IE. The value in the Length octet does not include either the one-octet Type or Length fields themselves (i.e., the Length expresses the amount of data that is carried within the TLV, not the length of the entire TLV, which is two octets larger).

Despite the interpretation of the "L" in TLV (as being the length of the "V" portion of the TLV), the "Size" column in Figure 5–11 reflects the entire TLV field, so that a direct comparison of field sizes can be made by remembering that TLV-encoded fields are actually two octets larger than the value in the table).

Following the fixed-length Capability Information subfield is the first TLV-encoded IE in the Probe Response MMPDU's payload. This subfield is used to transmit the SSID of the ESS in which the AP is operating. The SSID is a string of up to 32 ASCII characters that uniquely identifies the BSS. End users will encounter the SSID in their WLAN driver configuration utilities when they have to enter the name of the WLAN to which they are attaching their STA. Modern operating systems such as Microsoft's Windows XP can learn the SSID from the Probe Response or Beacon MMPDUs, which eliminates the need for the user to manually enter this information, and to enter it without making any typographical errors.

In the case of the example MMPDU of Figure 5–5, the SSID IE is interpreted in Figure 5–15. The first octet contains the "T" of the TLV, in this case 0x00, which agrees with the value in the table shown in Figure 5–11. The second octet, the "L" of the TLV, contains the value 0x07, meaning that the SSID is stored in the next seven octets.

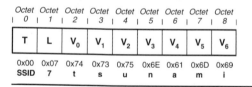

Figure 5–15   The TLV-Encoded SSID IE

In this case, the SSID string contained in the SSID IE is the ASCII string "tsunami" (the ASCII codes are all lowercase letters in this example). This TLV is nine octets long, overall, with seven octets of actual data. By observing that T=0x00 a receiver can properly interpret the octets in the Value field, since these octets are ASCII text in the SSID IE. The SSID field can be up to 32 octets in length, so the L field is from 1 to 32 (there is no good reason to send a null SSID in a Beacon or Probe Response; in a Probe Request, a null SSID corresponds to the "broadcast" or "wildcard" SSID, which is a mechanism that a STA can use to find out what SSIDs it may be near).

After the SSID IE, comes the TLV defined in Figure 5–16. Based on Figure 5–11, we can expect this next TLV to be the Supported Rates TLV. Since any implementation knows that this is a TLV (we have already seen all the fixed-length entries in this example), it can look at the second octet after the "i" in the SSID IE (i.e., the last letter of "tsunami") to see how long this next TLV is, since that's where the next TLV's length field would be. Even if this subsequent TLV isn't one that the implementation can decode, the implementation can at least skip over this TLV and hope to find a subsequent TLV that it *can* understand.

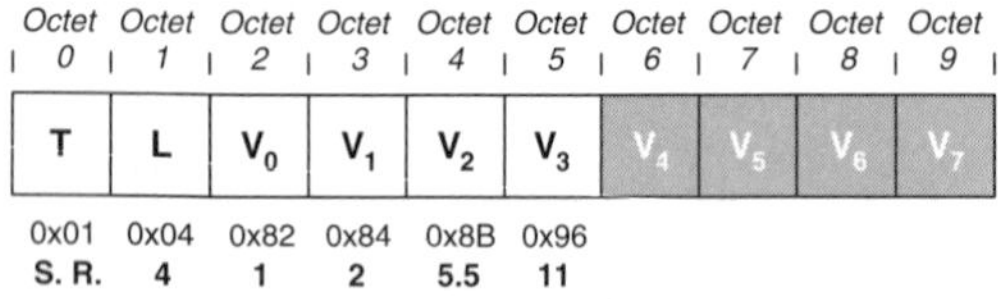

Octet 0	Octet 1	Octet 2	Octet 3	Octet 4	Octet 5	Octet 6	Octet 7	Octet 8	Octet 9
T	L	V_0	V_1	V_2	V_3	V_4	V_5	V_6	V_7

| 0x01 S. R. | 0x04 4 | 0x82 1 | 0x84 2 | 0x8B 5.5 | 0x96 11 | | | | |

Figure 5–16   Decoding the Supported Rates IE

By definition (per IEEE 802.11-1999 and IEEE 802.11*b*-1999), the Supported Rates IE can have up to a total of eight octets of payload; however, in this example only four octets are actually used. The Supported Rates IE must list at least one Supported Rate. Thus, this IE will always be at least three octets in length, but no more than 10 octets long. In the latter case, at its maximum size, this IE would list eight Supported Rates, each encoded in a single octet (expressed in units of 500 kbps). Thus, this mechanism may only express speeds from 500 kbps to 255×500 kbps (i.e., 127.5 Mbps).[9]

The Supported Rates is only used in the Beacon, Probe Response, and the Association and Reassociation Response MMPDUs. There are two types of rates, namely those in the "Basic Rate Set" and those that are not in the Basic Rate Set. The Basic Rate Set is the set of rates (known as "basic rates") that the AP expects all the STAs in the BSS to be able to support. If a STA does not

---

9. In certain circumstances, the most-significant bit is reserved to indicate whether the particular rate is in the Basic Rate Set (or not). By removing this bit from the field and giving it a special function, there are now really only 7 bits available to store the rate, which limits the top speed that can be indicated to 127×500 kbps, or 63.5 Mbps. Clearly some enhancement to this mechanism will be required as part of the IEEE 802.11*n* TG's work, since that new PHY will need to support speeds over 100 Mbps.

support all the basic rates advertised by an AP, it can choose to not associate with that AP. This decision on the part of the STA is not a requirement...STAs may still choose to associate in such circumstances, but while the standard never comes out and says it, this practice is not recommended.

The "B" bit is only significant in the four MMPDUs mentioned previously. When this IE is present in any type of MMPDU, the value of the "B" bit is ignored, although encoding the rate using more than seven bits is never allowed.

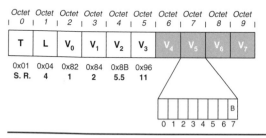

Figure 5–17   Supported Rates IE

Figure 5–17 shows the format of the Supported Rates IE, including the specific values from our example MMPDU, and includes a layout of each octet of the IE. A value of 0x02 equates to 1 Mbps, a value of 0x04 equates to 2 Mbps, a value of 11 (0x0B) equates to 5.5 Mbps, and a value of 22 (0x16) equates to 11 Mbps.

You will note that the values in the Value octets are not the same as those in the preceding sentence. When used, the "B" bit is interpreted as follows: The "B" bit is set to "1" when a rate is in the Basic Rate Set. Otherwise, it is clear for other non-Basic rates. The fact that each of the octets from the example MMPDU has the most-significant bit set indicates that these rates are part of the Basic Rate Set. The values in that case, for 1, 2, 5.5, and 11 Mbps, respectively, are 0x82, 0x84, 0x8B, and 0x96.

There are only two fields left in the payload of the example MMPDU in Figure 5–5. First, we have the DS Parameter Set, shown in Figure 5–18. The

Figure 5–18   The DS Parameter Set IE

fact that this is the DS Parameter Set is indicated by the fact that the Type octet contains 0x03. The Length field indicates a single octet in the Value portion, which is set to 6, meaning that this AP is using Channel 6 on which it is operating in DS Spread Spectrum DSSS mode.

The final field is depicted in Figure 5–19, and is proprietary to the vendor, so there is no way that we can decode the meaning of the final 32 octets of the MMPDU.

```
0030                  85 1e 00 00 4c 0d 07 00 ff 03
0040   11 00 41 50 33 35 30 2d 34 31 66 66 37 38 00 00
0050   00 00 01 00 00 22
```

Figure 5–19   A Proprietary TLV IE

The T-number for this IE is 0x85 (decimal 133), which is currently a reserved value and thus has no publicly defined meaning. The one thing we can decode is that the L field of the TLV is set to 0x1E (decimal 30), which does match the length of the mystery "V" field, so at least we can be confident that we have a complete IE, even though we do not know what it means.

If a STA encounters an IE that it does not understand, it can ignore that IE, and use the value in the L portion of the TLV to skip over the unknown TLV to the start of the next IE.

Summary

In this chapter, we explored a Probe Response MMPDU in detail. The interpretation of the fields in the various IEs, including how to interpret multi-octet fields (with respect to bit ordering issues) was also covered. With this knowledge, anyone familiar with a packet "sniffer" should be able to map between what they see on a packet analyzer versus what they see in the IEEE 802.11-1999 standard (or any of its derivative standards).

6

IEEE 802.11's MAC Sub-layer Protocol— Access, etc.

In this chapter, we examine the ways in which STAs share access to the WM, and the strategies that they employ to maximize throughput in a very challenging transmission environment.

Building Blocks: Joining a Wireless LAN

A station that wants to join a WLAN must first determine that a WLAN is present. This is accomplished either passively (by listening for a Beacon, a type of management frame that is sent by the AP), or actively (by transmitting a Probe Request on all available channels, until a Probe Response is received from the AP). The Beacon and Probe are two types of management frames, which along with Control and Data frames define the existing types of WLAN frames. Once it has determined that a WLAN is present, it must use local configuration to decide if it should join this WLAN.

In many WLAN clients, the user is asked to statically specify the SSID of the local WLAN; when a user of a product with such a driver roams to an area with a WLAN that has a different SSID, the user will have to manually update the SSID in order to join the new WLAN. Figure 6–1 shows an example of such a configuration screen.

Figure 6–1 shows an example configuration screen that allows input of the SSID from a product running on Windows 2000. In Chapter 3, we saw configuration screens from Red Hat Linux 9.0 and MacOS X.

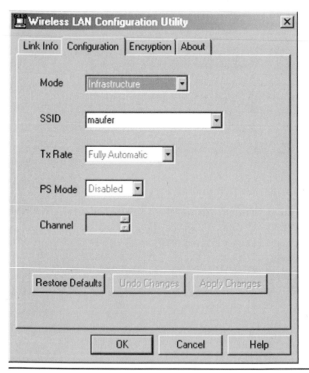

Figure 6–1   SSID configuration

To improve usability, it is also possible for the STA implementation to format the Probe Request MMPDU with a null SSID.[1] Any AP receiving such a Probe Request MMPDU with a null SSID will respond with a Probe Response MMPDU that lists its own SSID. After some time has passed, the STA will have accumulated a list of one or more available SSIDs. Based on these available SSIDs, or perhaps the configured SSID, the STA will either join the SSID that it has been configured to join, or it will present the user with the list of the available SSIDs, allowing the user to select which ESS to join.

The complete list of the IEEE 802.11-1999 Management frame Types and their associated Subtypes is in Figure 6–2, in which the structure of the Probe Request and Probe Response can be seen, as well as all types of Management frames.

Included here in Figure 6–3, for completeness, is the complete list of the IEEE 802.11-1999 Control frame Types and their associated Subtypes. The Control

---

1. The null SSID is interpreted as a broadcast, which is effectively a wildcard SSID that will match any SSID configured into any AP.

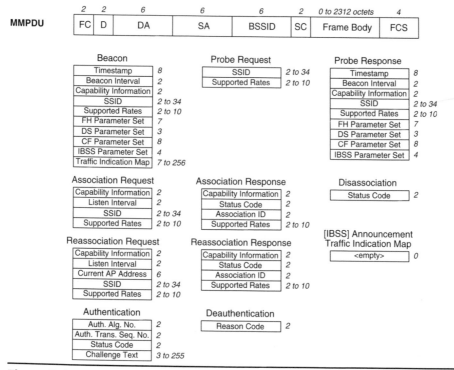

Figure 6–2   IEEE 802.11's Management frames

frames are primarily employed in the operation of the MAC sub-layer's access control protocol, and will be described in more detail later in this chapter. (The other type of IEEE 802.11-1999 frame is the Data frame (MPDU). It was described in detail in Chapter 4, *IEEE 802.11's MAC Sub-layer Protocol—Frames, etc.*).

IEEE 802.11 Frame Types and Usage

For each type of frame, there are situations in which it may (or may not) be used, as will be seen shortly. Note that in Figure 6–4, each frame type is classified as being Class 1, Class 2, or Class 3. These "classes" correspond to the state machine that governs the interaction between a STA and an AP (in infrastructure mode), or a STA and another STA (in IBSS mode).

The Data frame types in *italics* are associated with the IEEE 802.11*e* task group,[2] and will only become valid once that standard has been approved.

---

2. The working title for this draft standard is "Medium Access Control (MAC) Enhancements for Quality of Service (QoS)."

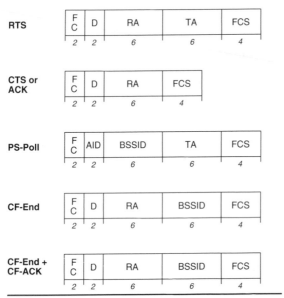

Figure 6–3   IEEE 802.11's Control frames

Note that in the case of Data type frames, each bit position has a defined meaning.

Basic STA State Machine

The first thing that happens when a STA wants to join a WLAN is that the STA does a passive or active scan. If an AP is within range, the STA will then move on to the authentication phase of the state machine, which is shown in Figure 6–5.[3]

In general, as a station progresses through the state machine of Figure 6–5, it will be able to send more of the possible frame types. In State 1, only Class 1 frames can be sent, but in State 3, all classes of frames may be sent (i.e., Class 1, Class 2, and Class 3).

The "Frame Class" column in Figure 6–4 associates each Type/Subtype combination with a corresponding state and/or class. As can be seen in that table, the Probe Request MMPDU is an example of a Class 1 frame, which means it

---

3. It is worthwhile to note that this state machine is not strictly representative of the states in which a STA can find itself, because of primarily the IEEE 802.11*i* work that is ongoing to improve security. There is considerable pressure to maintain the fiction that this state machine is still, essentially, correct. The state machine is accurate as a high-level representation, but it does not depict all the states that a STA may be in.

Type Value b3 b2	Type Description	Subtype Value b7 b6 b5 b4	Subtype Description	Frame Class
0 0	Management	0 0 0 0	Association Request	2
0 0	Management	0 0 0 1	Association Response	2
0 0	Management	0 0 1 0	Re-association Request	2
0 0	Management	0 0 1 1	Re-association Response	2
0 0	Management	0 1 0 0	Probe Request	1
0 0	Management	0 1 0 1	Probe Response	1
0 0	Management	1 0 0 0	Beacon	1
0 0	Management	1 0 0 1	Announcement Traffic Indication Message (ATIM)	1
0 0	Management	1 0 1 0	Disassociation	2
0 0	Management	1 0 1 1	Authentication	1
0 0	Management	1 1 0 0	De-authentication	2, 3
0 1	Control	1 0 1 0	Power Save Poll (PS-Poll)	3
0 1	Control	1 0 1 1	Request to Send (RTS)	1
0 1	Control	1 1 0 0	Clear to Send (CTS)	1
0 1	Control	1 1 0 1	Acknowledgment (ACK)	1
0 1	Control	1 1 1 0	Contention Free End (CF-End)	1
0 1	Control	1 1 1 1	CF-End + CF-ACK	1
1 0	Data	0 0 0 0	Data	3, 1*
1 0	Data	0 0 0 1	Data + CF-ACK *any PCF-capable STA or the Point Coordinator (PC)*	3
1 0	Data	0 0 1 0	Data + CF-Poll *only the Point Coordinator (PC)*	3
1 0	Data	0 0 1 1	Data + CF-ACK + CF-Poll *only the Point Coordinator (PC)*	3
1 0	Data	0 1 0 0	Null Function (no data)	3
1 0	Data	0 1 0 1	CF-ACK (no data) *any PCF-capable STA or the Point Coordinator (PC)*	3
1 0	Data	0 1 1 0	CF-Poll (no data) *only the Point Coordinator (PC)*	3
1 0	Data	0 1 1 1	CF-ACK + CF-Poll (no data) *only the Point Coordinator (PC)*	3
1 0	Data	1 0 0 0	QoS Data	3, 1*
1 0	Data	1 0 0 1	QoS Data + CF-ACK *any PCF-capable STA or the Point Coordinator (PC)*	3
1 0	Data	1 0 1 0	QoS Data + CF-Poll *only the Point Coordinator (PC)*	3
1 0	Data	1 0 1 1	QoS Data + CF-ACK + CF-Poll *only the Point Coordinator (PC)*	3
1 0	Data	1 1 0 0	QoS Null Function (no data)	3
1 0	Data	1 1 0 1	QoS CF-ACK (no data) *any PCF-capable STA or the Point Coordinator (PC)*	3
1 0	Data	1 1 1 0	QoS CF-Poll (no data) *only the Point Coordinator (PC)*	3
1 0	Data	1 1 1 1	QoS CF-ACK + CF-Poll (no data) *only the Point Coordinator (PC)*	3

QoS   CF-ACK   Null   CF-Poll

* May be used as a Class 1 frame only if both the ToDS and FromDS bits are clear (i.e., set to zero)

Figure 6–4   Management, Control, and Data Frames in IEEE 802.11-1999

can be sent from a STA that is neither authenticated nor associated, which corresponds to the usage of this MMPDU that has already been described.

Because the Authentication phase precedes the Association phase, it is possible for a STA to authenticate to multiple APs, even though a STA can only associate with one AP at any given time. This feature allows the STA to seamlessly roam from one AP to another, since it can simply disassociate from one AP and associate with the AP it is moving toward. The STA can use hints such as signal strength and signal quality to tell it which new AP it should associate with, since closer APs should have stronger signals.

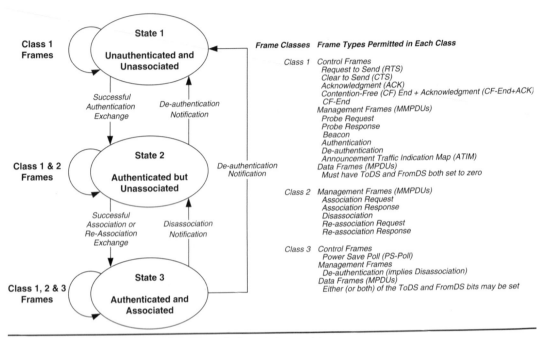

Figure 6–5   Authentication and Association state machine

Addressing in MPDUs

A data frame in a WLAN, just as in a wired LAN, must have a source and a destination MAC address (denoted MAC-SA and MAC-DA). However, in Chapter 4 you may have already observed that the MPDU frame format has no field with either of those names, yet it does have four six-octet fields named Address-1, Address-2, Address-3, and Address-4.

These four fields are all of the expected size necessary to accommodate a MAC address, but in IEEE 802.11's MAC sub-layer protocol, the Address fields in MPDU headers do not have fixed assignments; instead, the allocation of the Address fields to particular meanings depends on the setting of the ToDS and FromDS bits. There is a perfectly reasonable explanation for this.

In an infrastructure WLAN, it is not normal for a STA to send a frame directly to another STA...the frame is forwarded through an intermediate node, known as an AP.[4] This is done so that the AP can mitigate the effect of so-called

---

4. In IBSS mode, the STA-to-STA case is normal, but the dominant deployment of WLANs involves APs.

"hidden" nodes, which are nodes that can both hear the AP but cannot hear each other. The necessity exists for the address of an intermediate node (or of intermediate nodes) to be identified in the MPDU header so that the frame can be properly forwarded to its destination.

Influence of ToDS and FromDS on the MPDU Header

The settings of the "To Distribution System" (ToDS; bit 8) and "From Distribution System" (FromDS; bit 9) bits in the Frame Control field control the meaning and usage of the three (or four) Address fields in the MPDU header.

It is important to remember that (depending on the situation) there may not be a requirement for all four of the address fields to be present in the MPDU header. The layout and meaning of the individual Address fields for each combination of ToDS and FromDS is depicted on the left side of Figure 6–6, with the various combinations of ToDS and FromDS in the center, and a description of that particular scenario on the right.

Contents of the Address Fields (in Data and Management Frames)				ToDS/ FromDS		Meaning and/or Applicability (of ToDS and FromDS bits)
1	2	3	4	T	F	
DA	SA	BSSID	n/a	0	0	All Control frames. All Management frames. All intra-BSS Data frames. (Also, all intra-QBSS Data frames sent directly from one non-AP QSTA to another non-AP QSTA.)
DA	BSSID	SA	n/a	0	1	All Data frames from the DS to a STA (via an AP).
BSSID	SA	DA	n/a	1	0	All Data frames to the DS from a STA (via an AP).
RA	TA	DA	SA	1	1	All Wireless Distribution System (WDS) Data frames. In short, all Data frames that are being forwarded from one AP to another AP across the Wireless Medium (WM).

Figure 6–6   Usage of the Address fields in the IEEE 802.11 MPDU header[5]

Please remember that both IEEE 802.11 MAC Control frames and MMP-DUs have fixed header formats. The arrangement of the Address-n fields on the left-hand side of Figure 6–6 is *only* applicable to MPDUs, which are unique in

5. Adapted from IEEE Std. 802.11™-1999, copyright 1999, as amended by IEEE 802.11*e* draft 5.0 (a work-in-progress, which is subject to change before its publication). All rights reserved.

having this variable interpretation of the Address fields based on the settings of the ToDS and FromDS bits.

Whenever the ToDS and FromDS bits are set such that Address-4 is listed as "n/a" (i.e., not applicable), the Address-4 field is omitted from the MPDU[6] header, thereby reducing its size by six octets. The remaining bits in the FC field each control a particular feature that is provided by the IEEE 802.11 MAC sub-layer protocol. As a result, MPDU headers will either be short (24 octets) or long (30 octets).

The ToDS and FromDS bits do have an operational rule with respect to MAC Control frames and MMPDUs, which is that all such frames must be sent with both of these bits clear (i.e., set to "0").

On any given hop over the WM, it is possible that interference will require the use of MAC sub-layer retransmissions.[7] To accomplish this, the intermediate target needs to get the retransmission not from the originator of the frame, but from the most recent intermediate node that transmitted it (unsuccessfully, as yet). For this reason, in certain situations (e.g., particularly where a wireless distribution system is in use), all four of the Address fields will need to be populated (for the original sender, the ultimate destination, the current intermediate transmitter, and the current intermediate receiver).

Despite the presence of the four Address fields in the MPDU header, all four are not always populated in every situation. In the Wireless Distribution System (WDS) case, multiple APs must be traversed in order to reach the destination, so the intermediate node addresses will change with each successive hop across the WM.

For frames in the midst of being forwarded through a WDS, the Address-3 field contains the MAC-DA, and the Address-4 field contains the MAC-SA. In the WDS case (i.e., wherein both ToDS and FromDS bits are set to "1"), the Address-1 field contains the Receiver Address (MAC-RA) and the Address-2 field contains the Transmitter Address (MAC-TA). The MAC-RA may be thought of as an

---

6. The combination of ToDS and FromDS both being set to "1" is only valid for Data frames. Neither of these bits can be set in either Management or Control frames.

7. MAC sub-layer retransmission will be discussed later in this chapter, in the section covering medium access algorithms for WLANs.

"intermediate MAC-DA," and the MAC-TA may be thought of as an "intermediate MAC-SA," which may help with remembering their ordering.[8]

IEEE 802.11 WLAN Components

Before continuing with the discussion of the Access control methods and the Address fields in the IEEE 802.11 header, we will first briefly cover the terminology associated with the "intermediate nodes" (APs) in IEEE 802.11 WLANs. It is impossible to understand the reason for there being four Address fields in the IEEE 802.11 MPDU header unless one understands the nature and use of the AP.

Strictly speaking, an AP only serves to mediate communications between wireless stations in its vicinity, in particular those stations with which it has formed an "association." Figure 6–7a illustrates the AP function, which facilitates wireless communication between various STAs with which it has associated.

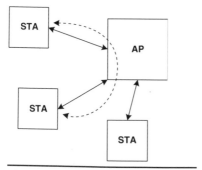

Figure 6–7a   Wireless LAN
components—wireless only

Devices called "APs" frequently also have integrated "Portal" functionality, which is specifically a gateway to a non-IEEE-802.11 wired LAN, so that a combined "AP + Portal" device effectively acts as a bridge between the wireless and wired domains. Devices that are commonly known as APs typically include a connection to the wired "Distribution System," so that the STAs in its local BSS can access devices outside their immediate vicinity.

---

8. The MAC-TA is an intermediate "source," and the MAC-RA is an intermediate "destination." The IEEE Project 802 LMSC tends to put destination addresses closer to the front of a frame.

The wired DS may link one BSS to a wired backbone, or link more than one BSS to other nearby BSSs such that they all form an ESS. An ESS is a collection of BSSs that appears to be one large BSS, as far as the LLC sub-layer is concerned. The DS that interconnects the BSSs may be any convenient medium, and is frequently wired (Ethernet, or IEEE 802.3). There is also the possibility to use the WM itself as a distribution system for the ESS, but that is not part of the IEEE 802.11-1999 standard.

Figure 6–7b illustrates a scenario that comprises a wired component[9] in which one STA is communicating through the Portal, while two other wireless STAs are exchanging data through the AP at the same time.

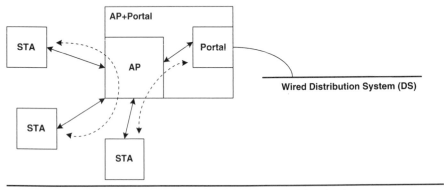

Figure 6–7b   Wireless LAN components—wireless with wired

Beyond the expected "usual case" that one AP will be in between any two communicating wireless STAs, there is the additional possibility that multiple APs may be needed to facilitate communication between two stations. This is why the IEEE 802.11 header needs enough space for up to four MAC addresses...the additional addresses in data frames represent an intermediate transmitter's address and an intermediate receiver's address.

The most common scenario for WLAN data traffic is probably a situation in which the two communicating stations are clients of the same AP, in which case only three Address fields would be present in the MPDU header. This case is illustrated in Figure 6–7a. Another very common scenario, shown in Figure 6–7b,

---

9. In IEEE 802.11 parlance, this wired "backbone" that interconnects the APs is known as the Distribution System (DS). When APs communicate over the WM without the presence of a wired DS, this mode of operation is known as Wireless DS operation.

would be that the wireless STA is communicating through a single AP to a station reachable via the wired LAN on the other side of the AP. In either case, only a single AP is involved in the data exchange. Because this situation may be logically equivalent to a single AP (e.g., if the APs and their common DS form a single broadcast domain), the format of the MPDUs on the WM is likely to require only three Address fields.

The case in which a frame must traverse multiple APs to reach a given station is not necessarily common, although it uses the two additional Address fields in a slightly different way compared to the two-stations-communicating through a common AP scenario. The meaning of the two additional Address fields is a slight generalization of the MAC-SA and MAC-DA concepts.

Other settings of the ToDS and FromDS bits involve defining one of the Address fields to hold a value known as the Basic Service Set (BSS) Identification[10] (BSSID), which is a unique number that, obviously, is used to identify a given BSS within an ESS. In an infrastructure BSS, the AP defines the BSSID to be the MAC address of the STA within the AP. In contrast, when a WLAN is operating as an independent BSS (IBSS), the first station in the IBSS defines the BSSID. The STA chooses a 46-bit random[11] number and concatenates those 46 bits with two additional bits to create a 48-bit locally administered MAC address (i.e., a MAC address that is not globally unique). This is accomplished by setting the least-significant two bits of the BSSID to "10" (where the least significant bit is "0"). Rather than confuse this definition by discussing bit ordering issues, simply note that the least-significant octet of the BSSID in the IBSS case can never be an odd number (i.e., it will be divisible by two because the least-significant bit is "0").

One of the other controlling factors in the selection of the values in the "ToDS" and "FromDS" bits is that certain combinations are only allowable for certain levels of association. For example, if a STA has not been associated or authenticated, it may not set either of these bits. In addition, certain management frames are sent with these bits clear, such as Beacons (sent by the AP). Once a STA has been fully associated and authenticated, it can set the ToDS bit. Only APs should be setting the FromDS bit.

---

10. The "ID" in BSSID is also sometimes used to mean "Identifier."

11. The random number is chosen in such a way that it is unlikely that another station would choose the same BSSID, even under very similar or identical initial conditions.

Frame Handling—Multicast

Because of hidden nodes, multicast[12] frames are not transmitted directly onto the WM by any STA (unless it is in IBSS mode, which has no hidden nodes by assumption). Multicasts must be sent by the AP, since that is the only way for all the STAs in the BSS to hear them. However, if the STA sent the multicast frame as a multicast, then all the STAs in range of its radio would hear the frame. However, the AP would then re-issue the frame into the BSS so that the other STAs could hear it, and that would result in the STAs within range of the STA that sent the frame in the first place getting a second copy of the multicast frame.

The way around this is that the STA sends the frame with the ToDS bit set to "1" and the Address-1 field set to the BSSID, the MAC address of the STA in the AP. The frame's ultimate MAC Destination Address (in the Address-3 field) is the desired multicast address. The AP understands this frame format and sends a new frame out as a native multicast, with the FromDS bit set to "1". In this case, the Address-2 field still contains the BSSID, since that allows a STA that can hear multiple APs to filter only the multicasts that are from the AP with which it has associated.[13]

MAC/PLCP Interactions

The PLCP is used to specify certain properties of the subsequent frame, most importantly its speed (which is intimately related to the modulation that is used to transmit the digital data over the inherently analog WM). By using PLCP, each transmitted PSDU is endowed with a label that lets it be transmitted at any of the valid speeds in the Operational Rate Set as specified by the AP.

The short-format PLCP header was introduced as an optional performance-enhancing feature in the IEEE 802.11b-1999 standard. The forthcoming IEEE 802.11g standard, if approved, will be the first 2.4 GHz PHY to mandate support for the short-format PLCP header.[14] The usage of the optional Short Pre-

---

12. Multicast includes broadcast, which is a specific type of multicast frame in which the MAC-DA contains the broadcast address (48 bits all set to "1").

13. **Note:** The Address-2 field *always* contains the MAC address of the transmitting entity.

14. IEEE 802.11a-1999 specifies a PLCP structure that is not directly comparable to the DSSS PLCP header, although its high-performance nature did cause the specification to require a PLCP header that was temporally shorter than that used in the DSSS PHYs.

amble primarily affects the efficiency of sending Data frames, since that type of frame will tend to dominate the traffic mix within any BSS.

STAs that use the Short Preamble option can spend more of their time sending data, and less time waiting to do so, so in that regard its use will improve the aggregate throughput of a BSS. Three things must happen for any frame within a BSS to be sent using short-format PLCP headers: 1) all the STAs must support the short PLCP header format, 2) the AP must enable the usage of the short PLCP header format, and 3) all the STAs must choose to use it (once the AP has permitted it, the STA is still free to transmit any of its frames with long-format PLCP headers).

The Beacon must be understandable by any PHY operating in the 2.4 GHz band, so it must be transmitted using the least-common-denominator PLCP header format; in other words, Barker/DBPSK modulation (at a rate of 1 Mbps) with a long PLCP preamble. The Beacon's Capability Information IE indicates whether the Short Preamble may be used within its BSS. The Association Response, Reassociation Response, and Probe Response MMPDUs also contain a Capability Information IE, which are also used to convey the same information.

For backward compatibility with DSSS PHYs (1 Mbps Barker/DBPSK and 2 Mbps Barker/DQPSK), Beacon MMPDUs must be transmitted using the long-format PLCP header. The original IEEE 802.11-1999 standard, which specified the 1 and 2 Mbps DSSS RF PHYs, only specified the long-format PLCP preamble, so the Beacons must still use the long-format PLCP preamble in IEEE 802.11*b*-1999 and IEEE 802.11*g*-2003, to maintain backward compatibility with any DSSS PHY devices that may be present in the BSS.

However, even in a BSS in which the usage of Short Preambles is permitted, all the frames are not necessarily transmitted in that mode. Beacons are still sent using Long Preambles, and any IEEE 802.11*b* STA that wants to do so can use the Long Preamble. The indication from the AP (in the Beacon and Probe Response MMPDUs) that Short Preamble mode is enabled is not a directive that all STAs that support Short Preamble mode must send all their frames in that mode. The AP is giving permission, not issuing an order.

Moreover, even when the AP allows STAs to send frames with the short-format PLCP header, all STAs must be prepared to receive a frame preceded by the long-format PLCP header. At a minimum, this will be the Beacon MMPDUs from the AP. In addition, any STAs that roam into this BSS cannot know in advance that the AP has enabled short-preamble mode, so any MMPDUs that newly arrived STAs transmit during the authentication and association phases will have to be sent in long-preamble mode, at least until the STA discovers that it is permitted to use Short Preamble.[15]

There is effectively a "preamble echo rule" that states that a response-MMPDU must be sent with the same type of preamble as the request-MMPDU that triggered the response-MMPDU. MMPDUs are sent between the AP and a STA, and those that are not request/response must be sent with the long-format PLCP header. For Data frames, how can the AP ensure that a STA which is only capable of using Long Preamble will be able to talk to a STA that supports Short Preamble PLCP headers?

The answer is quite simple. As soon as an AP associates with a long-format-only STA, it clears the "short-format PLCP header is ok" bit in its Beacon and Probe Responses. If the AP did not do this, the legacy STAs would not be able to participate in the MAC sub-layer access protocol, which depends on all the STAs being able to glean the Duration from each frame it can hear, either in the MPDU or MMPDU header, or in the RTS/CTS exchanges, in order for the operation of the Virtual Carrier Sense mechanism (in particular, the Network Allocation Vector (NAV)). The short PLCP preamble sounds like noise to a long-format-only PHY, so that PHY will not be able to make sense of the Duration field in the PSDU (MPDU), nor will it be able to tell that a valid IEEE 802.11 transmission is in progress. Also note that a short-preamble STA can recognize either preamble format, so there is no problem receiving long-preamble Beacons (or any other frame preceded by a long-format PLCP header), even if a STA is configured to transmit its frames with short-format PLCP headers.

Support for Short Preamble is optional-to-implement in IEEE 802.11-1999 DSSS PHYs and IEEE 802.11b-1999 HR/DSSS PHYs (CCK and PBCC at 5.5 and 11 Mbps), but mandatory-to-implement in IEEE 802.11g-2003 ER-PHYs (PBCC and CCK-OFDM; pure OFDM has its own distinct form of PLCP header; IEEE 802.11a-1999 uses the same form of PLCP header format that is unique to OFDM, and since it cannot interfere with STAs

---

15. Such a discovery would only be relevant to a STA that is capable of using the short-format PLCP header, since legacy STAs will not know how to interpret that bit in the Capability Information IE and will ignore it

operating at 2.4 GHz, there is no need to be backward compatible with them…although ER-PHYs based on OFDM may use an optional protection mechanism known as "CTS-to-Self" as one way to alert nearby STAs that an unintelligible transmission is imminent).

However, in the IEEE 802.11*g*-2003 standard, even though Short Preamble support is mandatory-to-implement, Short Preamble PLCP headers are still optional to use; the AP decides whether it is safe to do so. Due to the improved throughput, this feature is likely to be enabled by default for transmitted data frames as long as all STAs in a BSS support the short-format PLCP header.

Even though this feature is not required to be enabled, just supported, in practice, it is likely that many APs that support IEEE 802.11*g*-2003 will enable the use of short preambles as a default configuration. In IEEE 802.11*g*-based networks, the Beacon is still transmitted with the Long Preamble. The standard allows for a mode in which all STAs in a BSS must support the Short Preamble, since there is an error message that may be used by an AP at Association time to indicate to a STA that its association was denied because it did not support the short-format PLCP preamble.

When a STA joins a WLAN, it will find out if the WLAN supports the short preamble option. However, before it has joined, it does not know whether this is the case. Now, any STA that supports the short-format PLCP preamble must implicitly also be able to receive the long-format PLCP preamble. However, older STAs will only be able to send and receive frames with the long-format PLCP preamble.

In order to permit WLANs to effectively mix short- and long-preamble STAs, a rule has been defined that the author refers to as the "preamble echo rule": When a STA receives a PPDU (which encapsulates a Management frame) from another STA, it must remember the PLCP preamble format of the PPDU so that any PPDU (encapsulating a Management frame) sent in reply must use the same format of PLCP preamble. This rule allows a long-preamble STA to join a short-preamble BSS, since its long-preamble Probe Request will be answered with a long-preamble Probe Response.

A Usage of the CTS Control Frame: CTS-to-Self

This optional mechanism is designed to advise DSSS- or HR/DSSS-STAs that a transmission is ongoing, so that they will properly update their NAVs and not transmit during the ERP (i.e., OFDM) transmission. This mechanism is potentially useful because ERP-STAs may be exchanging frames using a modulation (e.g., PBCC, OFDM) that may be undetectable by the DSSS- or HR/DSSS-STAs. In a small BSS, without hidden nodes, this mechanism would suffice to alert pre-ERP[16] STAs that a legitimate frame transmission was about to commence, even if the frame would be undetectable to the pre-ERP STAs.

To keep the pre-ERP STAs from thinking it is safe to transmit, they need to be made aware that a frame is being transmitted, whether or not they can actually interpret its modulation while it is being transmitted. This mechanism, within certain limitations to be described later, allows all STAs to modify their NAVs so that they cannot transmit while the ERP-STA's frame is in progress. This feature is defined in IEEE 802.11*g*-2003, Clauses. 7.2.1.2, 9.2.11, and 9.7.

The CTS-to-Self MAC Control frame is only generated by ERP-STAs if the AP has signaled "protected mode" in its Beacon or Probe Response MMPDUs, which indicates to ERP-STAs (i.e., IEEE 802.11*g*-2003 STAs) that pre-ERP STAs (i.e., IEEE 802.11-1999 or IEEE 802.11*b*-1999 STAs) are present. The AP is allowed to turn protected mode off (even though it knows that some pre-ERP STAs are present) if it senses that the pre-ERP STAs are not sending much traffic. The AP has real-time discretion over this decision…there is no absolute rule on when protected mode shall be used.

It is clearly true that for *every* associated STA, the AP must be within range of that STA. From the STA's perspective, it is in range of the AP, and other STAs may be in range of that STA as well. If an ERP-STA has sent a CTS-to-Self MAC Control frame, we can assume that the AP has received it, and knows what it means. Of course, we are assuming that the AP is capable of understanding both HR and ERP transmissions. (The CTS-to-Self MAC Control frame is transmitted using CCK modulation, so any pre-ERP STA can hear and understand it.)

---

16. For clarity, the author will temporarily refer to DSSS and HR/DSSS STAs as pre-ERP STAs.

In Figure 6–8, the coverage area of the AP is shown with a solid line bordering its coverage area, and the coverage areas of the ERP and non-ERP STAs are indicated with different types of dashed lines.

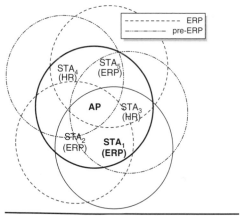

Figure 6–8   Hidden nodes and the
CTS-to-Self mechanism

As mentioned previously, all the STAs are in range of the AP. In addition, in Figure 6–8 both STA_2 and STA_3 are within range of STA_1's radio and thus can hear its transmissions. The other two STAs (STA_4 and STA_5) are both out of range of STA_1 (since they are outside of its coverage circle). Consequently, both STA_4 and STA_5 will not be able to hear *any* frame that is sent by STA_1, including any CTS-to-Self MAC Control frame. For the following example, let's presume that STA_1 does indeed send a CTS-to-Self MAC Control frame.

All STAs, including ERP-STAs and any older pre-ERP STAs, within range of STA_1's radio will understand the meaning of the CTS-to-Self MAC Control frame and update their NAVs accordingly. All the STAs will see this CTS frame as a normal CTS…only STA_1 knows that it sent a CTS-to-Self MAC Control frame. STAs do not need to keep state on whether they have seen an RTS Control frame in order to know if a CTS Control frame is a response to an RTS or a CTS-to-Self message. They must simply process the CTS Control frame statelessly. All STAs within range of STA_1—regardless of whether they are pre-ERP or ERP STAs—will update their NAVs (because the CTS-to-Self MAC Control frame is transmitted using a modulation that every STA within range should be able to understand).

Now, what about STA$_4$ and STA$_5$? This is different from a normal all-HR-STA hidden node scenario. It isn't a requirement that all MPDUs be preceded by an RTS/CTS exchange. In fact, each STA may have an RTS-threshold that can allow short unicast frames to be sent without using the RTS/CTS mechanism. When not using RTS/CTS, a STA senses the medium (only when its NAV permits it to transmit), and if the medium is not busy and its NAV permits it to transmit, then it simply does so. The MPDU is sent with the duration value in the D/I field set large enough to incorporate 1) the expected time to transmit the MPDU, and 2) the expected time to receive the corresponding ACK.

An out-of-range STA may send a data frame or an RTS while it is unaware that the AP is busy exchanging a frame with another STA. The frame from the out-of-range STA will interfere with the AP's transmission to or from the other STA—that's life. The way that such hidden-node collisions are normally avoided is by preceding the data exchange with an RTS/CTS exchange, so that all STAs will know how long to stay idle to accommodate the frame associated with the STA that sent the RTS.

In the case of frames arriving from the DS, the AP sends the RTS to the destination STA—and it is the RTS that all the STAs will hear—the STA responds with a CTS, and only the STAs within range of the destination STA's radio will hear the CTS from that STA. This is not a problem, because the RTS frame from the AP had its D/I field set to cover the entire duration of the RTS/CTS exchange, the frame transmission, and the transmission of the resulting ACK. Since all the STAs will hear the RTS, they will all update their NAVs so that none will attempt to transmit while the current exchange is in progress.

In the normal hidden node case (i.e., two wireless STAs communicating through a common AP with a third STA that is also in range of the AP but is out of range of at least one of the two communicating STAs), the AP sends the CTS in response to an RTS. The CTS is heard throughout the BSS, even though the RTS is only heard within range of the STA that sent it. Hearing the CTS from the AP allows all the STAs in the BSS to update their NAVs to prevent them from transmitting during the current frame.

Unfortunately, the CTS-to-Self MAC Control frame is not heard throughout the BSS (the AP does not forward such messages; if it did, this hidden node problem would be somewhat less acute;[17] however, the reason why CTS-to-Self exists in the first place is to improve throughput, and if the STA had to wait for the AP to echo a CTS-to-Self message, then that would reduce the throughput).

What if STA_4 or STA_5 sends a frame that "collides" with STA_1's frame transmission? The AP would not receive the complete frame from STA_1, so it cannot send an ACK back to STA_1. Eventually, STA_1 will time out and try again. Likewise, the interfering node will not get whatever response was appropriate to the frame it tried to send (i.e., if it sent an RTS, it would be expecting a CTS; or if it sent a Data frame, it would be expecting an ACK), so it will also eventually give up and try again as well. This event is treated like any other frame collision event—both STAs will choose a random back-off interval and try again at their next opportunity.

The CTS-to-Self procedure isn't perfect, but since faster modulations tie up the medium for as much as 80 percent less time (for a given packet size), it might be reasonable to suppose that the mechanism needn't be perfect. A 1500-octet IP packet becomes a 1536- or 1542-octet IEEE 802.11 frame, which takes about as much time to transmit at 54 Mbps as a 320-octet frame takes at 11 Mbps. Moreover, the CTS-to-Self mechanism isn't mandatory, and the IEEE 802.11g standard does still permit the use of RTS/CTS if desired. However, while the RTS/CTS exchange would seem to be sufficient to alert the BSS to the impending transmission (provided that the RTS and CTS are transmitted using a modulation that all HR- and ERP-STAs can understand), the RTS/CTS exchange incurs the cost of additional latency before an ERP-STA can begin to send data. This latency significantly reduces the maximum throughput that can be achieved.

Given that the CTS-to-Self mechanism can only be used by ERP-STAs, another issue is. When the STA should generate such a frame? It is a given that the AP must have enabled protected mode, but the STA needn't send an RTS before its frame. There does not appear to be any standards-based way to force the STA to use either RTS/CTS or CTS-to-Self, so this looks like a choice that implementers are free to make; this freedom extends all the way to legitimately ignoring the possibility of implementing CTS-to-Self.

The main reason to implement CTS-to-Self is that if the BSS is small, and if most of the STAs are in range of each other, then the CTS-to-Self mechanism,

---

17. It's still possible for a new STA to pop up after the CTS was transmitted and send a frame that would then interfere with the frame that had been protected by either the RTS/CTS exchange, or by the CTS-to-Self message.

coupled with the fact that the frame transmission times are shorter (due to the faster speeds), means that a STA that uses CTS-to-Self may see higher throughput. If a STA detects a collision after it had sent a CTS-to-Self, the implementation might choose to infer that there are hidden nodes and it is not safe to use CTS-to-Self for a while.

This behavior (of using collisions to infer the existence of hidden nodes) is not specified in the IEEE 802.11g-2003 standard, either as a mandate or a recommendation, but anyone who tries to implement CTS-to-Self should probably define their own decision tree governing the usage of this feature, since blindly enabling it all the time will not always give the best throughput. CTS-to-Self doesn't help throughput at all in a busy BSS that is large enough such that a significant fraction of the nodes are hidden relative to each other. The goal of any implementation should be to provide the end user with the best possible throughput. Again, CTS-to-Self is not mandatory, and it is perfectly reasonable to avoid implementing it.

DCF, PCF, Time, and Power Management

CSMA/CA is the basic method by which wireless STAs share access to the medium. IEEE 802.11's medium access protocol was designed to tolerate frame loss due to interference (which could come from any number of sources…misbehaving or hidden IEEE 802.11 stations, 2.4 GHz cordless phones, garage door openers, Bluetooth devices, microwave ovens, lightning, etc.). Interference is a much more common phenomenon in the wireless domain; if design accommodations were not made, the throughput of the IEEE 802.11 MAC might have been significantly limited.

Wireless versus Wired MAC Protocol Design Differences

Many readers are probably familiar with CSMA/CD, which was the algorithm that was defined for the initial shared-access Ethernet. In certain circles, the term "CSMA/CD" is interchangeable with Ethernet, although strictly speaking, CSMA/CD only applies to shared-media (half-duplex) Ethernets.

In a WLAN, stations can use whatever speed(s) are supported by their PHYs, as conditions warrant (i.e., if there is significant interference, slower speeds might be more successful than higher speeds); whereas in Ethernet, once a station has determined its speed, it continues to use that speed unless the station is manually reconfigured.

One advantage that designers of wired LAN MAC protocols have is that the media over which their protocols are designed to operate consist of environments with very high signal-to-noise ratios (e.g., copper twisted pair, or optical fiber), resulting in very low bit error rates. In such environments, since there is so little noise (either relative to the signal, or in absolute terms), there is a very high likelihood of successful transmission.

In addition, many wired LAN access protocols assume that all members can hear each other's transmissions, which is most definitely not a valid assumption in the wireless world. WLAN MAC protocols must be designed to support the much more challenging transmission environment[18] of wireless (particularly RF wireless). If a wireless MAC design ignored the reality of interference, and assumed that all stations were close enough to each other to hear each other directly, WLAN performance would be horrible, and usability would suffer. There are three main ways in which IEEE 802.11's MAC has been designed to tolerate interference.

The most common example of a wired LAN, Ethernet, began life as a half-duplex LAN that operated over a shared broadcast medium (initially coaxial cable, a.k.a. "thicknet," which evolved into shared 10BASE-T hubs that were still half-duplex, at least initially). In one very important way, the Ethernet's physical characteristics were similar to the RF environment that IEEE 802.11 is designed to operate in—they are both broadcast media, in the sense that when one station transmits, others can hear it. To fairly allocate access to the shared 10 or 100 Mbps half-duplex medium, Ethernet employed the CSMA/CD algorithm.

Note that in modern full-duplex switched Ethernet networks, there is no chance of a collision—a station may be receiving one frame while it is

---

18. In fact, the 2.4 GHz band that is used by IEEE 802.11, IEEE 802.11*b*, and IEEE 802.11*g* has been known as a "junk" band because of contamination by microwave oven emissions and more recently cordless telephone transmissions. Originally, the 2.4 GHz band was reserved because of interference from microwave ovens, expressing the FCC's feeling that no one else would ever want to try to use this band. However, the pressure to allocate more of the available RF spectrum to communications forced the FCC to create rules for unlicensed ISM operation in this allegedly worthless band.

simultaneously transmitting another—so the CSMA/CD algorithm is no longer used to control access to the medium.

However, CSMA/CD is not suited to operation over the WM. The radios cannot hear while they transmit, so they cannot hear a collision. Even if they could hear while they transmit frames, the fact that they didn't hear a collision didn't mean that one didn't happen. The STA that sent whatever frame interfered with the sender's frame may have been out of range of the sender's radio, but in range of the receiver's radio. This is the key difference. In half-duplex Ethernet, all STAs are presumed to be able to hear each other, but in IEEE 802.11, hidden nodes are a fact of life. A method of collision detection that can handle hidden nodes was required, which is known as CSMA/CA.[19]

The result of a collision in Ethernet and IEEE 802.11 is similar, in that a binary exponential backoff algorithm helps ensure that after a collision, one of the stations will have a chance to transmit a frame successfully. However, the IEEE 802.11 design places the collision backoff in front of the frame transmission, to help eliminate obvious collisions due to STAs simultaneously detecting an idle medium.

The big difference between Ethernet's CSMA/CD and IEEE 802.11's CSMA/CA is that in the case of half-duplex Ethernet, the LAN's collision domain is defined so that the sending and receiving stations are guaranteed to be able to hear each other's traffic within 512 bit-times (which is the reason why the minimum packet size is 64 octets; i.e., 512 bits). In IEEE 802.11, however, there is the possibility that the sender's transmission could be interfered with by a hidden node, a node that is within range of the receiver, but not of the sender. Of course, all these STAs are in range of the AP, and the IEEE 802.11 protocols incorporate several techniques for handling hidden nodes, one of which is the ACK mechanism, and the other is the virtual carrier sense mechanism that is explicitly enabled by the RTS/CTS exchange, and is implicitly enabled by any frame via its Duration field.

To detect if a collision has occurred, IEEE 802.11 STAs must acknowledge every frame that they receive; if no acknowledgment is received by the sender, the frame is retransmitted until it gets through or until the sender gives up and

---

19. CSMA/CA has also been used in some wired LANs; for example, Apple's LocalTalk 230.4 kbps LAN that was based on RS-422 cabling.

declares an error condition. It is important to note that the retransmissions are not meant to make the WM into a reliable transport service. IEEE 802.11 is still a LAN, and it still provides an unreliable datagram service. However, IEEE 802.11's designers realized that the sender may not be able to tell if its transmission has been corrupted, since the energy that was transmitted that stomped on the sender's transmission may have been from a hidden node, and the sender may not have been able to hear that hidden node—but the receiver did, and that's all that matters. In Ethernet, the sender can tell immediately if a collision has occurred, and can take steps to recover as soon as the error has been detected. In IEEE 802.11, the STA can't detect the collision until after the frame has been transmitted fully; even if more than half of it is garbled, the sender has no way to know that until after it realizes it never got an ACK for that frame.

One limitation of the IEEE 802.11 method of collision detection is that a lost ACK is equivalent to a sender inferring the occurrence of a collision. If a frame is re-transmitted by the sender, the frame is marked to indicate that it is a retransmission, and the receiver will ACK a retransmitted frame, multiple times (until the ACK finally gets through to the sender), but will only accept one copy of the frame. Each frame has a unique sequence number that can be used to eliminate duplicate frames due to retransmission. Remember, in the case of a lost ACK, the sender thinks the frame did not arrive successfully, although that is not really true.

The IEEE 802.11 access protocol uses several mechanisms to try to avoid collisions on the medium (/CA = Collision Avoidance), but these mechanisms are not foolproof. For example, each STA maintains a local "Network Allocation Vector," or NAV, which allows it to keep track of the imminent users of the WM so that the STA does not interfere with known imminent transmitters; there is also an RTS/CTS mechanism that can be used to ensure that all the STAs in the BSS will know that a transmission is coming, and therefore to be quiet until it is complete.

Third and finally, IEEE 802.11 supports MAC sub-layer fragmentation of large frames. In a WLAN, it is useful to break up the transmission of a large frame into smaller "fragments." Large frames are more likely to encounter interference because larger frames take longer to transmit at a given data rate. By breaking large frames into smaller pieces, the stations can increase their chances of a successful transmission, since each smaller piece may be able to get through without encountering interference. Consequently, if interference happens to be encountered during the transmission of a fragment, the damage will be localized to that fragment. As a result, only that fragment will need to be retransmitted, as opposed to the entire frame.

Before resorting to fragmentation, a STA will attempt to retransmit the entire frame, and possibly might reduce the speed at which it transmits, in order to use a more robust, albeit slower, scheme for encoding the bits at the Physical layer.

Besides the fact that this fragmentation[20] happens at the MAC sub-layer, the other major difference between IEEE 802.11 frame fragmentation and IPv4 packet fragmentation is that IEEE 802.11 fragments are transmitted one at a time, in order, whereas IPv4 packet fragments are independent packets on their own and may each take its own path through the network. IPv4 packet fragments are transmitted in order initially (from the point at which the fragments were created), but could potentially be re-ordered during their subsequent travels through the network before arriving at the ultimate destination of the original packet. Thus, it is possible for IPv4 packet fragments to arrive in an order that differs from the original order in which they were transmitted.

Alongside environmental differences between wired and wireless networks, there is also the fact that wireless devices are frequently battery-operated, at least some of the time, which makes power management a top priority for them. If a station's radio is kept active all the time, simply for the convenience of other stations that might want to communicate with this station, the result will be a big power drain. IEEE 802.11 specifically supports integrated "power management," in that the stations of a WLAN can tell each other how long they plan to "sleep" before they will be ready to accept data again. (This notion of "sleep" does not correspond to OS sleep states. The OS may or may not be awake the whole time, but the IEEE 802.11 MAC is conserving power by only being active when it needs to be.) Laptop users always

---

20. This MAC sub-layer *frame fragmentation* is independent of any higher-layer *packet* fragmentation; for example, IPv4 packet fragmentation. Not all higher-layer protocols support packet fragmentation, but some popular ones do, notably IPv4 (IPv6 only support end-to-end fragmentation).

appreciate power-saving features, especially when their laptop is running on battery power.

The IEEE 802.11-1999 standard specifies two different schemes that STAs can use to share access to the medium, namely the Distributed Coordination Function (DCF) and the Point Coordination Function (PCF). DCF is based CSMA/CA. PCF relies on a Point Coordinator (PC) (effectively, the WLAN's traffic cop) to tell each STA when it may transmit. Because the PC typically resides in the AP, the AP might use its superior knowledge of the traffic mix to provide a variety of class-of-service support.

Despite PCF being specified in the IEEE 802.11-1999 standard, the author is aware of very few implementations other than engineering demonstrations. As far as the author is aware, the Wi-Fi Alliance does not make PCF operation part of their certification test suite for Wi-Fi devices.

The operation of the PCF mode of medium access control is regulated and indicated by bits 2 and 3 of the Capabilities IE of all Beacon and Probe Response MMPDUs. As a preview of PCF, suffice it to say that in PCF mode, a central control entity (in the AP) acts to collect frames from WLAN STAs by polling each STA, rather than by allowing each STA with data to send to independently contend for access to the medium.

The "CF" abbreviation in each of the labels for bits 2 and 3 means "Contention-Free," as distinguished from the access method that is based on contention. Confusingly, the IEEE 802.11-1999 standard refers to the entity in the AP as a PC. Because PC is a ubiquitous acronym with a commonly interpreted meaning, the author will not use it. Beware that in the standard, when you see PC, it probably means Point Coordinator, not Personal Computer.

Distributed Coordination Function

The primary method of medium access control deployed in most real-world networks is DCF. CSMA/CA is the usual method employed by proximate IEEE 802.11 STAs to share access to their common WM. Like CSMA/CD, which is employed by half-duplex Ethernet, CSMA/CA is a "listen before talk" (CS) method of minimizing collisions resulting from simultaneous transmission of multiple radios.

In IEEE 802.11, collision avoidance rather than collision detection must be used, because the IEEE 802.11-1999 standard chose to rely on simplex radios, which are incapable of receiving while transmitting, or vice versa. Consequently, unlike conventional wired Ethernet nodes, a WLAN station cannot detect a collision while it is transmitting. When an Ethernet station (in half-duplex mode) detects that its current frame has been collided with, it stops its transmission immediately and initiates backoff procedures. This behavior is very commonly understood by people who get paid to manage networks, so they might be surprised to learn that WLAN devices do not operate using this basic functional stance.

In fact, the WLAN access protocol inverts the order of the backoff, placing it before the frame transmission. The reasoning is as follows: The most likely time that a collision would occur is immediately after a frame transmission completes. If multiple STAs were waiting to send frames of their own, and an in-progress frame concluded its transmission, the STAs with frames ready to send would immediately collide with each other as soon as they had determined that the medium was quiet. Therefore, in IEEE 802.11, the collision backoff happens *before* the frame is transmitted, which serves to reduce the likelihood of a collision.

The only way for an IEEE 802.11 transmitter to detect a collision is implicit: the transmitting STA will not receive an ACK control frame from the recipient STA (the STA to which the data frame was addressed). To help ensure that ACK control frames will make it through ahead of other traffic, they have a higher priority than all other network traffic, which derives from the fact that there is a short time window after the data frame is transmitted when only the receiver may transmit. This bit of time is reserved so that the receiver may transmit an ACK control frame.

Since all the other STAs know that the data frame had been in progress (because of the CS and CA parts of CSMA/CA), and can also all tell when it has finished, they all share the knowledge of how long to wait to allow the ACK to flow back to the sender. All the other STAs that had data to send while the frame was in progress must wait a pseudo-random period of time before transmitting, similar to the way that half-duplex Ethernet stations use a binary exponential backoff algorithm to regulate retransmissions after collisions. If the requisite ACK control frame is not received, the transmitting station may wait for a subsequent opportunity to retransmit the data frame, or if its retry threshold has been exceeded, it can indicate an error.

Timing Is Everything

The BSS is kept to a synchronized clock by the AP. Every Beacon is transmitted as close as possible to the TBTT (an AP may not transmit a Beacon if another frame is in progress...). Each Beacon and Probe Response begins with a fixed-length (eight-octet) IE known as the "Timestamp" IE. The Timestamp IE holds a 64-bit timer value expressed in units of microseconds, which allows for up to 18,446,744,073,709.551616 seconds before the timer must "roll over." This is equivalent to just over 584,542 years, if we define a year as 365.25 days long. Even if a manufacturer designs the perfect IEEE 802.11 product that never crashes, it would probably be obsolete long before the Timestamp field rolls over.

The reason why IEEE 802.11's Timing Synchronization Function (TSF) operates in units of microseconds is that the smallest time unit that can be precisely measured by *all* devices in an IEEE 802.11 LAN is the time to transmit a single bit by the slowest possible STA. The slowest modulation, Barker/DBPSK, runs at 1 Mbps, which implies that a bit is equivalent to one microsecond. An IEEE 802.11 STA running at 1 Mbps would find it impossible to measure any time interval with sub-microsecond precision—unless it were endowed with additional hardware to support a more precise clock, something that the standard does not require. To maintain backward compatibility for speeds all the way down to 1 Mbps, the IEEE 802.11 MAC sub-layer access protocol never expects STAs to be able to measure time more precisely than at one-microsecond intervals.

The eight-octet fixed-length Timestamp IE is immediately followed by another fixed-length timing-related IE, known as the Beacon Interval IE, which contains the TBTT. The Beacon Interval is a two-octet field expressed in units of "time units." The duration of a "time unit" is one "kilomicrosecond" (kµs). (Normally, one "kilo" (1000) of microseconds would just be one millisecond, but the power-of-2-sized 1024 microseconds is more useful for measuring time in the IEEE 802.11 MAC sub-layer protocol.) Thus, the TBTT can be anywhere from 1 to 65,535 kµs.

There are a number of "time windows" that govern the operation of the IEEE 802.11 MAC sub-layer protocol. To control access, it is critical that all the STAs understand a common time reference, since many timers are kept that are relative, and if the STAs had no common idea of what "time" it is, then they will be unsynchronized in their usage of the relative timers and the timers will not have the desired effects.

There are a number of inter-related aspects of the access control mechanism used by the IEEE 802.11 MAC sub-layer protocol. The following sections enumerate the mechanisms that have some bearing on each other. Because of the nature of the way these features are defined, it is difficult to explain any one of them in detail without referring to at least one other. The author will make every effort to avoid "forward references" to concepts that are not yet known to the reader by the use of sidebars and footnotes.

Time Intervals and Access Methods

There is one basic access mechanism known as the Distributed Coordination Function (DCF). It's clear why any access mechanism needs to be "distributed" if you're talking about WLANs. However, that doesn't explain the "coordination" aspect of DCF. It took the author a long time to figure out what the coordination was all about, and that's the most interesting part of the IEEE 802.11 MAC sub-layer's access mechanisms.

The Collision Avoidance mechanism is actually intimately interwoven with the Carrier Sense mechanism. A collision is when two STAs try to use the medium at the same time. When is such an event most likely to occur? Logically, such an event is most likely immediately following the successful transmission of a frame. Why? Again, remembering that a collision occurs when two STAs transmit at the same time, if we back up a bit before they transmitted, they must have both been waiting for the medium to go idle (because of their Carrier Sense mechanism). Once the medium was idle, they would both determine at about the same instant that this was the case and proceed to transmit their frame(s).

In Ethernet, collisions can be detected as they happen, and recovery (a binary exponential backoff procedure) can be initiated immediately. In IEEE 802.11, there is no way to detect a collision immediately, so the penalty for not detecting it is more severe, in that it takes more time to initiate corrective measures. Therefore, in IEEE 802.11's MAC sub-layer access method, the binary exponential backoff mechanism is applied *before* a STA attempts to transmit. If a STA believes it is next in line to use the medium, it will still randomize the start if its frame, in an effort to avoid a collision. Once the frame is under way, the other STAs in range of this one should perform their Carrier Sense (i.e., listen-before-talk) procedure and detect a transmission already in progress. If the random backoff were not implemented prior to transmitting, it would be virtually guaranteed that every time the medium went idle, there would be a collision. There are other mechanisms that are used to help control access to the medium, but the Collision Avoidance backoff is one of the more straightforward to understand.

Because IEEE 802.11 relies on simplex radios, the STAs cannot hear a collision while it is occurring. Why wouldn't requiring duplex radios solve the problem? The main reason not to require duplex-capable radios is the hidden node problem. Even if a STA *could* hear the medium as it was transmitting, it may be out of range of the STA with which it is interfering. The only place that interference is important is at the *receiver* of the frame. It is quite irrelevant to enable the sender to detect collisions, because the one device that can absolutely detect the collision is the receiver, and it needn't be burdened with a duplex radio to detect a collision. It will simply begin receiving a frame and never find a valid FCS during the frame's stated Duration.

This is one of the reasons for the hop-wise acknowledgment that is built into IEEE 802.11's MAC sub-layer access protocol. When a STA sends a frame to another STA, the frame is sent to the AP, which ACKs the frame. The sender can re-transmit if the ACK is not received. One might presume that the ACK mechanism confers some degree of reliability, but this is not the case. It is simply a way of validating the conditions that exist at the receiver's location. Without the ACK, the sender has no way of knowing if a collision has occurred. Contrast this with the case of Ethernet, in which a basic assumption of its MAC sub-layer access method is that all stations must be able to detect collisions as they happen, and all stations in a collision domain must be close enough to each other that the farthest two stations can exchange the shortest legal frame and still be able to detect a collision before the frame's transmission is concluded.

Given the likelihood of hidden nodes, there is no good reason to incur the expense of a duplex radio, since many collisions would be undetectable by the sender. To deal with the hidden node problem, the MAC sub-layer access protocol would have to find some way to detect collisions, and even if duplex radios were in use, some form of explicit acknowledgment would probably be required.

How does a collision manifest itself? The effect of the collision is to corrupt the frame such that the receiver cannot determine its complete contents (it might have seen a frame start that had its MAC address as the MAC-RA or MAC-DA, but it would never see an FCS within the stated Duration of the frame). The corruption could even happen early enough in the frame that even the D/I field is mangled, which could give the receiver a very long (or very short) value in the Duration field. Eventually, the sender will give up if it has not heard an ACK, and re-try the transmission.

The ACK is not a reliability enhancer; it is really nothing more than an implicit collision detection mechanism (it's implicit since it's a "no news is bad news" protocol, in which the lack of an ACK implies a collision, or some form of interference that prevented the frame from being successfully received; Ethernet's explicit collision detection mechanism involves actually being able to hear a collision as it happens). When a protocol designer is considering ways to increase reliability, it is indisputable that detecting collisions is an important component of a "reliability" solution. However, a collision detection mechanism alone does not constitute a reliability solution.

Ethernet is widely understood to be an "unreliable" Data Link layer technology. As with IEEE 802.11, that's not completely true. Ethernet's collision detection mechanism is not a reliability mechanism as such, but it *is* used to improve the reliability in half-duplex scenarios. Ethernet's reaction to the detection of a collision is the same as that of an IEEE 802.11 STA that has failed to receive an ACK—the frame is retransmitted after some randomly chosen back-off delay interval. The fact that Ethernet retransmits a frame after a node detects a collision does not make it a reliable Data Link layer protocol. A station could encounter a series of collisions (on a very busy LAN) such that the station can never successfully transmit its frame.

Ethernet's retransmission mechanism doesn't exist to provide reliability—it exists to increase the chances that a frame might get through. The mechanism is a throughput aid, not a reliability aid. IEEE 802.11's ACK mechanism provides the very same function, in a less direct fashion, but in a way that is ideally suited to operation over a WM in which not all nodes are in range of each other. In IEEE 802.11, the *lack* of an ACK serves as the collision detection mechanism, and this is a mechanism that can work in the face of the hidden node issue. Being able to perform collision detection in the presence of hidden nodes is the most important difference between the MAC sub-layer access protocols of Ethernet and IEEE 802.11.

These throughput-enhancing mechanisms do not make any guarantees that the frame will get through. This is an important distinction. Many people's only exposure to ACKs comes in TCP, and TCP is known to be a reliable transport protocol. However, ACKs do not always imply reliability. The unconscious binding of the concept of an ACK with the concept of reliability (because of the familiarity of TCP) is not generalizable to other scenarios.

Why is the ACK mechanism not a "reliable Data Link" mechanism? Certainly, reliable Data Link protocols do exist, and they are commonplace in WAN-oriented Data Link layer protocols; even IEEE 802.2 LLC supports a reliable mode, which is used by SNA when operating over LANs, such as IEEE 802.5 Token Ring. The ACKs in reliable Data Link protocols are end-to-end, not hop-by-hop. The only thing that an IEEE 802.11 STA gains from this ACK mechanism is the awareness that the frame got to the AP. The AP is now free to corrupt, drop, delay, or otherwise mistreat the frame, such that the frame that was received from the sender may never reach its intended destination intact. Effectively, the ACK mechanism in IEEE 802.11's MAC sub-layer access protocol is a "hope-by-hope" technique.

Before digging too deeply, there is a canonical timing diagram that seems obligatory. Figure 6–9 shows the relationships of the important timers defined in IEEE 802.11, including showing the relative lengths of the SIFS, PIFS, and DIFS intervals, and depicting the random backoff window (the contention window). At a minimum, a STA will defer access while the medium is busy, and then for at least a DIFS thereafter. Then, after a suitably chosen random backoff interval (some number of slot times), the STA will finally attempt to transmit its frame.

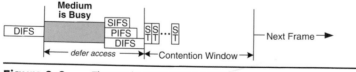

Figure 6–9   Timers in IEEE 802.11 DCF

The SIFS, PIFS, and DIFS timers are all PHY-dependent, as can be seen in Figure 6–10. The PIFS and DIFS are PHY-dependent because they are dependent on the SIFS and the PHY's "slot time." The slot time of a given PHY is a basic attribute of that PHY. The slot time for IEEE 802.11's DSSS PHY is 20 μs, which includes 5 μs for the PHY's Rx/Tx turnaround time and any MAC processing delay associated with its driving the evolution of the state of the medium, and 15 μs for the "energy detect" function (i.e., Clear Channel Assessment), which is taken to be long enough to accommodate the propagation delay between the two stations.

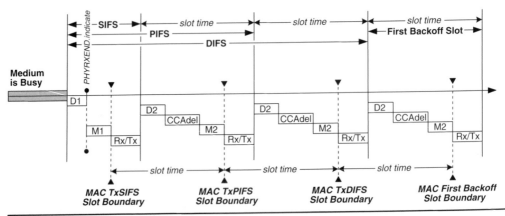

Figure 6–10   Relationship between slot time, SIFS, PIFS, and DIFS

In Figure 6–10, the D1 time interval reflects the time it takes for the PHY to indicate that a frame is complete, after it has received the last symbol from the medium. The D2 interval is the D1 interval plus a propagation delay component. The M1 and M2 intervals represent MAC processing, and are actually identical duration. The CCAdel interval is the CCA interval less the D1 interval. If one studies Figure 6–8, one finds that the slot time is the sum of the PHY Rx/Tx turnaround time, the CCA interval, and the air propagation delay on the medium.

The IEEE 802.11*b*-1999 standard specifies a slot time of 20 μs, with the same timing components as IEEE 802.11-1999. The IEEE 802.11*a*-1999 slot time is 9 μs. In the latter standard, the "energy detect" function is expected to take less than 4 μs, with the remainder of the time (5 μs) allowed for PHY Rx/Tx turnaround time and MAC processing.

Note that the IEEE 802.11*g*-2003 standard allows a "short slot time" option to be used in the 2.4 GHz band, in cases where all STAs in a BSS are based on the ERP-PHY. The optional "short slot time" is 9 μs, which matches the OFDM-based PHY in IEEE 802.11*a*-1999. If this new option is not enabled, the slot time for IEEE 802.11*g*-2003-based devices is 20 μs. This means that IEEE 802.11*g*-based devices will be able to interoperate with other IEEE 802.11 devices incorporating a 2.4 GHz RF PHY; in other words, devices based on either IEEE 802.11-1999 or IEEE 802.11*b*-1999.

A successful frame exchange in DCF is as shown in Figure 6–11, which also shows how the non-involved STAs use their NAVs to do their virtual carrier sense. Virtual carrier sense allows hidden nodes to be equally aware of transmissions that are happening for which either the sender or the receiver is out of range of the hidden node. If there were no possibility for hidden nodes, it is possible that the protocol could get by with only "physical" carrier sense mechanisms.

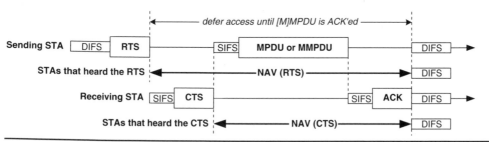

Figure 6–11   Successfully sending an MPDU or MMPDU using DCF

In Figure 6–11, time proceeds to the right. After it has seen previous activity conclude on the medium, the Sending STA waits for a DIFS and sends an RTS. All the STAs in range of the sender will hear its RTS and will use the Duration value in that frame to update their NAVs. That Duration is sufficient to encompass three SIFS intervals, plus the time to transmit a CTS and ACK, and of course the MMPDU or MPDU.

The Receiving STA responds with a CTS frame that is heard by a perhaps disjoint set of STAs, some of which will be out of range of the Sender's radio. The Duration value in the CTS is smaller than that in the RTS. Any STA that heard the RTS will not update their NAV because the IEEE 802.11 DCF procedures dictate that the NAV only be updated in one of two possible conditions.

- The frame[21] must not be addressed to a given STA for it to be able to update its NAV. In other words, the frame on the air must not be meant for a STA if that STA is to use the information in the frame's Duration field to update its NAV.
- The other condition is that a STA only updates its NAV if the received value in a frame's Duration field is greater than the value that the STA already knows.

As can be seen in Figure 6–11, the CTS is sent after a SIFS interval, and then after a second SIFS interval the MPDU or MMPDU is sent, and the ACK is sent after a third SIFS interval. The STAs that were not involved in the conversation, whether they heard the RTS or the CTS, will have their NAVs expiring at approximately the time when the ACK is complete. At that point, after another DIFS interval, a further Contention (i.e., Backoff) Window will begin among any other STA(s) that might have data to send.

The previous discussion can be examined in both the context of infrastructure BSS or IBSS mode. In the case of infrastructure BSS, the AP will be either sending or receiving a frame.

- If the AP is sending a frame, then the AP is the STA that sends the RTS, which means that all the STAs in the BSS will hear the RTS at essentially the same time. There are no hidden nodes with respect to the AP. The CTS will only be heard by the STAs within range of the receiver's radio, but they will not update their NAVs because the Duration field in the CTS is smaller than that in the RTS.
- If the AP is receiving a frame, then it is equivalent to say that another STA is sending a frame. In this case, the AP will hear the RTS, as will all the STAs in range of the sender's radio. The AP will send the CTS, which will be heard throughout the BSS. The Duration field in the CTS will not cause the sender-local STAs to update their NAVs, since the CTS has a smaller Duration value than the RTS.

---

21. The frame that could cause another STA to update its NAV could be any of the following types of frames: RTS, MMPDU, or MPDU.

By using this technique, the DCF procedures make an effort to eliminate hidden nodes from interfering with the operation of the MAC sub-layer's access control protocol.

DCF, PCF, and Timing

There are two levels of timing. One applies at the Beacon level, and applies to Beacons that contain Traffic Indication Message (TIM) IEs. Most timers in IEEE 802.11 are expressed in units of Beacon Intervals, including the STA Listen Interval, which is used by power-saving STAs to express the times when the AP can expect them to be awake, and the DTIM Interval, which is important in PCF mode and DCF mode. The sub-Beacon-Interval timing consists of intervals like SIFS, PIFS, and DIFS.

To control access to the WM, all stations that want to transmit (which have already sensed that the medium is busy) must wait for a time (the DCF Inter Frame Space, or DIFS) before attempting to transmit their frame(s). Even beyond waiting for the medium to be quiet for an entire DIFS interval, the STAs also randomize a backoff internal before sending a frame, just to help further reduce the chance that multiple STAs were waiting for the medium to go quiet and then two or more of them wait exactly one DIFS interval and BANG collide with each other.

There is one exception to the "next station to transmit must wait for the DIFS to expire before transmitting" rule, which is that any station that has just received a frame may transmit an ACK after only waiting for the Short Inter Frame Space (SIFS) interval. This ensures that the ACK will be given the highest priority access to the medium. Similarly, a CTS may be transmitted within one SIFS interval of the corresponding RTS.

When the BSS is operating in DCF mode, the Beacon Interval and the DTIM Interval are the same. In PCF mode, the DTIM Interval may an integer multiple of 2 or more Beacon Intervals, which allows the Point Coordinator in the AP an ample amount of time in which to operate in contention-free (i.e., polling) mode. The CFP begins when the DTIM Interval is at its time-zero point.

The benefit of CFPs is that during CFPs, data may be transmitted on an essentially regular basis, with predictable (bounded) latency. Thus, PCF enables the AP to support time-sensitive services for frames that can benefit from such treatment, such as frames that contain voice and/or video data. The CFPs repeat at a fixed rate that is determined by the AP, which may choose to reserve some portion of the available bandwidth for "isochronous[22]" or "plesiochronous[23]" (fancy words for "time-sensitive) data traffic.

When using this higher priority access, the AP issues polling requests to the stations for data transmission, hence controlling medium access. To still enable regular stations to access the medium, there is a provision that the Point Coordinator must leave enough time for Distributed Access in between the CFPs.

Not all STAs must implement contention-free operation. However, all STAs do need to be able to tell when a Point Coordinator has initiated contention-free operation so they can avoid interfering with the contention-free STAs. All the traffic sent during the CFP is sent with the Duration set to 32,768 (the protocol's version of the concept of infinity), and all the non-PCF STAs will set their NAVs so that they will wait essentially forever until they transmit. When the CFP ends, the AP sends a MAC Control frame,[24] which causes all STAs, PCF or otherwise, to reset their NAVs.

Power-Save Mode

The circuitry that drives the transmit side of the RF subunit draws considerable power even when there is no data to transmit. When there is data to transmit, it draws even more power. The receive-side circuitry also is a constant power

---

22. An isochronous signal is one that depends on some uniform timing, often from an external "clock" source; the timing information could also be embedded in the signal. Two signals that are isochronous should maintain synchronization over long time periods.

23. Two or more signals that are plesiochronous relative to each other have clocks that tick within some defined precision. The signals are not sourced from the same clock and so, over the long term, they will tend to become skewed relative to each other. Their relative closeness of frequency allows a switch to cross connect, switch, or in some way process the signals, but over time, that inaccuracy of timing will force a switch to repeat or delete frames (called frame slip events) in order to handle buffer under- or over-flow.

24. The Point Coordinator in the AP could send either a CF-End frame or a CF-End + CF-ACK frame.

drain, sensing the WM for incoming frames, or even just passing frames (to keep the STA's NAV updated). It is likely that the receive side circuitry's power demands do not vary as much as the transmit circuitry does. To maximize battery life, a reasonable strategy is to shut down all of the RF circuitry periodically. The MAC circuitry will stay awake, because it is the MAC subunit that wakes up the RF subunit in time to be ready for the next DTIM interval. Power-save mode is intimately dependent on the timekeeping functions of the WLAN, driven by the Timestamps in the AP's Beacon frames.

In the IEEE 802.11 specification, a STA that has temporarily shut down its RF circuitry is said to be "dozing." If a STA wants to do this kind of thing, it must tell the AP at association time. In particular, the STA tells the AP how often it will be awake to accept any queued data that is addressed to it. It is up to the STA to be awake when it has promised to be, and after it has received and sent whatever traffic it cares to, it may choose to "doze" until the next time it is obligated to be awake.

Clearly, when a STA is dozing, it can neither send nor receive frames. The latter constraint places a duty on the AP. When the AP knows that a STA is in power save mode, the AP must buffer any frames destined for that STA, so that the STA will not miss anything, although the relative order of multicast and unicast traffic may be affected when the STA wakes up. When a STA enters this mode, it gives up the ability to use the "Strictly Ordered" service that IEEE 802.11 optionally provides, whereby the delivery order of the frames is preserved. Any STAs that want to receive frames using the Strictly Ordered service may never doze. The default mode is known as "Re-orderable Multicast."

The mechanism by which sleeping STAs (sleeping and power save will be synonymous in this discussion; the power save mode of the WLAN STA has nothing to do with the ability of a laptop to enter a low-power "standby" or "hibernation" mode) are awakened is via the DTIM mechanism. In case anyone was wondering why the association IDs (AIDs) were numbered from 1 to 2007, it is because these numbers are used in the DTIM bit mask that is included in the DTIM IE that may be in a Beacon or Probe Response. Every Beacon does not include the DTIM IE...there is a DTIM interval that is a multiple of Beacon intervals that controls how often the DTIM is included in a Beacon frame.

Every Beacon includes a TIM IE. The TIM is used to indicate which STAs have traffic pending for them. The DTIM interval is a number of TIM intervals (a TIM interval is the same as a Beacon interval), and the DTIM contains information on the unicast traffic that is buffered, indicated in a bit-map on a per-AID basis. The TIM IEs in the usual Beacons provide a count-down to the next DTIM, and also indicate if there is any multicast traffic buffered. If any STAs are dozing, they all must wait for any multicasts that the STA receives, since every STA must be awake simultaneously if they want to receive the multicast.

One way this is accomplished is that the STAs join the WLAN and at Asso-ciation time they get to express their desired "Listen Interval." This is the inter-val at which the STA promises to be awake. The Listen Interval is expressed as some number of Beacon intervals, and the DTIM must be larger than the larg-est Listen Interval. Even if a STA expresses a Listen Interval when it joins the WLAN, it need not ever actually enter Power-Save mode. The Listen Interval exists so that if the STA ever does decide to doze, it will wake up at a predictable time and prevent the AP from needing to buffer traffic indefinitely.

Power Management Details

Due to the fact that wireless devices are often mobile devices, and therefore tend to be battery-powered, it is important that a WLAN solution minimize power drain to the maximum extent possible. For example, it would be wasteful of bat-tery power if a laptop were sitting idle for several hours, with nothing to send, but the wireless card was kept ever at the ready to receive (or send) data.

In IEEE 802.11, a station can "doze" after sending a frame, and it can wake up periodically to peek into the AP's Beacon frame to see if the AP is holding a packet for it. It can then wake up, get the packet from the AP, and go back to dozing...unless it has some data of its own to send. The STA tells the AP the rate at which it will promise to be awake (the Listen put in a space Interval), and the AP will buffer traffic for that STA if the STA decides to doze. Just because the STA indicated that it might doze, does not mean that it must doze.

There are degrees of strictness with respect to dozing. In the strictest mode, a STA will enter the "dozing" state every ListenInterval, and any delay in dozing will be due to an in-progress frame exchange running into the time when the

STA might have been dozing. The STA will, in this strict mode, doze as soon as it can, as close as possible to once per Listen put in a space Interval. In a less strict mode, the STA might decide to not doze right away, since it knows it is in the middle of an exchange of data, or it simply knows that it has a significant amount of data queued and ready to transmit. The STA may decide that sending a few extra frames might be okay, as long as it eventually does doze for a while before the next Listen put in a space Interval wakes it up. Finally, a STA may be configured to never doze, regardless of the consequences (i.e., increased power drain).

Power management state transitions are indicated by a bit in the "Frame Control" portion of the MAC header. Obviously, in order to be transmitting a frame, the station has to be awake. A bit in the Frame Control header is used to tell the other stations whether it will stay awake after successfully completing the current frame exchange.[25] If a large number of frames have already been dispatched to the wireless NIC, none of these frames will have had the Power-Save bit set. Therefore, whatever frames are buffered in the driver or hardware will have to drain prior to the station going to sleep. At that point, however, the STA must have something further to say or else it will not be able to doze. This is why there is a "null" Data subtype...a null Data frame can be sent that can trigger a change of state using the Power-Save bit.

Within the FC, which is the first two octets of the IEEE 802.11 MAC header, the "Power Management" state is carried in bit number 12 (the bits are numbered 0–15). A value of 0 indicates that the station will remain active after the current frame exchange, while a value of 1 indicates that the station will enter "power save" mode after the current frame exchange.

Since all traffic must go through the AP, the AP must keep track of which stations are dozing, and buffer the frames destined for those stations. The Beacon frames indicate to the stations when they need to wake up to receive frames that are destined for their MAC address. Observe that APs cannot be permitted to doze. In IBSS mode, it is possible for stations to doze, as long as at least one of them stays awake to send the Beacons. In an IBSS, the STAs use the ATIM MMPDU to indicate that traffic is buffered to a peer STA.

---

25. For unicast packets, the ACK from the receiving or destination station is considered part of this frame exchange, and the sending station will not go to sleep until it has received the ACK. After all, if the ACK is not received, the frame will need to be retransmitted.

Every Beacon frame has a TIM IE. The TIM IEs use a bit mask to indicate which Association IDs have buffered traffic. Association ID number zero is reserved to mean that multicast traffic is buffered. When any STA dozes, the multicast traffic in the BSS is only transmitted once per DTIM interval. Since multicasts can only be sent once per DTIM Interval, it is important that all the STAs be awake when this happens. In PCF mode, multicast traffic will be burstier than in DCF mode, in which it can come out at least as often as once per Beacon Interval (the only time that the multicasts are buffered is when at least one STA is dozing). If no STAs are dozing, multicasts are sent in essentially the order they are received.

In any BSS mode, an optional additional layer of control is possible, via the PCF, or "Point Coordination Function." If supported,[26] PCF is only active at one "point" in the network—the AP—as opposed to the Distributed Coordination Function, which is active simultaneously (distributed) in all the stations of a BSS.

When PCF is active, time is divided into two types of alternating periods: the CFP, and the Contention Period (CP). CFPs are only possible if PCF is active in the AP. The PCF makes use of a smaller PCF Inter Frame Space (PIFS) so that the AP can gain access to the medium before other stations, effectively giving the AP a higher priority.

Summary

The topics of medium access, MAC timing, power saving, fragmentation, and retransmission, are all inter-related. This can cause considerable confusion, since it is often difficult to remember which rule trumps another in a given situation. In this chapter, we have seen all the important bits and perhaps also exposed the reader to the complexity, in that the pieces are all inter-dependent and it is often necessary to mention special cases while trying to describe the "main mode" of operation.

---

26. PCF support is not mandatory in the IEEE 802.11 specification. IEEE 802.11e support, which may be shipping in many products sometime in 2004, pending approval of the IEEE 802.11e standard, will make QOS-enhanced operation available to more people.

DCF is that main mode, and it embodies the CSMA/CA access control protocol and a slew of timing-related rules. PCF is optional, and allows for polling-oriented access managed by an entity in the AP known as the Point Coordinator. PCF is built on DCF, and leverages mechanisms in the Beacon to control when CFPs begin. Only STAs that are capable of CF operation can participate in the CFP, and the rest of the STAs' NAVs are updated so they do not attempt to contend for the medium while the AP is in polling mode.

7

Security Mechanisms for Wireless LANs

There is much to learn about security as it pertains to IEEE 802.11 WLANs. Beginning this year, and continuing over the next several years, it appears that new WLAN products will be emerging that will attempt to prove that it is possible to truly secure a wireless infrastructure in a meaningful way, but as of yet, such a feat is effectively impossible. To be precise, it is currently impossible to achieve security for WLAN traffic using only MAC-layer techniques.

What is security anyway? When that word is used in the context of computer networks, it typically refers to a number of related services, among them authentication (for users and data), authorization (access control, which derives from authentication), and encryption (for confidentiality, or protecting data from being viewed by unintended third parties).

In networking, security is applicable at many layers. For example, a file system on a computer may be secure (e.g., encrypted), so that if someone stole the hard disk, he or she would not be able to read the data on it. Network devices, from switches and routers to terminal servers and file servers are typically protected by access control, to limit who can manage them, or to limit who can access them.

Users are familiar with logging on to a file server. This is a form of access control, but not all access control schemes are equally strong (some send the password in the clear across the network). It is even possible (commonplace, in fact) to "tunnel" a secure session across an insecure medium, which is what Virtual Private Network protocols (VPNs) do to safely extend the security perimeter of a private network to a remote user.

In the context of WLANs, security applies to access control (allowing only valid users to join the WLAN), mutual authentication (so the STA can be sure it is talking to a legitimate AP, and vice versa), and encryption (so the traffic on the air is unreadable by eavesdroppers). The encryption is enabled by the key distribution mechanism(s), since encryption is not possible without keys; ideally, keys are randomly chosen and securely exchanged, and only used once.

Introduction to Wireless LAN Security

Security at the Data Link layer is not a new topic. It has gotten a lot of press recently in the context of WLANs, but the IEEE 802.11 WG is only the latest subgroup of IEEE 802.11 to address the concept of security at the Data Link layer. The IEEE LMSC (a.k.a. Project 802) created the IEEE 802.10 WG in May 1988 and tasked it to create the Standard for Interoperable LAN/MAN Security (SILS). The introduction to the *IEEE 802.10-1998* standard states very clearly when[1] and why the WG was created.[2]

> The IEEE 802.10 Working Group was formed in May of 1988 to address the security [of] LANs and MANs. It is sponsored by the IEEE LAN/MAN Standards Committee (LMSC). The working group currently has representation from vendors and users of security technology, and previously has also had representation from the government and general interest communities. The standard is an interoperability standard that is compatible with the existing IEEE 802 and OSI architectures.
>
> Data networks, especially LANs and MANs, have become widespread. LANs and MANs are used by both industry and government for transferring vast amounts of information in the course of daily operations. Because of their ever-increasing use in the private and public sectors, the capabilities of these networks are being expanded to encompass more and more performance requirements. As a result, there is the growing

---

1. Note that this standard took 10 years to develop. Security standards are notoriously difficult to complete.

2. This passage is excerpted from IEEE Std. 802.10-1998 (copyright 1998). All rights reserved.

need to standardize network protocols wherever feasible, to ensure that data networks will interoperate effectively.

As standardization practices evolve, several key areas will become critically important. One of these areas is network security. Many LANs and MANs require the capability to exchange data in a secure manner. This is especially important in cases where disclosure of operational information to unauthorized parties would severely undermine an organization's effectiveness. It is often as critical to protect the integrity of the data as it is to prevent disclosure of operating information.

Financial and government institutions have traditionally been most aware of the importance of security. However, recent widely publicized cases of computer fraud and related crimes have made security a goal for many other industries as well. As the need for security on LANs and MANs gains recognition, the need for a standardized approach to providing such a capability also becomes a priority. Much security standardization has already been started. Where applicable, this standard attempts to incorporate this work.

The author is not aware of any LAN products that include implementations of IEEE 802.10's security mechanisms. However, the demand for products that incorporate security is present, and seems to be growing, as evidenced by the many different ways that exist to provide security services for networks.

The IEEE 802.10 WG was created because LANs and MANs do have some unique properties that distinguish them from point-to-point or point-to-multipoint WAN technologies. The chief difference, from a security perspective, is that the LANs and MANs may operate over a shared medium (frequently, these media are referred to as being "broadcast-capable," as opposed to WAN technologies, which are either point-to-point[3], or point-to-multipoint[4]), and it is

---

3. The best example of a point-to-point Data Link protocol is the IETF's Point-to-Point Protocol (PPP). Another such protocol is cisco's proprietary High-level Data Link Control (HDLC)-based serial line protocol. Various other point-to-point framing protocols have been invented over the years…it is even possible to send Ethernet frames over point-to-point WAN links.

4. Examples of point-to-multipoint media include X.25, frame relay, and Asynchronous Transfer Mode (ATM).

possible that traffic may be seen by a station even though it was not addressed to that station.

There are a number of reasons for this. First, in the case of a shared-medium LAN, such as half-duplex Ethernet ("classic Ethernet"), all stations will hear all the frames (but they only process frames that match certain filters based on a given frame's MAC Destination Address). It is a requirement of Ethernet's medium access control protocol (CSMA/CD) that a station be able to defer transmission of a frame if it detects that another station is transmitting. In effect, the protocol depends—at its lowest level—on the ability to eavesdrop on the medium. Moreover, a station that is transmitting must be able monitor the medium as it is transmitting, in order to determine if another station has collided with its transmission. Both of these "features" require that each station be able to detect *all* the traffic on the shared medium.

Moreover, in any bridged LAN, the first time a frame is sent to a MAC address, it may need to be broadcast (in the most literal interpretation of the word) across the LAN since the location of that MAC address has not yet been learned (once a bridge sees a frame from any new MAC Source Address, it remembers on which interface that MAC address was seen, so that future frames to that MAC address can be delivered only to the interface that is known to lead toward the actual location of that MAC address. Another aspect of bridged topologies is that any multicast or broadcast traffic that is sent by a station may be flooded to all the ports in the LAN.

The most popular[5] LAN technology, Ethernet, has evolved to the point where the most common access device is a switch, to which each attached station has direct, dedicated access (i.e., a wire, patched through to a locked closet where the wire attaches to a port on an Ethernet switch). In the beginning, however, Ethernet was a shared-medium protocol in which each station attached to a broadcast-capable bus comprised of coaxial cable, or a slightly evolved version of the bus, in which the bus was buried inside a network hub, allowing the convenience of star-wiring, but logically identical to a physical coaxial cable. In the shared mode, Ethernet was equivalent to a data-oriented party line. There was no privacy. As Ethernet evolved to be switch-based, the

---

5. For the moment, we will define popularity in terms of installed base, not in terms of desirability. It is clear that many people at the moment desire WLANs, but not necessarily to the exclusion of wired LANs.

traffic that a given station would see would be primarily only addressed to it, since the switch is a bridge, and it learned the station's MAC address.

An Ethernet switch isn't a perfect filter, since as mentioned previously, a station may see the occasional unknown-destination unicast frame that was broadcast (flooded) by the switch in an attempt to find the station to which the frame had been addressed. In general, though, the switch provides a weak level of privacy, in that each station cannot typically overhear the conversations between other stations. Eliminating eavesdropping is a significant advance in security, and it provides a very minimal level of privacy (the proper term is actually "confidentiality") due to physically separating the traffic.

Contrast the current state of the art in Ethernet bridging (i.e., layer-2 switching), where minimal confidentiality is an essential by-product of using the technology, with the fundamentally shared aspects of the WM, and we see a completely different situation. Within the range of its receiver, an IEEE 802.11 STA can hear everything that is transmitted by any other STA. The frame may be encrypted, which coverts the data portion of the frame into random-looking "noise" that only makes sense to someone who possesses the necessary decryption key.

However, the header of the MPDU is observable by all STAs, and the header's Duration/Identification field is used by the sending STA to indicate the amount of time it expects to use the medium, including both the time to transmit the frame and to receive the corresponding ACK, so that the other STAs can update their NAVs and know to remain quiet until that frame/ACK exchange is complete. The other STAs can remain quiet even if the data that is being sent is encrypted such that they cannot understand it. The fact that all the STAs can hear at least the headers of all frames is a basic unalterable fact of WLAN technology today.[6] The only way to prevent unwanted eavesdropping is to perform some sort of encryption of the frame's data, preferably using keys that are only known to a given (sender, receiver) pair. Such a key is known as a *pairwise* key.

It is fair to say that the state of the art in WLANs today, with respect to eavesdropping, is equivalent to where Ethernet was before the early 1990s, when high-speed multiport bridges (i.e., layer-2 switches) began to appear.

---

6. It is possible that a wireless equivalent to wired bridging (i.e., layer-2 switching) will be invented in the future, but no such technology exists today. However, even if there *were* a way to dedicate a frequency, or a time slot, to a given STA, that would still not prevent eavesdropping.

Security and the OSI Model

Network security encompasses several orthogonal services, including user authentication, message authentication, and confidentiality, which may be used together or separately. Authentication is a term that has at least two meanings in the context of network security.

One type of "authentication" in network protocols involves the use of cryptographic techniques to "sign" a message, in such a way that only the signing party could have sent it. Certain applications only need to know that the message has not been altered in transit, and it is not important to keep the "protected" messages secret. In such cases, the application programmer, or the person who has deployed and configured the system, has deemed that the application is not vulnerable to eavesdropping. The message authentication service can be used to provide for services such as non-repudiation, to guarantee that only a person who knew the key could have sent a given message. In practical terms, non-repudiation can never be proven, since if I were accused of sending a digitally signed packet, my logical defense would be to assert that my key had been compromised and that someone else had actually sent the message.

The "protocols" that provide message authentication are primarily one-way hash functions, also known as message digest functions. The output of such functions is variously called an Integrity Check Value (ICV), or a Message Integrity Code (MIC) or a Message Authentication Code (MAC), depending on the context. Examples of such algorithms will be given later in this chapter. The input to such functions typically consists of the data to be protected, plus a key (or a number derived from a key), so that only someone with knowledge of the key could have computed the resulting hash value. Without using a *keyed* hash function, anyone could save a copy of a valid frame, change the data, and re-compute a hash value that matches the new data. Such a fabricated frame would be accepted by the receiver if the only validity check was to verify the hash value.

Another aspect of authentication is used to determine how and when users may access a network and its resources. Via a suite of protocols and services known collectively as Authentication, Authorization, and Accounting (AAA), authorized users may be allowed access to a network and its resources. The AAA function is so important that (as of early 2003[7]) the IETF has an entire WG devoted to standardizing just these related aspects of security.

---

7. In the IETF, a WG only exists long enough to solve whatever problem(s) it was created to solve. Once a solution is at hand, the WG is typically disbanded.

Functionally, many AAA protocols have their roots in performing network access control functions for dial-up point-to-point networks. For example, a user of a certain ISP must be identified as a valid customer before he or she will be granted access to the ISP's network. The user might dial in to any of a number of the ISP's Network Access Servers (NAS; e.g., dial-in access concentrators), which all must be able to tell if this user is valid. The NAS devices rely on AAA protocols to provide an interface to a networked database of userIDs and their associated credentials. This networked database enables each NAS device to validate any user at any time, without needing to keep its own local copy of the entire credentials database.

The protocols most commonly associated with AAA services are the Remote Access Dial-In User Service (RADIUS; RFC-2865) and Diameter (not an acronym; a new protocol that some people think will eventually supplant RADIUS), but other protocols such as the Common Open Policy Service (COPS; RFC-2748) and the Simple Network Management Protocol (SNMPv3; STD-62; RFCs 3411 – 3418) may also be employed.

Early (proprietary) protocols in this space included Terminal Access Controller Access Control System (TACACS) and TACACS+, both of which were defined by cisco systems and supported on many vendors' terminal servers, and they were also used to protect access to terminal-oriented applications, such as the user interfaces of routers, and to provide access control for terminal servers. These early protocols, and many of their progeny, were used to provide a common interface by which various devices could query a server that contained user-based credentials (at a minimum, this would be a database of userIDs and their associated passwords). The follow-on protocols (e.g., RADIUS and Diameter) were improvements in the degree of extensibility and in the set of services that were offered (e.g., secure exchanges with the back-end AAA server(s)) to remove the chance of a man-in-the-middle attack—rogue users could masquerade as an authentication server once they have observed an unprotected protocol exchange between the authentication server and any network access device.

The deployment of protocols such as RADIUS was driven by the fact that all of a network's Network Access Servers[8] (NAS devices) needed to have access to the complete set of userIDs and authentication credentials. Now, if a corporation had only one such NAS device, there would be no need for RADIUS or its

---

8. The first example of such devices was access concentrators for dial-up modems.

friends, since the access concentrator would be able to store all that information locally (if it had adequate storage space, that is). However, once the organization deploys their second access concentrator, they will have to keep an up-to-date list of all the userIDs and related credentials on both concentrators. After all, they do not know to which concentrator the user will dial. Any organization that has more than a handful of access concentrators would benefit from being able to split the userID/credential management from the management of the access concentrators. That is one role of AAA protocols, to provide NAS devices with a common interface to a back-end database of user credentials. Any user can dial in to any NAS device, and be an equally valid user on every device to which he or she connects.

The IEEE 802.1X-2001 standard leveraged this back-end infrastructure in the context of the "Port-Based Network Authentication" standard. In many ways, Ethernet bridges (i.e., layer-2 switches) are like dial-up NAS devices, since the user is connected by a point-to-point link. If it supports IEEE 802.1X, an Ethernet bridge (i.e., layer-2 switch) can use the same back-end authentication database that already existed to support the dial-up users to determine if a user has a legitimate right to access a given network. In fact, if they already had a dial-up account, the IT department may not need to do anything to create new records for this user in the AAA database. The IEEE 802.1X-2001 standard does not mandate RADIUS support, but that is a protocol that is commonly employed in today's networks. Newer protocols (e.g., Diameter) may eventually displace RADIUS for the server-side (i.e., back-end) authentication engine functionality.

OPEN ACCESS NETWORK REQUIREMENTS

It's interesting to note that the reason why IEEE 802.1X was developed was to support network authentication for IEEE 802.3-based network access from shared places like computer labs and conference rooms (e.g., at universities) so that only valid users could access the network from those locations. This type of access control is also useful in corporate settings to ensure that only valid users can attach to the corporate network. However, it turns out that there was a big ease-of-use problem with the wired public-access usage scenario, in that users needed to drag along a patch cable in order to connect to the network. In addition, there was a non-trivial capital expenditure involved in wiring a classroom, dormitory, lecture hall, or library with network jacks. The primary source of the expense was (and is) the wiring itself, and the labor to install it, since the cost per port of Ethernet switches (bridges) has dropped so low as to be negligible when budgeting for such a project.

The need for access in public spaces, and in classrooms, was great, but in a practical sense, the usability of this form of "mobile" computing just wasn't suited to the requirements. The laptops were indeed mobile, but they were anchored to these network jacks, which constrained movement to within a small radius around the jack, dependent on the length of the user's patch cord.

It's ironic that the real demand for IEEE 802.1X-based authentication (and key management) has come from a LAN technology that was in its infancy when the IEEE 802.1X TG was completing its work. There are a few cursory mentions of IEEE 802.11 in the IEEE 802.1X-2001 standard, but it almost certainly would have been written differently if the TG had known that the "killer app" for their technology was going to be IEEE 802.11, not IEEE 802.3. (It is not the case that the authors of IEEE 802.1X would have known in 2001 that their technology was going to become the basis for the future authentication and key management schemes in IEEE 802.11, since at the time, the degree to which IEEE 802.1X was going to be leveraged was unknown.)

The design center for IEEE 802.1X authentication was clearly switched (i.e., bridged) IEEE 802.3 wired LANs. The operation of IEEE 802.1X to provide secure authentication and secure key exchange in shared media LANs was not thoroughly described. This is why the IEEE 802.11*i* TG has had to specify things like the four-way handshake...there was no secure way to do authentication or key exchange in shared-media LANs, especially shared-media LANs in which eavesdropping is absolutely trivial.

The need for user authentication is just as legitimate in a LAN scenario as it is in a dial-up WAN scenario. The use of IEEE 802.1X is not limited to Ethernet; it can be used with any LAN technology, although it is not particularly well-suited to operation over shared-media LANs such as IEEE 802.11. The IEEE 802.11*i* TG has needed to enhance the base IEEE 802.1X protocol(s) to support secure user authentication over a shared medium LAN.

Finally, confidentiality service is typically provided by using cryptographic algorithms to encrypt the data, using either secret-key (properly called "symmetric" algorithms) or public-key ("asymmetric") algorithms. In the former type of algorithm, there is a key exchange that limits knowledge of the key to the parties that negotiated it. In the latter type of algorithm, each party has a public and private key, and the public key is made available to anyone who wants to communicate with this party.

By virtue of some deceptively simple arithmetic, the party that possesses the private component of the key can encrypt data that can only be decrypted with the public component of the key, and vice versa: the public key can be used to encrypt the key such that only the holder of the private key can decrypt it. Because this cryptosystem uses two different keys—one of which is public, earning it the moniker "public key" cryptography—to establish a cryptographic "connection" between two machines,[9] it is also known as an "asymmetric" cryptosystem, since it uses different keys in each direction. Symmetric cryptosystems use only one key for a connection, and the key must be kept secret since anyone with possession of the key can decrypt the data.

Despite the apparent advantages of public-key cryptography, the one important quality that it lacks is speed. In most real cryptosystems, public key cryptography is used to establish a connection and to derive a symmetric session key, which is then used to encrypt and decrypt data with high performance. Public key cryptosystems, as they are usually known, implicitly provide a certain level of authentication (provided that the private keys are kept secret...if they are compromised, then whoever knows the private key can impersonate the user who is properly associated with the public key).

In secret-key ciphers, one key may serve only two parties, in which case it is known as a "pairwise" key, or it could be used by multiple parties, in which case it is known as a "shared" key. The terms "pairwise" and "shared" are generally used in the context of unicast confidentiality, whereas multicast or

---

9. More formally, such a cryptographic connection is often referred to as a "security association."

broadcast traffic is generally protected by a "group" key. It is possible that a pair of stations may be in possession of a pairwise and a group key at the same time, using the appropriate key based on the type of traffic that is being sent at any given instant.

There are many types of secret-key algorithms, including stream-oriented and block-oriented ciphers. The best example of a stream-oriented cipher is RC4, while examples of block-oriented ciphers are the Data Encryption Standard (DES), Triple-DES, and the Advanced Encryption Standard (there are many others as well).

The degree of control over which data is encrypted, and how it is encrypted, varies with the layer at which encryption is performed. In general, it can be assumed that each layer in the OSI model has had some form of security service defined. Typically, real systems will only apply security protection to a small number of layers, depending on the application's requirements. Moreover, certain services (e.g., message authentication) may be a better fit at certain layers than at others.

The Physical Layer

For decades (i.e., since the mid-1970s, at least), there have been Physical layer devices that organizations such as banks and governments used to encrypt sensitive or valuable data over point-to-point links. For example, a Physical layer security device might be designed to encrypt an entire bit stream between two WAN (typically) devices, one bit at a time, including any null data that may be transferred between actual data frames.

There is not necessarily any ability to encrypt only the most sensitive portions of the data stream, or even to limit the encryption to only data frames, and not the inter-frame null data that is often present to maintain clock synchronization. In some cases, it may actually be preferable to simply encrypt the entire bit stream, since an observer would not be able to tell the difference between an idle line and a line that was carrying protected data. To an encryption device operating at the Physical layer, all bits are probably equally important. As one considers progressively higher layers in the protocol stack, one observes increasingly finer control over how data will be encrypted, and over which data will be encrypted.

The Data Link Layer

At the Data Link layer, a device may be able to limit encryption within an entire LAN, or only among a set of MAC addresses. Optionally, it may be possible to protect broadcast and multicast frames differently than unicast frames. Note, however, that the frames cannot be completely encrypted, since the header at the front must be preserved (otherwise, the MAC addresses would not be available to the intermediate bridges (i.e., layer-2 switches), and even an end device would never be able to tell that a frame was meant for it).

Historically, encryption at the Data Link layer has not been much of an issue, since there are probably many router hops between a sender and receiver, and protecting each hop individually is not feasible. Furthermore, since every intermediate device would have to have the ability to decrypt the data it receives (so it can be re-encrypted on the outgoing interface), each of the intermediate devices is also effectively a wiretap, since it has access to the unencrypted frames.

The reason why this chapter is in this book, however, is that WLANs are a new form of LAN that is inherently shared, and fundamentally vulnerable to eavesdropping. In the original IEEE 802.11 specification, the standard specified a set of algorithms known as Wired-Equivalent Privacy (WEP), which was not designed to provide bulletproof protection; rather, the designers were only attempting to make eavesdropping on WLANs approximately as difficult as on wired LANs.

As we will see later, for a variety of reasons, WEP turned out to be an inadequate solution to that problem, and a new security paradigm is being finalized that will hopefully provide a trustworthy foundation for WLANs. The goal is to make WLAN security literally robust, which will actually supersede the security of a wired LAN in some ways.

Security in other LAN media is becoming an increasingly interesting topic, since the IEEE 802.3*ah* (Ethernet in the First Mile) group needs some sort of security to prevent their point-to-multipoint Ethernet-based access networks from leaking frames. Without security at the Data Link layer, it would be possible for a given customer to receive data that was meant for another customer. The IEEE LMSC Sponsor Executive Committee (SEC) has convened a Link Security Study Group to consider whether it would be worthwhile to define a security architecture that would apply uniformly across all LAN media; as of the March 2003 timeframe, this Executive Committee Study Group was moved into IEEE 802.1 WG. (The IEEE 802.10 standard may or may not be sufficient for this purpose; however, that WG is in a state that the IEEE LMSC refers to as "hibernation," which limits it to servicing interpretation requests made regarding the IEEE 802.10 standard(s) it has produced. As it was in this dormant state, there was not any active membership that could have worked on the new security architecture.)

The Network Layer

IP operates at the Network layer, and for IP, the Internet Protocol Security (IPSec) suite of protocols enables encryption between IP addresses (IPSec works with either IPv4 or IPv6), and supports authentication, either integrated with encryption or alone. In conjunction with the Layer 2 Tunneling Protocol (L2TP), or in conjunction with IP-over-IP tunneling or IPsec "tunnel mode" tunneling, IPsec may be used to provide VPN services.

At the Network layer, it is possible to encrypt traffic between two IP addresses, either for all traffic between them, or perhaps only for certain TCP- or UDP-based Application-layer protocols (although this filtering based on Transport-layer port is not, strictly, a Network layer operation, the encryption is carried out at the Network layer). As with the Data Link layer, the Network layer header information must be exposed to public view so that the packet can be properly delivered. However, at the Network layer, the situation is slightly more complex, since the Network layer header may contain certain "mutable" fields, which is a fancy word for "changeable," and these fields must be protected differently[10] compared to "immutable" fields, such as the Network layer Source and Destination addresses, which may not change en route. Some Data Link layer protocols also have mutable headers, and if they must be protected, then the Data Link layer encryption algorithms will be designed to do so.

The exact definition of which Network layer header fields are mutable and which are immutable will differ between various Network layer protocols, but any security applied at the Network layer will need to accommodate the differences between mutable and immutable header fields. In the case of IPsec, the

---

10. A field like the Time to Live (TTL) is expected to change in transit. Each hop decrements it. This is normal, and a security algorithm should not fail if the TTL at the destination is different than it was at the source. There are other fields in the Network layer header that are also mutable, but the easiest one to describe is the TTL field.

Authentication header protects the immutable fields by including them as input to its message digest calculation. If any of these fields change, or if the data itself is modified in transit—even by only a single bit—then the receiver's calculated integrity check value (ICV) will not match the ICV that was included in the packet after being calculated by the sender.

The Transport Layer

Many people use VPNs that are effectively unprotected packets tunneled through Secure Shell (SSH) connections, at the Transport layer. The security negotiations and the resulting encryption are provided by the VPN protocol itself, but the application being tunneled is unaware of the tunnel (except, perhaps being aware that the MTU of that link is smaller than it otherwise might be, due to the presence of the VPN header(s) that were added to the packet).

Other security schemes at the Transport layer include standards such as the Secure Sockets Layer (SSL) or its progeny Transport Layer Security (TLS), which provide for application-driven security services, for example to protect passwords or credit card information when accessing a secure Web site. At the Transport layer, one can employ SSL/TLS to enable encryption of entire sessions, or perhaps just to protect the information that the application developer believes should be kept confidential.

The Application Layer

When the application dictates the usage of encryption, it is likely to be applied judiciously—only where it is needed, whereas lower-layer approaches tend to be increasingly heavy-handed as one descends the protocol stack, and encrypt data as if it were all equally important. Taken to the extreme, Physical layer devices encrypt every bit that goes onto the wire.

In some cases, networked applications may include encryption and/or authentication services as an integral part of their operation. In general, while it is probably true that an application developer best knows the requirements for protecting (certain parts of) the application's data, and while it is probably also true that the security protection at the Application layer can be far better targeted at exactly what needs to be protected, it is unfortunately sadly true that the application programmer may not have adequate expertise in network security to put together a solid security architecture for his or her application.

From a user's perspective, the most familiar instance of an Application-layer security protocol would probably be "secure HTTP" (in a URL, the customary "http://..." is replaced by "https://..." for those Web sites that are protected by SSL encryption[11]). Any time you buy something on the Web, or log in to manage your checking account, the URL is probably indicating secure HTTP. When https is in use, the "padlock" icon in the Web browser is typically in the closed position. Whether or not https is an Application-layer protocol (http) that is simply taking advantage of Transport-layer security mechanisms (i.e., SSL or TLS), or is its own secure Application-layer protocol is mostly a semantic question. From the user perspective, https certainly appears to be a secure Application-layer protocol, and interpreting it that way is completely legitimate.

Well-known encryption and message digest algorithms are not likely to be broken, since they have been subjected to extensive peer review. Most attacks on networked applications manage to find the weakest part of the *system* and exploit that weakness. Systems with random number generators that were insufficiently random have been compromised. Attacks have been successfully mounted against systems with weak authentication schemes (strong authentication technology can be deployed in risky ways). Systems that make poor choices of keys and initialization vectors have been breached. The list goes on. People have written entire books on the weaknesses of various systems, detailing how they have been exploited.

The state of the art in network security has advanced quite far (although perfection is probably an unobtainable goal), but there are no guarantees that a programmer will put together the pieces in a way that has no weaknesses (obvious or subtle), or that a network manager will unwittingly deploy the system's components in a way that leaves the system vulnerable to attack. The fact is that most security systems are not broken directly. It is usually far easier to compromise a key than it is to break through a door. One might imagine that network security is one aspect of the construction of a structure, perhaps an exceptionally nice, well-balanced hammer. The fact that a superb hammer was used to build a structure is irrelevant if poor-quality nails and wood were used. In security, the whole system needs to be securely designed and securely deployed (and securely operated) to create the desired barrier to attack.

---

11. SSL was invented by Netscape. The IETF created Transport-Layer Security (TLS), a standards-based version of SSL, effectively.

A W0rd 0n P@ssw0rdz

From an end-user's perspective, the main (only?) difference between a system with security and a system without security is often just a password. Behind the scenes, there are many ways that a system can be secured, but these ways are most often invisible to end users. End users only see the user interface that prompts them for their userID and password, or whatever credentials are required for access to a system (e.g., smart cards, biometrics (e.g., retina or fingerprint scans), etc.), but those forms of credentials are far less common than the password. Unfortunately for the system operators, most people tend to be very bad at choosing passwords. Therefore, the security aspects (e.g., encryption protocols, authentication algorithms, etc.) of the secured system are not its weakest link; rather, the weak link is the user's inability to choose good passwords.

Imagine that the system administrator has designed a very secure system, loaded with strong encryption and all sorts of access controls, perimeter defenses, physical access control, and so forth, but has users who can't remember their passwords, so they leave them written on a scrap of paper kept strategically near their monitors. Now imagine a security-conscious individual who builds a house with solid steel walls, Kevlar windows, and an alarm system with motion detectors, then surrounds the house with thorny shrubbery, and a moat, and installs a high-tech door that is quite like the door to a bank vault, but whose teenager then forgets to lock the door when he goes out. Just as a parent would be really frustrated if they suffered a burglary simply because someone left their door unlocked, the system administrator would also be frustrated (at best!). In the case of system administrators, they could lose their jobs if they had spent tons of cash creating the perfect security for a system, and then the system was cracked.

Passwords should be easy to remember and difficult or impossible for others to guess. Best practices dictate that a password should be relatively long (at least six characters, preferably longer), contain a mixture of letters, numbers, and non-alphanumeric characters, be difficult or impossible to guess, and be only associated with one userID on one system at any given time. Moreover, it should be changed frequently. Unfortunately, end users (being human) have difficulty remembering a large number of different random-looking passwords.

What ends up happening is that end users keep "cheat sheets" to help them remember their passwords. In short, they write them down, creating the opportunity for others to find them—either accidentally or on purpose. Once a user's password has been compromised, anyone who knows that user's password can log in to the system as that user. After logging in to a system, a cracker can use numerous tools to elevate his or her privileges, and to extract useful information from the system. What's worse is the phenomenon of password re-use, in which an end user simplifies his or her life by using as few as one password on many systems. If a cracker manages to find that password, he or she doesn't have to work as hard.

Some end users are conscientious, and they *do* use different passwords on different systems. However, there are very few users that don't need to keep some form of record of which passwords are valid on which systems, especially since passwords typically have a fixed lifetime after which they are no longer valid. Moreover, some users have so many accounts on so many different systems that even the most security-conscious end user can be overwhelmed. It is not unheard of for people to keep an electronic file on one of their computers that lists all their userIDs and passwords. If an attacker manages to get this file, his or her workload is greatly reduced.

Even without finding a user's cheat sheet, it is usually not difficult to guess someone's password. If you know anything about a person, you can make a few guesses and have a reasonable chance of successfully logging in. Names of their children, spouse, their own name (perhaps written backwards), important birthdays, anniversaries, and other easily guessable personal data are typically chosen as passwords. The password "password" is seen far too frequently, and this sort of thing gives system administrators heartburn.

Imagine how frustrating this must be to IT managers—no matter how strongly they protect the payroll system (or any other business-critical system), it is vulnerable to malicious use if any of its users keep their system password on their computer in written or electronic form. If someone (an attacker) can manage to break in to an end-user's desktop machine, the payroll system has been compromised. Keep in mind that over two-thirds[12] of all corporate "cracking[13]"

---

12. Some studies have reported a higher fraction than this, so consider two-thirds to be the lower bound.

13. Such incidents are frequently also referred to as "hacking," but the hacker community (in this case, top-notch programmers) prefers not to be associated with people who deliberately try to gain unauthorized access to systems that they do not own.

incidents are launched from the inside. It is possible (even likely) that the security protecting the desktop machine is also password-based, and so breaking in to a very secure system on which a user has an account might only be as difficult as breaking in to the user's desktop PC.

How Can a User Create a Good Password?

One technique that the author has found useful is to use a telephone keypad as a number/letter substitution device. It is a convenient one-way function that everyone has access to. For example, if an end-user's prototype password is "lucky day," it can be obfuscated by converting the "y" characters to the number 9 (based on the telephone keypad). The letter "l" can be converted to the number 1 due to the resemblance, and the letter "a" can be replaced by the "@" symbol (over time, a user can build up a private list of transformations that make sense; some people convert the letter "o" into the number zero and the letter "l" into the number 1). The resulting password is "1uck9 d@9", which is relatively easy to derive from the phrase that the user can hopefully remember.

End users can even look at a number on the telephone keypad corresponding to the letter in the password that they are trying to obscure and replace the original letter with another one of the letters that are associated with that number on the telephone keypad. In the past, the author has had several passwords that were purely numeric, which were memorable words that had been converted to numbers, again using the mapping on the telephone keypad. For example, under such a transformation, the string

```
"Rumplestiltskin"
```

becomes

```
"786753784587546".
```

If the 1-to-1 substitution had been made, then the resulting string would have been:

```
"786713784187546".
```

An end user would probably not choose a password that long, because it might be difficult to remember such a long string of numbers, but having a private set of transforms that can be applied to a set of easily remembered words (or phrases[14]) might make it possible for the user to remember password(s) without needing to write them down—even if the user has to change passwords fairly frequently (some particularly draconian[15] system administrators may limit passwords to a lifetime of 60 days...*or less!*).

DILBERT reprinted by permission of United Feature Syndicate, Inc.

The way to make the system administrator happy, and keep end users from unwittingly enabling an otherwise secure system to be compromised and misused, is for end users to have some sort of personal system of transforms that they can use to help them derive all their passwords on-the-fly, without needing to have them written down on a cheat sheet.

No matter how fancy the authentication or encryption algorithms protecting a secured system are, if an attacker can obtain a valid userID and password, he or she can log in to a system and do whatever that user is allowed to do, and in addition could use that access to install software to, for example, elevate his or her status from "end user" to "system administrator," and then wreak all kinds of havoc. The attacker could also install "sniffer" software that would capture all the logins and store the userIDs and their associated passwords in a well-hidden

---

14. One technique is to take a favorite quote, such as the line from the Blues Brothers movie "We're on a mission from God," and abbreviate it down to the initial letters; in other words, "woamfg." Then, one can do some other substitutions; for example, change the letter "o" to a zero, and add some punctuation marks, which might produce the following: "*w0amfg!" As this example has shown, the use of phrases in passwords need not be limited to writing them out word for word.

15. Draconian is perhaps a bit harsh. *Security conscious* may be a better term. However, in their well-intentioned effort to make sure that passwords are fresh, they drive some users toward bad habits.

file for later retrieval by the attacker. All the attacker has to do to retrieve the file is to log in again (it's a reasonable assumption that the user will not have changed his or her password in the interim).

The weakness of passwords is legendary in security circles. In truth, any password-based scheme has its limitations. There exist "one-time password" algorithms that can generate a password that is only used once, which removes one of the biggest weaknesses in password-based systems; namely, that people never change them. Even with the best passwords, that consist of random-looking alphanumeric strings, and that are relatively long (10 or more characters), it is still possible to apply the password insecurely. In the WEP scheme that was part of IEEE 802.11-1999, the entire WLAN shares the same key(s). These keys are either 40-bit numbers, or in later products, 104-bit numbers. However, all the STAs must know the keys, and they are effectively static.

This creates problems, since any employees who leave the company can take their knowledge of the keys with them. Since WEP-based WLAN access control amounts to proving that you know the keys, it would be possible for the ex-employees (or anyone that they shared the keys with) to sit in the parking lot and access the WLAN, simply by entering those keys in their wireless STA. Newer WLAN security schemes rely on strong mutual authentication between the STA and the wireless infrastructure, which binds a randomly chosen session key to each individual association. The keys are never re-used, so there is no chance of someone walking away with the key(s). In addition, since the newer schemes are based on user-oriented credentials, it is easy to invalidate those credentials so that the user can not attach to the network again.

Security Is Hard—Network Security or Otherwise

Anecdotally, in the 1960s and 1970s, it became fashionable for wealthy homeowners near Los Angeles to install security systems on the windows and doors of their homes. At first, the burglars simply avoided those houses that had security systems, in favor of ones that had not yet been protected. However, eventually the proportion of houses with security systems got high enough that the burglars were forced to adopt a new approach. They knew that they would not be successful if they tried to enter through a door or window. They also knew that most of these houses were quite isolated from each other. Once they were sure that no one was at home, they simply showed up with a chainsaw and made their own entrance—right through a wall, without setting off the security system.

In general, an attacker will tend toward exploiting the weakest part of a system, similar to the way that electricity always follows the path of least resistance. One difficulty with designing secure *systems* is imagining where all the weaknesses might be. This difficulty applies whether or not we are talking about network security. The best-intentioned system designer might create a set of pieces that, when put together in just the right way, is quite secure. However, the designer is not involved in deploying his or her product, and it is all too easy to compromise a system by cutting a seemingly innocuous corner in the deployment phase. It is too easy to focus on the security aspects individually, and ignore their interaction with the rest of the system. The homeowners who had their walls breached never considered that form of attack in their security design, but by making it much harder to breach the windows and doors, their security system inadvertently made the walls an easier target.

Eventually, the homeowners countered with more advanced security systems that included motion detectors and infrared sensors, which made the system so difficult to bypass that the only reasonable way in became finding out how to turn the system off. There are a number of surprisingly easy ways to obtain this information. A thief could make a phone call and claim to be a representative of the security system vendor doing some sort of remote test (for which the pass code is allegedly needed). The thief could try to bribe the house staff. The thief could even dress up as a repair person and bribe a child who lives in the house. A candy bar might suffice to get the desired information. These types of attacks are known as "social engineering" in the cracker world.

The prospective thief could also simply cut the communications link that the home security system uses to alert the security service's command center when it detects a break-in. If the alarm is going off, but no one knows, the attacker is free to take whatever he or she wants. (To prevent this type of attack, the command center probably should poll every one of its client residences on a fairly regular basis; e.g., once every 90–150 seconds. If the system does not respond, an alarm could be triggered.)

The point of this discussion is that no matter how advanced a system's security is, the easiest strategy for an attacker is to find a way to bypass or nullify the security system entirely, perhaps by finding a way to disable it, or by finding a way to get inside the system in a way that the system believes to be legitimate. In network security, attackers rarely if ever try to break encryption algorithms; they try to find a way to obtain legitimate keys, so they can impersonate a real user.

Complexity is the enemy of security. A quote from C. A. R. Hoare on software design in general applies equally well to security design and deployment:

> *"There are two ways of constructing a software design:*
> *One way is to make it so simple that there are obviously no deficiencies, and the*
> *other way is to make it so complicated that there are no obvious deficiencies.*
> *The first method is far more difficult."*
> —Sir Charles Antony Richard Hoare

Summary of Motivations for WLAN Security

Given that the WM intrinsically enables eavesdropping, there is a natural tendency to want to do something to protect traffic between the STA and AP—so it is at least as confidential as a wired connection to a switch. The only way to accomplish this is to cryptographically manipulate the data such that no other STA can decode the frame (the AP must be able to decrypt traffic from all the STAs[16]).

Given that designers of WLAN protocols and products know that eavesdropping is possible, we must expect that eavesdroppers are present and behave accordingly. This may sound paranoid, but most people would probably say that at least *some* of their data is valuable enough that it is worth taking steps to protect against casual eavesdropping.

I have personally had the experience that my opportunistic downstairs neighbor associated with my AP and was using it as a source of free Internet access. I do not personally have a problem with people setting up mini-ISPs and sharing the cost of a common Internet link among

---

16. The requirement that the AP be able to accept encrypted traffic from each STA implies (at least) pairwise keys. Another arrangement that enables the AP to understand data from each STA is to have all the STAs share the same keying material; however, whenever the keying material is known more widely than necessary, there is increased risk that the keys will be exposed to parties that should not be aware of them.

their friends.[17] I *do* have a problem with someone taking service from me without asking. Therefore, I cut them off by configuring my AP to ignore frames sent from their MAC address. I don't personally have anything on my computers that anyone else would find interesting, but I pay money each month for broadband Internet access, and I'm not a nonprofit mini-ISP.

There have been numerous stories in the press about people driving to parking lots near businesses and using a WLAN card to access the Internet, and even in some cases the corporate network. In one case, a researcher was able to detect wireless LANs from 300 – 500 meters overhead while flying in a small plane (as Dave Barry would say, I am not making this up). Such stories have made it clear that existing wireless LAN deployments are not secure, especially if they do not take measures to protect against unauthorized access. To a certain extent, these stories have probably hindered the growth of the WLAN market, since many companies have almost certainly avoided investing in this technology until the security issues are resolved, or at least substantially improved.

These improvements are, in reality, imminent. The IEEE 802.11 WG created Task Group "*i*" (also known as IEEE 802.11 TG*i*, IEEE 802.11*i*, or simply "TG*i*"), with the objective of enhancing WLAN security beyond what was available in the most recent version of IEEE 802.11, namely IEEE 802.11-1999. On a related front, the Wi-Fi Alliance, in a quasi-standard, has endorsed part of the emerging IEEE 802.11*i* work-in-progress and refers to it as Wi-Fi Protected Access (WPA). WPA extracts the parts of IEEE 802.11*i* that are the most stable; however, due to considerations to be discussed later in the chapter, it is unfortunately not the most secure piece.

However, that compromise represents a tradeoff between enabling vendors to offer significantly improved (but admittedly imperfect) security that could be installed as a firmware upgrade on older hardware, vs. much better security that would require a "forklift upgrade" (i.e., deployment of new hardware). Despite the fact that it is not perfect, WPA is a real improvement over WEP, the security standard that has been part of IEEE 802.11 since IEEE 802.11-1997. WEP

17. The main reason why the author does not have a problem with this is that from the ISP's perspective, their exposure is limited to whatever can fit through just the one link, which is only capable of pulling down content up to the speed of the link, regardless of how many computers are attached to the link. Sure, the ISP would love it if each of those computers had its own access line, or at least was paying a marginal fee, but that's not economically feasible for many people.

and other security protocols pertinent to WLANs will be described in the remainder of this chapter.

Introduction to Wireless LAN Security

There are multiple types of "evasive maneuvers" that operators of WLANs can take to help shield their networks from attack. In the era when WEP was all that was available—and especially once WEP was known to be approximately the same as no protection at all—there were certain configuration techniques that did not rely on encryption, but tried to rely on subterfuge.

Non-Cryptographic Security Schemes

One of the earliest schemes by which some vendors tried to enable "security" is by supporting a feature that became known as "Closed WLANs." Normally, the AP includes the SSID in its Beacon MMPDUs, but a suitably modified AP may be configurable to omit the SSID from its Beacons. In order to join a "closed" WLAN, a STA must be pre-configured with the correct SSID…the AP will not reveal this information on a regular basis in its APs. How does this make anything more secure? In reality, it sounds better than it actually is. It is certainly true that the normal mode of operation of an AP includes the SSID in every Beacon, which does, in fact, enable user-friendly software to provide anyone with a dialog box to the effect of "I can hear the following SSIDs…which would you like to join?"

One would initially think that removing the SSID from the Beacon, and forcing the STA to know the SSID in advance, would be a step in the right direction. However, anyone with an ability to eavesdrop on the WM can learn the SSID by simply watching any legitimate STA associate with the AP. Remember, too, that the AP will still be sending Beacons, at a rate usually about 10 per second, so it is easy for an adversary to learn which MAC address on the WM corresponds to an AP. Probe responses from this MAC address will reveal the SSID that was formerly also included in the Beacon MMPDUs.

Another way to limit access to an AP is to restrict the AP to only accept traffic from a pre-defined set of MAC addresses, effectively creating an access-list of MAC addresses. It is easy, however, for an attacker to observe the WM and see which MAC addresses are successfully accessing the AP, so it will be possible for an attacker to spoof the MAC address of a valid STA and access the AP. The authentication and association procedures may not even be based on any credentials at all. In many WLANs, valid users join the WLAN but are effectively anonymous.

Both "closed" WLANs and "access lists" are perhaps useful to deflect an attacker who is looking for an easy target, but in order to repel a determined attacker, one needs to employ a range of techniques. The basis of all the techniques is user-based authentication, using some form of strong credentials. The authentication is the basis for key exchange, and that is what enables the use of encryption.

Cryptographic Security Schemes

If a protocol designer decides that encryption is the best way to protect frames as they transit the WM, then two ancillary decisions must be made. The means by which users are authenticated to the network (and the network to the users) must be defined, as well as the means by which the data is protected (e.g., encryption) both from the user to the network, and vice versa. The combination of the authentication and encryption algorithms that are used to protect data frames is known as a "ciphersuite." This new terminology has been added during the course of the work that is ongoing within TG*i*.[18]

End-User Authentication

The protocol designer must define how the user of a STA should prove his or her identity (so that the AP can decide if that user's STA should have access to the WLAN), a process known is "authentication." The simplest authentication scheme is to allow anyone in, without making them present any sort of credentials. The most rigorous scheme is to require that users be identified in a way that uses cryptographically strong techniques to prove that they are whom they claim to be. In fact, the best schemes not only authenticate the user to the network, but also authenticate the network to the user, a result known as "mutual authentication." Strong authentication schemes are almost certain to involve cryptographically protected exchanges, since the user's (and network's) credentials

---

18. TG*i* is defining a new set of security options for IEEE 802.11 WLANs; however, this standard is not yet complete and any references to it within this book will clearly state that it is a work-in-progress. The author will make every effort to try to refer only to aspects of IEEE 802.11*i* that are unlikely to change, but until it is complete, anything is fair game and might be changed at any time.

must be kept private so that an eavesdropper cannot listen to the authentication exchange and use those credentials later to impersonate that user (or to impersonate the network to an unwitting user).

In between the two extremes (i.e., no authentication to strong mutual authentication) are varying degrees of authentication strength, with one of the weakest being a simple static configuration of a "key" or set of keys that are used by the two parties to communicate (i.e., using the keys for encryption). The "user authentication" in this case is the simple-minded assumption that if the user has configured the correct key(s) into the STA, then he or she must be a valid user. This is a naïve approach, since there is nothing to confirm the users' identity other than their knowledge of these keys, meaning that anyone who discovers the keys can access the network, impersonate another user's STA, impersonate an AP, and so forth. There may be limited circumstances where a naive scheme like this would be appropriate, but in practice this level of "authentication" is not strong, and is easily spoofed by attackers.

There are other authentication schemes that are stronger than the "I know the key, so I must be a legitimate user" approach, and these may even use cryptographic techniques, without providing for mutual authentication. Such schemes are a step in the right direction, but the exposure to man-in-the-middle attacks is a significant weakness.

User authentication is the means for a STA to gain access to the network, based on the STA's user presenting the proper credentials or demonstrating knowledge of the keys. The user authentication algorithms are only employed when a user's STA is first joining a secure WLAN. This type of authentication happens once per association (at a maximum; the STA may be able to roam to APs other than the one that it originally authenticated to, and have the AP transparently hand off its connection to the next AP in such a way that the security of the user is preserved without the user needing to re-certify himself or herself at every hop). After that, a different form of authentication is used to protect the frames that are sent to and from the user's STA.

Message Authentication

In designing a ciphersuite, one must decide whether any cryptographic "message digest" will be applied to the message before it is encrypted and sent. The message digest is typically a hash function that is computed over certain fields in the frame header, plus the frame data, plus a key that only the sender and receiver know. A message digest serves as an ICV, since finding two sets of input data that have the same digest is computationally infeasible and highly improbable. This digest is used by the receiver to prove to itself that the results of its decryption are valid.

When a ciphersuite contains a message digest component, the message digest carries much of the burden of maintaining the security of the connection. It might appear that an encrypted message alone would be sufficient to ensure that the connection was secure, but the fact is that encrypted messages can be replayed or modified and then replayed. If the message were not protected by a digest, it is possible that it could have been modified in such a way that it can be successfully decrypted, without the attacker needing to know the encryption key. Besides maintaining the security of the system, keyed message digests also provide an essential tool in verifying that the received message was not modified or corrupted.

Message Verification

To a human, verifying that a message is correct upon decryption might seem like an easy test. Imagine that one has a message, such as "The quick brown fox jumped over the lazy dog." If one appends a message digest to the data, such as 0x3478619AB30CF781220AFE0E"[19], then the receiver can decrypt the data and re-compute the message digest, and know that if the result of its own calculation matches the value in the frame, that the chances are excellent that the frame is exactly what the sender intended for it to receive. In the preceding example, a human could tell that there was a problem if the sentence read "T%d qv0ch b#RUu fiC$hoiM3a avo1 i8R Eli4 Czy#." This is clearly nonsense...a human can tell that this "sentence" is not meaningful, but computers lack the intuition necessary to make such judgments, and moreover, most data is not ASCII human-language data.

To try to validate decrypted data without a message digest, computers could conceivably determine if the decrypted data consisted of ASCII text, and could even spell-check and/or grammar-check the text to see if it matched a known language. However, as can be seen in this next case, the computer would have no

---

19. That was a completely made up digest value, only accurate in its length, since 16 octets is the length of output from a popular one-way hash function known as Message Digest 5 (MD-5), which is used in this case for purely expository purposes.

way of knowing whether the message was correct, even if it had no spelling or grammar errors. The following two sentences are equally correct. 1) "`Transfer $1200 to account number 16372819.`" 2) "`Transfer $9999 to account number 76293971.`" The first sentence may have been what the sender intended, but the receiver would have no way to detect a forgery that would redirect a much larger amount of the sender's money to a different account. The forged sentence is syntactically correct, contains no spelling errors, and even has the same number of characters in the sentence. Despite the fact that it is not the message that the sender intended to convey, the receiver has no way of knowing that the message is invalid, and will happily process any directive that it can understand—provided that sufficient funds are available in the account from which the money is being transferred.

In the typical case, wherein a frame contains non-ASCII, non-human-language binary data, a receiver needs to have some sort of ICV that it can use to determine if a string of hexadecimal (binary) data was correctly decrypted. Any useful ICV will do its job properly regardless of whether the frame contains binary data or ASCII data. Depending on the level of certainty desired, the integrity check could be anything from a Cyclic Redundancy Check (CRC) code to a cryptographic keyed message digest based on a cryptographically strong one-way keyed hash function, the latter being the strongest known type[20] of ICV. Again, the validation of the message digest is what enables the receiver to be sure that it has the correct data. Without this check, the receiver would have absolutely no clue that it was being tricked.

In many ciphersuites, the message digest is computed from a keyed hash function, which means that the data to be signed is combined with a secret key, and then the resulting data is fed into a cryptographically strong one-way hash function. The result is a fixed-length output that depends very strongly on the inputs to the function.

One definition of a cryptographically strong hash function is a function that takes an arbitrary amount of input data and distills it to a fixed-length output value, with the additional property that changing just a single bit of the input

---

20. Emerging technologies such as quantum cryptography have been demonstrated in the laboratory, and may someday offer non-mathematical ways to transmit messages securely, and implicitly prove that a message hasn't been tampered with, but practical applications of such technology are not imminent.

will change, on average, half of the bits of the computed hash value. The fact that the sender and receiver agree on a secret key, which is used as part of the input to the one-way hash function, enables the receiver to be virtually certain that only the sender (or someone who has compromised the sender's authentication key) could have computed the hash that was appended to the data.

To summarize, a message digest is frequently computed by using a keyed one-way hash function, that can take an arbitrary amount of input data and render it into a fixed-length output (the "hash" value). The most common hash functions in use today are Message Digest 5 (MD-5), which outputs 128 bits of hash, or NIST's Secure Hash Algorithm number 1 (SHA-1), which outputs 160 bits (i.e., 20 octets) of hash value. SHA-1 was defined in the Federal Information Processing Standard (FIPS) publication 180-1, which was standardized on April 17, 1995.

The description of SHA-1 has been carried forward into FIPS publication 180-2, which was approved as a standard on 26 August 2002 and came into force effective February 1, 2003. In addition to SHA-1, FIPS publication 180-2 defines three new hash algorithms that have larger output sizes: SHA-256, SHA-384, and SHA-512. SHA-256 outputs 256 bits (32 octets), SHA-384 outputs 384 bits (48 octets), and SHA-512 outputs 512 bits (64 octets).

Message Encryption

To complete the definition of a ciphersuite, a protocol designer must define what cryptographic encryption algorithms will be used, and exactly what mode of operation must be used (if more than one mode is possible). The complete transformation of the data, including appending the keyed hash result and encrypting all or part of the data and ICV (with a different keys for encryption and authentication), probably including the hash, is known as "encapsulation." Encryption algorithms that are commonly used in network security are block-oriented ciphers, including the Data Encryption Standard (DES), Triple DES, and the increasingly popular Advanced Encryption Standard (AES).

Many other ciphers have also been defined, including RC4, which is a stream-oriented cipher. Other block-oriented ciphers include IDEA, Blowfish, CAST, RC-2, RC-5, and RC-6; there are not many stream ciphers that are commonly used in the context of network security (RC4, in its use within IEEE 802.11 WEP, and in TLS/SSL, is an exception). An exhaustive list of encryption algorithms is not warranted here, but readers interested in encryption should read Bruce Schneier's book entitled *Applied Cryptography: Protocols, Algorithms, and Source Code in C, 2nd Edition.*

For a given ciphersuite, the length of the authentication and encryption keys will be chosen appropriately for the constituent authentication and encryption algorithms. For example, AES may use encryption keys of 128, 192, or 256 bits. The choice of key length is related to the issue of key derivation, since keys of the appropriate length must be derived for the use of the encryption and/or authentication algorithms.

Derivation of Encryption and Authentication Keys

There are at least two reasons why one might need a key. One is to use in a keyed hash function, to create a cryptographic digest of the data (so that the device that decrypts the data can verify that the receiver can verify that the decrypted data is exactly what the sender had encrypted). Another is to encrypt the frame for transmission. To enable the proper operation of the selected authentication and encryption algorithms, a set of mechanisms must be defined to allow both of the communicating entities to derive the same keys. The key derivation mechanisms must derive keys of the appropriate length for the chosen hash or encryption algorithm.

As was previously implied, the "algorithm" for key derivation could be as simple as having all users statically define the relevant keys into their WLAN configurations using the configuration tools that are provided with the WLAN card. For more sophisticated approaches, keys can be chosen dynamically. At one extreme, keys pertain to only a single connection. At the other extreme, keys could be dynamically defined for an entire set of stations, with the disadvantage that they would all re-key at the same time. In the latter case, each new participant in the encryption scheme would need to be told the key in such a way that he or she would end up knowing the key that all the other stations were using, without revealing the key to any eavesdropper. Figure 7–1 shows the classification of key derivation schemes.

To limit the knowledge of the keys to only the intended parties, the key exchange must not reveal enough information to allow an eavesdropper to determine the resulting key(s). Luckily, techniques exist to allow two parties to exchange a secret over a public channel, in such a way that eavesdroppers can

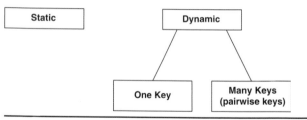

Figure 7–1   Classification of key derivation schemes

extract no information, even if they have a copy of the entire exchange. One of the better-known examples of such an algorithm is the Diffie-Hellman protocol, but there are many other functionally similar algorithms. The message authentication and encryption keys could be derived in one pass, from a single exchange, or there could be separate exchanges to derive each key.

Once the keys are known to both parties, the keys are used to both transform the data from plaintext into ciphertext (a process known as "encapsulation") and transform the ciphertext into plaintext (a process known as "decapsulation"). If the chosen ciphersuite indicates that a message digest function is to be used in addition to an encryption algorithm, then keys for both will need to be derived. When both message authentication and encryption are used together, the message is typically authenticated before being encrypted. Figure 7–2 shows the encapsulation and decapsulation processes with encryption only.

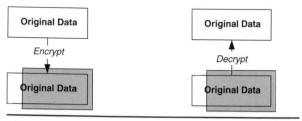

Figure 7–2   Encapsulation (encryption only)

Figure 7–3 shows the encapsulation and decapsulation processes when message authentication is also included. Note that the ICV may not be computed over all of the original data, since certain header elements may be expected to change in transit, and thus should not be part of the ICV computation. The exact fields over which the ICV is calculated would be specified by the message authentication protocol rules.

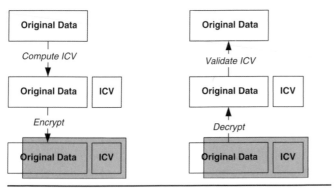

Figure 7–3   Encapsulation (message authentication plus encryption)

Note that in both cases, the encryption (indicated by the gray shading) cannot cover all of the original frame's data, since the header must remain visible for the data to be delivered. However, the ICV calculation can include (or "cover") parts of the header that cannot be encrypted, so that the receiver can tell if the packet has been altered in transit.

Ciphersuite Selection

To provide flexibility for implementers, a protocol designer may, at his or her discretion, also provide a way for a STA and AP to select a ciphersuite from a list of mutually supported ciphersuites. When multiple ciphersuites are defined, one of them is typically designated as "mandatory-to-implement." This is to ensure that any two implementations that want to use security services can find at least one common set of authentication and/or encryption protocols.

Wired-Equivalent Privacy (WEP)

During the standardization of IEEE 802.11-1997, there was a strong desire to include a set of minimal (but adequate) security services that could challenge the potential eavesdropper in the same way that a physical wire challenges an eavesdropper (or, in that case, wiretapper). WEP was carried forward, unchanged, in the next version of the standard, IEEE 802.11-1999.

WEP was designed to be a simple, yet secure-enough technology that could be implemented in software or firmware for little or no cost. Unfortunately, the design of WEP turned out to include a number of fatal flaws. In the course of describing how WEP works, we will have the opportunity to describe what is broken.

Unfortunately, security is a notoriously digital endeavor…either you have it or you don't. It is difficult to cut corners and still maintain a desired level of security. Once a security system has been implemented, it is inevitable that many people will attempt to find its weakness (or weaknesses), especially if it is popular and/or widely used. There are quite a few network security researchers, including many candidates for Masters or Ph.D. degrees in Mathematics or Computer Science who like nothing more than an opportunity to write a paper (or a thesis) on how to exploit the weaknesses of a given security scheme.

One aspect security is that it might take an extremely talented individual quite some time to find such a weak point…but once a weakness has been found, software tools that exploit the weakness can be distributed over the Internet, and anyone (regardless of IQ) can use those tools. Just because a security system has not yet been compromised does not mean that it is truly secure in any absolute way, it just means that it is secure *for the moment*. WEP is a case in point, in that it was defined and deployed for over four years before tools became available to reduce its security value to zero.

Authentication within IEEE 802.11's MAC-Layer

There are two modes of user authentication defined for WEP. The first is not really a form of authentication at all. The second is a simple challenge-based exchange that relies on WEP encryption for protection. In IBSS mode, an association is never possible since there are no APs, and by definition an association must include an AP and a STA. Now would also be a good time to note that in IBSS mode, MAC-layer Authentication is optional.

Before a STA can join a WLAN, it must identify itself. The degree to which it is trusted depends on the configuration of the STA and the credentials of the user. In traditional WLANs (i.e., those based on the IEEE 802.11-1999 standard), a station must first "authenticate" itself to an AP within range of its radio, which requires one of the following two packet exchanges.

When using encryption to form a link, the two parties form a "security association," which is a formal name for the set of characteristics that define a given binding between a STA and an AP (in infrastructure mode) or between two STAs (in IBSS mode). A security association may enumerate some (or all) of the following characteristics pertinent to the connection: the authenticated key management protocol in use (if any), unicast and multicast ciphersuites, cryptographic keys, key lifetimes, and other parameters governing the operation of the cryptosystem.

The first step to defining a security association is to perform an authentication step, to make sure that each party finds the other acceptable in whatever way they care to check. There are three "states" in which a legacy IEEE 802.11-1999 STA may be in, relative to an AP. First, there is the state in which the STA is are unauthenticated and unassociated. In this state, the STA can only send management frames to establish authentication. It is also permissible to send certain control frames that are necessary to participate in the MAC protocol, such as Request to Send (RTS) and Clear to Send (CTS) frames. It is also possible to send data frames in this state provided they do not need to go beyond the AP (i.e., if they are contained within the STA's local BSS). This capability enables STAs in IBSS mode to exchange data without performing authentication (which is ultimately up to the user who is driving the STA). If the STA has successfully authenticated with at least one AP, it can move to the second state, in which it can proceed to association. The second state is characterized by the STA being authenticated, but as yet unassociated. In this state, the STA can send more kinds of frames, specifically MMPDUs that have to do with Association, Re-Association, or Disassociation. Remember that a STA may only be associated with one AP at a time. Finally, the third state is reached when the STA has associated with an AP, and thus is referred to as the "authenticated and associated" state. In this state, data frames may be sent that can cross the AP and access the Distribution System Service (DSS) provided by the wired LAN to which the AP is attached.

Figure 7–4 shows the relationship between these three states, and enumerates all the different types of frames that can be sent in each state. In each state, all the frames in the lower state or states are explicitly permissible, so in State 2, it is possible to send all frame types permissible in both State 1 and State 2; likewise, in State 3, all frame types are permissible.

Because IBSS mode does not have an AP (so there is nothing to associate with, since an association requires an AP), or its associated Portal functionality (so there is no DSS (wired LAN), which is only accessible to a STA via an AP and it associated Portal), STAs in IBSS mode can never be in the third state; in

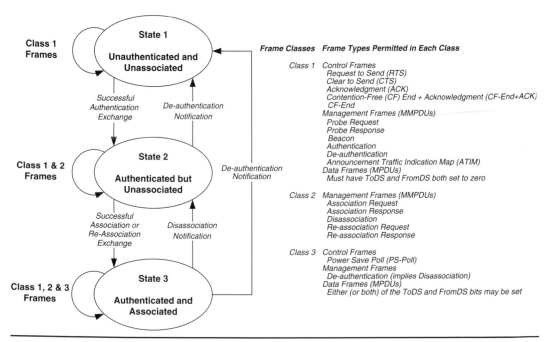

The following table appears within the figure:

Frame Classes	Frame Types Permitted in Each Class

Class 1	Control Frames
	    Request to Send (RTS)
	    Clear to Send (CTS)
	    Acknowledgment (ACK)
	    Contention-Free (CF) End + Acknowledgment (CF-End+ACK)
	    CF-End
	Management Frames (MMPDUs)
	    Probe Request
	    Probe Response
	    Beacon
	    Authentication
	    De-authentication
	    Announcement Traffic Indication Map (ATIM)
	Data Frames (MPDUs)
	    Must have ToDS and FromDS both set to zero

Class 2	Management Frames (MMPDUs)
	    Association Request
	    Association Response
	    Disassociation
	    Re-association Request
	    Re-association Response

Class 3	Control Frames
	    Power Save Poll (PS-Poll)
	Management Frames
	    De-authentication (implies Disassociation)
	Data Frames (MPDUs)
	    Either (or both) of the ToDS and FromDS bits may be set

Figure 7–4   Connectivity states of a STA

other words, they may be either "unauthenticated and unassociated," or "authenticated but unassociated."

User Authentication: "Open System"

The term "Open System authentication" is semantically equivalent to "no authentication." In Open System authentication, the WLAN is open to any potential user, who needs only go through a basic "authentication" exchange, which serves little purpose other than to identify the new STA's MAC address to the AP. In the case of IBSS mode, this form of user authentication can be used between two STAs, although MAC-layer user authentication is not mandatory in IBSS mode.

The IEEE 802.11-1999 "legacy" authentication exchange is comprised of management frames. The MMPDU's Frame Control (FC) field is depicted in Figure 7–5. The MMPDUs used to negotiate authentication are indicated by a Type of "00" (management) and a Subtype of "1101" (authentication) or "0011" (de-authentication).

Open System authentication consists of just two messages, as shown in Figure 7–6.

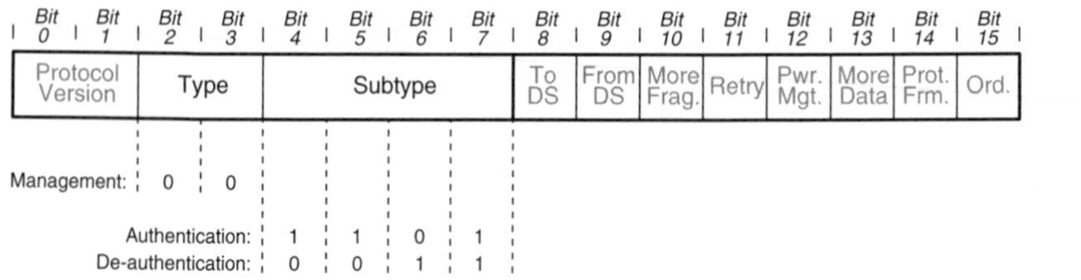

Bit 0	Bit 1	Bit 2	Bit 3	Bit 4	Bit 5	Bit 6	Bit 7	Bit 8	Bit 9	Bit 10	Bit 11	Bit 12	Bit 13	Bit 14	Bit 15
Protocol Version		Type		Subtype				To DS	From DS	More Frag.	Retry	Pwr. Mgt.	More Data	Prot. Frm.	Ord.

Management: 0   0

Authentication: 1   1   0   1
De-authentication: 0   0   1   1

Figure 7–5   FC Field of the IEEE 802.11 MMPDU showing sub-types for authentication and de-authentication messages

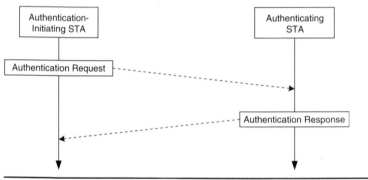

Figure 7–6   User authentication: Open System

Each message carries different information, but has the same structure, which is shown in Figure 7–7. Not shown in the diagram is the MMPDU header (which is functionally similar to the MPDU header), nor the FCS. The diagram only shows the format of the payload MMPDU that is used in Authentication messages.

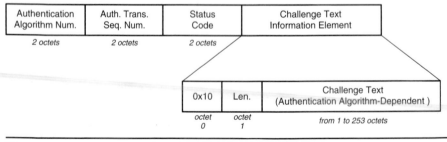

Figure 7–7   Contents of Authentication MMPDU[21]

21. As with all IEs containing a Length field, the Length field applies to the data field of the IE. In the case of the Challenge Text Information Element, the Challenge Text field must be at least one octet in length, and may be up to 253 octets in length.

The first message flows from the Authentication-Initiating STA to the Authenticating STA.[22] The purpose of this frame is to initiate the Open System authentication negotiation. Keep in mind that in infrastructure mode, a STA can authenticate with as many APs as it can hear. The first frame of the Open System authentication exchange contains the following information:

Authentication Algorithm Number: 0^{23} (i.e., "Open System")
Authentication Transaction Sequence Number: 1^{24}
Status Code: Reserved (i.e., set to 0^{23})
Challenge Text: Not present when Authentication Algorithm Number is zero
Station Identity: (From the MMPDU header's Source Address (SA) field)

The second (and final, in the case of Open System authentication) message flows from the Authenticating STA back to the Authentication-Initiating STA. This frame is only ever sent in response to the first authentication frame, and the contents of this frame are as follows:

Authentication Algorithm Number: 0^{23} (i.e., "Open System")
Authentication Transaction Sequence Number: 2^{25}
Status Code: (i.e., successful or otherwise)
Challenge Text: Not present when Authentication Algorithm Number is zero

The complete list of status codes is listed in Table 7–1. The codes that might apply during the Open System authentication exchange are numbers 0, 1, 12, 13, 15, or 16. It is possible that the Authenticating STA would

---

22. When the WLAN is in infrastructure mode, the Authenticating STA lies within the AP. When two STAs are in IBSS mode and they are configured to perform authentication, each STA will play the role of both the Authentication-Initiating STA and an Authenticating STA.

23. The decimal number "0" is encoded in a little-endian two-octet field (i.e., 0000 0000 0000 0000).

24. The decimal number "1" is encoded in a little-endian two-octet field (i.e., 1000 0000 0000 0000).

25. The decimal number "2" is encoded in a little-endian two-octet field (i.e., 0100 0000 0000 0000).

refuse[26] to authenticate an Authentication-Initiating STA if it were trying to use Open System authentication. In such a case, the Authenticating STA would respond with a Status Code of 13, the meaning of which is listed in Table 7–1, along with all the other Status Codes that have been defined in IEEE 802.11-1999. Note that some of the codes in this table pertain to association exchanges, while others are only usable in the context of authentication exchanges.

Table 7–1   Status Codes Used within the Authentication MMPDU

Status Code	Meaning
0	Successful
1	Unspecified failure
2 – 9	Reserved
10	Cannot support all requested capabilities in the Capability Information field
11	Reassociation denied due to inability to confirm that association exists
12	Association denied due to reason outside the scope of this standard
13	Responding station does not support the specified authentication algorithm
14	Received an Authentication MMPDU with authentication transaction sequence number out of expected sequence
15	Authentication rejected because of challenge failure
16	Authentication rejected due to timeout waiting for next frame in sequence
17	Association denied because AP is unable to handle additional associated STAs
18	Association denied due to requesting STA not supporting all of the data rates in the BSSBasicRateSet parameter
19 – 65,535	Reserved

WARNING: THIS PART IS CONFUSING   In the IEEE 802.11-1999 standard, when in infrastructure mode, the Authentication step is followed by a step called Association. A STA can only be associated with one AP at a time, but it may be authenticated with as many APs as it can hear. This enables a mode of operation known as "pre-authentication" in which a STA may easily roam from one AP to another, because all it needs to do is disassociate from one AP and associate with the other, since it has already authenticated itself to the AP prior to associating with it. In the next section, we discuss the Association procedure.

Now, for the confusing part: Later in this chapter, you will learn that in the IEEE 802.11*i* work-in-progress, the order of Association and Authentication has

---

26. For example, in the case of infrastructure mode, in which the Authenticating STA would be inside an AP, or in the case of IBSS mode, in which the Authenticating STA is simply another STA in IBSS mode, if the Authenticating STA was configured by the Authenticating STA's administrator to enforce a stronger level of authentication than Open System authentication, then the Authenticating STA would refuse to authenticate using the Open System authentication method.

(apparently) been reversed. Actually, a new kind of Authentication, based on IEEE 802.1X-2001, has been introduced that happens *after* Association. (IEEE 802.11 MAC-layer Open System authentication is still permissible prior to Association, but it is optional under the new rules specified in IEEE 802.11*i* as of this writting.) Remember, these statements apply to infrastructure mode, not IBSS mode.

For infrastructure mode, the current design of IEEE 802.11*i* dictates that a STA may first perform an IEEE 802.11 MAC-layer Open Authentication (this is optional, but may be required on certain APs or STAs that require MAC-layer authentication to begin the process that culminates with the ability to send data frames), which is then followed by IEEE 802.11 Association,[27] and finally IEEE 802.1X-based strong authentication.

To summarize, we have MAC-layer authentication (which is optional), followed by association, followed by IEEE 802.1X-based authentication. The last authentication step is where the real work of user authentication happens, and it happens after association. The reason why the current design forces the "real" authentication to happen after association is that IEEE 802.1X authentication frames are data frames, and a STA can only send data frames after it has associated with an AP.

Note that the IEEE 802.11*i* standard is still very much a work-in-progress, and it is quite possible that the ultimate state machine will change; for example, to encode the IEEE 802.1X messages in MAC-layer management frames (i.e., MMPDUs) instead of in data frames (i.e., MPDUs). At this point, the best I can do is to describe the current design of IEEE 802.11*i*, and to make the reader aware that this is likely to change. Once the IEEE 802.11*i* TG has completed its work (hopefully that will happen in 2003), anyone who is interested will be able to see what the final design was.

User Authentication: "Shared Key"

The overall procedure employed in Shared Key authentication follows the template established by Open System authentication. Note that "Shared Key

---

27. APs that support IEEE 802.11*i* will allow unauthenticated STAs to associate (i.e., IEEE 802.11 MAC-layer "Open System" authentication is optional).

authentication" is a proper name and refers to an authentication method that is specific to IEEE 802.11-1997 and succeeding versions. The term "Shared Key authentication" refers to the fact that all the STAs share knowledge of the same (set of) key(s), which they use to prove that they should be allowed to join the WLAN.

In the broader context of cryptography, there is a concept of "pre-shared keys." There is no relationship between "pre-shared keys" and "Shared Key authentication." At some point in the future, it is possible that Shared Key authentication will be removed from the IEEE 802.11 standard, but that is not even a consideration at this point in time. The frame exchange used to implement Shared Key authentication is illustrated in Figure 7–8.

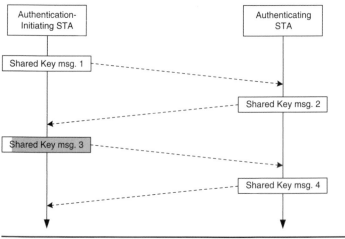

Figure 7–8   Shared Key authentication negotiation

The format of the messages in the Shared Key authentication negotiation is identical to those in the Open System authentication exchange, which is illustrated in Figure 7–9. The main difference is that Open System authentication does not make use of the Challenge Text Information Element, while Shared Key authentication does.

Even though the Challenge Text Information Element is capable of containing up to 253 octets of challenge text, only 128 octets are required in order to negotiate Shared Key authentication. Figure 7–9 shows the maximum capacity of the information element, rather than illustrating a special case that would only be applicable to Shared Key authentication.

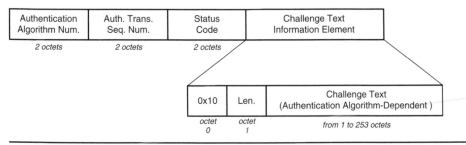

Figure 7–9   MMPDU format for IEEE 802.11-1999 authentication negotiations

As in Open System authentication, the first message of the Shared Key authentication exchange flows from the Authentication-Initiating STA to the Authenticating STA. All of the MMPDUs that are used in the Shared Key authentication negotiation have their two-bit message Type set to 00 (Management) and the four-bit message Subtype set to $0xB$ (Authentication).

The first message of the Shared Key authentication negotiation contains the following information:

> **Authentication Algorithm Number**: 1^{28} (i.e., "Shared Key")
> **Authentication Transaction Sequence Number**: 1^{28}
> **Status Code**: Reserved (i.e., set to $0x0000$)
> **Challenge Text**: Not present in this message
> **Station Identity**: (From the MMPDU header's Source Address (SA) field)

The second message of the Shared Key authentication negotiation flows from the Authenticating STA back to the Authentication-Initiating STA. If the status code is not "successful," then this Authenticating STA is either configured to not accept Shared Key authentication, or it may have insufficient resources to handle this Shared Key authentication negotiation at this time. In this case, the second message would be the final message of the aborted Shared Key authentication exchange.

This frame is only ever sent in response to the first authentication frame, and the contents of this frame are as follows:

> **Authentication Algorithm Number**: 1^{28} (i.e., "Shared Key")
> **Authentication Transaction Sequence Number**: 2^{29}

---

28. The decimal number "1" is encoded in a little-endian two-octet field (i.e., 1000 0000 0000 0000).

29. The decimal number "2" is encoded in a little-endian two-octet field (i.e., 0100 0000 0000 0000).

Status Code: (i.e., successful or otherwise)

Challenge Text: *128 octets of challenge text (generated by WEP's pseudo-random number generator seeded with any initialization vector (IV) and key)*

The third message of the Shared Key authentication negotiation is only sent if the second message indicates "successful" in the Status Code. The message flows from the Authenticating STA back to the Authentication-Initiating STA. The third frame is *encrypted* using one of the statically defined WEP[30] keys, and contains the following information:

Authentication Algorithm Number: 1^{31} (i.e., "Shared Key")

Authentication Transaction Sequence Number: 3^{32}

Status Code: (i.e., successful)

Challenge Text: *128 octets of challenge text (generated by WEP's pseudo-random number generator seeded with any initialization vector (IV) and key)*

The receiver of the third frame (the Authenticating STA) can tell from the WEP header which key was used to encrypt the frame, and if the frame is successfully decrypted, it will attempt to match the challenge text with the text that it sent out in the second frame. WEP uses the CRC-32 algorithm to generate an ICV. The CRC-32 algorithm is more commonly found in Frame Check Sequences, and it is well-known to be fairly weak, in that errored frames have a reasonable chance of having the same CRC as the original frame. The ICV is calculated over the data frame and appended to the data frame before the data frame and the CRC-32 ICV, are encrypted. If, once the frame is decrypted, the ICV in the frame is found to match a CRC-32 separately calculated over the data then the frame is taken to have arrived intact.

Note that anyone with knowledge of this BSS' WEP keys could forge the second frame in this exchange. The fact that the third message is encrypted is only

---

30. The mechanics of WEP will be discussed shortly. Unfortunately, there is a bit of a catch-22, in that a STA can't join a BSS unless it can do WEP, since the Shared Key authentication exchange depends on encrypting the third message. Rather than discuss WEP encapsulation and encryption in between Open System and Shared Key authentication, the author chose to finish describing authentication first.

31. The decimal number "1" is encoded in a little-endian two-octet field (i.e., 1000 0000 0000 0000).

32. The decimal number "3" is encoded in a little-endian two-octet field (i.e., 1100 0000 0000 0000).

proving that the Authentication-Initiating STA knows the WEP keys, which is a fairly low barrier to entry. An imposter could easily interfere with the Authenticating STA's transmissions, and impersonate it (e.g., by spoofing its MAC address), once the challenge text has been chosen.

The final (fourth) frame of the Shared Key authentication exchange is a confirmation that the Authenticating STA received the third frame, and that the Authentication-Initiating STA is now authorized to use the BSS. Note that the BSS may be in either infrastructure or IBSS mode, although authentication is optional in IBSS mode.

Authentication Algorithm Number: 1^{33} (i.e., "Shared Key")
Authentication Transaction Sequence Number: 4^{34}
Status Code: (i.e., successful or unsuccessful, depending on the ICV check)
Challenge Text: *128 octets of challenge text (generated by WEP's pseudo-random number generator seeded with any initialization vector (IV) and key)*

Association

Regardless of the order of authentication and association, the association procedure is quite simple. Remember that there is no AP in IBSS mode, so there are no associations. Associations are, by definition, only between a STA and an AP, and an AP will only accept data from a STA if they are associated with each other. STAs can only send and receive frames to the wired world on the far side of the AP if they have completed association.

There are actually three different types of association messages: "Association," "Re-Association," and "Disassociation." The first type is used to establish an association, and the latter is used to terminate an association. The Re-Association message is used to either change the parameters of an existing association with an AP, or to move a STA to a different AP.

The process of association, which occurs after IEEE 802.11-1999 MAC-layer authentication, consists of just two messages, as shown in Figure 7–10. The Association Request message flows from the Association-Initiating STA

---

33. The decimal number "1" is encoded in a little-endian two-octet field (i.e., 1000 0000 0000 0000).

34. The decimal number "4" is encoded in a little-endian two-octet field (i.e., 0010 0000 0000 0000).

to the AP,[35] and the Association Response message is sent in the opposite direction.

Association Initiating STA
Access Point (AP)
Association Request
Association Response

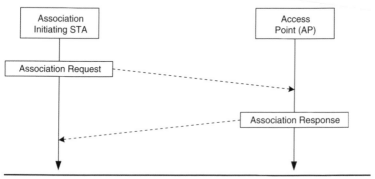

Figure 7–10 Association of a STA to an AP

Figure 7–11 shows the encoding of the MMPDU Frame Control field for each of these message types, both of which have a message type indicating that they are "management" frames (i.e., "00"). The message subtype for the "Association Request" MMPDU is "0000", and the message subtype for the "Association Response" MMPDU is "1000".[36]

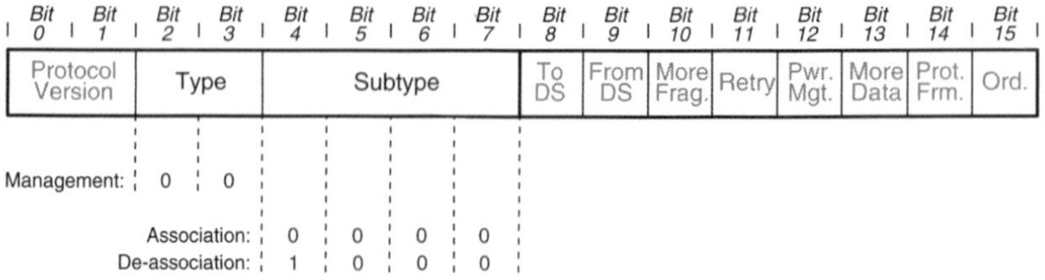

Bit 0
Bit 1
Bit 2
Bit 3
Bit 4
Bit 5
Bit 6
Bit 7
Bit 8
Bit 9
Bit 10
Bit 11
Bit 12
Bit 13
Bit 14
Bit 15
Protocol Version
Type
Subtype
To DS
From DS
More Frag.
Retry
Pwr. Mgt.
More Data
Prot. Frm.
Ord.
Management: 0 0
Association: 0 0 0 0
De-association: 1 0 0 0

Figure 7–11 Type and subtype encoding of Association MMPDUs

Each association message carries different information, and therefore has different payload structure. The Association Request MMPDU conveys the following information:

Association-Initiating STA's Identity: (from the MMPDU header's SA field)

AP's Identity: (from the MMPDU header's DA field)

35. Association can only occur when the WLAN is in infrastructure mode, since an AP must be involved in an association. In IBSS mode, associations are not performed.

36. Note that the message subtype fields were written with the least-significant bit on the *left*.

(E)SS ID: (Ensures that the STA is joining the correct WLAN). The SSID is an ASCII string that serves as a sort of "VLAN name." A STA wanting to join a WLAN must know its name, which is accomplished either by having the user enter the name statically, or by having the OS dynamically detect the name of the WLAN, after which the user can be prompted to see if he or she would like to join that WLAN.

Various control information such as ESS versus IBSS mode, whether Privacy is enabled in this WLAN, whether the Association-Initiating STA supports Contention-Free operation, and the rates at which the Association-Initiating STA can operate. The AP will use this information to determine whether it should accept the association. The Association-Initiating STA also can inform the AP how long its "Listen Interval" will be. The Listen Interval is the amount of time that the STA will spend in power-saving mode, and is expressed in units of Beacon intervals, so the STA can "sleep" for anywhere from 1 to 65,535 Beacon intervals.

The format of the Association Request MMPDU is shown in Figure 7–12.

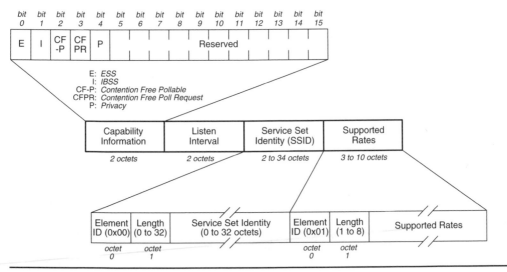

Figure 7–12 Contents of Association Request MMPDU

The Association Response message flows from the AP back to the Association-Initiating STA if the proposed association is accepted. This MMPDU is only ever sent in response to the Association Request MMPDU. The Association Response MMPDU conveys the following information:

- Association Identifier. The Association ID is a 14-bit number between 1 and 2007, inclusive. The two most-significant bits of the 16-bit Association ID field are set to 1. This is a number assigned by the AP, which is used as a shorthand way to refer to this association. The only other frame type that has an Association ID field is the Power-Save Poll control frame, which the AP uses to indicate to a STA that traffic is queued for it in the AP. As with other fields in the various IEEE 802.11 frame headers, the least-significant bit of the Association Identifier is written on the left. The values in Figure 7–13 reflect the proper bit ordering. Note that the most-significant two bits of the AID field are both set to "1" in accordance with the specification.

- The AP will return a list of its own supported rates, so that the Association-Initiating STA can limit itself to the intersection of its own set of supported rates against the set of supported rates which the AP supports.

- Status Code. The Status code will be chosen from the values in Table 7–1 that are applicable to association events. Given that we have assumed that the association was successful, the Status Code field will contain the value zero.

The format of the Association Response MMPDU is shown in Figure 7–13.

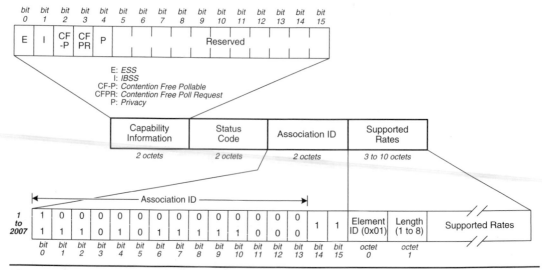

Figure 7–13   Contents of Association Response MMPDU

Once completed, the associated STA will be able to send frames to any other MAC address within its own BSS, or accessible via the DSS (i.e., the wired LAN that interconnects the APs of the ESS).

Encryption

In the beginning, there was WEP. Despite the "P" in its name, "Privacy" is not what WEP was attempting to provide…it was trying to provide a minimal level of "confidentiality." There is a reference that defines various security terms very precisely, and I do my best to follow it. RFC-2828 is an informational RFC entitled "Internet Security Glossary." The concept of privacy has to do with controlling information; for example, about yourself (i.e., keeping information about what books you read, or what stores you shop at, etc., from being disseminated too widely), whereas the concept of "confidentiality" has to do with preventing your communications from being understood by others.

WEP was completely inadequate for its intended purpose…protecting traffic as it flowed across the air so it would be just as secure as traffic that is traversing a wire. WEP was designed to be strong enough to prevent casual eavesdropping. The mechanisms it used to provide "security," however, were not well thought out, and in retrospect it turned out that WEP was quite easy to break. In fact, given the proper tools in the hands of miscreants, WEP-protected networks were no more secure than networks that operated in the clear. In fact, WEP might have been slightly dangerous, in that it may have conveyed a false sense of security to users that enabled it.

This chapter concerns itself with all forms of WLAN security, including WEP, although it must be re-stated that WEP is not secure and should not be used if better alternatives are available. The IEEE 802.11 WG is in the process of defining new procedures that are collectively known as "Robust Security Network" protocols, which are able to provide much more secure operation for WLANs. In fact, in some ways, WLANs using RSN procedures may be more secure than their wired counterparts.

WEP employs RSA Security Inc.'s RC4 stream-oriented cipher algorithm. Curiously, RC4 used to be a trade secret of RSA, but the algorithm was leaked and a publicly available implementation now exists that can be used without license. It is known as "Alleged RC4" or "ARC4" (which can still be pronounced the same as RC4, if you stretch the rules of English pronunciation a bit, pronouncing the "AR" as if it were just an "R"). RSA[37] has even admitted that it is, in fact, the actual RC4 algorithm, so anyone can effectively use ARC4 for free, even though RSA Security, Inc. still claims it as their intellectual property (RC4 is at least a registred trade mark).

Stream-oriented ciphers take a seed value (in the case of RC4, this seed is comprised of a 24-bit number that is included with the frame, known as an IV) plus a key (can be variable size; in the case of WEP's use of RC4 it is either 40 or 104 bits long[38]) and generate a pseudo-random string of bits (via RC4's Pseudo-Random Number Generator, or PRNG) that is known as a "keystream." This keystream is exclusive-OR'ed against the data to be encrypted, effectively scrambling it.

In WEP, the seed is either 64 or 128 bits long, corresponding to a 24-bit IV concatenated with either a 40-bit or 104-bit key. RC4 keys can be as small as eight bits (one octet), and as large as 2048 bits (256 octets), and can have a length that is any intermediate multiple of 8 bits. RC4 keys are not limited to multiples of, for example, 32 or 64 bits, as you might conclude from looking at the key sizes used with WEP.

The bitwise exclusive-OR operator is also known as the "not equal to" function, since the result of an exclusive-OR operation is only true when the inputs are unequal. If either input matches (either both are zero, or both are one), the output of the bitwise exclusive-OR operator is zero. In summary: the result of the logical exclusive-OR operation is 1 only if the two inputs do not match. The truth table diagram for the exclusive-OR operator is shown in Figure 7–14, with the logical "OR" operator provided for the sake of comparison.

Due to an interesting property of the exclusive-OR function, it is just as easy to decrypt a frame as it is to encrypt it. The following simple equation says that if you take some plaintext (P) and XOR it with a keystream (K), and *then* you XOR the resulting ciphertext (C) with the same keystream, the result is the

---

37. RSA is an acronym representing the names of the three people who co-invented a popular form of public-key cryptography: Ronald L. Rivest, Adi Shamir, and Leonard M. Adleman. RSA is also a company that was founded in 1982 by the three co-inventors in order to commercialize their invention. Today, RSA is a premier data security company, selling everything from cryptographic toolkits for software developers to consulting services. RSA Security Inc. is the most recent name for the company.

38. The author is aware of products that have claimed to have WEP implementations based on RC4 with 152-bit seeds. Presumably, this consisted of the usual 24-bit IV, plus a 128-bit key. It is also possible that the spec sheet on which the author saw this claim was in error.

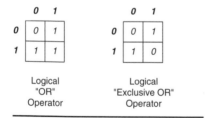

Figure 7–14 Truth table for the Exclusive-OR operator

same plaintext that you started with. If we take "⊕" to be the exclusive-OR operator, then we have the following equations that represent the encryption and decryption procedure:

$$C = P \oplus K \text{ (encryption)}$$
$$P = C \oplus K \text{ (decryption)}$$

By combining the two equations algebraically, we have the following identity:

$$P = C \oplus K$$
$$P = (P \oplus K) \oplus K$$

Because the exclusive-OR function obeys the associative rule, we see that

$$P = P \oplus (K \oplus K)$$
$$P = P$$

Therefore, if a peer can re-create the keystream, it can decrypt a frame. In order to perform the decryption, the receiving peer needs to know the proper IV, plus the key. The RC4 PRNG will do the rest. In WEP, the IV is sent as part of the frame, but the key is kept secret (well, it's supposed to be...). The receiver can use its knowledge of the secret key plus the IV (which is included as plaintext in the frame) to generate its own keystream with which to decrypt the frame, which is accepted provided the ICV is verified to be correct.

In WEP, the ICV is the CRC-32 function (the same function that is used in the Ethernet and IEEE 802.11 Frame Check Sequence). In a moment, when the frame encapsulation and decapsulation rules are shown, it will be clear that even though the ICV is a CRC-32, there is still an FCS at the MAC layer.

WEP is more than just a way to use an encryption algorithm. As was noted earlier, an ICV is required to enable the receiver to verify that what was received was the same thing that was sent by the sender. One thing to keep in mind about WEP is that it was designed to be able to be implemented in software or firmware. RC4 is a fast algorithm, and it is not CPU-intensive compared with other encryption algorithms, making it ideal for implementation in APs and PC Cards.

As noted earlier, the frame header must remain exposed to the intermediate devices (e.g., the AP), so that it can be properly forwarded. Consequently, there is a need to "encapsulate" the original data frame (MSDU), which consists of 1) computing the ICV, 2) appending the ICV to the MSDU, 3) encrypting the MSDU and ICV (using the IV and a secret key), and 4) pre-pending the IV to the encrypted data. WEP encapsulation transforms the frame as shown in Figure 7–15. The gray box in Figure 7–15 that surrounds the MSDU at the top of the figure is meant to symbolize that the ICV is calculated over that entire MSDU. Visually, and actually, the ICV covers the MSDU.

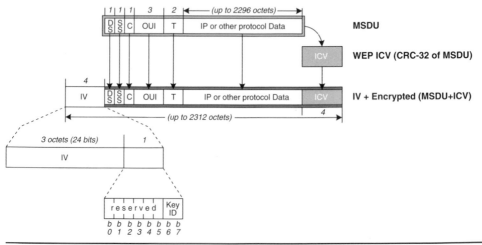

Figure 7–15   WEP encapsulation

When a STA or AP is configured to use WEP, there is typically a user interface that permits the entry of up to four RC4 keys. The values are either 40 bits (i.e., 5 octets), or 104 bits (i.e., 13 octets) in length. When an MSDU is encapsulated with WEP, the sending STA may choose any of the four keys that are at its disposal. It is a pre-requisite that all STAs and APs that want to communicate must have their WEP keys statically pre-defined before they can use WEP to protect frames that they exchange between each other.

To use WEP, at least one key must be defined in the AP or STA. Because the KeyID field in the IV header provides for up to four WEP keys, many implementations allow the entry of up to four 40-bit keys. To provide an example, Figure 7–16

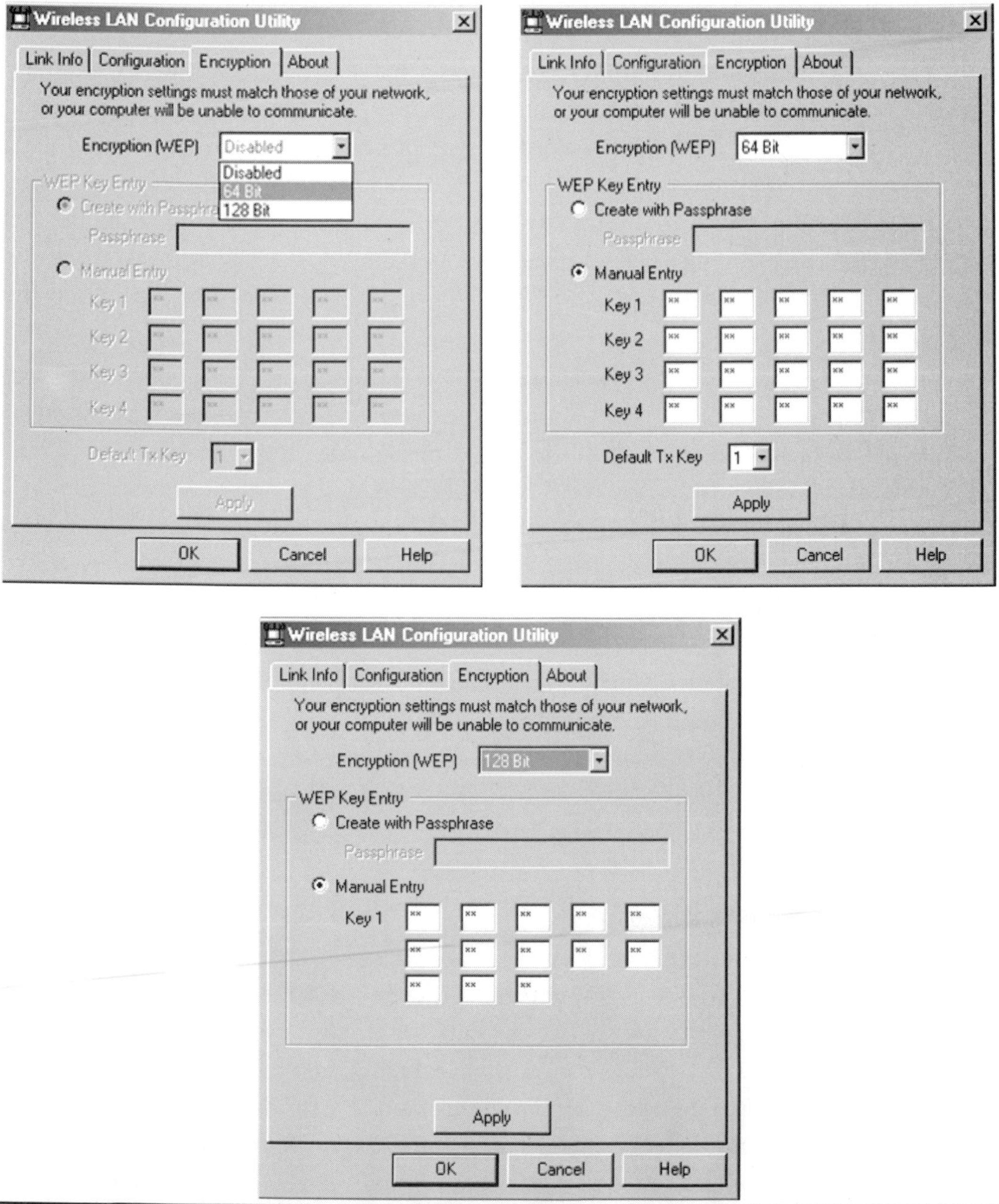

Figure 7–16 User interface for configuring WEP keys

shows the user interface for the author's WLAN PC Card. Remember in Chapter 3, we saw that the Red Hat Linux 9.0 "neat" user interface for WLAN configuration allowed the WEP key to be entered in the top-level configuration dialog box.

Note that as an alternative to typing in 20 hex octets (five for each of the four keys), the user interface supports entering a "pass phrase" from which the keys are derived. The mapping between pass phrases and keys is not defined in the standard, so if a user wanted to configure a STA or AP that way, that user might have to use equipment from one vendor. Also note that, in the case of WEP-104, the user interface of my product only supports entering a single key (although in principle, it should also be possible to enter four keys, since the KeyID field only enumerates the key number, it does not care how large the key(s) is(are)).

The STA that receives a WEP-encrypted frame can tell it is encrypted since the WEP bit in the MPDU's Frame Control field is set. The first four octets of the MSDU are then known to be the WEP IV, and the final two bits of that four-bit field constitute the WEP Key ID. By selecting one of the four possible values of the Key ID field, the receiving STA knows the key to use to combine with the IV to determine the seed from which the pseudo-random keystream may be calculated. A complete MPDU, showing the full MPDU header and the WEP pieces that surround the original MSDU, is shown in Figure 7–17.

Once the decryption step is complete, the receiving STA has recovered the original frame, plus the ICV that was supplied by the sending STA. The receiving STA calculates its own ICV, from scratch, over the received MSDU, and compares this to the ICV that was inside the WEP-protected MPDU. If the two ICVs match, the frame is accepted.

What Can Go Wrong? (Or: What's So Bad about WEP?)

There are a number of flaws in WEP; some are obvious, and others less so. As to the obvious flaws, we see that the initial authentication is very weak. Shared Key authentication is virtually no better than Open System authentication, since knowledge of the WEP keys can be very easy to come by. The very idea that it makes sense to operate a large network based on WEP is foolish, since the entire user population needs to have the same static key configuration. Consequently, the keys are not exactly a secret. When an employee leaves a company, or loses

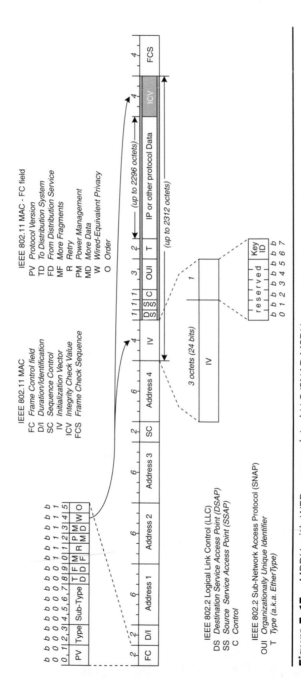

Figure 7-17 MPDU with WEP-encapsulated LLC/SNAP MSDU

his or her laptop, all of the remaining machines' keys should all be changed to protect the integrity of the corporation's network; however, in reality that is really quite unlikely to happen. The administrative overhead necessary to change what might be hundreds (or even thousands) of system configurations in a relatively short period of time makes changing the keys a prohibitively expensive operation. Anyone who knows the key can access the network, since no strong authentication is used.

On the topic of message authentication, even though WEP includes an ICV, it is not a keyed hash function, so its value is essentially zero. As we now know, the ICV is just a simple CRC-32 checksum, which WEP "protects" by appending it to the original MSDU and encrypting the whole thing. However, since the CRC-32 function is mathematically linear, flipping any bit in the ciphertext message results in a deterministic set of bits in the ICV that must be flipped to repair the ICV in the modified (and still encrypted) message. The location of the ICV in the encrypted frame can be found by working backward from the end of the MPDU...the ICV is the four octets that immediately precede the MPDU's FCS.

The bits that must be flipped are knowable even without knowing the key (i.e., an attacker does not need to have access to the plaintext to re-compute the encrypted ICV!). The modified MPDU's ICV can be repaired because any bits that the attacker flips in the encrypted ICV field are flipped in the plaintext that the receiver will recover after it decrypts the frame (by the properties of the exclusive-OR operator). Therefore, the attacker can flip arbitrary bits in an encrypted message and correctly adjust the checksum of the encrypted frame such that the resulting message appears valid, and can do this without first needing to decrypt the message.

This type of attack is known as a "bit flipping" attack, and it is not inherent in stream ciphers. If WEP employed a nonlinear ICV, bit-flipping attacks would be far more difficult, especially if the ICV depended on a secret key (separate from the encryption key) that was only known to the two communicating entities.

The biggest problem with WEP is that it specifies a ridiculously small IV, and the IEEE 802.11-1999 standard only *recommends* that it be changed periodically. The original standard makes the following statements about the IV (see Clause 8.2.3, page 63).[39] The second paragraph of this excerpt is a virtual recipe for many of the attacks that were subsequently successfully mounted against WEP.

---

39. Excerpted from IEEE Std. 802.11™-1999, copyright 1999. All rights reserved.

The IV extends the useful lifetime of the secret key and provides the self-synchronous property of the algorithm. The secret key remains constant while the IV changes periodically. Each new IV results in a new seed and key sequence, thus there is a one-to-one correspondence between the IV and k. The IV may be changed as frequently as every MPDU and, since it travels with the message, the receiver will always be able to decipher any message. The IV is transmitted in the clear since it does not provide an attacker with any information about the secret key, and since its value must be known by the recipient in order to perform the decryption.

When choosing how often to change IV values, implementors [sic] should consider that the contents of some fields in higher-layer protocol headers, as well as certain other higher-layer information, is constant or highly predictable. When such information is transmitted while encrypting with a particular key and IV, an eavesdropper can readily determine portions of the key sequence generated by that (key, IV) pair. If the same (key, IV) pair is used for successive MPDUs, this effect may substantially reduce the degree of privacy conferred by the WEP algorithm, allowing an eavesdropper to recover a subset of the user data without any knowledge of the secret key. Changing the IV after each MPDU is a simple method of preserving the effectiveness of WEP in this situation.

Despite the recommendation that the IV be changed (as frequently as on a per-MPDU basis!), the frequency at which that should happen was never actually specified, nor did the standard make it mandatory for an implementation to support changing the IV at all. It turns out that even if you do change the IV once per packet, an attacker won't have to wait long before one is re-used, and if a keystream is used twice, the attacker can begin to deduce quite a bit about the keys, eventually recovering the "secret" keys.

The ways the IV and keys are used in this particular application of RC4 make WEP extremely vulnerable to chosen plaintext attacks. The topic of cryptanalysis is beyond the scope of this book, but suffice it to say that it is easier to break a code if you can see some examples of ciphertext, especially if you know the plaintext that was used to create that ciphertext. It is easier to do this than you might think: If a cracker parks near a company, he or she can send packets to that subnet and see what they look like when encrypted. A cracker can do this by using a dial-up connection to an ISP over a cell phone to send a packet to one of the local machines (if it can determine the ISP subnet address of the WLAN). The AP will happily encrypt the frame before sending it to the destination STA, so the attacker will know the plaintext, the ciphertext, and the IV (from the encrypted frame itself).

As we know, WEP's IV is only 24 bits long, and it is sent in the clear, immediately following the MPDU header, and just before the encrypted MSDU+ICV. Given that the only thing that makes the keystream unique is the IV, and given that it is likely that the IV may not change for many frames, and given that the total space of initialization vectors is so small, virtually guarantees that a given keystream will be reused. How bad is this? It's much worse than one might think. If an AP had only one STA associated with it, which was receiving a steady stream of 1500-octet frames at 11 Mbps, all possible IVs would be used after only about five hours.

How do we arrive at this surprising result? There are 1500*8 (i.e., 12,000), bits in a 1500-octet frame. This corresponds to a frames-per-second (fps) rate of about (11,000,000 bps / 12,000 b), or a little more than 910 fps. To be precise, the theoretical best-case throughput of an IEEE 802.11b WLAN operating at a bit rate of 11 Mbps is just under 6.25 Mbps. This is the theoretical maximum bit rate, allowing for all types of overhead and all mandatory quiet intervals between frames. So, in reality, 910 fps at that frame size is absolutely unachievable.

The maximum frame rate for 1500-octet frames is more like (6,245,8560 bps / 12,000 b), or 520 fps. If the 2^{24} (16,777,216) IVs in the 24-bit IV space were used at the worst-case rate of one IV per frame (presuming for the moment that they were changed that rapidly), a cracker would be guaranteed to see an IV re-used in at most (16,777,216 / 520) seconds, or about 32,200 seconds. This is about 540 minutes, which is about nine hours. If the AP were not sending large-sized frames, then it could be sending more frames per second, which would further reduce the amount of time it would take to cycle through the 16 million or so IVs. Moreover, given that all the STAs and the AP share the same WEP keys, either 40- or 104-bits long, any frames sent to or received from other STAs will help eliminate the IVs that the cracker hasn't seen that much more quickly.

In practice, it's unlikely that an attacker will have to wait more than a few hours to observe a keystream being reused.

If an attacker can collect two frames that were encrypted with the same keystream, he or she can perform statistical analysis to recover the plaintext. If the cracker originated some of the frames that are subsequently "recovered," then the attacker knows the plaintext plus the IV, and has at least two different frames that were encrypted using the same keystream.

The five-hour figure is the worst-case length of time that an attacker would have to wait in order to have enough information to begin such an analysis. If the IV isn't changed that frequently, or at all, the attacker won't have to wait very long to find two frames that were encrypted with the same keystream. In such a scenario, attackers may not have to do very much at all before they know all the keys, especially if they send the frames and know what the plaintext looks like. Therefore, it's clear that making the WEP key longer (from 40 to 104 bits) did nothing to improve the security of WEP, since the weakness is in the small IV space and the fact that the keys, regardless of their length, are static.

Besides the ability to literally choose the plaintext in such an attack by sending packets that will cross the wired LAN for the attacker's examination, the structure of the MSDUs for many packet types is well known. Simply knowing the structure of the packets, and knowing that certain values always appear at certain offsets in the plaintext, may be sufficient to give just enough information that, if enough frames are harvested, enables a cracker to determine one or more of the keys. Remember that the keys are the only thing that stands between a legitimate user and a cracker in legacy IEEE 802.11-1999 WEP-based security. Software exists to allow a cracker to determine keys, hijack existing associations, impersonate APs or STAs, and so forth. The only thing the cracker needs is time. He or she doesn't even need to be present to carry out an attack...the cracker can drop a laptop in a concealed location, such as under a shrub on the outside of a building, which can then harvest the necessary information for a few days, so that by the time the cracker returns, the laptop will have derived enough information to enable the cracker to join the LAN as an (apparently) valid user. The only enemy of the cracker in such a scenario is the weather.

As a side note, WEP *does* support per-association keys, via a "key mapping key" table. The table can associate a WEP key with every (RA, TA) pair. The

IEEE 802.11-1999 standard requires that implementations shall support[40] a minimum of 10 key mapping keys, but provides no way to install the keys, other than manually. The MIB in which the key mapping key table is stored is mandatory-to-implement, according to the normative text of the standard, as well as the Protocol Implementation Conformance Statement (PICS). However, the initial test suite that was used to grant Wi-Fi logos did not require that key mapping keys be supported, so it is unclear how many implementations actually support this feature. (To be precise, the earliest Wi-Fi logo testing did not require that an AP or STA support more than one WEP key.) The lack of secure dynamic key distribution dooms any static scheme, due to the other weaknesses in the WEP encryption design.

If WEP had been designed with a better ICV, and a secure authentication and key management protocol, then it's possible that certain attacks might have been impractical, but the IV space was still too small, and the BSS would have to re-key at a fairly high rate to keep from reusing a keystream.

The Post-WEP Era: WLAN Security Evolves

The first "patch" to WEP was to allow longer keys. As we have seen, WEP's key length is not its weakness, and products that support longer (104-bit) keys have no security advantage over those that are limited to 40-bit keys. The only advantage of longer keys is in product marketing, since consumer perception is that bigger is usually better. That's the implicit (and incorrect) assertion that vendors of big-key WEP were making.

There were several inadequate attempts at an improved WEP, including WEP+, but the most effective initial "patch" to WEP was the Temporal Key Integrity Protocol (TKIP), that allowed per-association keys and provided for secure, dynamic key management based on IEEE 802.1X-2001. TKIP has evolved somewhat, but it is still based on the RC4 algorithm, which is not bad, since the algorithm was never the problem (although the stream-oriented cipher did enable certain kinds of attacks—e.g., bit flipping—that would not have been

---

40. The author has never seen a Wi-Fi product that supports key-mapping keys via the user interface, although the author would also like to state for the record that he has not seen everything. To qualify this statement, it's possible that a given implementation supports the MIB table that stores the key-mapping keys, but provides no user interface from which to configure them. However, given that the Wi-Fi Alliance does not make this feature part of their certification test suite, it would be easy for an implementer to justify not supporting this "mandatory" feature.

possible with a block-oriented cipher. The original TKIP still had a too-small IV space, and still used 40- or 104-bit keys. An upgraded version of TKIP (with fixes for those problems, plus a stronger ICV) is part of the IEEE 802.11*i* draft standard, and is the basis for the Wi-Fi Alliance's Wi-Fi Protected Access (WPA) specification.

The third "patch" to WEP is effectively a complete alternative to WEP. The IEEE 802.11*i* TG is defining new encryption schemes for WLANs, based on the Advanced Encryption Standard (AES). The AES-based based protocol is called <u>C</u>ounter-mode with <u>C</u>ipher-block-chaining <u>M</u>essage authentication code (i.e., <u>C</u>ounter-mode with <u>C</u>BC-<u>M</u>AC) <u>P</u>rotocol (CCMP), and it leverages the same secure dynamic key distribution protocol that is based on a four-way handshake using IEEE 802.1X-inspired frames, while offering a much stronger encryption algorithm. The combination of TKIP and CCMP, with IEEE 802.1X, is known as Robust Security Network, or RSN.

Even though there is no way to be sure what will emerge when IEEE 802.11*i* is complete, it is a fairly safe bet that there will be one AES-based ciphersuite (almost certainly CCMP), one RC4-based ciphersuite (TKIP), and IEEE 802.1X-based authentication and key management protocols. The precise details of the final standard may differ from what they are today, but the author feels safe stating the current frame transformations that are involved in TKIP and CCMP, and in stating the current authentication and key management protocol, because he believes that any changes are likely to be in the tiny details, not in the overall functions achieved by the protocols, and it is highly unlikely that the features defined today will be dropped. It is likely that modifications will be made to the IEEE 802.1X-based authentication and key management protocols, to support fast roaming (for handing off associations quickly from one AP to the next...fast enough that, for example, VoIP telephony connections will not be interrupted).

IEEE 802.11*i*—Robust Security Network

Once the IEEE 802.11*i* draft standard is complete, there will be a total of three authentication and key management architectures in IEEE 802.11, namely the two that were originally defined for use in the context of WEP in IEEE 802.11-1997 (i.e., "Open System" and "Shared Key"), and the newer IEEE 802.1X-based authentication mechanisms that are defined for use in the context of an IEEE 802.11*i* RSN. In fact, the term "RSN" is synonymous with "an IEEE 802.11 LAN that uses an IEEE 802.1X-based Authentication and Key Management Protocol." The terms "RSN" and "IEEE 802.1X" are effectively synonymous, since an RSN is defined in the IEEE 802.11*i* draft as "An IEEE 802.11 ESS relying on IEEE 802.1X for its authentication and key management services."

There are two different RSN ciphersuites, one based on AES (CCMP), and one based on RC4 (TKIP). TKIP is a significant improvement over WEP, and is designed to be implementable on most hardware platforms that already support WEP. This allows an upgrade path for end users who have already made substantial investments in WLAN technology, since TKIP can be installed in many older devices by simply upgrading the firmware and/or driver software. However, despite the fact that TKIP is a massive improvement over WEP, it is not the best available security solution. To achieve this level of security, end users must purchase and deploy new AP hardware that includes support for AES encryption. The new hardware will probably support both TKIP and CCMP, so that STAs can support either type of encryption.

In fact, the IEEE 802.11*i* draft includes support for what it calls "transition security networks" or TSNs, in which APs may support a mix of WEP and RSN STAs. This is horrifically insecure (in fact, it is no better than WEP, since every frame that is super-encrypted by RSN between an RSN STA and the AP is then only WEP-encrypted to a legacy STA). If an attacker can crack WEP (and we know that tools to do that are readily available), then the attacker can intercept traffic that an RSN STA sends to a pre-RSN STA. The benefits of RSN do not begin to accrue until the entire LAN is migrated to RSN-capable status.

RSN Authentication and Key Management Mechanisms

IEEE 802.1X "Port-Based Network Authentication" was originally designed for bridged (i.e., layer-2 switched) networks, in which eavesdropping is infeasible (or at least somewhat challenging) due to the fact that each station is endowed with a dedicated link to a bridge (i.e., layer-2 switch). The original IEEE 802.1X standard was designed based on the assumption that tapping into the communication link between the station and the bridge/switch was nontrivial, and would be relatively easy to detect.

By the time that implementations of the IEEE 802.1X-2001 standard first appeared, networks had been rapidly adopting bridged (i.e., layer-2 switched) topologies for quite some time, rapidly moving away from shared-media hubs, so there was no strong demand for IEEE 802.1X-2001 to support shared-media LANs, although the standard does not prohibit operation over shared LAN topologies. As IEEE 802.11 LANs increased in popularity, the need for a properly designed authentication and key management protocol manifested itself. It was natural for the IEEE 802.11*i* TG to want to leverage mechanisms that had already been defined in another IEEE 802 standard, rather than inventing something that was totally specific to IEEE 802.11. However, in shared-medium networks such as those based on IEEE 802.11, extensions to IEEE 802.1X needed to be defined such that its network authentication services could be provided securely, because eavesdropping was not only possible, it was easy.

IEEE 802.1X-2001 defines a framework based on operating the Extensible Authentication Protocol (EAP)[41] over LANs, via a protocol known as EAPoL (or EAPOL). IEEE 802.11 is an example of the cryptographer's worst-case threat model: the adversary is the channel, in that an attacker can choose to deliver or block any frame, misroute frames, corrupt and modify frames, or even create forged frames from scratch (given sufficient information). The implication of this is that no shortcuts to security are possible. The wireless environment is, if not inherently hostile toward valid users then at least it is inherently friendly toward malicious users.

Because the original IEEE 802.1X was unsuitable for use in the IEEE 802.11 environment, extensions to IEEE 802.1X were defined to ensure that the network authentication services provided by the extended IEEE 802.1X would be as secure in IEEE 802.11 wireless shared-medium networks as the IEEE 802.1X procedures that are used in dedicated-media networks such as bridged (switched) IEEE 802.3 LANs.

---

41. The EAP was originally designed to support authentication over PPP, and is a product of the IETF. The use of EAP within the PPP context is defined by RFC-2284. As of August 2003, the EAP specification is being updated to specifically broaden its applicability beyond PPP, as well as clarify (and in some ways, extend) the specification.

The EAP is not tied to any particular authentication algorithm, hence its extensibility (and hence also why it cannot define a secure keying scheme[42]). The EAP defines a small number of messages that are used to communicate between the EAP Client (in the device seeking to be authenticated) and the AS. This design allows the two peer EAP entities to mutually determine whether the device seeking to be authenticated should be granted access to the network (based on the algorithm-specific authentication credentials, such as the user's identification and password). In IEEE 802.11i, there is a strong preference for choosing EAP methods that provide for strong mutual authentication, so that both sides know that they are communicating with the intended party, and not an impersonator implementing a man-in-the-middle attack. The EAPoL Authenticator (resident within the AP in the case of IEEE 802.11, or in an Ethernet bridge (switch) in the case of IEEE 802.3) is only required to interpret the outcome of the negotiation without being required to participate in the negotiation itself.

EAPoL is used to exchange the EAP messages that are actually performing the authentication between the STA that is seeking to be authenticated (the EAP Client) and an EAP "server" entity known as the Authentication Server (AS). The EAPoL Supplicant is an EAP and EAPoL "client." The Authentication Server is not an EAPoL entity, unless it is embedded in the same machine as the EAPoL Authenticator. The station seeking to be authenticated uses EAPoL to communicate across its local LAN segment with a device that enforces the authentication; for example, an Ethernet bridge (i.e., layer-2 switch) or an IEEE 802.11 AP.

Again, the EAPoL exchange takes place between two entities, one associated with the station desiring to be authenticated, an EAPoL entity known as the "Supplicant," and the other associated with the device that enforces the access to the network (e.g., the bridge (i.e., layer-2 switch) or AP, an EAPoL entity known as the "Authenticator." Besides restricting network access only to authenticated stations, the Authenticator also acts as a mediator

---

42. The entire EAP exchange is vulnerable to spoofing and man-in-the-middle attacks. Thus, it is critical to choose an authentication method that was designed to defend itself from these attacks. Moreover, the EAPoL message conveying the EAP-Success can be forged as well, so the authentication method should also be sure to derive a fresh key that is used to protect all EAP messages subsequent to the key derivation.

in the EAP conversation between the EAP Client and the AS. Table 7–2 lists the five types of EAPoL packets that may be sent, according to IEEE 802.1X-2001.

Table 7–2   EAPoL Packet Types

0x00	EAP-Packet	Indicates that an EAPoL frame contains an EAP packet
0x01	EAPoL-Start	Used to initiate EAP protocol processing
0x02	EAPoL-Logoff	Not recommended for use with IEEE 802.11
0x03	EAPoL-Key	Used by the Authenticator and Supplicant to derive or exchange cryptographic keying information
0x04	EAPoL-Encapsulated-ASF-Alert	Used by a Supplicant's STA to send Alert Standard Format (ASF) alerts (e.g., Platform Event Traps* prior to the STA being fully authenticated)

* ASF alerts are known as Platform Event Trap (PET) frames, and are a specific kind of SNMP trap.

EAP packets are encapsulated in EAP-Packet frames to enable them to cross the LAN segment between the Supplicant and the Authenticator. EAPoL also provides some control features; for example, an EAPoL-Start message was defined to initiate the EAPoL exchange; similarly, an EAPoL-Logoff message was defined to terminate a connection. Even though these two control messages are part of IEEE 802.1X-2001, the IEEE 802.11i draft does not require them. IEEE 802.1X-2001 also defined an optional capability to use the EAPoL-Key [Descriptor] message[43] to exchange cryptographic keys, but no mechanism was defined to enable keys to be exchanged securely. Note that the format of the EAPoL-Key [Descriptor] message in IEEE 802.11 is different from that in IEEE 802.1X-2001. The format of the EAPoL-Key Descriptor that is used in IEEE 802.11i is shown in Figure 7–18.

---

43. Note that the format of IEEE 802.11's EAPoL-Key [Descriptor] is different from that of IEEE 802.1X-2001.

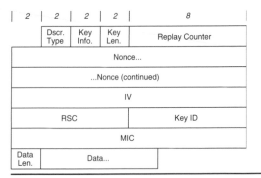

Figure 7–18   Format of the EAPoL-Key Descriptor

Figure 7–19 depicts the protocol relationships among the Supplicant (associated with the EAP Client's STA), Authenticator (associated with the AP's STA), and the AS. It also shows the relationship of EAP to EAPoL (and of EAP to RADIUS), which is one example of a protocol that may be used to implement a secure channel between the Authenticator and the AS). The Supplicant and the AS exchange messages encoded in the EAP, and these EAP messages are encapsulated in EAPoL frames as they are transmitted between Supplicant and the Authenticator across their common LAN segment.

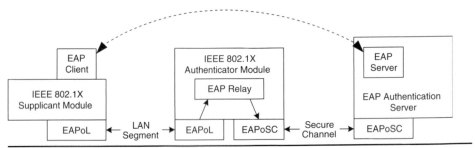

Figure 7–19   Authentication and key management protocol peer relationships

At the EAP layer, the EAP peers are unaware of the presence of the Authenticator, which simply serves as a relay between the EAPoL and EAP-over-Secure-Channel domains. The EAPoL Authenticator[44] simply acts as a relay for these EAP packets by extracting the EAP packets from within the EAPoL frames and sending those EAP packets to the Authentication Server over the

---

44. In IEEE 802.11's use of IEEE 802.1X, the Authenticator is associated with the AP's STA.

secure channel that is required to exist between the EAPoL Authenticator and the EAP AS. EAPoL employs a small number of frame types to carry the various EAP messages between the Supplicant and the Authenticator across their common LAN segment.

The IEEE 802.11i draft will neither specify nor mandate the protocol(s) to be used to secure the Authenticator-to-AS channel. A typical implementation of IEEE 802.11i, for example, might be based on RADIUS.[45] Even though RADIUS is not mandated by the IEEE 802.11i or IEEE 802.1X standards, it is a convenient protocol that many early implementations of IEEE 802.11i will use for securely exchanging EAP messages between the Authenticator and AS, as well as a secure out-of-band channel for Pairwise Master Key (PMK)[46] distribution from the AS to the Authenticator.

RADIUS, or any protocol with similar attributes that can provide a secure channel over which the EAP packets can flow, is logically equivalent to EAPoL, in that it is used to encapsulate the EAP packets between the Authenticator and the AS, after the EAP packets have been extracted from the EAPoL frame.

RADIUS has messages to augment EAP; for example, special RADIUS packet types have been defined that may be used to transmit the PMK from the Authentication Server to the Authenticator, over the secure channel[47] between the AS and the Authenticator. Any other protocol used to implement the Authenticator-to-AS secure channel would also need to support additional message types such as this, to support the proper operation of EAP. The transmission of the PMK to the Authenticator is not accomplished using EAP messages, since EAP is an end-to-end protocol between the Supplicant (EAP Client) and the AS (EAP Server).

EAP Packets and EAPoL Frames

All EAPoL frames are normal IEEE 802.11 data frames, thus they follow the format of IEEE 802.11 MSDUs and MPDUs. With reference to the IEEE

---

45. Another protocol that may become useful for this purpose is Diameter, which is in the early stages of standardization by the IETF.

46. All the cryptographic keys used to protect the link are derived from the PMK. Each peer confirms the other peer's validity, since each peer's use of the PMK confirms that the IEEE 802.1X authentication phase authorized the peer-to-peer channel created by this association.

47. The secure channel must be present, and is provided by RADIUS or a protocol with similar capabilities.

802.11 frame format defined in IEEE 802.11-1999 Clause 7.1.2, an MPDU may be up to 2346 octets in length, which encapsulates an MSDU payload that is up to 2312 octets in length. The remaining 34 octets in the MPDU comprise the IEEE 802.11 header (24 or 30 octets) and the four-octet Frame Check Sequence that concludes the frame. For practical reasons, it is safer to presume that the long form of the MPDU header will be used, so that the MSDU will not need to be fragmented.

EAPoL messages, like other data packets (MSDUs) that are transmitted over IEEE 802.11 LANs, are de-multiplexed using information contained in the LLC (or LLC/SNAP) header, which comprises the first three (or eight) octets of the MSDU. In the particular case of EAPoL frames, LLC/SNAP encapsulation is used. Figure 7–20 illustrates an MPDU that contains an EAP packet, encapsulated in an EAPoL (IEEE 802.1X) header.

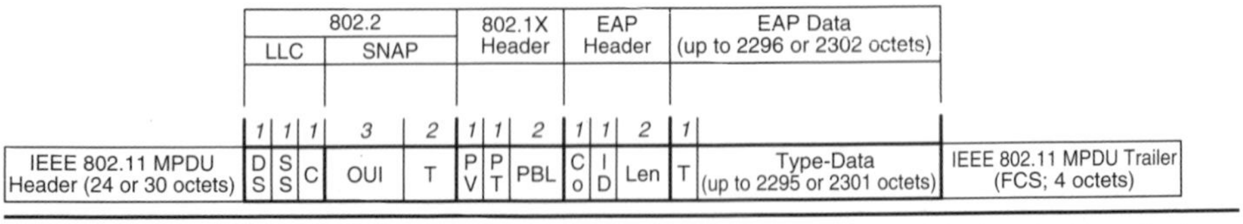

Figure 7–20   Format of an IEEE 802.11 MPDU with an embedded EAPoL packet

Referring to Figure 7–20, the IEEE 802.2 LLC header's DS (Destination Service Access Point, or DSAP) and SS (Source Service Access Point, or SSAP) fields are both set to a value of 0xAA, indicating that an IEEE 802.2 SNAP header follows the LLC header. The IEEE 802.2 LLC header's Control field is set to 0x03, indicating that this is an unnumbered information frame. To indicate that a standard Ethernet type is being used in the IEEE 802.2 SNAP header's Type field, the IEEE 802.2 SNAP OUI field is set to a value of 0x000000. A value of 0x888E in the SNAP header's Type field indicates that an IEEE 802.1X frame header is next.

The IEEE 802.1X header begins immediately after SNAP's Type field, starting with the Protocol Version (PV) field, the value of which is defined in the current IEEE 802.1X specification. The version specified in the IEEE 802.1X-2001 specification is 0x01. The next field is the one-octet IEEE 802.1X Packet Type (PT), the five values of which were listed previously, in Table 7–2.

The IEEE 802.1X Packet Body Length (PBL) follows the Packet Type. Because the LLC/SNAP header is eight octets long, and the IEEE 802.1X header is an additional four octets, a total of 12 octets of the available MPDU payload is consumed, leaving 12 octets less for the MSDU, so the IEEE 802.1X PBL value can be at most 2300 octets (based on the fact that the MSDU can be at most 2312 octets). The limit of 2300 is for unencrypted EAPoL-Key messages. Note that in cases where the EAPoL-Key message is encrypted—using CCMP or TKIP—additional octets will be consumed, which will have the effect of further reducing the MPDU's payload capacity; hence the maximum PBL will not be able to be as large as if encryption were not performed. In the case of EAP, the need to transmit large-sized frames that would bump up against this restriction is dependent on the authentication method being used.

When the Packet Type field in an EAPoL packet is set to a value of 0x00 (meaning EAP-Packet), an EAP header follows the IEEE 802.1X (EAPoL) header. The EAP packet header begins with a one-octet Code field that defines the function of the EAP packet. The EAP packet format is shown in Figure 7–21:[48]

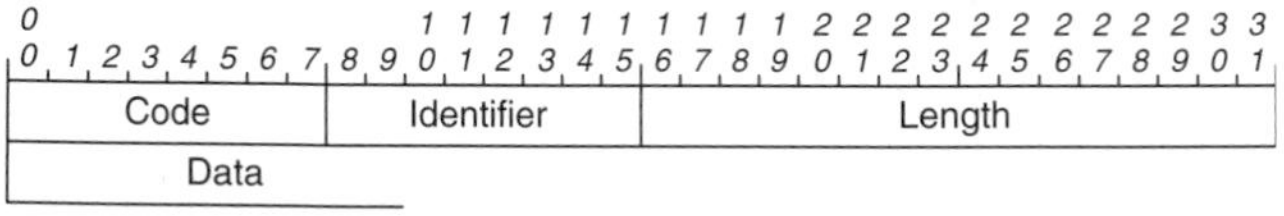

Figure 7–21   EAP packet format

There are four EAP Codes: 0x01 (Request), 0x02 (Response), 0x03 (Success), and 0x04 (Failure). For EAP-Request or -Response packets, the one-octet Identifier field contains a value that is used to match Responses to Requests. An EAP packet need not have a Data field, but a Data field will be present if the Code is set to Request or Response. For such EAP-Request and EAP-Response packets, the first octet of the Data field is a Type field that indicates which authentication algorithm is in use (e.g., EAP-TLS, EAP-PEAP, EAP-TTLS, etc.). The remainder of the Data field will be algorithm-specific data.

The STA initiates the association process. Once the STA and AP have completed setting up their association, the AP and STA will indicate success via one of the following APIs:

---

48. Note that the IETF's EAP WG is busy updating the EAP specification, so it is possible that this packet format will change. See RFC-2284 or its successor, for the current specification of EAP.

- MLME-ASSOCIATE.indication
- MLME-ASSOCIATE.confirm
- MLME-REASSOCIATE.indication
- MLME-REASSOCIATE.confirm

If the AP is RSN-capable and configured such that RSN is enabled, the Authenticator sends an EAPoL EAP-Packet message to the Supplicant, which contains an EAP-Request (Identity) packet. The entire packet exchange is shown in Figure 7–26. Before we examine that entire exchange, we will see how the peers prepare for this exchange.

The EAPoL-Start message is triggered once the STA and the AP have completed their association, a condition that is detected by one of the APIs listed previously. The Supplicant's STA includes the RSN Information Element (RSN IE) in the management frames that are used to facilitate association, which lets the Authenticator's STA (in the AP) know that this particular STA desires to join the RSN. The AP constructs its RSN IE based on whatever subset of its RSN capabilities are enabled, and the AP then includes the RSN IE in its Beacon and Probe Response frames.

After the association has been established, only IEEE 802.1X protocol messages (i.e., EAP and its associated authentication method) flow across the link until authentication completes; the IEEE 802.1X Port Access Entity (PAE) in the Supplicant filters all non-EAP traffic during this period. The AP also has a per-association PAE and all traffic to and from this STA will also be filtered at the AP. Until upper-layer authentication completes, the PAE ensures that only EAP packets are sent or received between this STA and the WM.

The IEEE 802.1X-based Authentication and Key Management protocols and selected EAP method allows the Authenticator and the Supplicant to prove to each other that they both know the PMK. It is essential that this be done without divulging the PMK to eavesdroppers. Even though the EAP-Client (EAPoL Supplicant) has been successfully authenticated by the Authentication Server, it cannot use the link until it has successfully derived the necessary encryption and authentication keys, which depend on the ciphersuite chosen in the RSN IE in the AP's Beacon and Probe Response frames. The format of the RSN IE is depicted in Figure 7–22.

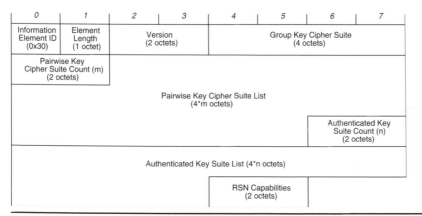

0	1	2	3	4	5	6	7
Information Element ID (0x30)	Element Length (1 octet)	Version (2 octets)		Group Key Cipher Suite (4 octets)			
Pairwise Key Cipher Suite Count (m) (2 octets)							
Pairwise Key Cipher Suite List (4*m octets)						Authenticated Key Suite Count (n) (2 octets)	
Authenticated Key Suite List (4*n octets)				RSN Capabilities (2 octets)			

Figure 7–22   Format of the RSN IE

The ciphersuites and the Authenticated Key Management Protocol suite selectors all have the same format. They consist of a three-octet OUI field, which allows for vendor extensions (the value 0x000000 is reserved for ciphersuites described in the forthcoming IEEE 802.11*i* standard, which will eventually be integrated into a future version of IEEE 802.11, presuming that IEEE 802.11*i* succeeds in producing a ratified standard). Figure 7–23 shows the format of a generic suite selector.

Organizationally Unique Identifier (3 octets)	Suite Type (1 octet)

Figure 7–23   RSN IE ciphersuite selector format

Vendors that have their own OUI may define up to 256 suite types per OUI using this structure. Figure 7–24 shows some of the currently defined suite selectors (taken from the IEEE 802.11*i* draft, version 5.0). Note that there is no defined Authentication Suite selector for either Open System or Shared Key authentication, since these selectors are only usable in the context of pre-RSN devices. Only an RSN-related authentication method would need to be specified within an RSN IE.

An alert reader may wonder why, if there is no authentication suite selector for Open System or Shared Key authentication, are there not one but *two* ciphersuite selectors for WEP? The answer is that WEP encryption can be used as a group ciphersuite, while at the same time CCMP or TKIP is used as

Authentication and Key Management Protocol Suite Selectors	
0x000000:01	Auth: IEEE 802.1X (EAP) Key Mgmt: IEEE 802.1X (RSN Key Hierarchy)
0x000000:02	Auth: \<none\> Key Mgmt: IEEE 802.1X (PSK)

Pairwise or Group Cipher Suite Selectors	
0x000000:00	Use group key
0x000000:01	WEP-40
0x000000:02	TKIP
0x000000:03	WRAP (historical)
0x000000:04	CCMP (RSN default)
0x000000:05	WEP-104
0x000000:06	\<reserved\>
⋮	⋮
0x000000:FF	\<reserved\>

Figure 7–24   IEEE 802.11*i* ciphersuite selectors

a unicast ciphersuite. The rule for unicast versus multicast ciphersuite selection is that the unicast cipher must always be stronger than the group ciphersuite. It is, therefore, not possible to use WEP as a unicast ciphersuite in the context of RSN, because there is no weaker ciphersuite that one might choose as the group ciphersuite.

Note that the protocol specification related ciphersuite number 0x03 (WRAP) has been removed from the IEEE 802.11*i* draft specification. WRAP was an AES-128-based encryption algorithm based on Offset Codebook (OCB) mode, and the acronym WRAP stood for "Wireless Robust Authenticated Protocol." WRAP last appeared in the 3.0 version of the IEEE 802.11*i* draft. WRAP's ciphersuite selector ID value assignment will be preserved so that vendors who had already implemented WRAP still have a legal way to identify that ciphersuite within the RSN IE.

EAP Negotiation Procedure

An EAP authentication method is negotiated as follows. One peer proposes an EAP authentication method to the other by sending an EAP-Request packet with the Type field's value set to the assigned number of the desired authentication method. If the receiving peer supports that authentication method, it will respond with an EAP-Response using the same Type as was proposed by the first peer. If the receiving peer does not support this authentication method, its EAP-Response packet will have the Type set to "NAK", and the original peer may then attempt to authenticate using a different method by proposing a different Type. A successful EAP authentication message flow is documented in the upper portion of Figure 7–26.

In the case of IEEE 802.11*i*'s usage of IEEE 802.1X messages, the Authenticator initiates the EAP exchange by sending an EAP-Request to the Supplicant, which then responds. The Authenticator passes the response to the AS, which then begins to send messages to implement its preferred EAP method; for example, EAP-TLS (the *de facto* EAP method in early implementations of IEEE 802.11*i*). The Authenticator is triggered to begin the exchange by noticing that the association has completed properly.

At the completion of a successful EAP authentication exchange, the AS informs the EAP Supplicant that the authentication has succeeded by sending an EAP-Success packet (Code = 0×03). The Authenticator is able to detect the EAP-Success code, and registers the fact that this EAPoL Supplicant now represents an authenticated station. Using the secure channel between the AS and the Authenticator, the AS also sends one other essential piece of information to the Authenticator, the PMK that has been generated by both the EAP-Client (EAPoL Supplicant) and the AS. By virtue of the EAP-Client's authentication exchange with the AS, the EAP-Client already knows the PMK.

Neither the Supplicant nor the Authenticator can trust the channel for communication until they have securely determined that each party knows the PMK, because neither has authenticated the other (only the AS and EAP-Client have mutually authenticated). Hence, the AP (Authenticator) does not yet know it is communicating with the party that the AS authenticated, and the STA (Supplicant) does not yet know it is communicating directly with a legitimate AP.

In order to establish a secure channel, the Authenticator and Supplicant use a "four-way handshake," in which each peer can convince itself that it is communicating with the intended peer for this association, and to use the PMK to derive the operational cryptographic keys that will protect this session. The four-way handshake demonstrates to each peer that the other peer knows the PMK, without leaking any useful information to a computationally bound attacker, active or passive. The four-way handshake provides each peer with proof that the other peer knows the PMK, and therefore that they both are whom they claim to be.

The bottom portion of Figure 7–26 includes the steps involved in the four-way handshake, which is comprised entirely of EAPoL-Key messages. A replay counter is part of each EAPoL-Key message, which enables detection (and thus prevention) of replay attacks. The replay counter is incremented by 1 for each successive message in the four-way handshake. Each retransmission of a given message uses the same replay counter value as was used when the message was first transmitted.

Filtering (from the STA's Perspective)

Until the four-way handshake is complete, the only unicast frames that are permitted to be sent by the STA are IEEE 802.1X (EAPoL) frames. The IEEE 802.1X Port Access Entity enforces this constraint. Once the four-way handshake is complete, the STA has unicast pairwise keys and can receive encrypted unicast frames; for example, the frames involved in the group key handshake, which follows the four-way handshake. Once the group key handshake (which is only two messages) has completed successfully, the STA is now able to decrypt multicast traffic encrypted with the group temporal key by the AP. (In infrastructure mode, the only device that sends encrypted multicast traffic is the AP.)

Before delving into the four-way handshake, it might be a good idea to review how we got here. Figure 7–25 shows the sequence of messages that leads from a STA joining a WLAN up to when it needs to begin the four-way IEEE 802.1X authentication phase. Remember that the messages related to Open System authentication only exist to retain backward compatibility with the IEEE 802.11-1999 state machine that governed the ordering of initial events; in other words, the original standard dictated that Authentication preceded Association.

The complete four-way handshake is depicted in Figure 7–26. The figure shows the four-way handshake in the context of the entire access process, picking up where Figure 7–25 left off. The EAPoL exchange is the authentication exchange, and the four-way handshake is the key management exchange.

The First Message of the Four-Way Handshake

The first EAPoL-Key message of the four-way handshake is sent from the Authenticator to the Supplicant. The main purpose of the first message is to carry the randomly generated Authenticator Nonce (ANonce). Any observer could eavesdrop on this message and learn the Authenticator's chosen ANonce. Upon receiving the first message, the Supplicant has learned the

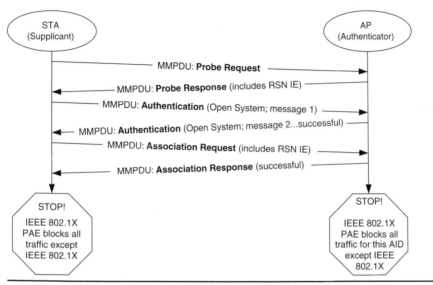

Figure 7–25   Prerequisite messages to the four-way handshake

ANonce. Subsequent messages in the four-way handshake ensure that only the legitimate Authenticator is in communication with the Supplicant.

Any eavesdropper could also have attempted to impersonate the Authenticator by forging an EAPoL-Key message after it saw the EAP-Success packet. However, such an impostor would not know the PMK; thus it will not be able to successfully forge future EAPoL-Key messages, so the only exposure at this point is possibly to denial-of-service (DoS) attacks.

What the heck is a nonce? It's a very important type of unique number. The definition from Clause 3 of IEEE 802.11*i* is very strict: "A [random] value that is never reused with a key. 'Never reused within a context' means exactly that, including over all re-initializations of the system through all time." The nonces are used to guarantee that a fresh key is generated each time the four-way handshake is executed between two given peers.

It is of the utmost importance, from a security perspective, to make sure that each new negotiation is as unique as possible, not just in the PMK, but in the nonces as well. In the context of IEEE 802.11*i*'s four-way handshake, the nonce is required to be random (or at least pseudo-random), and it must absolutely never be used again. One could imagine concatenating

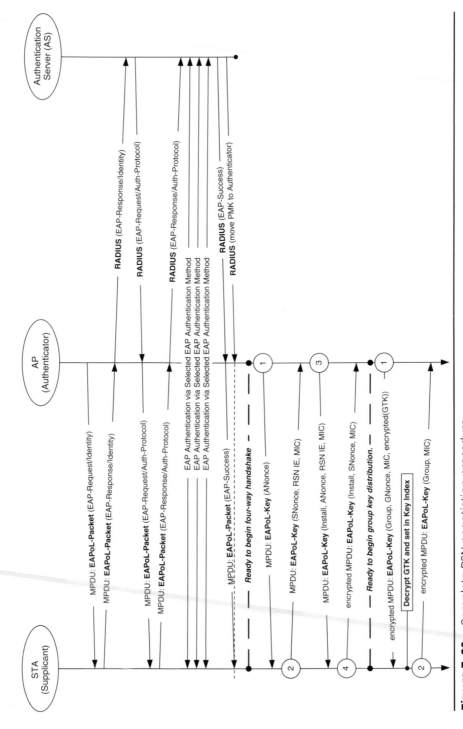

Figure 7-26 Complete RSN negotiation procedure

a system clock value,[49] or a hash of a system clock value, with a random value, to make a number that is guaranteed to be a) randomly chosen, and b) unique for all time.

The Second Message of the Four-Way Handshake

This message acknowledges receipt of the first message, flowing back from the Supplicant to the Authenticator. Of course, the act of sending this message does not serve as an acknowledgment until after the Supplicant can tell that the Authenticator has received this message. Using MAC-layer ACK procedures, the Supplicant may be able to tell that the Authenticator has received the second message, but the MAC-layer ACK could be forged, so the only real proof that the Authenticator has received the second message is for the Supplicant to receive the third message. If the Supplicant does not hear the third message within a reasonable amount of time, it will re-transmit the second message (up to three times). Because of the cryptographic protections on which the four-way handshake is built, the second through fourth messages of the four-way handshake can only be forged if the PMK has been compromised.

The second message carries the RSN IE (see Figure 7–22) that the Supplicant's STA has constructed based on the ciphersuites it supports, and is the same RSN IE that the Supplicant's STA used during the association process with the AP. The EAPoL-Key Descriptor's Data field is used to transport the RSN IE. To be specific, the STA indicates the authentication suite and key management suite, as well as the unicast and group ciphersuites that it supports, in the Association Request message that it sent to the AP well before the four-way handshake ever started.

When the Authenticator receives the second message of the four-way handshake, it knows that there is no man-in-the-middle. The contents of the second message are sufficient to prove (in a cryptographically sound sense) that this is the case. After receiving the second message, the Authenticator also knows that the Supplicant has computed the PTK, and now the Authenticator has the necessary information to do the same.

The AP has created its own RSN IE that defines which ciphersuites are allowed to be used within this ESS. By sending its RSN IE to the Authenticator's STA in

---

49. For example, the time expressed as a Julian day, which is a monotonically increasing value, would be a possible choice.

the second message, the Supplicant's STA informs the Authenticator's STA of which ciphersuites it supports, which controls how the keys are derived, and it is confirming that it is the same STA that associated with the AP. The STA's choice of valid cryptographic algorithms is made from the intersection of the set of ciphersuites that are supported by the STA and the set that is supported by the AP (which the STA learned from either a Beacon or Probe Response that was generated by the AP).

The Supplicant randomly chooses[50] its own nonce, known as the SNonce after it received the first message. At this point, the Supplicant has sufficient information to generate the temporal keys used for directed packet transmission and reception. Moreover, derived cryptographic keys protecting [51] the remainder of the key exchange are derived from the ANonce contained in this first message, as well as being based on the SNonce and the STA's RSN IE.

A message digest of the second message is included as part of the second message. This message digest protects (i.e., is computed over) this entire EAPoL-Key Descriptor and uses one of the keys that the Supplicant has derived from the PMK and the two nonces, among other inputs. Specifically, the Supplicant has derived the EAPoL-Key MIC Key (MK). This key is more generically known as a Key Confirmation Key, or KCK. The next subsection describes the key derivation procedure in more detail.

The message digest of the second message is included in the MIC field of the EAPoL-Key Descriptor, which is illustrated in Figure 7–27.

The Authenticator will be able to verify this message digest once it has received the second message from the Supplicant, and will be able to derive the EAPoL-Key MK for itself once it has received the second message (the Authenticator cannot calculate the MK until after it has received the SNonce from the Supplicant). Only a Supplicant that knew both of the nonces *and the PMK* could have sent this message, since it contains a message digest that could only have been computed if the PMK were known.

---

50. Once the Supplicant has generated its SNonce, it has sufficient information to derive the necessary encryption and authentication keys that will be used throughout this security association, pending successful completion of the four-way handshake. Of course, the Authenticator does not yet know the SNonce, which is one of the purposes of the second message.

51. By protecting, we mean that knowing the keys enables the message integrity and confidentiality services.

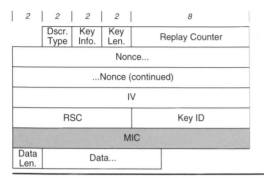

Figure 7–27   EAPoL-Key Descriptor format with the MIC field highlighted

To summarize, the second message of the four-way handshake serves to transmit the SNonce to the Authenticator, and this message also includes a cryptographic message digest that allows the Authenticator to verify that it is communicating with the same STA that had associated with it earlier. This message confirms to the Authenticator that the Supplicant is legitimate and that there is no "man-in-the-middle" attack under way. Like the first message, the second message is also sent in the clear (but as noted previously, it is protected by the message digest that is computed over the EAPoL-Key Descriptor and which is included as part of the EAPoL-Key Descriptor, in the MIC field of the Descriptor).

The second message can also be observed by third parties, who would now have seen the ANonce in the first message and the SNonce and second message, as well as the Supplicant's RSN IE, but who nonetheless cannot forge the message digest (MIC) in the EAPoL-Key message without knowledge of the PMK.

DERIVATION OF CRYPTOGRAPHIC KEYS

The EAP method in use may generate a Master Key, from which a session-specific PMK will be derived. Regardless of whether a Master Key is generated, the EAP negotiation will conclude with the AS and Supplicant (the EAP peers) knowing a PMK. They may also, depending on the EAP method, know a Master Key. The Master Key, if known, is kept private to the EAP peers. The PMK is sent to the EAPoL Authenticator (the AP), and is used by the Supplicant and the Authenticator to prove to each other that they are both who they claim to be. Note that once the user has successfully authenticated, the AS is supposed to maintain no record of the PMK (i.e., after the AS is sure that the Authenticator has the PMK, the AS will delete it).

The key derivation procedure establishes a chain of trust, which is based on the user's credentials and the configuration of the network. The configuration of the network ensures that the Authenticator and the Supplicant share a common LAN segment, and that the Authenticator and the AS are connected by a secure channel (which probably crosses multiple router hops, but is logically a direct link between the two of them). The EAP method is used to establish the credentials and validate the user, to form the basis for the network access control that is performed by the Authenticator.

The key derivation process alluded to previously, which is performed in parallel by both the Supplicant and the Authenticator, is known as the "Pairwise Key Hierarchy." The Pairwise Key Hierarchy defines how to combine the ANonce, SNonce, the Authenticator's MAC address (AA), the Supplicant's MAC address (SA), a specific ASCII string, and the PMK as input to a pseudo-random function (PRF). The PRF outputs a large enough number of bits sufficient to define the EAPoL-Key Encryption Key (EK), the EAPoL-Key Message Integrity Check (MIC) Key (MK), and the necessary Pairwise Temporal Key(s) for protecting unicast data traffic (the PTK material is used for both authentication and encryption). The length of the output of the PRF depends on the ciphersuite that was determined based on comparing the RSN IEs during the association process.

Specifically, the PRF output is separated into the following components: the MK (used to create a keyed message digest of certain of the EAPoL-Key Descriptor messages, to bind the Supplicant and Authenticator to the PMK), the EK (used to encrypt the EAPoL-Key Descriptor's Key Material field during the Group Key Exchange, but it is not used in the four-way handshake that implements the pairwise key exchange), and the temporal key(s) for the ciphersuite defined in the RSN IE. The Pairwise Key Hierarchy is illustrated in Figure 7–28.

The complete output of the pseudo-random function (PRF) is known as the Pairwise Transient Key (PTK), of which bits 0–127 are the MK, bits 128–255 are the EK, and bits 256–383 represent temporal key number 1 (TK1). Temporal key

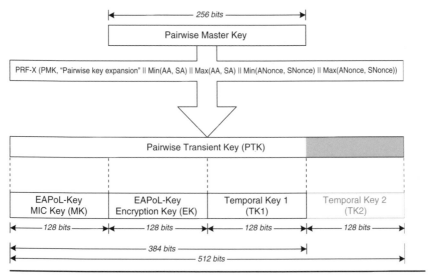

Figure 7–28   The Pairwise Key Hierarchy

number 2 (TK2), if present (which depends on the needs of the ciphersuite defined in the RSN IE), is found in bits 384–511.

Note again that the Authenticator cannot perform the PTK derivation until it has received the SNonce from the Supplicant, since the SNonce is part of the input in the PTK derivation. In other words, the Authenticator cannot derive the EAPoL-Key MK, EAPoL-Key EK, and the Temporal Key(s) until after it has received the second message of the four-way handshake. The Authenticator and the Supplicant both derive identical temporal keys because they both compute the Pairwise Key Hierarchy using the same inputs. Because only this Supplicant and this Authenticator (and the Authentication Server) are presumed to know the PMK, no eavesdropper can learn enough information from simply observing the four-way handshake to impersonate the Supplicant or the Authenticator.

The Third Message of the Four-Way Handshake

This message is sent by the Authenticator to the Supplicant, and its most basic function is to acknowledge receipt of the second message by the Authenticator, and to direct the Supplicant to install the derived temporal key(s) in the Supplicant's STA. The Authenticator need not tell the Supplicant what those keys are…it knows that the Supplicant knows the keys.

When the Supplicant receives the third message of the four-way handshake, it also knows that there is no man-in-the-middle; in other words, it knows that the Authenticator is a component of the same AP that it has associated with prior to beginning the four-way handshake. Similar to the second message, the contents of the third message are sufficient to prove to the Supplicant (in a cryptographically sound sense) that this is the case.[52] After receiving the third message, the Supplicant also knows that the Authenticator has computed the PTK. All that remains is to transition from the phase where the two parties know the keys to the phase where the two parties are *using* the keys.

This message contains the ANonce (again), which is the same randomly chosen value that was sent in the first message. The third message also includes the Authenticator's RSN IE (must be identical to the RSN IE that was sent in the AP's Beacons and/or Probe Responses), and a message digest computed over the third message's EAPoL-Key Descriptor by the Authenticator using the EAPoL-Key MK that has now been derived by the Authenticator. Finally, the EAPoL-Key Descriptor's "Install" bit is set for the first time in the third message of the four-way handshake. As in the second message, the Authenticator's RSN IE is transported within the EAPoL-Key Descriptor's Data field.

When it is set, the EAPoL-Key Descriptor's Install bit directs the receiver to configure its local STA with the derived temporal key(s). Since the Supplicant is the receiver of the third message, it is being told to prepare to receive encrypted unicast traffic. The third message is similar to the first message, but conveys much more information, built on what has been learned through the exchange of the first and second messages.

The Fourth Message of the Four-Way Handshake

As with all other messages after the first message, the final message serves to acknowledge receipt of the previous message. This message of the four-way handshake may appear superficially similar to the second message, but its role is much more important, in that it confirms that both sides can now send

---

52. Knowing that a man-in-the-middle is not present is predicated on the assumption that the PMK is only known to the Authenticator and the Supplicant. If the PMK has been compromised, all bets are off, and a rogue STA could impersonate either any Supplicant or any Authenticator. Any message in the four-way handshake could be forged by an eavesdropper who knows the PMK.

encrypted unicast traffic. The fourth message implicitly tells the Authenticator that the keys are installed on the Supplicant's STA (since the fourth message acknowledges the third message), and that the Authenticator's STA (in the AP) should now install the temporal keys for this security association into its STA. The fourth message is also stating that the Supplicant has installed the temporal key(s) in its STA, as directed by the third message, and is ready to receive unicast data encrypted using the ciphersuite specified in the RSN IE.

As with the second and third messages, the fourth message contains a message digest that is computed over the EAPoL-Key Descriptor using the EAPoL-Key MK. At this point in the four-way handshake, both parties have derived the temporal keys and both know the ciphersuite that has been negotiated. Therefore, (in contrast to the previous messages) the entire fourth message is encrypted using the derived unicast temporal key(s) using whatever unicast ciphersuite was defined in the RSN IE; thus, the fourth message will be encrypted using CCMP or TKIP. The fourth message is not explicitly acknowledged, but the exchange can be judged a success when bi-directional encrypted traffic begins to flow.

The "Install" bit in the third and fourth messages directs the IEEE 802.1X entity in the Supplicant or the Authenticator, respectively,[53] to configure its local STA with the keying information derived from the Pairwise Key Hierarchy. By virtue of the Install bit being set in the fourth message, the Supplicant is directing the Authenticator to install the temporal keys for this security association into its STA (i.e., in the AP's STA). The IEEE 802.1X software uses the MLME-SETKEYS.request API to convey this information to either the Supplicant's or the Authenticator's STA, respectively. In the event that an Authenticator or Supplicant decides to terminate an association, the MLME-DELETEKEYS.request API is used.

What Can Go Wrong?

An issue can arise when the fourth message is lost, since the third message indicated that the Authenticator's STA has had the PTK installed (and thus, all unicast traffic will be encrypted using the PTK). Therefore, if the third message needs to be re-transmitted, the frame will be encrypted using the PTK with the

---

53. In both messages, the Install bit is telling the recipient of the message to do something. It is not telling the receiver that the sender has done something.

encapsulation depending on the rules of the selected ciphersuite. The Supplicant's STA, then, might receive an encrypted frame before it thinks it should be able to do so. There is, unfortunately, no way out of this situation (this is the "Two Armies" problem, described in detail in the context of Transport layer protocols in Dr. Andrew S. Tanenbaum's *Computer Networks, 4th Edition*). At some point, each STA has to be committed to sending and receiving encrypted traffic, and if something goes wrong, the only recourse would be to restart the process and derive a new PTK. If the third message is received, but the fourth message is lost in transit, there is really not any impact, since after transmitting the fourth message, the Supplicant's STA's MAC will have the PTK installed.

If the fourth message does not reach the Authenticator, the Supplicant's STA must still be prepared to accept unencrypted traffic from the Authenticator (which would most probably be a re-transmission of the third message, since the Authenticator will not have received the fourth message from the Supplicant, which, among other functions, serves to acknowledge the third message from the Authenticator).

Provided the fourth message has been properly received and interpreted by the Authenticator, the per-association keys are installed on the Authenticator's STA, and future unicast data is encrypted using TK1 and/or TK2, as required by the RSN IE. Once the four-way handshake is complete, the Authenticator's and Supplicant's IEEE 802.1X PAE permits unicast traffic to flow through their respective STAs, which encapsulates the packets according to the ciphersuite(s) indicated in the RSN IE.

We're Not Done Yet

Now that the unicast Pairwise Key Hierarchy calculations have been completed, unicast traffic must be sent in encrypted form, using the derived unicast temporal key(s). However, multicast and broadcast traffic would still need to be sent in the clear, which is why there is a small additional handshake (just two further messages) in which the Authenticator transmits the Group Transient Key (GTK) to the Supplicant. Even though the IEEE 802.11*i* draft defines a "Group Key Hierarchy," the GTK that the Authenticator sends to its associated Supplicants is indistinguishable from a random number. Moreover, contrary to the case with the Pairwise Key Hierarchy, the Supplicant does not need to do anything to "co-compute" the GTK; each Supplicant simply receives it (securely) from the Authenticator.

All the STAs in the BSS use the same GTK to decrypt the multicast and broadcast transmissions that they receive from the AP. Multicasts and broadcasts that are sent by the STAs are actually sent as unicast messages to the AP (the MAC-RA set so that the AP consumes that frame), and the MAC-DA of the frame is the desired multicast or broadcast address. The STA encrypts the unicast frame with the unicast temporal key(s) as it would any other unicast frame. When the AP receives the frame, it can tell that it is a non-unicast frame based on the address in the MAC-DA field. If the AP can successfully decrypt the frame using the unicast temporal key(s), it can then create a new output frame that is encrypted with the GTK.

The Group Transient Key is derived from the Group Master Key, the Authenticator's [MAC] Address (AA), and a nonce (the GNonce, chosen by the Authenticator), as shown in Figure 7–29.

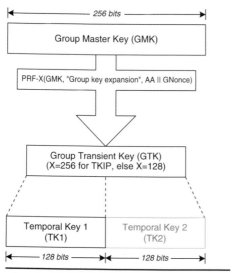

Figure 7–29   The Group Key hierarchy

The difference between the GTK derivation and the PTK derivation is that the GTK is only derived inside the Authenticator, whereas the PTK is derived in parallel in both the Supplicant as well as the Authenticator. The critical issue with the group key is that all the STAs know the same group key, so that they can decrypt multicast and broadcast traffic from the AP. There is never a need for a STA to encrypt its own multicast or broadcast frames with the GTK.

As noted in Figure 7–29, when TKIP is the ciphersuite indicated in the RSN IE, the PRF is set to output 256 bits of GTK, so that the GTK 2 will also be derived, which is the second 128 bits of the output of the PRF. Otherwise (i.e., in the case of CCMP), the GTK is only 128 bits long. In CCMP, the PRF's output is just 128 bits long, and those 128 bits are directly mapped into the GTK 1.

Both of the EAPoL-Key messages in the Group Key Exchange are digitally signed by the MK, after the EAPoL-Key EK has been used to encrypt the Key Material field of the EAPoL-Key Descriptor, which holds the [encrypted] GTK. The Group TK1 (and possibly also TK2), are subsequently configured into the Supplicant's STA and the Authenticator's STA via the MLME-SET-KEYS.request API. When this procedure is complete, the Supplicant's STA can now send encrypted broadcast and multicast traffic, in addition to the prior ability to send encrypted unicast traffic.

When the Group Key exchange is complete, the Supplicant's STA can now decrypt encrypted broadcast and multicast traffic from the AP, in addition to the prior ability to encrypt and decrypt unicast traffic. The EAPoL-Key messages of the GTK exchange are encrypted using unicast key(s) derived from the PTK.

MODIFICATIONS FOR IBSS MODE

In IBSS mode, each STA generates its own GTK and sends it to each of the other STAs. To decrypt a non-unicast frame, the receiver needs to look up the GTK associated with that frame's MAC-SA. Therefore, in IBSS mode, each STA generates its own GTK to protect the non-unicast traffic that it sends, while in infrastructure mode, the Authenticator defines the GTK for the entire BSS, and distributes it to each new Supplicant.

MODIFICATIONS FOR TRANSITION SECURITY NETWORK (TSN) MODE

In TSN mode, an AP will speak any form of authentication, and allow any form of encryption, except no encryption. Thus, in TSN mode, an AP will enable a legacy WEP STA to communicate with an RSN-capable STA, by receiving the WEP-encrypted frame from the first WEP STA, and then encrypting it for transmission to the RSN-capable STA. The reverse operation is performed for RSN-encrypted frames that are destined for a WEP STA.

An AP in TSN mode will happily receive a WEP-encrypted frame and forward it to an RSN-enabled STA, re-encrypting it using TKIP or CCMP, or vice versa. As a result, a user of an RSN-capable STA may prefer to configure it so that it does not associate with an AP that is configured to be in TSN mode.

What If You Want Better Security than WEP, but You Don't Have a RADIUS Server?

By separating the functions of the AP and the AS, the designers of IEEE 802.1X (and by extension, IEEE 802.11i) have enabled the system to scale up into really huge deployments. Centralizing the user credentials is the key to scalability. However, there are many users who have WLANs at home who would like to have security superior to WEP. It is highly unlikely that many users have a RADIUS server at home (unless they have a *very* large family!).

The IEEE 802.11i draft defines a way to use a "pre-shared key" (PSK[54]) instead of a RADIUS server. (Once again, note that RADIUS is the *de facto* standard for the back-end user credentials database protocol, but it is not endorsed or required by the IEEE 802.11i standard, nor is it likely to be the *de facto* standard for this function forever. Better protocols (e.g., Diameter) are in the works, and while they are not perfect either, they offer many improvements and are likely to be supported in the not-too-distant future.) The PSK offers a way to effectively integrate the AS and Authenticator functions into the same device (the AP). In general, PSKs are not secure, but if a separate PSK is assigned on a per-STA basis, that is secure.

The PSK is a 256-bit (i.e., 16-octet) number, and is probably derived from a pass phrase. The Authenticator and Supplicant are both configured with the PSK (hence, the reason it is described as being pre-shared), and when the time comes for the four-way handshake, the Supplicant and the Authenticator both use the PSK as their PMK. The PTK is derived as usual, mixing in the ANonce and SNonce to derive fresh temporal keys to protect the session.

---

54. This PSK has ABSOLUTELY NOTHING to do with Shared Key authentication.

The PMK is taken directly from the PSK since there is no end-to-end EAP method that can generate the PMK. Again, the use of PSKs is adequately secure only if the PSK is used on a per-STA basis. Sharing the same PSK among multiple STAs would have the same effect as if an attacker managed to discover the PMK for a given association. Once a PMK is known, the attacker can masquerade as either party in the association.

PSKs are likely to be the preferred method of RSN usage, if the current trends of WLAN deployments at home continue. PSK usage is likely to scale up to the level of dozens of separate PSKs, before the administrative overhead of managing a large database of users and their PSKs makes a RADIUS server look like a good investment.

From a usability standpoint, RSN security is likely to be far more user friendly than WEP was. It is much easier to enter a pass phrase (to generate the PSK) than it was to enter four 40-bit numbers (or one or more 104-bit numbers). It will be much easier for managers of small networks to keep track of the PSK allocations…it is likely that network management tools for APs will provide the ability to configure PSK-generating pass phrases on a per-MAC-address basis. The STA/Supplicant configuration is just absolutely simple in IBSS mode. Simply enter the SSID of the ESS within which the pass phrase is valid, and you're done.

An encrypted frame may be identified by the receiver because it has a bit set in the Frame Control field indicating that it is encrypted. The bit is known as the "Protected Frame" bit in IEEE 802.11i parlance, but in IEEE 802.11-1999, it was known as the "WEP" bit. The newer nomenclature is generic enough to apply to WEP, TKIP, and CCMP, and whatever new ciphersuites are invented in the future. This one bit is sufficient to indicate the presence of the IV field (between the MPDU header and the MPDU payload). Those frames encrypted with either TKIP or CCMP have an additional "Extended IV" bit, just prior to the Key ID field in the IV header.

However, beyond this point, there is nothing in the frame to distinguish between TKIP and CCMP…the receiver must look up the MAC-SA of the frame in its table of security associations and see what type of encryption was negotiated with that peer. This lookup has virtually zero cost, since the receiver already would have had to look up the MAC-SA in its table of security associations in order to retrieve the appropriate keying material with which to decrypt the frame. Given that RSN encryption and decryption will probably be implemented in hardware,[55] this "extra" lookup (i.e., to determine which encryption protocol was used to encrypt the frame) will have no performance impact at all.

RSN Ciphersuites

At the moment, the draft IEEE 802.11*i* specification describes two ciphersuites, namely TKIP (an RC4-based encryption algorithm) and CCMP (an AES-based encryption algorithm). The two algorithms have advantages and disadvantages, but their operation is driven by the key management protocols that have already been described. Without a source of secure keys, it does not matter how good your encryption algorithm is.

Temporal Key Integrity Protocol

By some accounts, the Temporal Key Integrity Protocol (TKIP) is the perfect protocol, since no one is happy with it. The purpose of TKIP is to provide a wrapper around WEP, so that hardware that supports WEP could be upgraded to have better security than WEP, which is effectively the same as no security. TKIP can be added as a software layer that pre-processes MSDUs such that the WEP hardware can do a halfway effective job of providing some level of security.

TKIP provides a greatly expanded IV space, as well as a cryptographically almost-strong-enough Message Integrity Code (MIC), called Michael (cute, huh?). Michael is actually quite weak. The MIC had to be designed to be implementable on computationally bound older hardware (which typically has few CPU cycles lying around unused), which meant that it could not be very strong. The designer of Michael was able to find a compromise that works (or doesn't, depending on your point of view) under very constrained circumstances.

Michael protects the MSDU plus the MAC-SA and MAC-DA addresses that get passed down via LLC's MA-UNITDATA.request API, as well as the rest of the frame's contents, from the LLC header onward. Because it protects

---

55. This statement is almost certainly true of APs and low-end (i.e., CPU-bound) devices. However, it is conceivable that a PC-based STA could implement CCMP in its driver software. Today's PCs have more than adequate CPU to perform CCMP in software. Newer devices, however, will probably begin incorporating CCMP logic in hardware.

the MSDU, Michael can be implemented in software, independent of the underlying WEP hardware.

The MA-UNITDATA.request LLC primitive is the means by which the LLC entity within a STA requests that a MAC sublayer entity transfer an MSDU from the local LLC sublayer entity to a single peer LLC sublayer entity. If the destination address parameter indicates a multicast or broadcast address, then the MSDU is intended for multiple peer LLC sublayer entities. The parameters of the MA-UNITDATA.request primitive are as follows:

```
MA-UNITDATA.request (
                    source address,
                    destination address,
                    routing information,
                    data,
                    priority,
                    service class
                    )
```

- The source address (MAC-SA) parameter specifies an individual MAC sublayer address of the sublayer entity to which the MSDU is being transferred. This parameter is used by the LLC sublayer entity to select from which of the possible output MAC interfaces the MSDU should be transferred.

- The destination address (MAC-DA) parameter specifies either an individual or a group MAC sublayer entity address. This is the address of the remote LLC entity to which the MSDU is being transferred.

- For IEEE 802.11, the routing information parameter must be null. The routing information parameter specifies the route desired for the data transfer (a null value indicates source routing is not to be used).

- The data parameter specifies the MSDU to be transmitted by the MAC sublayer entity. For IEEE 802.11, the length of the MSDU must be less than or equal to 2304 octets. This size seems to contradict the 2346-octet MPDU total length and the worst-case 30-octet header and four-octet FCS, which would appear to leave space for up to 2312 octets of MPDU payload. However, the API is reducing the offered payload by eight octets to allow for the possibility that a four-octet WEP KeyID field and a four-octet ICV may need to be added, which (if the MSDU were allowed to be larger than 2304 octets) would necessitate fragmentation of the frame, which would degrade performance much more than reducing the payload of each MPDU by a small amount (eight octets).

- The priority parameter specifies the priority desired for the data unit transfer. IEEE 802.11 allows two values: Contention or Contention-Free.
- The service class parameter specifies the service class desired for the data unit transfer. IEEE 802.11 allows two values: Re-orderable-Multicast or Strictly-Ordered.

Michael has been estimated to have a cryptographic strength on the order of 2^{-20}. This means that if an attacker modified a frame and modified the ICV, the attacker would have an approximately million-to-one shot at getting the ICV correct, just by guessing. Given the weakness of Michael, TKIP has certain "countermeasures" built into it. As the countermeasures are currently defined (in draft 3.2 of the IEEE 802.11i specification), attackers cannot be allowed to repeatedly send modified frames until they find one that works. If TKIP detects that it is under attack—which is defined as two MIC failures in any 60-second period—it will shut down the WLAN for 60 seconds, and then re-key everyone. This limits the rate at which an attacker can forge frames.

The reason why the WEP ICV is not changed is that the expectation is that the WEP support is in hardware, and the opportunity for a software or firmware upgrade means that the WEP hardware is a given. If an end user is replacing his or her hardware platform, that user is probably going to want to get one with more serious encryption, such as CCMP, which is based on a mode of the Advanced Encryption Standard (AES). The RC4 encryption that is ultimately applied to the frame protects the entire payload of the MPDU, including the eight-octet Michael MIC (that protects the MSDU) has been appended to the MSDU, and the four-octet WEP ICV that is computed exactly as it was in legacy WEP...it is still a CRC-32 over the MSDU (however, in this case, the WEP ICV sees the TKIP MIC as part of the MSDU).

Figure 7–30 shows the construction of a TKIP-enhanced WEP frame. Note that TKIP adds four additional octets to what is now the Extended IV field, and the Michael MIC adds an additional eight octets over and above the WEP ICV. Thus, the available MPDU payload for TKIP is, at best, 2292 octets (WEP was 2304, and TKIP takes away 12 additional octets from the available MPDU payload).

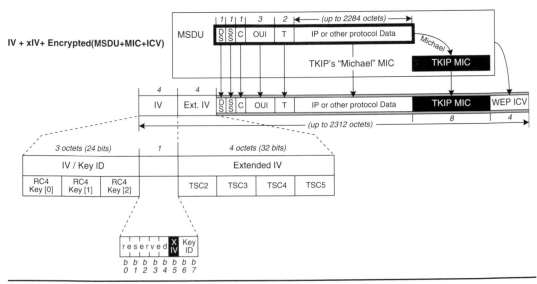

Figure 7–30   Encapsulation of an MSDU using TKIP

It is trivial to modify a set of bits in a WEP-protected MPDU such that the WEP ICV will not be able to detect the change, but the Michael MIC is stronger, and it *will* detect the change. However, Michael is not invulnerable, and it is still important to protect the BSS from active attackers; hence the countermeasures. If a TKIP device detects a Michael failure, it will start a clock, and if there is a second Michael failure within 60 seconds, then the BSS shuts itself down to limit the damage that an attacker can do.

TKIP was designed as a "wrapper" for WEP, to enhance it so that it was not so easily breakable. TKIP extended the size of the initialization vector, and provided an extra MIC (Michael) to protect the MSDU, as can be seen in Figure 7–31. There is some debate within the IEEE 802.11 TG*i* community regarding TKIP's "countermeasures"; in other words, whether they are too draconian. The Michael MIC was designed to be "just strong enough" to give an acceptable level of security given the expected low-end platforms on which it would be deployed, and the countermeasures were designed to limit the rate of attack to an acceptable level, given the generally accepted strength of Michael.

The countermeasures are designed to keep TKIP from being undermined by a clever attacker. If there are two MIC failures in a "short enough" period of time, the AP will shut the BSS down, temporarily, to limit the rate at which it can be attacked. To quote the IEEE 802.11*i* (draft 5.0):

> "The first MIC failure shall be logged and a timer initiated to enforce the countermeasures. If the MIC failure event is detected by the Supplicant [STA], it shall also report the event to the AP by sending a Michael failure report frame.
>
> If a subsequent MIC failure occurs within 60 seconds of the preceding failure, then a device shall disassociate itself (if a Supplicant [STA]) or disassociate all the associated STAs (if an Authenticator [AP]). Furthermore, the device will not receive or transmit any TKIP or WEP encrypted class 3 data frames other than IEEE 802.IX messages, if not an IBSS to or from any peer for a period of at least 60 seconds following the second detected failure. If an IBSS, the device shall not receive or transmit any unencrypted class 1 data frames other than IEEE 802.IX messages to or from any peer for a period of at least 60 seconds following the second detected failure. If the device is an AP, it shall disallow new associations using TKIP during this 60 second period; at the end of the 60 second period, the AP shall resume normal operations and allow STAs to (re)associate. If the device is a Supplicant, it shall first send a Michael failure report frame prior to revoking its PTK and disassociating (if not an IBSS)."

Much has been made of the fact that the countermeasures are effectively a built-in DoS attack against TKIP, since two packets in a one-minute period can shut down the BSS for a minute or more. It would be difficult to track down the source of an attacker who was sending malformed frames at a rate slow enough to trigger the countermeasures. Such an attacker may not even care about breaking in to the BSS. This would be a purely DoS-style attack. This is a genuinely good point, but if the alternative is having weaker countermeasures, and thinking you are more secure than you actually are, and not being able to detect an attack when it happens, which would you choose?

The issue boils down to this question: How strong is Michael? If it is stronger than generally accepted, as some have suggested, then shutting down a WLAN for 60 seconds seems to be erring on the side of caution in an overly aggressive manner. Efforts are under way to quantify the strength of Michael, so that the countermeasures can be tuned to a level that is commensurate with the threat. Some have suggested that Michael is strong enough that the countermeasures will only need to shut the BSS down for on the order of one second, or even less. If Michael is stronger than had been presumed and the countermeasures can be tuned to the actual strength of Michael, such that they would be less of a penalty to the BSS, everyone would be happy.

However, the important thing is that TKIP should actually offer some enhanced level of security, and if the countermeasures need to be draconian to do that, then that's what needs to be in the standard. If end users want high security and they do not want to deal with the TKIP countermeasures (that only exist to bolster the presumably weak Michael MIC), then they should be investing in products that support stronger encryption and message integrity check algorithms, specifically products based on CCMP.

AES Counter Mode with CBC-MAC (CCM) Protocol (CCMP)

TKIP is limited by the fact that it is designed to be a firmware or software upgrade to a device that did, and will, support WEP in hardware. The IEEE 802.11*i* group has defined an AES-based algorithm that offers considerably more strength, but in order to implement CCMP in a real BSS, a customer needs STAs and APs that support AES, and that means hardware upgrades. The author contends that anyone who wants a secure WLAN will be willing to pay the small incremental cost to have AES-enabled devices, especially since catering to the installed base is overlooking the large pool of people who would love to invest in WLAN technology but who have been waiting for (and will be willing to pay a slight premium for) seriously strong security.

CCMP operates at the MPDU level, as depicted in Figure 7–31, and incurs a four-octet smaller penalty than TKIP against the MPDU payload since the baggage of the WEP ICV is no longer required.

Figure 7–31 looks really complicated, but it really isn't as bad as it may appear. The first two rows of the diagram are the expansion of the Extended Initialization Vector (Ext. IV) field of the CCMP-protected MPDU, which is depicted on the third and fourth rows of the diagram. The third row shows the ultimate structure of the CCMP-protected MPDU, whereas the fourth row gives the

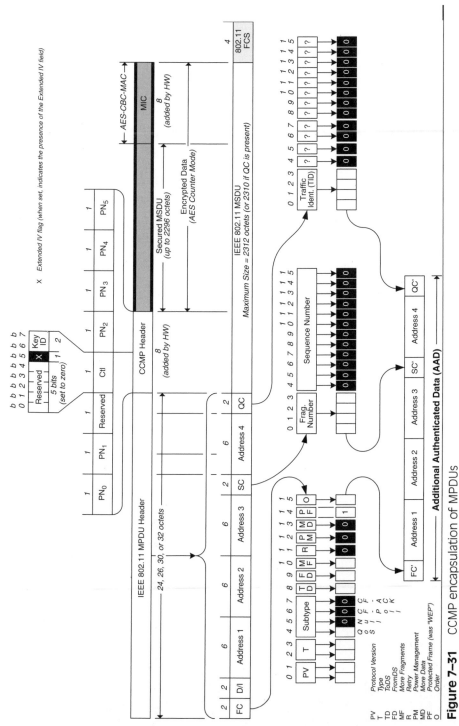

x Extended IV flag (when set, indicates the presence of the Extended IV field)

Figure 7–31 CCMP encapsulation of MPDUs

PV   Protocol Version
T   Type
TD   ToDS
FD   FromDS
MF   More Fragments
R   Retry
PM   Power Management
MD   More Data
PF   Protected Frame (was "WEP")
O   Order

283

details of the MPDU header that are used to build the "Additional Authenticated Data" that drives the AES CBC-MAC calculation (CCMP's Message Integrity Check).

The AAD field is comprised of parts of the MPDU header, but the FC and SC fields must be transformed before computing the MIC. Only certain of the fields of the MPDU header need to be included in the MIC calculation. The QC header, if present, is also transformed and is included in the AAD so that it is protected by the MIC. Finally, all the pieces come together, as shown in Figure 7–32.

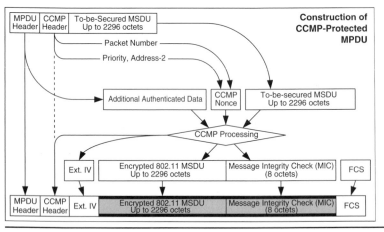

Figure 7–32   Construction of CCMP-protected MPDU

CCMP, as it is based on AES, is efficient to implement in software, provided adequate CPU horsepower is available. For example, a PC running Windows should be able to implement CCMP in software, since it is running on a CPU that is 2+ GHz. CCMP is also efficient in hardware, and as enhanced security products start coming to market, providing AES will be a significant value-add, we can expect to see AES emerging as a standard feature in new hardware over the next 18 months or so.

Wi-Fi Protected Access

To get more-secure products to market in a timely fashion, the Wi-Fi Alliance decided to take excerpts of the IEEE 802.11*i* draft 3.0 specification and create Wi-Fi Protected Access (WPA). WPA-logoed products will start appearing in late 2003. There are some who question the wisdom of basing products on a draft of a standard that is still very much in flux, but the vendors in the Wi-Fi Alliance seem to think that is a risk worth taking (i.e., the risk is that the WPA spec will be rooted in the past, based on IEEE 802.11*i*-draft 3.0, while the IEEE 802.11*i* group will move forward and possibly diverge from the feature set of WPA). In practice, now that WPA exists, TG*i* is very sensitive about touching any part of their draft that might have implications on WPA.

WPA is a simple idea, really. Take the parts of IEEE 802.11*i* that seem fairly solid and build products based on those parts while the IEEE is finishing the rest of the document. The pieces that WPA has selected are the TKIP cipher-suite (which is optional in IEEE 802.11*i*, but mandatory in WPA) and the IEEE 802.1X-based authentication and key management (i.e., the four-way handshake and such). WPA even supports CCMP as an option (the IEEE 802.11*i* draft mandates CCMP for devices claiming to support RSN, but requiring CCMP in WPA was a non-starter, since that would have required hardware upgrades).

It is the author's opinion that WPA will become the public face of RSN. It is unlikely that terms like RSN and IEEE 802.1X will be exposed in the market-place, since the level of user education necessary would be too great. A WPA logo is a nice simple way to get the message across, without the user needing to know too much. At least it simplifies the purchasing decision.

Installing WPA and getting it configured securely will probably be a challenge. There will be phases of deployment. Early products will use IEEE 802.1X for the four-way handshake, but may not be tied into a RADIUS infrastructure, which will mean that APs will need to support some kind of user interface for entering a per-STA "pass phrase" which is converted to a pre-shared key. The integration of RADIUS or Diameter as a back-end protocol will ease this management burden, but there will undoubtedly be deployment issues with getting the EAP exchanges and the Authenticator-to-Authentication_Server secure channels working properly. These types of issues will mainly occur when the new hardware and software system is being brought up to speed, and should cease to be issues once everything is installed and configured properly.

The author does not mean to imply that getting real security (whether you call it WPA or RSN is irrelevant) to work on a WLAN will be too difficult...once it is up and running, it will be far more usable than WEP (from an end-user's perspective). From a network manager's perspective, the ability to have per-association keys that are securely exchanged to drive modern encryption protocols is certainly worth some effort to get working.

There are likely to be two key deployment scenarios...home and corporate. In the home, managing per-STA pass-phrases won't be a big deal. It's unlikely that there will be many homes with RADIUS infrastructures, so the pre-shared key approach will be important to support. In corporate settings that already have RADIUS infrastructures, it should not be too difficult to integrate EAP and IEEE 802.1X into the mix. The corporate deployments will probably benefit from much more sophisticated management and configuration tools to aid deployment and troubleshooting.

Another deployment scenario has the flavor of corporate, and is the potential for wireless ISPs (WISPs), which might provide secure access (for a price). These WISPs are likely to have access to all the necessary back-end software databases and systems to enable such services, even more readily than a corporation, which may need to install a RADIUS server to support user-based authentication for their WLAN. For a WISP (or ISP), user-based authentication is what their business depends on. If they don't have that, they can't do billing....

In a WISP scenario, users of various ISPs might be separated onto different VLANs, at least so that the unencrypted users (which will hopefully be on a declining trend) won't be able to interfere with the secure subnetworks that are overlaid in the same space, be it a coffee shop, a bookstore, or an airport lounge.

By 2005, the default for wireless devices, as far as security is concerned, should be the opposite of what it is today. By then, the default will probably be secure mode.

8

Applications and Deployment of Wireless Technology

Wireless technology is seeing widespread deployment in many types of environments, which are roughly classifiable into the following categories:

- Personal-Area Networks
- Home and Small Office (SOHO) deployments
- Medium-to-Large Enterprise deployments
- Wireless "last-mile" carrier deployments
- Wireless "hotspots"

The first bullet is supported by standards from IEEE 802.15, whereas the second and third are both different applications of IEEE 802.11 with the difference being the scale of the deployment. IEEE 802.11 technology is also pertinent to the final bullet. The fourth bullet is the domain of IEEE 802.16, "Fixed Broadband Wireless Access." IEEE 802.16 is specifically designed with capabilities that make it more suitable to operation on the scale of metropolitan areas, which makes the protocol quite different from IEEE 802.11. However, the payoff is that it is more scalable, and it has features that are specifically designed to support this type of application, including support for security and for different grades of service.

Other emerging wireless networking standards will address *mobile* broadband wireless networking. The IEEE 802.16 WG (Task Group "*e*") and the IEEE 802.20 WG are both creating standards based on unique approaches. At this point, adding mobile broadband wireless access to the previous bulleted list would be premature, but this technology will be maturing over the next several years.

IEEE 802.11: Wireless LANs and Beyond

The standards that define WLANs will continue to evolve, at least in that new PHYs will be defined that provide for progressively higher speeds. As this book is going to press, the first mentions of the new IEEE 802.11n TG are being seen in the trade press.[1] As we have seen, additional capabilities such as improved security or QoS are also being added, and new PHYs are being defined that extend the reach of WLANs into more regulatory domains. The target deployment, however, will remain *local* (as far as the IEEE 802.11 WG is concerned), but end users will not be intentionally constrained in their ability to creatively deploy WLAN technology in legally permissible ways.

"LAN" is a term that has a surprisingly confusing meaning. It used to be the case that LAN was primarily defined by the "LA" portion of the acronym (i.e., local area), but certain applications of Ethernet allow operation over distances on the order of a few kilometers, stretching the meaning of the term "local." The same is true in WLANs, in that they typically are a "local area" network, covering on the order of 300 feet, but some people have found ways to extend their reach over distances that don't seem to be local (i.e., 10 miles, with special antennas…).

I would not bother to mention this, except that I had someone ask me this very question at an IEEE 802.11 meeting. The answer is that all LAN technology was originally designed for applicability in a certain domain, but that original intent does not limit the creativity of vendors or customers in deploying the products in a way that is not consistent with the term "local." The products are still based on standards, and if the standards have multiple domains of application, that is probably a good thing, as long as the cost of products is not unduly driven up by the additional capabilities that the equipment and/or the standard is able to support.

---

1. These mentions are a bit early, since TG*n* will not formally exist until September 2003, and the work of TG*n* in defining a new high-speed PHY (perhaps as fast as 250 Mbps) will take on the order of two years. At this point, it would be irresponsible to do more than mention the imminent existence of TG*n*, since they have not even been formally chartered, and so there is no proposed standard on the table. Almost anything written about TG*n* in 2003 would be highly speculative.

This book has focused on IEEE 802.11-based devices, and while these are very popular, they are not the only class of wireless devices. In the late 1990s, another wireless technology was being developed that many people mistakenly perceived to be competitive with IEEE 802.11*b*. One reason for the implied competition was that both of these technologies used the 2.4 GHz ISM band. The name of this technology was, and is, Bluetooth®. It is still in existence…primarily because it has applications to which it is uniquely suited, and for which IEEE 802.11 is *not* suited.

Bluetooth® and IEEE 802.15.1: Wireless Personal Area Networks (WPANs)

Bluetooth® uses Frequency Hopping Spread Spectrum techniques and can coexist with IEEE 802.11*b* devices, and it serves a completely different application. The interference with a DSSS-based IEEE 802.11*b* WLAN is going to be minimal, but it's possible that two FHSS-based technologies operating in the same proximity would cause each other grief. In an effort to mitigate the effects of proximate operation, the IEEE LMSC has created the IEEE 802.19 TAG to study "coexistence" issues.

Bluetooth® was conceived as a very low power, and thus short-range (i.e., 3 to 10 meters), wireless "cable replacement" to enable devices to communicate in very small *ad hoc* networks (termed "piconets"). A Bluetooth® piconet can have up to a total of eight devices, with one being a master and the others known as slaves.[2] A set of proximate piconets can merge into what's known as a "scatter-net" by the fact that each Bluetooth® station can be a slave in one piconet, and be a master in another.

The "race" between IEEE 802.11*b* and Bluetooth® that was covered in the trade press would have had readers believe that only one could survive. This type of overly simplistic "winner takes all" analysis is not limited to the trade press.… It is especially telling that few people look at 2.4 GHz cordless phones and imagine that they compete with WLAN devices[3] (except in the sense that they

---

2. The author would have preferred if the Bluetooth® SIG had chosen less socially charged naming, perhaps "primary" and "secondaries" instead of "master" and "slaves." However, it is a fact that the standard does use these terms.

3. In the near future, ultra-portable WLAN devices that look a lot like cellular phones will support VoIP over IEEE 802.11 WLANs. Once such products exist, then a comparison against cordless phones will be meaningful.

can both use the same band of RF spectrum). In fact, microwave ovens and other devices, such as new forms of lighting based on using microwaves to excite glowing plasma, all share this 2.4 GHz ISM band.[4]

The standardization of Bluetooth® began in an *ad hoc* fashion with an industry group known as the Bluetooth® Special Interest Group (Bluetooth® SIG), and the specification grew quite complex because certain members of the SIG wanted to endow Bluetooth® with LAN-like capabilities. As it was originally conceived, Bluetooth® had no "broadcast" capability, which was not a limitation in its target application as a cable replacement technology. Because of its intended application in the cell phone world, it supported synchronous data transfer, so that voice communications between a cell phone and a wireless headset would have acceptable quality, theoretically on par with what a wire could deliver.

Had the scope of the specification been limited to the original vision, of a short-range cable replacement supporting wireless point-to-point "links," interoperable Bluetooth®-enabled devices may have entered the market much sooner. As it happened, the first Bluetooth® "interoperability" event was attempted in late March 2001 at the giant CeBIT[5] trade show in Hannover, Germany. At this trade show, a very spectacular public relations disaster happened when the high-profile new technology, Bluetooth®, did not work as advertised. A Bluetooth® network that was meant to span an entire exhibit hall did not work as advertised, primarily because of the fact that each vendor was using a slightly different version of the standard, and interoperability was just not possible at the time.[6]

Rather than leave the reader with the impression that Bluetooth® is a failed technology, if we fast-forward to 2003, we find many late-model cell phones with Bluetooth® support, such as for "connecting" to a wireless headset, or to exchange data with another phone, or a PC. The standard for Bluetooth® has now stabilized to the point where multiple interoperable implementations are

---

4. For more information on this new type of lighting, do a Web search on "RF lighting."

5. CeBIT is a German acronym that stands for "Centrum für Büro, Information und Telekommunikation" (which may be loosely translated into English as [World] "Center for Office, Information, and Communication" [Technology]. CeBIT is one of the largest trade shows in the world, perhaps *the* largest.

6. For more information on this event, one can do a Web search on "CeBIT Bluetooth demo 2001."

the norm, not the exception. It would appear that Bluetooth® has found its niche in the technology marketplace, but getting to this point was not easy!

While the Bluetooth® SIG may have created the initial Bluetooth® specification, the Bluetooth® SIG is not a legally recognized standards body, and so its specification(s) would be effectively *de facto* standards. To make them official *de jure* standards, the IEEE LMSC created a WG—IEEE 802.15—to formally standardize Bluetooth® and related WPAN technologies. The first of the standards from this WG has already been published: IEEE 802.15.1-2002, which was "derived from the Bluetooth® core, profiles, and test specifications" and contains "unaltered or minimally altered text of the Bluetooth specifications." To summarize the features of Bluetooth®, here is an excerpt from IEEE 802.15.1-2002, Clause 8.1:[7]

Bluetooth® is a short-range radio link intended to replace the cable(s) connecting portable and/or fixed electronic devices. Key features are robustness, low complexity, low power, and low cost.

Bluetooth® operates in the unlicensed ISM band at 2.4 GHz. A frequency hop transceiver is applied to combat interference and fading. A shaped, binary FM modulation is applied to minimize transceiver complexity. The symbol rate is 1 Msymbol/s. A slotted channel is applied with a nominal slot length of 625 μs. To emulate full duplex transmission, a Time-Division Duplex (TDD) scheme is used. On the channel, information is exchanged through packets. Each packet is transmitted on a different hop frequency. A packet nominally covers a single slot, but can be extended to cover up to five slots.

The Bluetooth® protocol uses a combination of circuit and packet switching. Slots can be reserved for synchronous packets. Bluetooth can support an asynchronous data channel, up to three simultaneous synchronous voice channels, or a channel that simultaneously supports asynchronous data and synchronous voice. Each voice channel supports a 64 kb/s synchronous (voice) channel in each direction. The asynchronous channel can support maximal 723.2 kb/s asymmetric (and still up to 57.6 kb/s in the return direction), or 433.9 kb/s symmetric.

---

7. Excerpted from IEEE Std. IEEE 802.15.1-2002, copyright 2002. All rights reserved.

The IEEE 802.15.2 draft standard is entitled "Telecommunications and Information exchange between systems – Local and metropolitan area networks Specific Requirements - Part 15.2: Coexistence of Wireless Personal Area Networks with Other Wireless Devices Operating in Unlicensed Frequency Bands," and it is intended to help devices based on IEEE 802.15.1, and other forthcoming IEEE 802.15 standards, coexist with other devices in this band.

IEEE 802.16: Fixed Broadband Wireless Access

Another class of wireless devices is based on the fixed (initially) and mobile (eventually[8]) broadband wireless metropolitan area network (WirelessMAN™) standards being created by the IEEE 802.16 WG. The reason why the IEEE 802.16 standard is referred to as a metropolitan-area standard is that the technology supports inter-node distances of up to 31 miles (50 km), and some of its PHYs do not require line-of-sight in order to operate.

The initial application of IEEE 802.16 technology will be as a high-speed last-mile access technology, so that a networking company can deliver services over microwaves instead of over wires that it must lease from another company (or over wires that it owns, but had to pay to install). IEEE 802.16 infrastructures could be used to wirelessly interconnect IEEE 802.11 wireless "hotspots," or to provide "T-1"-class[9] access circuits to corporate customers, or as an alternative to using wires to deliver DSL services. In the latter case, it may be possible to provide hundreds of DSL-class access "circuits" from a single base station.

IEEE 802.16 provides integrated support for privacy and QoS in its MAC sublayer protocol, because it is unlikely that a business would purchase a wireless T-1 circuit unless they could be certain that no eavesdroppers could intercept their traffic, and the provider could meet contractually mandated service level

---

8. The IEEE 802.16 WG's TG "*e*" is developing a standard for mobile broadband wireless access (MBWA). There is another MBWA effort under way in the IEEE 802.20 WG.

9. A T-1 circuit operates symmetrically at 1.544 Mbps, with a bi-directional payload capacity of 1.536 Mbps, sufficient to carry 24 digitized voice channels, each running at 64 kbps. A T-1 circuit may be configured to support a "channelized" service, for use as a voice trunk between a company's private branch exchange (PBX) and a telephone company's central office, or as an "unchannelized" service, in which all of the payload capacity is used to carry data. This type of circuit is frequently also referred to as "DS-1" (digital signal level one).

agreements. More information on IEEE 802.16 and related technology can be found on the Web at www.wirelessman.org.

There are currently two varieties of IEEE 802.16 standards, the original IEEE 802.16-2001, which operates in the 10–66 GHz RF spectrum (where licenses are required), and the newer IEEE 802.16a-2003 standard, which operates in parts of the 2.5–11 GHz RF spectrum (which supports operation over both licensed and unlicensed portions of this spectrum). The introduction to the IEEE 802.16-2001 specification describes the standard as follows:[10]

This standard specifies the air interface of a fixed (stationary) point-to-multipoint broadband wireless access system providing multiple services in a wireless metropolitan area network (MAN). The WirelessMAN™ medium access control layer defined here is capable of supporting multiple physical layer specifications optimized for the frequency bands of application. The standard includes a particular physical layer specification applicable to systems operating between 10 and 66 GHz. This 10–66 GHz air interface, based on single-carrier modulation, is known as the WirelessMAN-SC™ air interface. An amendment to this standard, to support 2 – 11 GHz using an enhanced version of the same basic medium access control layer along with new physical layer specifications, is in development in IEEE-SA Project 802.16a.

One important difference between IEEE 802.11 and IEEE 802.16 devices is that the latter standard operates in licensed spectrum. One of the enablers of the growth of the market for IEEE 802.11 devices has been that they are designed to operate in unlicensed spectrum, which means that the owners of such devices need not get permission from the FCC before turning them on. It is appropriate for a provider of IEEE 802.16-based fixed broadband wireless services to get a license to operate in a given geographical area, since they will want assurance that no other provider will be interfering with them. The IEEE 802.16 WG created a TG*b* to work on a PHY that could operate in the unlicensed 5–6 GHz band, known as the Wireless High-speed Unlicensed MAN (or, WirelessHUMAN™). Eventually, IEEE 802.16 TG*b* was merged with IEEE 802.16 TG*a*, so the

---

10. Excerpted from IEEE Std. 802.16a-2003, copyright 2003. All rights reserved.

finished IEEE 802.16a-2003 standard includes support for unlicensed operation in the 5–6 GHz band, as well as for licensed operation in the 2.5–11 GHz band.

The speed of networks based on IEEE 802.16 depends on several factors, notably channel width and physical distance separating the devices. The further two devices are apart, the more the transmitted power is attenuated (by the inverse square law), which means that more robust modulations must be used to overcome the poor signal-to-noise ratio. Such modulations cannot transmit as many bits per symbol, so a side effect of increasing distance is that the maximum achievable transmission speed decreases (this effect is also present in IEEE 802.11, although on a much shorter distance scale). In particular, devices that are designed to operate in wider RF channels can achieve higher speeds.

Devices based on the IEEE 802.16 standard can use any of three channel widths in the 10–66 GHz band, viz. 20, 25, or 28 MHz. Depending on the selected modulation scheme and the available RF channel size, speeds of 32–44.8 Mbps are achievable with QPSK, the "slowest" modulation scheme; speeds of 64–89.6 Mbps are achievable with the intermediate-speed modulation known as 16-QAM; and the fastest modulation, 64-QAM, can achieve speeds in the range of 96–134.4 Mbps. Table 8–1 summarizes the speeds attainable with the various combinations of modulation and channel width in the 10–66 GHz band. A typical deployment may deliver aggregate network bandwidth on the order of 70 Mbps.

Table 8–1   IEEE 802.16 Speeds and Modulations

Channel Width	Symbol Rate (Megasymbols per second)	QPSK (2 bits per symbol)	16-QAM (4 bits per symbol)	64-QAM (6 bits per symbol)
20 MHz	16	32 Mbps	64 Mbps	96 Mbps
25 MHz	20	40 Mbps	80 Mbps	120 Mbps
28 MHz	22.4	44.8 Mbps	89.6 Mbps	134.4 Mbps

Due to the increasing maturity of WirelessMAN standards and the expected new products that will be based on these standards, a group of vendors has formed an organization to promote interoperable implementations of the technology, known as the Worldwide Interoperability for Microwave Access (WiMAX) Forum, which is logically equivalent to the Wi-Fi Alliance, which provides a similar interoperability testing and promotion function for IEEE 802.11.

The WiMAX Forum (on the Web at www.wimaxforum.org) was announced on April 15, 2002, and will certify IEEE 802.16 products throughout the entire

2.5–66 GHz range (i.e., covering products based on either the IEEE 802.16-2001 or IEEE 802.16*a*-2003 standards). The full text of the press release announcing the WiMAX™ Forum is provided here (in the time since the four companies listed here formed it, the WiMAX™ Forum membership has increased to 26 members):

The WiMAX™ Forum is formed to promote interoperability standards for broadband wireless access. Executives from Nokia, Ensemble Communications, Harris Corporation, and Crosspan resolve to support interoperability standards.

ANTIBE, FRANCE --April 15, 2002-- Representing a significant step forward in catalyzing the growth and future viability of the global fixed broadband wireless market, leading equipment and component manufacturers have formed the Worldwide Interoperability for Microwave Access (WiMAX™) Forum. As a non-profit organization, the objective of WiMAX™ is to promote wide-scale deployments of point-to-multipoint networks operating between 2.5 and 66 GHz by leveraging new global consensus standards and certifying the interoperability of various products and technologies from multiple manufacturers.

As has been proven many times in the past, true market success of a particular technology can only be realized through a global standard and a concerted effort to ensure the interoperability of multi-vendor products which in turn result in economies of scale and, ultimately, a healthy competitive environment.

The recent completion and formal approval of IEEE® Standard 802.16™ ("Air Interface for Fixed Broadband Wireless Access Systems"), which defines the IEEE 802.16 WirelessMAN air interface, was achieved through successful collaboration of many individuals and companies in the wireless industry. Together, they produced the industry's first broadband wireless access standard to be published by an accredited standards body.

As the next step in widespread adoption and use of the WirelessMAN standard, WiMAX™ has been created to further define and commercialize this global specification.

IEEE 802.11 Wireless LAN Devices

Clearly, to make a WLAN, one needs at least two devices to make an *ad hoc* network, and at least three devices to make an infrastructure network (an infrastructure network with one STA and one AP would be possible, but the STA would not have any other STAs with which to communicate...). As a practical requirement, one also needs a wired network (the Distribution System in IEEE 802.11 parlance) to which the AP may be attached.

APs are available at a variety of price points. Entry-level IEEE 802.11*b* APs for home use might be available (refurbished) for less than $40. On the opposite end of the price spectrum, APs designed for corporate deployment will cost up to $750 or more. The latter type of AP distinguishes itself by supporting features like manageability, upgradeability (e.g., the ability to add IEEE 802.11*a* and/or IEEE 802.11*g* support to an IEEE 802.11*b* AP), as well as robust support for the full range of features in the standard, even those that may not be required for the necessary testing to acquire Wi-Fi certification. The more expensive APs also may have higher quality components, such as their RF components (power amplifiers and such), and antennas.

In many current laptops, IEEE 802.11*b* is almost an afterthought. (Would you like that new laptop with or without a WLAN? Well, duh...*with*, of course!) In fact, the incremental retail cost of WLAN STA capabilities in a laptop is rapidly approaching $0; in other words, it is becoming a required component, like a CPU or a keyboard. Another trend is that by the end of 2004, it is likely that IEEE 802.11*g*-2003 support will be at least as prevalent as IEEE 802.11*b* is today.

The hardware necessary to implement a STA is generally divided into a chipset that implements the MAC sublayer protocols, and a chipset that implements the PHY, including the modulation schemes (in the BBP), and the RF subunit, which actually transmits the modulated digital data onto the WM. IEEE 802.11*b* implementations are available as both PCI[11] cards for desktop PCs and as PC Cards (formerly known as PCMCIA[12] cards). Wireless PC

---

11. PCI stands for "Peripheral Component Interconnect."

12. PCMCIA stands for "Personal Computer Memory Card International Association." This mouthful was replaced by the much shorter "PC Card," which doesn't appear to be an acronym. The joke used to be that PCMCIA stood for "People Can't Memorize Computer Industry Acronyms." The original PCMCIA standard provided an interface bus that was 16 bits wide and ran at 8 MHz (maximum throughput, 128 Mbps, or 16 megabytes per second (MBps)). The newer CardBus interface runs at 33 MHz, and is 32 bits wide, for approximately eight times the throughput (132 MBps, or 1,056 Mbps; i.e., just over a gigabit per second).

Cards can be used in certain PDAs (those that have PC Card slots) to make the device into a WLAN STA. Other nontraditional devices, such as printers, digital cameras, and so forth, are appearing with integrated WLAN capabilities.

Integration of WLAN components has progressed in an orderly fashion so far, tending to follow similar integration steps that wired LAN components have already taken. Initial WLAN cards were isolated products that could be easily added to any laptop (or desktop...WLAN cards for desktops do exist). This add-in card product category is not likely to go away any time soon, especially since the rapid pace of change of WLAN standards means that whatever built-in hardware a laptop has might become obsolete.

The early days of Ethernet were dominated by the add-in card business. For cost saving reasons, and higher reliability, the second phase of WLAN integration was reminiscent of the evolution of Ethernet progressed from a NIC-oriented (i.e., add-in card) to so-called "LAN-on-motherboard" (LOM) implementations. From a customer's perspective, Ethernet had been integrated onto the motherboard, even though it was still a set of discrete components. Eventually, Ethernet controllers were further integrated into the core logic of the motherboard, although they may or may not still be logically a PCI device. The adoption of progressively faster Ethernet speeds tended to be NIC-driven, meaning that 10/100 desktops were commonplace before the network infrastructure was upgraded to support 100 Mbps to the desktop. The evolution of gigabit Ethernet is proceeding in the same way, with 10/100/1000 NICs being readily available today, well in advance of widespread deployment of gigabit-to-the-desktop.

The integration of WLAN components into PCs (i.e., laptops) has progressed in a similar fashion. In laptops, WLAN support has now reached the first level of integration, which is not to say that there is no need for the add-in cards...any laptop that was built prior to the newer WLAN-on-motherboard (to coin a term) designs is a potential customer for an add-in card. The add-in card manufacturers will be able to leverage the cost reductions in the components that the higher volume WLAN-on-motherboard chipsets will create, and the add-in card designs are likely evolve to ultimately use the same components or some closely related derivative components.

The most modern motherboard designs have the Ethernet hardware logic built in to the PCI South Bridge chip. In the early days of PCI, the South Bridge chip was simple and basically just provided an interface through which the add-in cards on the PCI bus could access the memory and CPU in the

PC—via the PCI North Bridge chip, which interfaces to the CPU and acts as a memory controller. As an aside, it is typically the case that the graphics controller interfaces to the North Bridge chip via the AGP[13] interface, or it may even be integrated into the North Bridge chip in some designs.

One trend in current PC design is to have the South Bridge chip be a package that includes Ethernet MAC logic, USB[14] and FireWire interfaces, and any other type of logic that is involved in talking to a peripheral device (even storage interface protocols like SCSI[15] and IDE[16] could be integrated into the South Bridge itself, thereby eliminating the need for standalone disk controllers). Figure 8–1 shows the evolution of the PC motherboard, in terms of block diagrams that identify the major components.

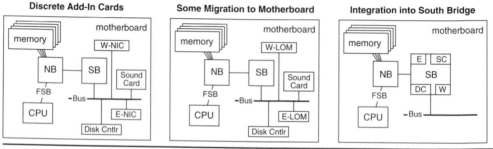

Figure 8–1   Evolution of PC motherboard design[17]

The evolution of WLAN designs can be expected to follow the same course as Ethernet did, for much the same reasons. Newer PCs (especially laptops) will probably have integrated WLAN capabilities embedded in their core logic (i.e., in their PCI South Bridge chip, which already houses integrated Ethernet and other interfaces; e.g., USB, FireWire, etc.). This level of integration is desirable for PC motherboard OEMs,[18] since their design and production costs are lower

---

13. AGP stands for "Accelerated Graphics Port."
14. USB stands for "Universal Serial Bus."
15. SCSI stands for "Small Computer System Interface."
16. IDE stands for "Integrated Drive Electronics."
17. In the diagram, the following abbreviations are used: Cntlr (Controller), CPU (Central Processing Unit), DC (Disk Controller), E (Ethernet), FSB (Front-Side Bus), LOM (LAN on Motherboard), NB (North Bridge), NIC (Network Interface Card), SB (South Bridge), SC (Sound Card), and W (Wireless).
18. OEM stands for "Original Equipment Manufacturer."

than if they have to accumulate all of those functions via separate PCI cards. Ultimately, these cost savings translate into some combination of increased profits and lower prices at retail. There are really two major metrics that are used to compare laptops...battery life and weight. In laptops, it is conceivable that the integrated solution might be thriftier when it comes to using the battery, but that's not necessarily true. The weight shouldn't be that different either way (integrated or not).

Besides the degree to which WLAN hardware could be integrated with PC motherboards, the actual implementation of the WLAN product has evolved considerably. First- and second-generation WLAN products tended to implement the MAC sublayer protocol in a small CPU, with the BBP and RF subunits being external to that CPU, connected by proprietary interfaces (these interfaces did not need to be exposed to third parties because, generally, these chipsets were sold as a package—from the beginning, the MAC and BBP were trending toward integration with each other—so there would be some ability for product designers to choose their own radio, much as they can choose their own Ethernet PHY today).

Newer designs are integrating the MAC (which is sometimes still implemented as firmware running on a CPU core, with that CPU core embedded in the South Bridge package, or perhaps implemented as purpose-built logic circuitry in the South Bridge) with the BBP inside the same package (the BBP has always been purpose-built logic). Thus, the MAC alone or MAC and BBP can be physically integrated in the South Bridge chip.

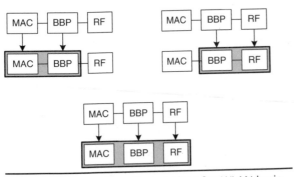

Figure 8–2   Integration choices for WLAN logic
components

Figure 8–2 shows some ways in which the various WLAN components could be combined with each other. The fully integrated solution is likely to be useful for add-in cards (where minimizing the cost is especially critical), but "complete integration" may not be desirable for motherboard applications. The RF subunit is likely to remain separate for motherboard applications, since it is desirable to keep the high-frequency analog signals as close as possible to the antenna.[19] The trend for the MAC and BBP components is clearly toward integration within the South Bridge chip.

Over the next several years, it is highly likely that most laptops will ship with WLAN interface logic, in much the same way that Ethernet has become ubiquitous in laptops (and everywhere else).

Wireless LANs at Home

WLANs can extend over a range of 200 to 1000 feet,[20] but coverage depends on the density of the obstructions between the AP and the STA. Empirical evidence based on experiments at home indicates that every time an IEEE 802.11*b* signal needs to pass through a wall (e.g., sheetrock a.k.a. drywall), it loses approximately 20 to 30 percent of its power. If there are three or four walls between a STA and their nearest AP, the STA may not be able to hear the AP at all (or vice versa). The easiest solution to this situation in a home is to strategically locate two or three APs throughout the home, so that there will be adequate signal strength in locations from which the user might want to be able to access the WLAN.

The most APs are likely to be sold (relative to the number of STAs that they support) into the home/SOHO market. In any given home or small business, an AP might serve only one to 10 STAs. In corporate settings, an AP may serve up to dozens of STAs. To date, the market for WLAN products has been approximately equal between home and corporate purchasers, but several studies indicate that the unit sales of APs into home/SOHO environments will exceed the number sold to corporations for deployment in larger networks.

---

19. These signals are close to the clock frequencies of modern PCs, so the issue of interference is real. The analog signals probably wouldn't interfere too badly with the CPU clock, but the CPU clock's square wave harmonics could make a real mess of the WLAN RF signal.

20. In fact, it is even possible to build a low-cost directional antenna that can send all of the RF energy in one direction. Several people have posted online instructions for using a pair of Pringles® cans to build antennas for extending an IEEE 802.11*b* link for several miles without illegally boosting the signal beyond the limits set by the FCC.

In a way, this makes sense, since there are potentially many more home networks than there are corporate networks.

Because WLAN technology will be slower than wired LAN technology for the time being, it is likely that any WLAN deployments in medium-to-large enterprises will be made as a parallel network to the existing wired LAN. However, in home and SOHO WLANs, the WLAN may be the *only* LAN. The implicit benefit of WLANs is that they are wireless. The need to have a network jack in each room of the house where you might want to use the computer and Internet is eliminated, and the clutter of all those extra wires in the office is reduced.

To share access to the Internet, the PCs or other networked devices must have a common network through which such access may be obtained. In the late twentieth century, essentially all home networks were Ethernet-based,[21] using wiring installed by the homeowner, providing connectivity to the rooms of the house that needed access to the network. The cost of adding a network drop within a house is about $100, including parts and labor (for each drop, although the cost per drop may be cheaper if the homeowner had them all installed at once; many new homes advertise pre-installed category-5 network cabling as a selling point).

Initial applications for home networks included the usual PC-based networked applications, such as file sharing, printer sharing, and so forth. Technologies such as Universal Plug and Play (UPnP) allowed a PC to access pictures on a digital camera that was attached to a different PC by using a common network to discover the camera and to access the picture files within it. The number of types of devices that can be accessed over a network is increasing rapidly. A PDA may have a network interface, probably wireless. Emerging classes of home appliances will allegedly have integrated networking capabilities (e.g., a refrigerator that can automatically re-order bread or milk if you run out, or a light switch that is remotely controllable via a central control station).

Other devices that may be attached to a home network are home weather stations, fire and burglar alarm systems, game consoles (which can now support multiplayer gaming over local LANs or the Internet), and satellite or cable TV

---

21. Although WLAN products did originally begin to emerge in the early 1990s, they were nonstandard, slow (not just by today's standards), and very expensive, compared to what we have today. The technology did not get much traction in the market until higher-speed standards-based WLAN products began to appear.

set-top boxes. A set-top box may provide audio/video access to or from a PC; for example, to support Personal Video Recorder (PVR; also known as Digital Video Recorder, or DVR) functionality. A set-top box with integrated PVR functionality (a DIRECTV® tuner with integrated TiVo® functionality) costs approximately $200 at the end of 2002, for a unit that can record 35 hours of programming; these prices will only drop, especially since new PCs have sufficiently large hard drives, and sophisticated graphics cards, that the PC itself can become a PVR, leveraging a home network to share recorded video throughout the household.[22]

Eventually, even the television set may evolve to include a network interface. It is even possible that a near-future home entertainment system will be networked using simple low-cost Ethernet patch cords to move digitally encoded audio and video data between devices, rather than the clumsy analog wiring of today's systems. Survey after survey shows that the key driving application for home networking is streaming audio and video between rooms of the house.

Evolving WLAN Technology Enables Future Applications

The currently most popular home-oriented application of WLANs is sharing Internet access among multiple WLAN devices at home (e.g., laptops or PDAs with integrated WLAN capabilities, or add-in PC Cards, or desktop PCs with add-in WLAN cards). As WLAN speeds increase, ever more bandwidth-intensive applications will become possible over future home-based WLANs.

For example, it is not uncommon for a new PC today to have over 100 GB of disk space. There are a substantial number of people who would love to copy their own CDs onto their hard drive, and use a small WLAN-based device to access the songs from anywhere in the house. This would be like having your own radio station that only played songs that you like. This sort of "audio jukebox" scenario is likely to be an early use of higher-speed WLANs (provided that Congress does not revoke the consumers' right to fair use of items they purchase).

---

22. The author is not endorsing any particular device or service. In fact, the author has not personally used any such device. This class of device is discussed only as an example of another type of network application, nothing more.

Eventually, once sufficient bandwidth is available (and presuming that disk storage will continue to get denser and cheaper), it's not difficult to imagine that it will be possible to one day (within three to five years) store your collection of DVD movies on your PC, for playback on a laptop or future WLAN-equipped TV screen anywhere in the house, or even on a portable video viewer (or a laptop). It's conceivable that a future television set will have integrated WLAN capabilities, and will be able to discover the video jukebox in the home, from which it can access stored movies, recorded TV programs, and so forth. This would be like a super-enhanced version of today's PVRs. Such applications of WLANs are not far away, and there are surely others that we can't even imagine yet.

Wireless LANs at Home: WLAN-Enabled Gateways

The most significant trend in the market for so-called "home gateway" devices has been the addition of WLAN AP and Portal functionality. Typically, the "Portal" is not explicitly mentioned; in other words, a wireless home gateway usually is described as having an integrated AP. The fact that the AP is internally connected to the rest of the gateway is not usually explicitly stated, nor does it need to be—if the wireless gateway did not provide packet forwarding service between the Internet and the users on the WLAN, the utility of the wireless AP would be greatly diminished. Before the widespread existence of WLAN devices, a home network was typically limited to operation in a single room, or wherever one was able to get the wires.

Before WLAN devices existed, wires were the only medium over which home networks could be operated. However, now that home gateways have evolved to support WLANs, the ease of deploying home networks has been greatly enhanced. Now, instead of figuring out how to get a wire to another room, one just has to add a WLAN card to each PC and put an AP in a common location such that all of the computers have reasonably good reception.

Clearly, home networks make sense for the same reason that corporate networks made (and make) sense—they enable family members (or employees, as the case may be) to work together more effectively, and to share common network resources. Corporate networks have become mission-critical infrastructure, but it is a reasonable question to ask why an individual might want to install a network in his or her home. The answer is the same as the reason why networks are valuable to corporations...they provide a means to exchange data among a group of networked devices, particularly PCs. Other classes of devices are emerging that can also benefit from a network connection, from PDAs to intelligent refrigerators, to light switches, to home security systems. WLANs break down the barriers to deployment of networks in the home, by making installation easier, and by lowering the total cost of ownership.

Until recently, most homes had only one PC. However, as multiple-PC households became more common, there is an increasing desire to share data among the PCs[23] within the home, or to access networked resources such as printers. Internet access, especially broadband Internet access over DSL or cable modems, has been another key driver for a home network, since it would be terribly expensive to have a separate Internet connection for every PC in the home. It would no doubt please the currently cash-strapped telephone companies and ISPs if all their customers purchased a separate Internet connection for each of their home-based devices, but let's be realistic and observe that no residential customer would be stupid enough to blindly pay for separate phone lines (or DSL or cable modem connections) for every PC in the home...even if there were only two PCs in the home.

In addition, it is not the case that every PC needs to be online all the time, so paying for more than one access line would be a serious waste of the end-user's money and the resources necessary to provide the connection—including extra ports on the access server, more usage of copper pairs from the central office, more electricity to operate all the extra home access devices, the extra labor necessary to install all the other devices, and so on.

Of course, no rational customer would ever consider spending so much more money every month for the additional physical access circuits and Internet accounts. In fact, it would be foolish to *not* share the Internet access, since the very nature of packet-switched networks, which are based on statistical multiplexing, encourages (or at least enables) multiple packet streams to share a common physical access circuit. When the access circuit is free, another packet can

---

23. Some people define "home networking" to be any form of connectivity among PCs in a multi-PC household (besides Ethernet and other LAN technologies, this might include serial or parallel data connections, Universal Serial Bus (USB) or IEEE 1394 (a.k.a. FireWire) connections, etc.), but for the purposes of this book we will focus on the LAN-oriented connectivity provided by Ethernet (a.k.a. IEEE 802.3) and IEEE 802.11.

use it at no incremental cost to the end user. Whether the provider's network is unduly stressed by the unplanned-for extra activity depends on the extent to which their network design "oversubscribed" (i.e., how many simultaneous end users is their backbone designed to accommodate?).

Due to the slow speed of even broadband access circuits (which top out at around 600 to 2,000 kbps in the downstream direction), a single end-user's PC can easily soak up the full capacity of the access line. Since any given customer is throttled by the speed of their link, even if it were 100 percent utilized, there is no way that the customer could generate more traffic than the link can carry, regardless of the number of PCs at that location. In fact, several PCs sharing a common link may use less backbone capacity than several individually connected PCs, since the access device may drop packets during busy periods, thereby throttling certain connections to a rate lower than the link could carry if the PC had a dedicated link.

From the backbone provider's perspective, a set of PCs sharing Internet access through a common link is equivalent to the situation in which all the PCs have dedicated access, since the aggregate traffic that the PCs would cause to traverse the provider's backbone would be the same whether or not they shared a common physical access link. In fact, the provider may even be better off with the PCs sharing a link, since they will be throttled by the link speed and won't be able to do more damage collectively than a single active PC with a single access link.

This argument is not 100 percent true, because when providers design their backbone infrastructures, they rely on certain models of expected customer traffic patterns based on the number of customers they expect to serve, and the assumption that most of their customer access links will be idle most of the time, since it really is the case that most customers' access links are idle for most of the time, except for certain peak usage times, when many customers might be causing traffic to cross the Internet provider's backbone. Therefore, if the Internet access provider's customers are using more cumulative bandwidth than the provider's backbone network was designed to carry, the overall performance may degrade, causing the provider to need to upgrade their network sooner than they otherwise might have. This will either cause the provider to lose customers (who leave in search of better performance) or make some strategic upgrades to their backbone infrastructure.

What Is a Home Gateway?

To connect the LAN at home with the Internet, a router needs to be deployed that has the necessary interfaces. In this case, the router is typically called a "home gateway." The home gateway has a feature set that is appropriate for its application (a generic router would work, but would have a number of inadequacies, such as the lack of NAT, and perhaps the lack of an integrated WLAN interface).

Figure 8–3 shows a "physical" view of a wireless home gateway. The illustrated gateway integrates at least three logical interfaces (previous generations of home gateways contained approximately the same components, with the obvious difference that they lacked the integrated WLAN AP):

- A connection to the Internet. This connection is most often a 10BASE-T[24] Ethernet port that attaches to a separate device, typically an external broadband modem (e.g., a DSL or cable modem) that is actually a layer-2 bridge between the gateway's Ethernet interface and the provider's access technology. It is also possible for home gateways to have an integrated broadband chipset (e.g., Digital Subscriber Line (ADSL) or Data-over-Cable Service Interoperability Specification (DOCSIS) cable modem), which eliminates the need for the external Ethernet-to-broadband bridge. In the latter case, the "Internet" connection really is a WAN port, for connection to a coaxial cable or to a "phone jack" through which a DSL line is reached. This interface is labeled with a "0" in Figure 8–3.

- A set of LAN interfaces[25] (labeled "1" through "4" in Figure 8–3) for attachment to "local" Ethernet devices (e.g., PCs, or other wired devices, such as hubs or switches).

- A WLAN "interface," also for attaching to "local" devices (labeled "5" in Figure 8–3). This interface does not appear as a physical jack on the

---

24. The interface is limited to operation at 10 Mbps, since there is no need to connect to an ISP at a speed greater than 10 Mbps; for example, 100 Mbps.

25. Usually, there are four RJ-45 interfaces that comprise a single subnet, via either an integrated hub or a switch. In the latter case, the interfaces can do either 10BASE-T or 100BASE-TX based on the results of Ethernet autonegotiation. If the local LAN interfaces are components of an integrated Ethernet hub, they will all be running at the same speed—10 Mbps or 100 Mbps—since a hub is a shared-medium and all the devices must be running at the same speed in that case.

gateway, but as an antenna that is used to send and receive data. Some gateways have two antennas, so that they can select the one that is receiving the best signal on a moment-to-moment basis.

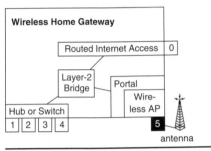

Figure 8–3 Physical diagram of a typical wireless home gateway

The home gateway's components may be easier to visualize if you consider the logical components that are integrated into the device, as depicted in Figure 8–4. The fact that they are all in one box does not change what the pieces do, or affect their relative inter-relationships. The most significant feature in a home gateway, besides WLAN capability, is Network Address Translation (NAT) which allows multiple devices to access the Internet and to appear to the external observer as if there was only a single device sending data to and receiving it from the Internet.

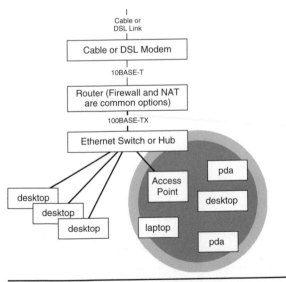

Figure 8–4 Logical components of a wireless home gateway

It is also possible to get a home gateway that does not have a WLAN interface, which would clearly omit the AP, but otherwise be functionally similar. Such home gateways do tend to cost less than gateways with integrated APs, and if a homeowner already has an AP, there may or may not be a need to have a second AP located in the gateway. There is a case study on home gateway deployment (in which the AP was separate) later in this chapter.

Many studies indicate that the penetration of broadband Internet access over the next several years is likely to continue to increase at a steady pace. Given that WLAN interfaces are only a small incremental cost when purchasing a home gateway, it is likely that at least some of the WLAN growth in the home market will be due to the effective "bundling" of WLAN capabilities into the home gateway devices that will be sold as broadband access becomes more popular. Figure 8–5 illustrates one projection of the growth of the broadband Internet access market in terms of what percentage of households have broadband access.

Sources: Jupiter Media Metrix; Jupiter Access Models

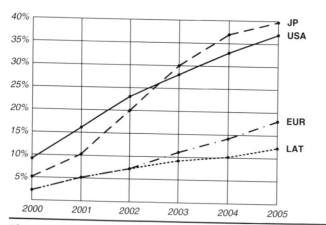

Figure 8–5   Actual and projected broadband Internet access penetration[26]

WLANs are far more attractive in the home than in the corporate setting, since at home there is typically no high-quality wired infrastructure (or even

---

26. Other studies show lower penetration rates for broadband Internet access in the 2005 timeframe, but not by more than 5 percent or so. One should not take market projections too literally. I tend to look at where the market is going, realizing that it is just an educated guess that someone has made regarding the precise market size on a given date.

low-quality wired infrastructure!). Everyone seems to agree that wireless devices are more desirable than wired ones, due to the freedom of operating without being limited to moving within the radius of the patch cord, but in corporate networks, WLAN capability is just an adjunct to the existing wired LAN. It is even true that in corporate networks, wired [Ethernet] LAN jacks are numerous, and it is usually not difficult to find an attachment point.

For the deployment of wired LANs at home (e.g., to interconnect multiple APs), wall jacks were convenient, but not required...since a 10BASE-T or 100BASE-TX Ethernet patch cord can be up to 100 meters long, the patch cords can stretch beyond a single room and plug directly into a remote PC or other networked device.[27] The interconnection of APs by long patch cords may save a homeowner from having to invest in a small switch or hub to sit between the two APs (the switch may need to be in a place that does not have convenient power access, which is a further reason to prefer the "long patch cord" approach. In addition, the failure modes of wires are easier to diagnose than those of switches.

Home Networking: Why?

Beginning in the 1960s, networks became increasingly pervasive as the foundation for corporate computing environments. Early computer networks served to interconnect mainframe computers with each other, and with special-purpose devices such as terminals,[28] printers, and so forth. These early networks (e.g., IBM's Systems Network Architecture (SNA)) were based on connection-oriented packet switching principles and on point-to-point wiring; for example, terminals were connected to "cluster controllers" that multiplexed the packets from a set of terminals onto a common link toward the mainframe. Logically, these terminals operated as if they were directly attached to the mainframe, even though there were, in fact, active intermediate devices mediating the exchange of packets.

Beginning in the late 1980s and continuing through the early 1990s, LAN-based networks began to be deployed by corporations. Early LANs were wired

---

27. In a house with central heating, it might be feasible to snake the patch cord from one room to another—or one floor to another—without needing to make holes in the walls and install actual wall jacks, by using the central heating ducts.

28. Early terminals were sometimes application-specific; in other words, if workers needed to access multiple applications, they would have needed to have multiple terminals at their desk.

using inexpensive coaxial cables that were easier to install, but more difficult to maintain. Initial deployments were in workgroups, where knowledgeable users set up small file servers and LANs so that people in the group could share access to a printer, and share files.

Eventually, corporations embraced LAN technology and installed (and managed) production-quality infrastructures. LANs based on "structured wiring"—first LAN hubs, and then switches (wire-speed bridges)—became available. Once the initial investment in structured wiring had been made, the network was much easier to maintain. Faults can be easily isolated to a single hub or switch port, which can be administratively disabled until the problem is solved, which prevents the problem from affecting other users. LANs were based on another form of packet switching, referred to as "connectionless" packet switching.

In connection-oriented networking protocols, each layer is responsible for ensuring that its data units are delivered intact. Therefore, each layer implements some form of error detection and retransmission, which complicates the design of the protocol. Such protocol features are important when transmitting over media that have high amounts of noise (relative to the signal). In contrast, connectionless networking protocols just send the data and hope it arrives intact. This is an adequate mode of operation over most modern media where errors due to noise are rare. LANs fall into this latter category. LAN protocols have a "frame check sequence" that is used to detect errored frames, so that the low-level network interface card can discard frames that it knows are corrupted. The missing frame will be detected by higher layer protocols, which will arrange for a retransmission (if the protocol is connection-oriented; some higher-level applications do not need reliable delivery, so the connectionless concept can extend right up through the Transport layer).

In these new LAN-based networks, the end-user's device was attached to the *network*, not the mainframe, and the attached device could access many different network resources (including, perhaps, mainframes) over its network connection. In other words, the PC becomes part of the network when it is attached, but there is no longer (necessarily) a single centralized computing entity like a mainframe. Mainframes do still exist, but they have morphed into high-end file servers and transaction-processing systems, which are applications that can benefit from their high-powered I/O capabilities.

Home Networking: Who?

The drivers for increased adoption of WLANs at home can be traced to two primary sources. First, there is a motivation to take advantage of the easy deployment of WLANs in the home, to support mobile intra-home computing, or to allow multiple PCs to wirelessly share network resources such as the Internet, or a household file server or printer. The printer need not be connected to the wired LAN...HP is now making a printer with an integrated WLAN interface. As other devices evolve to have integrated WLAN support, the value of the home-based WLAN will continue to increase.

Corporate Drivers of Home Networking

The corporate world has also been driving the adoption of broadband Internet access and home networking, to support workers who spend some (or all) of their work day at home. Not only have broadband network access technologies such as cable modems and DSL enabled better performance for networked applications, VPN and other security technologies have enabled the extension of a worker's workspace from the office into the home office. Companies are increasingly distributing their employees to their homes (for some or all of the work day) due to the widespread availability of inexpensive broadband Internet access, over which the user may run VPN software to obtain secure access to the corporate network.

Such a home worker is logically equivalent to a worker who is physically present, although this mode of working may not be efficient for everyone (people who frequently need to meet face to face with others would find it less attractive to work at home, but with the availability of high-speed Internet access and VPNs, employees have the flexibility to work when it is convenient (e.g., to work at home in the morning, avoiding being on the road during peak commuting hours), and employers have the flexibility in deciding the best location for a given employee, be it in the office or at home. The following list enumerates the types of workers that might work at home:

- **Day extenders**: Employees who work extra hours at home (e.g., in the mornings, evenings, or on weekends), in addition to the time they spend in the office

- **Part-time teleworkers**: Employees who telecommute some hours of each day, or perhaps certain days of the week. This category also applies to people who are sick enough that they do not want to pollute the office with their germs, but not sick enough that they have to take a sick day and stay in bed.
- **Full-time teleworkers**: Employees for whom their home is their primary work site. This category includes people with home-based businesses.

The common thread here is flexibility. The full-time teleworkers represent flexibility for the employer (saves on office space), while the other categories represent flexibility for both the employer and employee. Some companies are beginning to modify their business processes to include (and encourage) teleworking programs, to integrate home-based workers into their corporate network infrastructure. Not all companies will compensate employees for the installation or service charges incurred as a result of the broadband Internet connection, but given that the Internet connection is always on, and the employees would not be using it if they were in the office, there is a reasonable case to be made that the employer should not pay for the monthly charge. If the service was installed for the convenience of the employer, it's conceivable that the employer would help pay for the installation charges.

For those employees who decide to (or must) work at home, a WLAN is often part of the package—this is simply because home gateways with WLAN capabilities are hardly more expensive than home gateways without them... and if employees have a choice in which gateway to purchase, they will probably opt for the one with the WLAN interface, simply for the reasons that a typical home network user would want a WLAN—ease of installation, mobility throughout the dwelling without needing to install wires and drag along Ethernet patch cords, and so forth.

The categories of workers listed in the following section might benefit from a WLAN at home (which from the corporation's perspective, is enabling an extension of the corporate network—via the VPN—to the user's home desktop or laptop). Note that some home gateways support VPN termination, but because of WLAN security limitations, many companies consider it bad form to have a VPN tunnel to the corporate network with an insecure WLAN at the end of the tunnel. However, when the VPN tunnel terminates in the laptop or desktop PC, there is much less security exposure.[29] For one example, I can state that it is against my current employer's corporate Information Technology policy to have an "open" WLAN attached to a device that is terminating a VPN. Any wireless devices in homes must terminate the VPN session within the device itself. Other employers will have their own rules, and it's best to not make any assumptions…always check before you do anything that might get you fired!

Security Aspects of Home WLAN Deployment

Several different scenarios may affect what level of security a user wants to a) pay for, and b) deploy. The good thing about the emerging RSN-capable devices is that they reduce the deployment headaches, leaving only the issue of cost.

Deployment for One's Own Use—Isolated Deployment

Some people will just want WLANs for the mobility, ease of installation, and other killer features. In this setting, there is little need for security to be enabled, although newer RSN-capable products can be secured with only a minimal impact on usability. This scenario is relatively independent of the growth of broadband, and its coupled growth of teleworking.

If you are far from neighbors, it's less likely that you will need security to protect yourself from the casual STA associating with your AP and "borrowing" your Internet access. However, certain individuals may be worth spying on, and if you are one of these individuals, you would be well advised to buy RSN-capable APs and STAs just as soon as they are available and deploy them.

Deployment for One's Own Use—in Close Quarters

In closer quarters, if users want to have a WLAN and restrict access to it, they will want RSN-level encryption, authentication, and key management. Other features may be used in conjunction with encryption (or without) such as MAC address filtering. Yes, it is possible that MAC addresses can be spoofed, but that requires a moderately motivated attacker. A casual wireless moocher will probably look for an easier target.

---

29. It is a fact that some VPN solutions are better than others…if a good VPN is used, the security exposure is minimized. In the world of security, it is rare to find any absolute truths.

Deployment for Shared Use—Implicitly in Close Quarters

Users in this case will explicitly not care about security between their WLAN clients (who they may not even know) and the Internet. They may care about security between "trusted" and "un-trusted" WLAN clients. An AP suitable for such a deployment may want to support RSN and non-RSN STAs at the same time, perhaps by using VLANs to keep them in different subnets. This way, the RSN STAs can securely talk amongst themselves, while the freeloaders can access the Internet and not have access to the RSN STAs at all, at least not in any direct way.

WLANs in Medium-to-Large Enterprise Networks

WLANs are being rapidly adopted in corporate settings, perhaps even more so than the Internet was, primarily because there is now an existing network infrastructure to which the APs can be attached. This parallels the Internet's rapid growth, because the catalyst there was a killer app (i.e., the World Wide Web) and the enabler was an abundance of PCs that had already been attached to a LAN. Adding IP to such a PC was easy. In a similar way, the deployment of WLAN infrastructures is enabled by the existing networks that have, by now, become ubiquitous.

Anyone who has a network can easily add wireless to it, simply by purchasing APs. The user-based access control that is integrated into products based on IEEE 802.11*i* will also leverage other existing network services; for example, RADIUS servers that are already used to store user credentials in support of network authentication. These university deployments probably don't qualify as hotspots, per se, since they are typically limited to use by students and faculty, and are not available to the general public.

The biggest difference between a home-based (or SOHO-based) WLAN deployment and a medium-to-large enterprise deployment is simply one of scale. Due to the fact that radio frequency energy does not propagate equally well at all frequencies, designs must allow for the fact that if a corporation decides to deploy WLANs that use the 5 GHz frequency band, they will need to place their APs closer together.

The typical deployment of IEEE 802.11*b* or IEEE 802.11*g* may require APs to be located approximately every 120 feet apart, to cover a floor. In a corporate setting, the APs will typically be located in the ceiling. Because of the geometry of the situation, the coverage is maximized when the APs are arranged in a two-dimensional crystal shape known as "hexagonal close packing." The arrangement is comprised of equilateral triangles with sides that are 60 feet (18 meters) long. For IEEE 802.11*b* deployments, it is only necessary to populate every other "node" in the diagram with an AP, since a spacing of 120 feet (37 meters) between APs is sufficient for this application. Many current WLAN rollout design plans are based on 60-foot cells, with the initial deployment only using every other cell position (e.g.., effectively, creating 120-foot cells). Such designs are "future-proof" in that it is possible to put power outlets, wired connections, and so forth in the center of every cell when the network is being installed, and then add APs as necessary (it is trivial to add more in the future).

Figure 8–6 illustrates the arrangement of APs. Note that the empty circles correspond to places where APs could be added to make the spacing tighter (to cells based on 60-foot separation of APs). Note that it takes considerably more APs to cover the space when there are APs at the 60-foot spacing than at the 120-foot spacing. The reason one might want to have the denser distribution of APs is that certain WLAN technology (i.e., IEEE 802.11*a*) operates at a higher frequency, and its signals do not propagate as well as the lower-frequency signals of IEEE 802.11*b* or IEEE 802.11*g*.

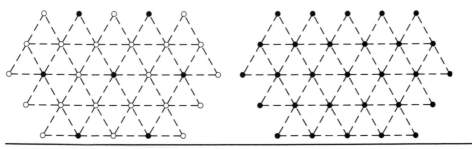

Figure 8–6   120-foot inter-AP spacing versus 60-foot inter-AP spacing

To maximize the usage of the spectrum, the three non-overlapping channels in IEEE 802.11*b* can be situated so as to ensure that no two channels are ever adjacent. For example, in Figure 8–7, we see that channel 1 always borders channels 6 and 11, but never needs to border another cell using channel 1. This arrangement will work whether the 60- or 120-foot cell spacing is used. The coverage circles around each AP extend beyond the radius of the inter-location distance, which reflects the reality that the signals do not stop at exactly 60 feet, they gradually decrease in power.

Outside of any of these circles, a STA is more likely to find a better signal from another AP. However, there may be locations in which a STA is approximately equally served by more than one AP, and local events, such as someone walking between the user and one AP will make the other AP appear stronger. Thus, an apparently stationary node will be "roaming" from the perspective of the APs.

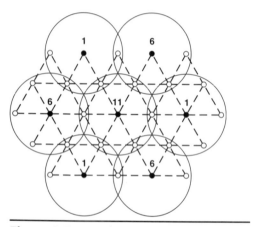

Figure 8–7   Using non-overlapping channels to cover an area

It is important to note that the coverage circles are not monolithic. When a STA is closer to an AP, it will be able to achieve the highest performance, whereas at progressively greater separations, the optimal transmission speed will gradually decrease, since the modulations used to achieve lower speeds have better range due to the fact that they can tolerate a lower signal-to-noise ratio.

When a STA is experiencing transmission difficulty, which it can detect by the need to fragment or retransmit frames, it may decide that another strategy for optimizing its successful transmission would be to lower the speed at which it is transmitting, to employ a more robust modulation technique. While this choice may seem counter-intuitive, the result may be superior to using a "faster" speed, since at the faster speed the STA may be spending more time waiting for frames to be successfully transmitted than actually transmitting frames.

What about Site Surveys?

It was necessary in the early-to-middle 1990s to plan the location of pre-standard "access points" very carefully. This was because they were much more expensive[30] than today's IEEE 802.11 standards-based APs, so users wanted to make sure that they got the most coverage for the fewest APs. As can be seen from the design methodologies in use today, the coverage is implicit in the layout of the APs, which are presumed to cover the entire desired area. In the event that a soft spot is discovered, where the signal isn't what it should be, an IT department could simply elect to incur the minimal marginal cost to locate an additional AP closer to the area with a weak signal.

Moreover, site surveys only give information on physical RF parameters such as signal quality (an abstraction of the signal-to-noise ratio) and signal strength. What the IT department really wants to do is provide sufficient capacity to handle the expected number of users, but the site survey doesn't give useful information here. The design of the WLAN, especially including the layout of APs with respect to the channels on which they operate is more likely to affect capacity, given that there are assumed to be sufficient APs to cover the area with adequate signal strength.

New products just now appearing on the market may herald the return of the site survey, in a way. Applications allow a user to feed in their floor plan, and the composition of the various materials in the cubicles, the walls, and so on, and can then provide a list of suggested locations in which to place APs. The APs are even configured so that their coverage area matches your floor plan almost exactly, thereby minimizing the extension of your WLAN into, for example, your parking lot.

There is a significant advantage in IEEE 802.11a, in that even though the APs must be spaced closer together, there are many more non-overlapping channels (at least 8, and frequently as many as 12). The larger number of channels means that the channels can be laid out on successive floors such that the "no two adjacent APs use the same channel" rule is extended into the third

---

30. An AP that supported no more than 2 Mbps could easily have cost $2000 or more.

dimension. If you think about it, there is no way to do this with three channels. Any channel that is put above or below any of the channels in Figure 8–7 will have to overlap with one of the others. There are only three channels from which to choose. In the plane (i.e., on a floor of a building), it is just sufficient that there are three non-overlapping channels. If only two non-overlapping channels existed, there would be no way to arrange the layout of the channels such that no two channels were ever adjacent. Therefore, with IEEE 802.11*b*, it is virtually guaranteed that signals from a floor above or below may interfere with signals on the floor in between, although the signal's ability to cause interference may be limited by the attenuation caused by the materials in the floor or ceiling.

For the optimal arrangement of the WLAN cells in a three-dimensional deployment (i.e., a multi-floor deployment), try to visualize stacking cannon-balls or oranges or other approximately spherical items. To extend Figure 8–6 into the third dimension, you need more channels to ensure that the "no two adjacent cells use the same channel" rule is observed. We can safely assume that the AP's coverage does not extend up and down two to three floors…the floors are far more substantial than the walls, and so are much more effective at atten-uating the signal, and the antennae in commercial APs tend to be designed such that they radiate most of their energy in a horizontal plane, not uniformly in all directions. Thus, it is fair to assume that a given AP will only be able to "inter-fere" with those on the floors immediately above and below it.[31]

There are two ways to stack the cells. In the easiest way, the APs on a given floor are directly above or below those on another floor. In the slightly less easy way, the APs are arranged in a three-dimensional hexagonal close-packing arrangement[32] in both dimensions, so that the number of APs is minimized. In the latter case, one can get away with a smaller number of channels and still meet the rule that no two adjacent cells will use the same channel. However, the tetrahedron need not be an equilateral tetrahedron, because the signals do not

---

31. Caution: non-linear propagation effects (i.e., through elevator shafts or heating and ventilation ductwork) can create situations where this is not the case, wherein signals reach well beyond one floor above or below the device emitting the signal. Such cases will probably be discovered by a process of trial and error.

32. Imagine a stack of billiard balls, oranges, or any roughly spherical shape. Each layer, as in Figure 8–6, is a two-dimensional hexagonal close-packing arrangement, and a similar arrange-ment of each higher layer will nest into the gaps in the layer below. As multiple layers are built up, the resulting stack is known as a three-dimensional hexagonal close-packed structure.

propagate as well in the vertical dimension. In the three-dimensional hexagonal close-packing arrangement, I believe that at most six[33] channels would be required to cover an arbitrary number of floors such that no two adjacent cells would interfere with each other. Whether five or six non-overlapping channels are required is irrelevant, since IEEE 802.11*a* has a minimum of eight non-overlapping channels, which is more than enough to do the job.

To help visualize the stacking of the cells, Figure 8–8 attempts to show how the floor above (APs indicated in gray, which cover the intersections of the coverage circles) nestles among the coverage circles of the middle floor (in black), and how on the floor below (in gray, but which are drawn under the intersections of the coverage circles), the APs nestle in the opposite intersections of the coverage circles. On either floor, the gray (below) or gray (above) circles are arranged exactly as the black circles on the middle floor are arranged, in a hexagonal array with 60-foot spacing.

The author, using his limited drawing capabilities, has tried to indicate the main floor as the one with the black central APs, and the concentric circles indicating the APs' coverage areas on the main floor. The APs below are indicated by gray circles which are visible under the intersection of the coverage circles, and the APs on the floor above are indicated by gray circles that block the intersection of the coverage circles on the main floor.

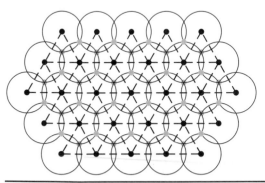

Figure 8–8   Locating APs on floors above and below

Incremental RSN Deployment Using Channel Overlays

An optional capability for devices (in particular, APs) that support RSN is that of the TSN. TSN allows a mix of RSN and pre-RSN STAs to associate with a

---

33. It's possible that only five channels are required, but I can't prove that to myself at the moment. As far as I can tell, six will work for sure.

given AP. When TSN is enabled, traffic to or from the AP is encrypted using WEP, TKIP, or CCMP (whereas WEP is not allowed in a pure RSN situation). In a WLAN that is configured for encryption, all data frames (MPDUs) will be encrypted, once the key derivation is complete. It is illegal to send unprotected traffic in such a WLAN. However, even without allowing for unencrypted traffic, it should be obvious that this situation is ridiculously insecure. Because it supports WEP, TSN is as insecure as WEP was (which is just about as secure as sending data in the clear).

TSN is more appropriately discussed in this chapter, which is concerned with deployment-related issues, versus Chapter 7, *Security Mechanisms for Wireless LANs*, for two reasons. First, TSN is not secure, and second, TSN is purported to exist solely to aid deployment of RSN (the author finds this to be a highly dubious assertion). The TSN approach does not enhance security unless it is used very rapidly as it was intended—as a transition mechanism. Then, it will have improved security by aiding the elimination of the old technology that was insecure.

There is no performance or other benefit to running a WLAN in TSN mode. In fact, due to the complexity of TSN, the AP may have software implementation errors that create their own security vulnerabilities. The author has seen "transitional" technologies or designs implemented too many times in the past, after which people got used to them and the transitional schemes became "operational" (i.e., part of the expected mode of operation). Thus the author is pre-disposed to advise against starting down that path, if it can be avoided, since it is likely to make it more difficult to step off that path, human nature being what it is.

For security reasons, most corporate WLANs are maintained outside of the corporate firewall, and users must use VPN software to access the "inside" of the corporate network (even if they are physically inside the corporate office space). Even when proprietary techniques such as cisco's Lightweight EAP (LEAP) are used, which offer much better authentication than WEP's Shared Key authentication, but which do nothing to improve key management, operating a WLAN still represents a sufficient risk such that it makes sense to take a security stance that distrusts all WLAN STAs.

However, there is a way to avoid the complexity and insecurity of TSN and still maintain the goal of mixing RSN-capable and pre-RSN STAs. Imagine that all of the APs in Figure 8–7 are pre-RSN APs. As an alternative, consider a deployment that effectively creates a "secure parallel universe" overlaid on the existing floor plan. In order to deploy RSN technology, new RSN-capable APs could be rolled out and mounted near the existing APs. Rather than replacing the old with the new, it would be better to run both together for a short time. The configuration of the original APs need not change at all. The new APs would be configured to run on different channels (e.g., if a new AP were mounted next to an AP that was on channel 1, the new AP could be on channel 6, or similarly, a new AP next to an existing AP on channel 6 could be configured to use channel 11, and finally, a new AP on channel 1 would be situated next to an existing AP that was on channel 11).

If an RSN-capable STA arrived in any of the cells, it would perform an active or passive scan and discover that one of the APs was sending out RSN IEs in its Beacons or Probe Responses, which would cause the RSN-preferring STA to associate with that AP (and use the RSN AP's channel) rather than the other AP that it hears, which is advertising that it supports WEP (the legacy APs could even be configured with no encryption, a capability that is impossible in the context of TSN). When the RSN and pre-RSN APs are mixed in this way, the transition to RSN is straightforward. Simply watch the old network and once very few STAs are using it, work out how to migrate these stragglers to RSN capability.

When is TSN useful? There are two cases of "WLAN upgrades" that could enable TSN. Remember, to be able to use TSN, users must upgrade their APs to support it. Such an upgraded AP will (at a minimum) probably support TKIP, IEEE 802.1X, and WEP.

- A firmware/software upgrade for existing deployed APs. This will provide basic RSN capability (i.e., TKIP).
- A newly purchased AP device. This will support both TKIP and CCMP, and perhaps optionally WEP (either in the context of TKIP, or alone).

The latter type of device is the one that could be rolled out in parallel with an existing WLAN infrastructure. The former, as it is a software upgrade, is not really going to provide an opportunity to co-locate two APs in the same vicinity. An upgraded AP that supports RSN (i.e., TKIP) may or may not support TSN, but it will certainly support WEP (since TKIP is built on WEP). Even a newly purchased RSN-capable AP will support WEP if it supports TKIP, but the hope is that customers will be eager to migrate to the most secure configuration as soon as it is available.

Just because an AP supports WEP does not mean it can use it—keys are required for a device to successfully participate in WEP. If the network manager does not configure WEP keys into the device, then the device will not be able to perform Shared Key authentication, nor will it be able to perform WEP encryption. For the case of devices that receive firmware and/or software upgrades, the customer who performs such an upgrade is probably interested in investment protection at least as much as in security, and for this type of customer, the TSN capability will probably be quite valuable, especially since both new and old STAs will be able to access the newly upgraded AP. However, the customer who purchases new APs would be well advised to configure them in pure RSN mode. Besides the fact that they are much more secure, the usability is much better on the part of the end users, since they only need to enter the necessary credentials to enable their chosen EAP method to successfully authenticate the user to the network.

In the event that the EAP method consists of per-STA pre-shared keys,[34] each user only needs to enter his or her pass phrase, from which the PSK is derived. Given that we have assumed that there is an existing WLAN, there is reason to expect that the TSN capability is not that useful, since there is a presumed infrastructure that is already in place that supports WEP. The new RSN-capable APs can support the new RSN-capable STAs without needing to enable TSN mode. There is already a network in place that allows the pre-RSN STAs to attach to the WLAN. The usefulness of TSN is maximized when an AP is upgraded from pre-RSN to TKIP capability, since the "new" APs are just upgraded old APs, which can support RSN-capable STAs without needing the pre-RSN STAs or APs to be changed at all. Any new RSN-capable APs can implicitly support all forms of encryption, authentication, and key management.

Is this overlay technique superior? For one thing, the availability of strong security for WLANs is likely to unleash a torrent of purchasing by corporate IT departments who have not yet invested in WLANs because of the lack of security. These fence-sitters will start purchasing APs rapidly once they are comfortable that the security issues have been resolved. The author has reason to believe that the installed base, which TSN is designed to protect (in the sense of investment

---

34. Remember that the PSKs in use at any given time should all be unique on a per-STA basis. A shared PSK, across multiple STAs, is more vulnerable to attack and is not recommended.

protection, not security protection), will soon be dwarfed by RSN-capable (or WPA-capable) devices. In a market where the legacy devices are outnumbered by the next generation, the motivation to produce patches to the old generation is greatly reduced, and the larger market for RSN-capable (or WPA-logo-ed) devices will drive down the prices for the new technology, making a "forklift upgrade" economically feasible for early adopters of WLAN technology. It's very likely that many existing corporate WLAN deployments have stalled pending the resolution of the well-publicized security issues, so any new RSN-capable equipment that will be purchased starting later in 2003 could simply be used to build out the parts of the wireless network that were on hold, and eventually the original APs could be swapped out in favor of the RSN-capable APs as they either fail or are replaced due to the network manager wanting a common RSN-capable hardware platform throughout his or her WLAN implementation.

In general, TSN seems like a solution in search of a problem (in some ways, it's a problem in search of a solution!). TSN is only useful in a limited set of circumstances, and it is unfortunately perpetuating a security model that is known to be broken. The IEEE 802.11*i* TG has emphatically stated that TSN is only meant to be a short-lived approach, and that any organizations that use TSN should migrate to RSN as quickly as they can. It is also in the economic interest of hardware vendors to enable this transition to new RSN-capable hardware, since the profit margins on selling a new RSN-capable AP should exceed the profit derived from selling software/firmware upgrades to the installed base. Not only is this not terribly profitable, it is also likely to be a support nightmare, since the number of things that can go wrong in a TSN is significant. It is likely that there are many corner cases lurking that are not obvious, and so are not easily tested. The result is that the end users become the beta testers.

The inclusion of TSN was done with the best of intentions, but it will probably not be widely used (at worst, it risks giving IEEE 802.11*i* technology a bad name by association, if poor implementations of TSN get bad press), but if an overlay design is chosen, there is no need for the complexity of TSN. The other reason why the overlay technique is superior is that the STA side of the equation will rapidly evolve toward RSN, as new equipment (e.g., laptops with embedded Wi-Fi support, newer model PC Cards, etc.) is likely to support RSN (or the Wi-Fi Alliance's WPA) in its "out-of-the-box" configuration. The market for legacy pre-RSN devices should quickly drop to near zero.

Wireless LANs in Public Places

This category of WLAN deployment is the least well-defined, and has the most potential to change the way we use networks in our everyday life. As I write this, I am sitting in a coffee shop accessing the Internet and my corporate IPsec-based VPN via a WLAN. Many are attempting to get WLANs deployed in as many public spaces as possible, hopefully to garner revenue from such deployments. Currently, WLANs may be found in coffee shops and other restaurants, airport gate waiting areas, bookstores, and other places. One of these "other places" in which WLAN access will soon be available is on airplanes. Boeing has already tested a flying WLAN, with satellite-based Internet connectivity. In fact, the service has been tested live by Lufthansa. The satellite link limits the responsiveness (due to the roundtrip time[35] of the signal between the plane and the ground via the satellite).

The practical downside for WISPs is that—by far—most people's interactions with computers occur either a) at work, or b) at home. Personally, I only lug my laptop around when I have to have it with me. I'd love to be able to use my WLAN card on the train when I am commuting to and from work. As of yet, that service is not available. At best, WLAN hotspots will provide highly localized coverage. While in a hotspot, you could enjoy Internet access at speeds on the order of 1 to 2 Mbps, but when you leave the hotspot your access speed drops to zero Mbps.

Some influential telecommunications market analysts think that WLANs are the wave of the future, and that eventually APs will be densely distributed (at least in densely populated areas) simply because they are so cheap to buy, deploy, and operate. It's not clear to the author if there will be a business case for these wireless islands (archipelagos?), or if it is all supposed to be free. The author fully supports people building shared community networks, but networks need maintenance, and that costs money. I'm rambling a bit here, but I know that some Bell Labs researchers proved that you can make an arbitrarily reliable system out of arbitrarily unreliable components, as long as it was possible to characterize the "unreliability" of the components and ensure that the system was designed to compensate for it (i.e., by

---

35. The delay, in one direction (i.e., from the ground station to a satellite in geosynchronous orbit, and back down to the plane, or vice versa) is approximately one half of one second.

increasing redundancy in certain aspects of the system design). One might suppose that if enough people in a given area were operating overlapping WLAN "cells," that connectivity could be available as long as at least one of the cells was still operational. Time will tell whether a "service" that is, at its most fundamental level, best-effort can succeed.

The current deployment platform of WLAN STAs is primarily laptops, which are not exactly so portable that people take them everywhere they go. However, as PDAs with IEEE 802.11*b* capabilities become more common (even cell phones with Internet access via integrated WLAN hardware have been announced, especially if 3G and 4G cellular doesn't take off), the potential user base for WISPs will get larger, since more people will tend to have a WLAN device with them. The WISPs' main competition, ultimately, will be the public-access WLAN deployments that many activists are setting up. Whenever WLAN users have the option of choosing free access over paying for it, it's easy to presume that they'll go with the free one. The WISPs will need to offer more than just vanilla Internet access for people to be willing to pay for the service (and the price will have to be right).

The ability of WISPs to derive revenue is obviously tied to the number of people who are carrying a device with them through which a WLAN could be accessed. Clearly, business travel is the one case where people will be likely to carry their laptop along with them (hopefully they won't take it on vacation!). Thus, WLAN deployments in airports, hotels, and on planes make a lot of sense, since these are places in which larger-than-average concentrations of business travelers may be found.

Despite "cherry picking" the best locations that are frequented by business-people on the go, the total user base of traveling WLAN users is still going to be small, compared to those using WLANs on a regular basis at home or at work. Besides the limited user base, WISPs are also under price pressure because many *ad hoc* organizations are also setting up low-cost or no-cost WLANs in many of the same places as the WISPs, so it's not clear how many people will be willing to pay for this service (or how much they will be willing to pay, which is a separate question altogether).

A well-known example is a certain popular coffee shop chain that has signed up a nationwide WLAN access provider, but in certain branches of the chain, cheaper alternatives are available. The price structure of the nationwide provider is seen by some to be too expensive. If so, simple laws of supply and demand should tend to equalize the price such that the provider is able to attract sufficient customers to cover their operating costs. The nationwide plan does have some inherent advantages that would be worth paying a small premium for, in that a customer can count on finding a WLAN-equipped coffee shop in most places in the country, even in less populated areas that may not be served by multiple WLAN access providers. In the cities, more alternatives are likely to exist, so perhaps a tiered pricing structure will evolve that will reflect where you are when you use the WLAN.

Today, roaming and staying connected (via a laptop) is not exactly what you might call "seamless," at least not from an ease-of-use perspective. The advantage of this cellular phone based approach is that it is going to work over a wide geographic area—so, it is slow but widely available.

The cool thing about WLANs in public places is that they enable end users to be truly mobile, not only in the sense of being able to move, but in the sense that they can remain connected, at high speeds, while moving (or while sitting in a coffee shop, after they have stopped moving temporarily). The bandwidth that a roaming WLAN user will have access to is much larger than other current mobile alternatives, which may be limited to 128 to 256 kbps (perhaps up to 1 Mbps in a couple of years, if 3G wireless technology is deployed as promised), but probably much less, via a cell phone connection to carry data communications to and from a PC, either over a wire between the PC and the phone, or over a wireless short-hop connection such as Bluetooth.

The real trigger that would get people to carry devices with them is not just making them smaller and lighter, but also having them fully leverage mobile-related networking technologies. When these devices fully leverage so-called "presence-based" services, the users may want to be able to be reachable whenever their PDA (or whatever) is within range of a WLAN. Today's presence-based applications, such as Instant Messaging, rely on "buddy lists" that enable the service provider to tell each user when his or her friends are online. One can imagine a service that not only knows that a friend is online, but also knows the spatial distance between the two of you. If you knew that a friend was several blocks away, you might want to meet him or her at a location in between, and a service that could help enable such meetings might be very popular, especially if it was package-able into cellular phones that are already being used as text messaging "terminals" but that really don't rely on presence (the way Internet-based Instant Messaging does). Many forms of presence-based applications present themselves; for example, you could find out what movie start times were within walking distance of your closest (in the sense of distance) friends. The service could even buy the tickets for you, to save you from standing in line.

Public Access WLANs: Universities Exploring the Future

A clue to the transformations that such pervasive WLANs might have on society in the next 5 to 10 years is described in the October 2002 issue of *Wired* magazine. A case study on Dartmouth College is presented, in which the effects of the pervasive WLAN technology are analyzed. Later in this chapter, I will summarize some of their findings. One of the more amusing is that the bell tower on campus can be controlled wirelessly, allowing students to change the tune. The bell, for whatever reason, was attached to the university network, allowing it to become a resource available to any wireless user; in the case mentioned in the story, the wireless user is actually a "bell-hacker."

A university campus is more like a hotspot than a typical corporate deployment, since the university is likely to experiment much more with unexpected applications based on pervasive wireless connectivity. One user even modified the software that triggers reminders in his PDA, so that the distance from the appointment would be taken into consideration (based on the location of the user at a given point in time).

But is a university campus a wireless hotspot? Such deployments as have happened at Dartmouth are happening all over the country, at perhaps hundreds of schools, including Carnegie Mellon, Stanford University, the University of Texas at Dallas, the University of Minnesota, Virginia Tech, and so on. It is indisputable that at those universities where WLANs have been deployed, the WLANs have transformed the way the students and faculty work, play, and communicate.[36] The impact on society once these über-wired people get into the workforce is difficult to estimate, but today's trends toward "mobile lifestyles" will

---

36. When one student user was asked to name the biggest difference between Dartmouth and another school that he was attending, it was that at Dartmouth, no one knows anyone else's phone number! All communications are via email or instant messaging, and soon VoIP over the WLAN.

almost certainly accelerate. The "mobile professionals" of today, with their cellular phone and laptop will surely seem old-fashioned in a short time.

Deploying WLANs at Home: A Case Study

As a case study, I will describe a series of events that actually happened to me when I was visiting friends after Christmas 2002.

The friends had broadband Internet access via a cable modem, which was attached to their only PC (they had another PC, but it was not part of the home LAN…it turns out that it wouldn't have worked if they tried to connect it, for reasons that will become clear in a moment). My friends had purchased an AP so that they could use their laptop at home, but they were frustrated because even though their laptop worked wirelessly in the office, it did not work at all at home. This was supposed to be easy. The AP just had a simple Ethernet interface, and the laptop appeared to associate with it, but it couldn't access the Internet through the cable modem. They both had a Wi-Fi logo, so what was wrong? I guessed correctly what was wrong, and it had nothing to do with the wireless functions of either the laptop or of the AP.

The AP was working properly. The cable modem was the problem. The cable modem was also working properly, within a definition of "proper" that suits the cable company, but that is counter-intuitive to the user, and in this case made it look like it was the AP that was broken. The cable modem has an integrated Ethernet-to-DOCSIS bridge. As part of the fundamental operation of this (and any) bridge, it watches all frames arriving on each of its interfaces, looking for MAC-SAs that it hasn't seen before. The bridges in cable modems are specially modified to help the cable companies make more money, in that they are limited to learning only one MAC address on the interface to which the home network is attached. This is to allow the cable company to sell you connectivity for multiple devices at a higher marginal cost per month. This is not surprising…the cable company does a similar thing with extra TV connections.

However, there is no reason to pay extra. Many home gateways have a "MAC Address Cloning" feature. It works as follows: First, disconnect your PC from the cable modem. Connect the PC to the new home gateway and connect to its configuration utility (probably Web-based). On the PC, open a DOS window (click the Start button / select "Run…" / type cmd and click OK). Under Linux and the MacOS, there are utilities that can be used to determine the local MAC address (the `ifconfig` program and the TCP/IP control panel, respectively).

Figure 8–9 illustrates the previous steps to open a DOS command window in Windows 2000 Professional, the OS that I happen to have on my laptop. Windows XP requires similar steps to open a DOS command window. Screen shots are provided here as a convenience for the Windows users of the world.

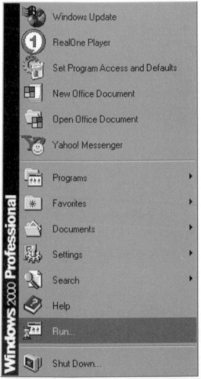

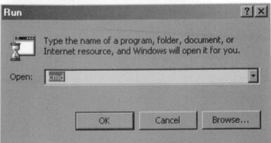

Figure 8–9   Accessing a DOS command (cmd) window from the Start button

Unfortunately, it is not practical to include screen shots of every OS, but all OSs will have a way to display the MAC addresses of their network interfaces.

After the DOS command window appears, you can type "`ipconfig /all`" (note that this command is not usable on all versions of Windows...on some versions, the command may be "`winipcfg`", and in some versions of Windows, that command or a similar one may be launched directly from the "Run" dialog box, without needing to open a DOS command window). Figure 8–10 shows the DOS command window with the output of the "`ipconfig /all`" command (the MAC address of my laptop's built-in Ethernet interface is highlighted).

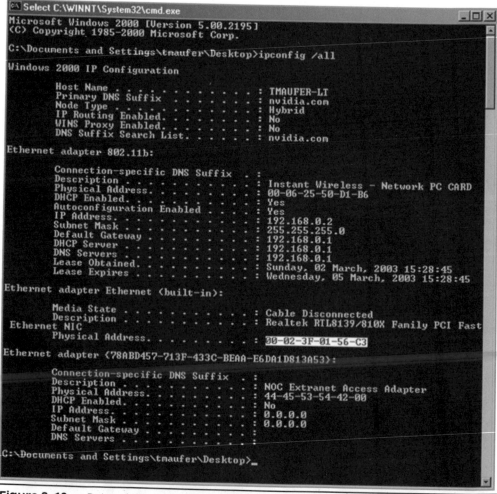

Figure 8–10   Determining a PC's MAC address

Once I had written down the PC's MAC address, I went to the portion of the home gateway's user interface in which one may adjust the MAC address of the Internet interface of the gateway. My own home gateway does not have this feature, so I cannot easily show you a screen shot of this configuration step. Suffice it to say that I made sure that the feature was listed on the box when we went to the office supply store to purchase a home gateway for my friend.

Once the home gateway was configured with the PC's MAC address, I connected the home gateway to the cable modem. As far as the cable modem was concerned, it was once again talking to the PC. The fact that the PC is still using the same MAC address on a different interface of the same home gateway is not a problem, since the gateway is acting as a router. It is trivial to disambiguate the two instances of the same MAC address, since each is associated with a different IP address.

Speaking of which, on the PC, after I connected it to the home gateway, I typed one further command into the DOS command window before closing it, namely "`ipconfig /renew`", which forced the PC to forget its old IP address and use DHCP to request that a new IP address be assigned to it. The home gateway integrates a DHCP server, which quickly complied with that request. The old IP address, which was valid when the PC was directly attached to the cable modem, would no longer work now that the PC had been moved to a different IP subnet on the other side of the router from the cable modem.

As with my laptop's configuration (as shown in Figure 8–4), my friend's PC was assigned a private IP address from the range `192.168.0.x`. After the PC had obtained a new IP address, I typed "`exit`" to close the DOS command window.

The home gateway also supported NAT, which means that multiple devices can be active in the home, simultaneously accessing the Internet, and on the Internet side, all of the connections will appear to be emanating from the external (public) IP address of the home gateway. Therefore, after the original PC was plugged back in, now to the home gateway instead of the cable modem, and verified to be working properly, the next step was to attach the AP to the one of the home gateway's Ethernet interfaces and try to access the Internet from the wireless laptop.

It worked, but this whole experience shows an important lesson in networking and troubleshooting. It was very easy to look at the situation that first presented itself and conclude that the AP must be misconfigured or broken. After all, the laptop worked in the office, but not at home. My friend had no reason to suspect his cable modem, or to have a clue as to why the cable modem's basic operation might be causing this problem. Moreover, knowing that a home gateway with NAT and MAC address cloning could solve his problem was simply way beyond his level of knowledge. And, to be honest, this stuff is still way too complicated for normal people. I was happy to help him, and I'm happy to admit that it's not normal to know how to fix what was broken in his setup.

Even if the AP had some diagnostics that would show that it was passing frames to the Distribution System (i.e., the wired LAN), that would not even have helped much, since the AP would have indicated that all was well.[37] The AP, even with diagnostic capabilities, would have had no way of knowing that the problem was in the cable modem. What looked (to my friend) like a problem with the WLAN was actually not a problem at all…it was working fine all along. The cable modem was just eating all the frames that didn't come from the one MAC address it was allowed to know about, the original desktop PC's MAC address. No reasonably intelligent person would suspect that this was happening.

After the original PC's MAC address was programmed into the home gateway, the cable modem was none the wiser, and everything worked the way my friend thought it should have all along. You've never seen someone so happy to be able to be checking email via his corporate VPN while watching a football game downstairs.

Back to that nonconnected PC that was mentioned earlier. The reason it wouldn't have worked was the same as why the wireless laptop ultimately did not work…the cable modem had locked on to the MAC address of the primary PC, and would not accept traffic from any other device (more properly, it would not have accepted traffic from any device with a different MAC address). Had my friend ever connected the second PC to his home LAN, surely the fact that it didn't work would have been extremely mystifying, perhaps even more so than

---

37. Of course, one might have suspected that something was amiss when no frames were ever seen to be coming back in the other direction, but who would suspect the cable modem? Most people would probably jump to a conclusion that something was wrong on the Internet, but when the desktop PC was working fine, and the laptop wasn't working at all, it was very frustrating for my friend. The cable company could have helped him, by giving him another cable modem and charging him more per month, but they probably never would have been able to explain what was broken.

the case of the wireless laptop, since there was another PC right next to it that worked fine. Even basic troubleshooting tricks, like trying to have only the second PC connected, without the first one, would have failed. Now that the home gateway with NAT was installed, my friend could have a very large number of PCs and other devices sitting behind the gateway, appearing (to the cable company) to be the one PC that they originally knew when the cable modem was first installed.

Summary

Wireless penetration into the home is being driven by the adoption of broadband Internet access, which in turn was driven by trends toward more flexible work arrangements and also the simple desire for speedier access to the Internet. Conversely, people buying wireless LANs probably will upgrade to high-speed Internet access, simply because of the integration of the gateway and access point.

Corporations will, once they are comfortable with the emerging much improved security aspects of WLANs, adopt them rapidly due to the advantages of mobile computing. As this decade progresses, the speeds of wireless LANs will likely approach or exceed 1 Gbps (which sounds fast, until you realize that wired networks will by then be running at 100 Gbps or 1 Tbps). Within this decade, wireless technology will be able to support whole new classes of applications, including delay-sensitive traffic like Voice-over-IP, and bandwidth-intensive applications like streaming media, for whom a little jitter is no big deal.

Eventually, wireless LANs will get fast enough that they will become the primary form of connectivity. Our grandchildren will look back at our wired devices the same way they'll look back on our gasoline-powered cars in the rear-view mirrors of their Hydrogen-powered fuel-cell vehicles. Actually, the author doesn't expect that it will take that long for wireless to become the default form of "connectivity" (that term should become increasingly quaint as the years go by!).

The standards that are being written today are laying the foundation for this futuristic-sounding wireless world, and will form the basis of the next generation of network access and applications. The future is definitely wireless.

Index

informIT